MONOPOLY IN ECONOMICS AND LAW

DONALD DEWEY
Duke University

Monopoly
IN ECONOMICS
AND LAW

Rand McNally & Company
Chicago

RAND MᶜNALLY ECONOMICS SERIES
Walter W. Heller, *Consulting Editor*

For my mother and father

Preface

In this small treatise I have tried to give an account of what economists and lawyers have thought about monopoly since the subject first received their serious attention. The time has long since passed when anyone could sanely claim to know—much less summarize—*the* literature on monopoly which, in the United States alone, now runs to hundreds of books and articles, thousands of government reports on trades practices, and an incalculable amount of relevant material locked in the small print of law reports and court records. In the face of this mass of information the aspiring author can only draw upon his limited store of knowledge to illustrate or test those generalizations which strike him as most worthy of emphasis. A treatise on monopoly is therefore, of necessity, a highly personal work far removed from the judicious anonymity of the annotated case book. My qualifications for attempting such a book are meager enough— some years' experience as a teacher of economics and a smattering of law picked up from associating with lawyers. I am fortified in my temerity only by the knowledge that the men who could write a better treatise have, in recent years, been occupied with other tasks.

This book has no particular claim to originality in viewpoint or organization. My political convictions are those of the bourgeois liberal who esteems Frank Knight as the best of economists and Learned Hand as the best of lawyers. The specialist in monopoly problems will probably meet most of his old friends somewhere along the way—Robinson and Chamberlin, *Mitchel v. Reynolds,* the reports of the Industrial Commission, the rule of reason, etc. If this book has any special claim to novelty, it derives from a conviction that economists and lawyers who are interested in monopoly as a policy problem cannot get along without one another. The important issues in the control of monopoly are "economic" in the sense that judges and administrators are compelled to make decisions in the light of what they think the business world is "really" like, and it is the task of economists through research and reflection to provide them with an increasingly accurate picture. But no policy is good or bad independently of the way in which it is enforced or the interests that must be sacrificed to achieve it, and lawyers are the guides to the complexities of administration and litigation.

In the course of writing this book, I have imposed on many friends, acquaintances, and total strangers and met with naught save kindness. My heaviest debts are to Professor Harlan M. Blake of the University of Minnesota Law School who read the entire penultimate draft with sympathetic severity; and to Dr. E. J. Mishan of the London School of Economics who patiently helped me over the rough terrain of Chapters VII and VIII. It is also a pleasure to acknowledge the aid of the following critics who have read and commented on various parts of the manuscript in its varying degrees of unreadiness: Professor Fred Weston of the University of California at Los Angeles, Professor Warren Nutter of the University of Virginia, Dr. Simon Whitney of the Federal Trade Commission, Professor William Letwin of the Massachusetts Institute of Technology, Professor Lionel McKenzie of Rochester University, Professor Ralph Pfouts of the University of North Carolina, and Professors Charles Ferguson, Frank de Vyver, and Charles Livengood of Duke University. I would also like to thank Professor G. C. Allen of University College, London, and the Monopolies Commission for his kind assistance in gathering the materials for Chapter XIX during my tenure as a Fulbright scholar in the United Kingdom, 1956–57.

The generosity of critics, of course, does not leave them open to a charge of guilt by association. The sins of omission and commission in this book are all my own work.

The Appendix to Chapter VIII appeared in slightly altered form in the February, 1958, issue of the *Journal of Political Economy*, and Chapter XVII draws upon material included in my article, "Romance and Realism in Antitrust Policy," which appeared in the April, 1955, issue of this journal. Chapters IX and X are a revision and elaboration of my article, "The Common-law Background of Anti-trust Policy," which was published in the October, 1955, issue of the *Virginia Law Review*. I am indebted to the University of Chicago Press and the editors of the *Virginia Law Review* for permission to borrow from these articles in the construction of this book.

DONALD DEWEY

Durham, North Carolina
September 15, 1958

Table of Contents

Chapter I

MONOPOLY AS A POLICY PROBLEM

Businessmen have always known that any sudden increase in the supply of whatever they sell will cause its price to fall and, conversely, that any sudden decrease in the supply of whatever they sell will cause its price to rise. Likewise, businessmen have always known that a higher price and lower output may mean greater profit for themselves. Naturally they have often sought to turn this knowledge to profitable account by restricting the flow of their own wares—or their competitors' wares—into the market, and in the pursuit of this private gain they have irritated the people from whom the higher prices were to be exacted.

In modern textbooks on political economy the "fact" that the price of a commodity varies inversely with its rate of output is conveniently, if pretentiously, called the "law of diminishing demand." In this book we shall be concerned with the efforts of businessmen—including some labor leaders—to use this law for their own ends, that is, to secure and exercise monopoly power, and we shall examine the obstacles which courts, legislatures, and civil servants feel it prudent to place in their way.

Over the years the case against monopoly has rested mainly on the popular conviction that its possession confers on the fortunate party an unfair advantage in the competition for the good things of life. Monopoly has been condemned on other counts as well; it has often been charged with undermining efficiency and impeding progress—and even with subverting the foundations of liberal democracy. But monopoly has reached the status of a problem in the United States affording employment to hundreds of lawyers, civil servants, private detectives, and economists largely because of the sense of injustice that it inspires.

Positive action to preserve or promote competitive markets has always been difficult since it requires the sacrifice of other values. Such action necessarily involves interference with freedom of contract—a

1

liberty rightly prized by reasonable men for themselves and others. Monopoly is often the unavoidable by-product of a measure designed to attain a goal of undoubted worth. Thus we must rely upon the medical profession to prescribe the qualifications of persons who would practice as surgeons and physicians lest we be unnecessarily punctured, bled, and drugged; we cannot be sure that the members of the profession will not abuse this power by imposing more restrictions on potential competitors than are needed for our reasonable protection. Again, labor unions by virtue of the monopoly powers they possess are enabled to do good by protecting workers from the petty harassments of superiors and by giving political support to civil liberties and improved social services. Then, too, it is possible that monopoly is a condition of technical efficiency, for if one industrial plant can supply all shoe machinery needed by the economy, a policy that compels the continued operation of more than one plant is perforce wasteful.

Finally, there is always the problem of how to interfere intelligently with freedom of contract with the object of restraining monopoly. Intelligent intervention—at any rate in the area of monopoly policy—involves more than a mechanical appraisal of alternative courses of action in the light of "given" ends. The ends we would set for economic policy depend, in large measure, on what we think the business world is "really" like, and our views of business "reality" are often blurred and generally changing. The reluctance of many nineteenth-century judges to concern themselves with monopoly problems was not due primarily to a respect for freedom of contract that we no longer share. Many judges who upheld contracts between rival businessmen to divide markets, maintain prices, and share profits simply doubted that a profitable monopoly position could long be maintained when new firms were legally free to enter the field. Other judges who refused redress to persons injured by the tactics of aspiring monopolists were not unsympathetic to the plaintiffs or skeptical of the virtues of competition. Rather they rightly doubted that they could determine intelligently where the public interest lay on the basis of evidence and arguments produced in a private lawsuit.

In the present day there are few important ideological differences among persons who concern themselves with monopoly policy in the United States. The main division—and it generates a surprising amount of acrimony in debate—is between persons who view big business as a good way of life and people who dislike the habits of mind it fosters and rewards, but the assumption that production and distribution should be entrusted to business firms committed to the pursuit of private gain now goes virtually unchallenged. Gone from the American scene are the deviationists who once made life more interesting—Marxists, populists, Christian democrats, syndicalists, social democrats, and so forth.

Differences of opinion on monopoly policy can usually be traced to different views of how the economy functions. (Admittedly, one often has good grounds for suspecting that a particular individual's mental image of the business world is influenced by his attitude toward big business as a way of life.) The late Henry Simons could favor a vigorous trust-busting program because he traced economic progress to the efforts of hard pressed small firms to avoid bankruptcy by cutting costs and improving the product.[1] J. K. Galbraith can take a dim view of such drastic measures because he sees economic progress flowing from the laboratories of large corporations that have the resources to gamble on research and development.[2]

One further difficulty of interfering intelligently with freedom of contract also deserves mention. The economic policy of any society—good or bad—must necessarily rest to a considerable extent on faith and conjecture. "Problems" commonly emerge ahead of the evidence that would allow the discovery of the "best" solution; indeed it is the discussion—or conflict—accompanying the emergence of a problem that generates the facts and ideas needed for a solution. The makers of policy, however, cannot always wait for all relevant facts to be gathered and weighed. The federal courts have been ruling on the probable economic consequences of business mergers since 1893; yet surveys which throw light on the economic consequences of business mergers have only appeared in the last twenty years. The Supreme Court encountered the problem of "oligopoly"—business behavior in a market containing only a few sellers who cannot, or will not, form a cartel—as early as 1920 in *United States v. United States Steel Corp.*[3] Oligopoly received almost no attention in the works of economists until the 1930's.

Moreover, it often happens that no amount of research or reflection will suffice to confirm or discredit the assumptions on which a policy is based. Consider the question, How would a merger of Ford, General Motors, and Chrysler that creates a firm controlling 90 per cent of domestic automobile production probably affect the price of automobiles in the next ten years? Clearly no incontestable answer is possible for this question. The effects of the merger cannot be known in ad-

---

[1] *Economic Policy for a Free Society* (1948), especially 56–62.
[2] *American Capitalism* 89–99 (1952).
[3] 251 U.S. 417.

vance. If the merger is allowed, one can never know what would have happened had it been blocked by government action. Nevertheless, some answer to this question is necessary if our object is to establish sensible criteria for screening mergers. Nor can we escape the need to adopt some assumption about the probable effect of such a merger on the price of cars by saying that it should be disallowed if it promises an "injury to competition." (Some authorities strongly oppose any effort to judge the "economic performance"—past, present, or future—of a defendant in an antitrust case because they fear it gives him too much scope for clouding the issues and delaying the outcome.) Possibly there is somewhere a professor of economics or a lawyer too long immersed in antitrust work who will sacrifice any amount of efficiency and progress in the interest of frustrating monopoly, but most of us are reasonable men who place a high value on comfort, leisure, and national self-preservation. We would promptly scrap all measures directed against monopoly if we became convinced that they were grossly wasteful.

How then does one go about forming an estimate of the probable effect of a major merger in the automobile industry on the price of cars? The information on which an informed estimate can be based must be obtained mainly from people in the trade—the parties to the merger, dealers, engineers, suppliers to the industry, and the remaining manufacturers of cars. But since the superior knowledge of the trade derives from self-interest, the evidence obtained from this source will probably conflict, and little of it can be accepted at face value. One can, for example, confidently predict that supporters of the merger will assert that consolidation will reduce the price of cars, while spokesmen for the remaining independent firms in the automobile industry will maintain that it will raise the price of cars.

What help can persons responsible for devising a policy toward mergers expect from economic analysis? The representative economist invited to offer an opinion would probably reason as follows. A merger that brought 90 per cent of domestic car production under the control of one firm would represent a substantial increase in monopoly power, that is, the new firm could more easily raise price by restricting output than could its three predecessor companies with their jealousies and conflicting interests. Foreign companies would probably be unable to offer comparable products at any price which the combination is likely to select, and the high cost of founding a new automobile company means that a higher price for cars will not draw new producers into the industry. A merger of Ford, General Motors, and Chrysler would produce a combination that could raise price, and since a business firm is not a charitable institution, this combination can be expected to raise price if its profits are thereby increased.

The representative economist would then point out that only one consideration would restrain the combination from raising price or cause price to fall. Conceivably a consolidated enterprise could produce a given quantity of cars more cheaply than three smaller firms, and this saving might be so great that it would gain by lowering price in order to increase revenue by selling more cars. Our economist would add that if the combination proposes to keep existing plants in operation, the economies of scale cannot lie in manufacturing—they will have to be sought in advertising, centralized purchasing, standardization of parts, etc. At this point the economist ceases to be useful to the makers of policy unless he is also a specialist on the automobile industry. As a specialist he may properly presume to say whether, in this particular case, downward pressure on price of scale economies resulting from the merger would suffice to offset the upward pressure on price resulting from an increase in monopoly power.

In short, economic analysis is mainly useful because it helps the makers of policy to put the right questions to specialists. Given, however, the uncertainty surrounding future developments in research, consumer preferences, and the factors that make for efficiency in business organization—not to mention the difficulty of finding specialists who do not have a stake in the outcome of the cases—it is improbable that specialists will give uniform answers to the questions put to them. Ultimately, the makers of policy—legislators, judges, or civil servants —must weigh the evidence and reach a decision. Their decision can never be indisputably "right." We can only hope that it exhibits a firm grasp of economic principles, has the support of some business specialists, and reveals a handling of evidence that commands the respect of lawyers.

The reasonable man's approach to monopoly policy—or indeed any branch of economic policy—must therefore combine the courage to act on unsatisfactory evidence and unprovable presumptions with a disinclination to regard any important issue as settled. It follows that anyone who believes, as an unalterable article of faith, that the progress of technology "inevitably" increases the scale of efficient production is not a reasonable man. Nor can anyone be admitted to this category who preaches that the family farm and family business are technically the most efficient ways of organizing an economy at all times and places.

Given the diversity and complexity of the issues that arise because individuals seek to use the law of diminishing demand for their own ends, the organization of a treatise on monopoly must be quite arbitrary. This book is organized on the following plan with the following hopes. Chapters II, III, and IV consider the light that current economic analysis can throw on two of the enduring problems of monopoly policy —agreements among rival businessmen to restrict output and mergers. Chapters V and VI examine the extent and tendency of industrial concentration in the American economy in the light of the available statistics. Chapters VII and VIII consider some of the finer points of economic analysis relevant to monopoly policy. The remaining portion of the book, Chapter XIX excepted, traces the growth of monopoly policy in the United States from its common-law origins to the present as it relates to cartels, market tactics, oligopoly, and labor unions. Chapter XIX, which considers the drift of monopoly policy in Britain since 1890, is intended to afford a perspective on the American effort.

Chapter II

THE THEORY OF CARTELS

1. *First principles of monopoly*

Most of the important propositions of political economy are plain and obvious—if not trite—once they are stated correctly in language intelligible to non-specialists. The collection of postulates and inferences that economists call the theory of monopoly is no exception. But since people who seek or possess monopoly power generally take care to disguise their motives—and since they are often pilloried by their opponents in highly emotional language—much nonsense is talked and written about monopoly. Let us, therefore, begin our study by recognizing the obvious.

This mainly involves remarking two corollaries to the law of diminishing demand which posits that the price of a commodity varies inversely with the quantity offered for sale in a market. The first corollary is that the amount added to the industry's total revenue by the marketing of an additional unit of product—that is, the industry's "marginal revenue"—is always less than the price for which this incremental unit sells. Since equal units of the same commodity cannot sell for different prices in the same market, the incremental unit depresses the price at which all other units of the commodity would sell if the incremental unit were withheld from the market.[1] The second corollary is

---

[1] Readers experienced in economic analysis will perceive that the above statement of the "law of one price" side-steps the difficult problem of defining "commodity" and "market." If equal units of substance X—say X_1 and X_2—sell for different prices in the same geographical area, then either they are not the same commodity or they are not sold in the same market. One can only suggest hypothetical tests for deciding whether and how far the price differential should be ascribed to "product differentiation" or market "imperfection."

Suppose that X_1 and X_2 are placed side by side for sale. If a small cut in the price of X_1 now causes the sale of X_2 to fall to zero, so long as any portion of X_1 remains unsold, then X_1 and X_2 are the same commodity.

that the industry will maximize profit (or minimize loss) by producing at that rate of output at which (a) its marginal revenue is equal to its marginal cost—or as nearly equal as the necessity of marketing the commodity in discrete units permits—and (b) its marginal cost is rising.

It follows that an industry containing two or more firms whose owners wish to maximize their profits in the short run will embrace co-operation and abjure independent action in selecting prices and rates of output. The failure of the member firms to carry co-operation to the length of matching the industry's marginal cost and marginal revenue generally indicates the presence of one or more of the following complications. (1) A policy of co-operation is illegal—as it is in many American industries. (2) The industry is unable to solve the administrative problem of assigning production quotas and sharing out the industry's aggregate profit among member firms. (3) Established firms fear that their success in raising the industry's short-run profit to its maximum rate will encourage new producers to enter the industry. (4) Established firms do not know which rate of output would yield the industry its maximum profit in the short run. Thus the "competition" of businessmen—as the term is commonly understood—is rooted in the prohibitions of the law, avarice, distrust of actual rivals, fear of potential rivals, and simple miscalculation. For our purpose, competition is "perfect" when each of the businessmen who deal in a particular product believes that it is beyond his poor power to influence its price by buying more or less.[2] In this circumstance he docilely equates

---

The test for determining whether X_1 and X_2 are sold in the same market is equally abstruse. If a small cut in the price of X_1 causes the quantity offered for sale to be taken "immediately" with no visible effect on the price of X_2, then X_1 and X_2 are sold in a perfect market. If a small cut in the price of X_1 merely causes some increase in the quantity sold while simultaneously causing some fall in the sale of X_2, then X_1 and X_2 are sold in an imperfect market.

One cannot measure the degree of product differentiation or market imperfection; hence the study of monopoly as a policy problem must always proceed in terms of inexact and shifting definitions of "commodity" and "market." Frequently the definition of these key words is the crucial issue in an antitrust case, and the difficulty of selecting the right pair of working definitions is wonderfully illustrated by Times-Picayune Publishing Co. v. United States, 345 U.S. 594 (1953). In this case the Court had to decide how far advertising space in morning and evening newspapers in one city was the same commodity and how far readers of morning and evening papers—often the same people—were the same market for advertised wares.

[2] Readers who wish to examine attempts at a more rigorous definition of "perfect" competition may care to consult G. J. Stigler, "Perfect Competition, Historically Contemplated," 65 J. Pol. Econ. 1 (1957). Personally, I doubt the

his own private marginal cost to market price and hopes for the best.

If competition is less than perfect, each producer knows that he has a choice of price policies and that his own marginal revenue and price are not, for decision-making purposes, the same thing. The size of his particular marginal revenue, however, is always problematical since it is influenced by the price and output policies of rival firms. Consequently, in an imperfectly competitive market, the industry's output is "indeterminate" in the sense that it depends upon the formula that rival firms can evolve for getting along with one another and upon how much they fear "potential" competition.

2. *Cartel policy in the simplest case*

Let us examine the limiting case where the members of an industry can restrict their own outputs in accordance with a common plan and do not fear the entry of new firms. On these assumptions we may infer the following rule of action:

> If owners wish to maximize the rate of return upon the capital they have committed to the industry, they will collectively disinvest so long as the value product of an increment of capital transferred to other employments is greater than the loss of income sustained by curtailing the industry's rate of output.

This rule may also be expressed as follows:

> If owners wish to maximize the rate of return upon the capital they have committed to the industry, they will collectively transfer capital to other employments at a rate which (a) maximizes the difference between total receipts and total costs in the industry when total receipts exceed total expenses and (b) minimizes the difference when total expenses exceed total receipts.

This rule implies, of course, that the firms comprising the industry will foreswear competition and form a cartel.[3] For the sake of con-

---

usefulness of hornbook-type definitions in law or economics; hence the absence of capsule definitions of such terms as "competition," "monopoly," "market," and "restraint of trade" in this book.

[3] The rule that an industry organized by a cartel maximizes profit or minimizes loss, in the short run, by matching its marginal cost and marginal revenue where marginal cost is rising, in turn assumes that at every rate of output, price

venient exposition, let us introduce three additional assumptions, namely:

1. No firm acting alone can perceptibly influence the price of its product or the costs of its raw materials by varying output.

FIGURE 1

The Single Firm in Competitive Equilibrium

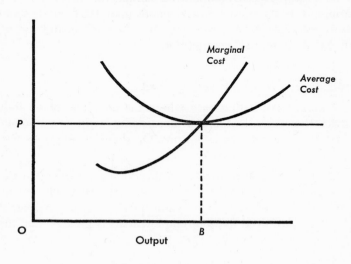

OB = The Single Firm's Output
OP = The Equilibrium Market Price

---

falls less rapidly than marginal revenue. This relation of marginal revenue to price is depicted in virtually all economics textbooks.

An examination of this assumption and its alternatives would involve us in a dreary and unrewarding discussion of methodology. Suffice it to say that one could only construct a real world demand curve by varying price for the express purpose of observing what happens to quantity sold—and this is manifestly impossible. Consequently an industry organized by a cartel can never hope to equate marginal cost and marginal revenue in any exact sense. The orthodox industry demand curve of the textbooks that makes marginal revenue fall more rapidly than price is therefore no more and no less unreal than any other kind. Since it greatly simplifies the study of how businessmen would behave if they had "perfect" knowledge of their operations, we use it exclusively. For examples of "unorthodox" demand functions, see Joan Robinson, *The Economics of Imperfect Competition* 57 (1933), and Arthur Smithies, "Monopolistic Price Policy in a Spatial Market," 9 *Econometrica* 63 (1941).

2. All firms have identical costs of production for each rate of output.
3. The industry has achieved long-run equilibrium, *i.e.*, (a) average cost equals average revenue in each firm, (b) production is distributed among firms of optimum size, and (c) the industry's output is neither increasing nor decreasing.

The cost-revenue position of the single firm that acts unilaterally is given in Figure 1. The cost-revenue position of the industry is given in Figure 2. The reader will note that in long-run competitive equilibrium, the industry operates under conditions of increasing average cost and hence, if its output is reduced, average cost of production will

FIGURE 2
The Industry's Competitive Equilibrium with
Firms of Equal Efficiency

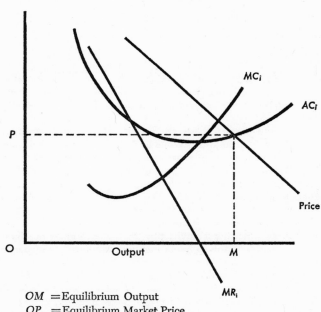

OM = Equilibrium Output
OP = Equilibrium Market Price
AC_i = Industry Short-Run Average Cost
MC_i = Industry Short-Run Marginal Cost
MR_i = Industry Marginal Revenue

fall in each firm;[4] yet no firm acting alone can cut its average cost by curtailing production. This seeming paradox is merely another illustration of the adage that in unity there is strength; when the firms act in concert they exercise monopsony power and so force down the costs of labor and raw materials by buying less of them.

If a cartel is formed in the above circumstances, its rational course is clear enough. It must reduce the industry's rate of output and assign production quotas among member firms that will minimize the total cost of producing whatever output is decided upon. The latter goal is achieved by devising quotas so as to equalize marginal costs in all firms so long as marginal costs fall as the rate of output is decreased. Since all firms have identical cost conditions, each will suffer the same reduction in its output until marginal cost has been minimized in every firm. If profit maximization for the cartel requires a further cut in production, some firms must suspend operations entirely, and the cartel must devise some method of pooling profits in order to compensate the owners of the firms selected for closing down. Short of this point, however, the gains of mutual restraint can be shared out equally among the cartel members without resort to pooling of profits—at least in the short run.

---

[4] While some textbooks still distinguish increasing, decreasing, and constant-cost industries, there are, strictly speaking, only increasing-cost industries. This proposition is introduced here because it is only when an industry has decreasing total average cost that technical efficiency requires that the industry's output be produced by one firm.

Decreasing and constant costs are merely the optical illusions which result from narrowly defining an industry. When an industry's rate of output is increased, its total average cost must also rise for two reasons. (1) Manpower and raw materials are not equally suited for the production of all commodities; consequently, additional units of the industry's product can only be obtained by sacrificing increasing amounts of other goods. (2) The law of diminishing demand ensures that as the output of these other products declines, ever increasing rewards must be paid to attract resources away from the industries which produce them.

Of course, by invoking a sufficiently narrow definition of "industry," any collection of firms can be resolved into a number of industries which, when viewed in isolation, have decreasing or constant costs. Consider the extreme case where one firm owning one plant is deemed to constitute an "industry." Given overhead costs, the single plant has a U-shaped curve of total average cost of production; therefore at low rates of output it is a "decreasing-cost industry."

We might also note that when the firms grouped together to form an industry incur losses, then the industry has the decreasing average cost that is the concomitant of "excess capacity." This sort of decreasing cost is a short-run phenomenon provided that producers react "rationally" to their unprofitable plight. Excess capacity disappears as obsolescence permits capital to be transferred to other industries.

In the long run, pooling cannot be avoided if co-operation is to yield the greatest possible profit, for if quotas are not revised as equipment becomes obsolete, the firm making capital replacement will elect to build plants that are of optimum size from its own standpoint but of less than optimum size for the cartel's purpose. (We assume that there is some one best way of building a plant for every anticipated rate of output.) Figure 3 gives average cost per unit in four possible plants.

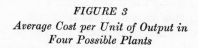

FIGURE 3
Average Cost per Unit of Output in
Four Possible Plants

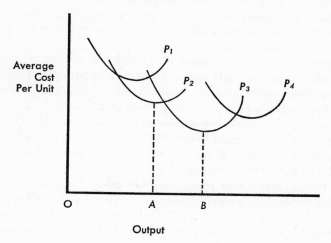

If the cartel member is limited to a quota of *OA* units, he will choose plant design p_2 in preference to p_1, p_3, or p_4. If, however, the cartel is to maximize profit, it must produce efficiently, and this requires the construction of plants of p_3 design and the production of *OB* units in each plant. Now if the cartel desires that the firm should replace with plants of optimum size, the quotas of producers constructing new plants must be increased and the quotas assigned to producers with older facilities correspondingly reduced. The latter, as the price of their continued co-operation, will demand some share of the greater profits realized by the firms which receive the increased quotas.[5]

---

[5] For a more detailed discussion of cartel policy in the simple case where all firms have identical costs, see Don Patinkin, "Multiple-Plant Firms, Cartels, and Imperfect Competition," 61 *Q. J. Econ.* 173 (1947).

3. *Cartel policy with firms of unequal efficiency*

When the firms comprising the cartel do not have identical cost conditions, income pooling may be necessary for maximum profit even in the short run. Since attainment of the maximum rate of return on capital requires that marginal costs be kept equal in all firms, the greatest restrictions must be borne by those firms whose marginal costs decline least rapidly as the rate of output is reduced. Conceivably, joint maximization of profits can be secured merely by sharing out the benefits of restraint unequally among the cartel members. But the cutback in production required for this joint maximization may be so great that high-cost firms will have to accept quotas that, in the absence of pooling, will lower the rate of return on their initial investment. In the extreme case, joint maximization may even require the shutting down of plants which, at the lowest feasible rate of output, cannot match the marginal costs of the remaining plants.

To state what a cartel must do in order to maximize profit is to suggest why, in fact, cartels never achieve—or even seriously seek—this goal. Any close approximation to full monopoly pricing is precluded by (a) the impossibility of continuously revising quotas to take account of obsolescence and capital replacement in member firms, (b) the administrative difficulties involved in negotiating the distribution of monopoly earnings among member firms, and (c) the uncertainty that surrounds the future of the restrictive agreement.[6]

Actually cartels that resort to profit pooling for the purpose of increasing profits by reducing costs are exceedingly difficult to uncover.[7] Most of the so-called "pools" that have figured in government investigations and court cases have been little more than collection

---

[6] For a unique discussion of the obstacles to profit maximization by a Danish economist who has participated in a cartel negotiation, see Bjarke Fog, "How Are Cartel Prices Determined?" 5 *J. Ind. Econ.* 16 (1956). Fog records that even in Denmark, where cartel agreements are enforceable at law, the inability of business rivals to trust one another makes it difficult to negotiate price and output policies that would be mutually profitable.

[7] Authentic cases where a cartel, lacking government support, has so restricted an industry's output that closing of some plants was necessary to achieve its ends are difficult to discover. Cartels apparently are seldom this ambitious or foolhardy. It is recorded, however, that in Britain during the 1920's the Federation of Calico Printers—a textile cartel with about twenty-five members—on two occasions bought and shut the plants of non-members. "The printing plant in each case was scrapped and the premises disposed of subject to a covenant precluding their future use for calico printing." Monopolies and Restrictive Practices Commission, *Report on the Process of Calico Printing* 19 (1954).

agencies formed to supervise co-operation among the members and bear witness to everyone's good faith. (One British cartel aptly described its earnings pool as a "fidelity fund."[8]) Hence, the practical

FIGURE 4
Two Protected Cartels in Long-run Equilibrium

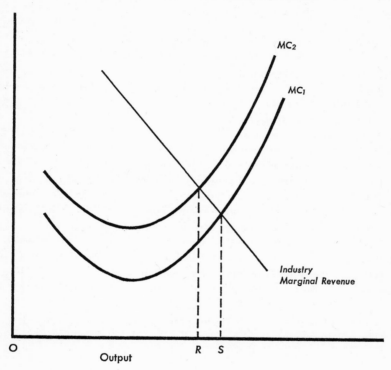

MC_1 = Industry Marginal Cost with Plants of Optimum Size
MC_2 = Industry Marginal Cost with Plants of Less than Optimum Size
OS = Equilibrium Output of a Protected Cartel That Pools Income
OR = Equilibrium Output of a Protected Firm That Does Not Pool Income

[8] Monopolies and Restrictive Practices Commission, *Report on the Supply of Standard Metal Windows and Doors* 17 (1956).

objection to pooling rests not so much upon its use to promote full monopoly pricing as upon its value for insuring that cartel members abide by whatever agreement they have negotiated.

4. Cartels and economic efficiency

In the short run, both the pooling and the non-pooling cartel are wasteful to the extent that they assign quotas which fail to equalize marginal costs in all firms, and the approach to this equality will, of course, prove more difficult in the non-pooling cartel. In the long run, the non-pooling cartel is clearly the more wasteful type since adherence to fixed quotas will lead to the construction of plants of less than optimum size.

It does not follow, however, that the non-pooling cartel imposes the greater restriction on output in either the short run or the long run, for pooling is employed by cartels both to reduce the cost of the agreed-upon output and to share out the gains of monopoly among the member firms. If we postulate (a) identical cost conditions for member firms—even in the long run—and (b) no entry of outsider capital, the pooling cartel will impose a smaller reduction of output than the non-pooling cartel (see Figure 4). This proposition holds because, as noted above, the absence of pooling will ultimately produce plants of less than optimum size, so that in long-run equilibrium, the short-run marginal cost curve of the non-pooling cartel lies above the marginal cost curve of the pooling cartel. But if one does not assume both identical cost conditions for member firms in the long run and protection against outsider capital, it is not possible to determine (a) the degree of restraint short of full monopoly pricing which the industry will attempt, (b) the type of plants which will be constructed, or (c) the industry's short-run costs of production. The pooling cartel is always more efficient and more profitable than the non-pooling cartel. It may or may not impose a greater restriction on the industry's output and exact a higher price.

5. Cartels as a short-run policy problem

Actually, few useful insights are to be gleaned from contemplating the long-run economic consequences of the pooling as against the non-pooling cartel. If the industry enjoys no legal protection against the invasion of newcomers, the design of new equipment is unlikely to be tied closely to the firm's current quota. If the industry does enjoy a legally protected position, quotas are likely to become property rights which it will pay someone to acquire and distribute among plants of optimum size.

In the absence of enduring barriers to entry, there is no stable long-run equilibrium for the cartel. For a time, it may pay the members to pay something for the limited co-operation of newcomers. The amount of blackmail which can be collected by any particular new-comer depends mainly upon the size of the cartel's monopoly profit, the ability of its established members to survive a return to competitive conditions, and the size of the investment which the newcomer can bring to the industry. The total amount of blackmail that the cartel will pay to enlist the co-operation of newcomers cannot, of course, exceed the loss which its members would suffer through the complete collapse of the quota system.

In the case of the non-pooling cartel the bribe will probably take the form of a quota for the newcomer bestowed on condition that he play the game. But as more new firms are taken into the group, the quota that the members are willing to assign to each successive new-comer shrinks in size and the type of plant that he must construct to produce it most cheaply becomes smaller. Eventually the quota offered by the expanded cartel to a newcomer will not suffice to dissuade him from building a larger plant and equating his marginal cost to price. The return to competition has then begun.

The disintegration of a pooling cartel will follow substantially the same path. The only difference is that the total bribe may be more or less than the quota given to the newcomer. He may exact a cash pre-mium for not exceeding his quota or, alternatively, in return for a quota that enables him to construct an optimum-size plant, he may agree to surrender part of his income to the older members.

It is perhaps unnecessary to remark that no "rules" govern the conduct of the "rational" cartel that is not in a position to protect itself permanently against the entry of new capital. Decisions relating to price policy, willingness to accept new members, and the design of new equipment must turn upon how rapidly new capital enters the industry once restriction of production has made the industry profitable, and upon how these decisions, in turn, affect this rate of capital movement.

Chapter III

THE INFERENCES FROM
CARTEL THEORY

1. *The improbability of full monopoly pricing in the cartel*

So far we have seen that on a premise of *ceteris paribus*, competition—
which we may define as the making of decisions affecting price and
output without consulting one's rivals—is irrational whenever the members of an industry have it within their power to restrict output among
themselves and to delay the entry of new producers who would share
the fruits of concerted action. Our examination has also suggested that
rival firms—even when they find themselves in this enviable position—
are unlikely ever to exact the full monopoly price in either the short run
or the long run. The administrative difficulties are too formidable to
allow the "joint maximization" which such a price policy requires. In
any event, few cartels enjoy unlimited protection against the entry of
newcomers.[1]

2. *The temptation to chisel*

The main obstacle to the success of a cartel lies, of course, in the incentive to cheat that is dangled before the members. Honesty is a
foolish policy for the single participant so long as the others can be
relied upon to play the game, for when a single firm produces only its
assigned quota, marginal cost is always below marginal revenue. On the
assumption that the cartel functions in what would otherwise be a
purely competitive industry, Figure 5 depicts the temptation to cheat
facing the producers who have been assigned the quota *OA* when the
ruling market price is *OI*.

---

[1] For a more extended examination of the obstacles to profit maximization
by cartels, see W. J. Fellner, *Competition Among the Few* 142–97 (1949).

18

Therefore, the less temptation the cartel puts in the way of its members, that is, the lower its price, the more likely it is to command their trustworthy co-operation. It also follows that whenever the cartel price is set much above the competitive price, the combination is destined for early disintegration unless its managers have access to reliable information on the operations of its members. When firms are few, chiseling can be detected and its perpetrators traced without much difficulty, otherwise some formal organization for the purpose of gathering data is indispensible.

FIGURE 5
The Cartel Member's Temptation

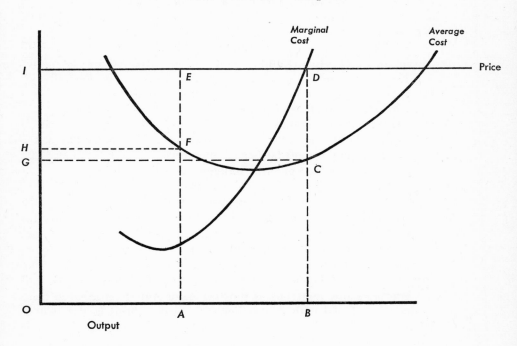

OA   =Honest Member's Authorized Output
OB   =Cheating Member's Output
HFEI =Honest Member's Authorized Profit
GCDI =Cheating Member's Profit

19

3. *Barriers to entry*

The barriers to entry which a cartel may erect or shelter behind are of five main sorts.[2] We might emphasize that these entrenchments need not permanently exclude potential rivals for co-operation to prove profitable. It is enough if they merely delay the entry of outside capital.

1. The cartel may enjoy the protection of the law. A legally protected market position is the highest desideratum for established producers, and, unhappily, the proliferation of legislation granting special favors to influential interests is everywhere so great that a systematic classification of such benefits is probably out of the question. The least disputed of the legal barriers to entry is the patent grant for a limited period of time;[3] the most vehemently condemned by economists is the licensing law which requires a showing of public "convenience and necessity" before a new firm is allowed to challenge established producers.

2. The cartel may employ methods which are palpably unlawful —even indictable—to discourage competitors attracted by its profits. A loose federation of sovereign members, however, is generally ill-suited to attempt the intimidation of rivals by threats aganist the person or malicious destruction of property. Given a reasonable level of law enforcement, illegal activity is more likely to be the work of the single firm with its better chance of escaping detection and conviction, or the work of labor unions and farmer co-operatives whose roughhouse tactics are more likely to enjoy the indulgence of the public.

3. The cartel may resort to "unfair" methods of competition to preserve its monopoly gains against outsiders. (Technically, such methods have been both actionable and indictable in this country for many years, but the standards of proof set by the courts make cases against unfair competitors difficult to win.) The members of the combination may concertedly cut price or incur heavier selling costs when rivals appear on the scene, or they may deliberately bid up the prices of the industry's raw materials as did the major American tobacco companies when faced with the challenge from new firms in the 1930's.[4] When the industry has only a few members, these tactics may prove

---

[2] For a detailed discussion of the nature of barriers to entry, with some reference to cartel policy in manufacturing industries, see J. S. Bain, *Barriers to New Competition* (1956), especially 1–41.

[3] The American patent system has been attacked often enough, but criticism is generally directed at its administration rather than the principle of patent protection for deserving inventors.

[4] American Tobacco Co. v. United States, 328 U.S. 781 (1946).

effective in discouraging potential rivals, but again, if flexibility in cartel policy is made difficult by the presence of many members, it is more likely that newcomers will receive an invitation to join the group.

4. The members of the cartel may turn to their own account the imperfections of the market. News of their success may travel slowly, and if either the future of the cartel or the industry itself is uncertain—a most probable circumstance—the rate of return on capital secured by the combination may be insufficient to offset the investment risk which newcomers must assume in order to enter.

5. The cartel may take advantage of the existence of "excess capacity" in its operations. So long as the industry is not covering average cost even with a policy of output restriction, no reasonable investor will desire entry. Even though the firms are receiving something more than the "prevailing" rate of return on their committed capital, new producers will not hastily enter the industry if it is probable that an outbreak of competition will drive price below average cost.

We may note that even on static assumptions, excess capacity is a wasting asset as a barrier to entry since it presumes a gradual withdrawal of capital from the industry. On the more realistic assumption that technology is improving (or at least changing), outside rivals capable of starting operations with new plants have even less cause to fear a return to competition with the passing of time.

4. The "ideal" conditions of cartel management

Our brief examination of the theory of combination and its more obvious implications enables us to discern the conditions which favor the formation and persistence of the successful cartel. If we were to embark upon cartel management as a profession we should, of course, above all else wish to enjoy the patronage of the State.[5] Like Mr. Dooley's businessman in politics we should prefer to make it a penitentiary offense for anyone to patronize our rivals. But forming a cartel with the aid of the State is too much like shooting fish in a barrel. Indeed, given free entry into our profession, we would soon find ourselves doing the work—and drawing the wages—of bookkeepers and private detectives. Let us, therefore, assume that we face the more

---

[5] That cartel management could become a profession if the law were not so hostile is strongly suggested by the role of free-lance industrial consultants in the promotion of trade associations. See, for example, Salt Producers Ass'n v. Federal Trade Commission, 134 F.2d 354 (7th Cir. 1943), or United States Maltsters Ass'n v. Federal Trade Commission, 152 F.2d 161 (7th Cir. 1945).

challenging (and rewarding) task of promoting co-operation in an industry whose members enjoy no legal protection against the entry of outsider capital. In this circumstance, we should wish to enjoy as many of the following "natural" advantages as possible.

The industry should consist of relatively few firms in order that our job of inspection and co-ordination may be easily handled. Preferably the member firms should have similar costs of production over a wide range of output since, as we have seen, given equally efficient producers, it is possible to make extensive use of the law of diminishing demand without the pooling of income or a redivision of the market. The demand for the industry's output should be highly inelastic at its precartel price, so that any reduction of output will cause a perceptible increase in the industry's total revenue. Such inelasticity simplifies our task of selling our members on the advantages of co-operation and the unwisdom of chiseling once some part of monopoly profit has been realized. That is, we prefer that the advantages of mutual restraint should be capable of easy demonstration.

Likewise, the success of the cartel will be assisted if we can secure control of the better supplies of some essential raw material and so render the entry of new producers more difficult. Our task will be further simplified to the extent that the industry consists of firms which must incur high overhead costs in order to operate efficiently. A large optimum size for the firm will increase the difficulty faced by potential competitors in raising capital and make easier our task of driving out newcomers who give battle with firms of less than optimum size.

Finally, we should wish to organize our cartel in an industry which in the short run is unprofitable without co-operation, modestly profitable with it. This condition will serve to discourage chiseling among the members since there is a good prospect for profits for everyone if restraint is practiced, and the probability of profits for no one if our admonitions are ignored. If the industry is so lacking in hope that some firms face bankruptcy even if they play the game, desperation may drive them to cut prices or exceed their quotas on the chance that they may survive through a policy of beggaring their more honest or less enterprising neighbors. If the industry is already earning appreciably more than the prevailing rate of return on capital, its members are probably thinking in terms of expansion rather than contraction, and if our cartel cannot long delay the entry of new firms, they are right to do so. In any event, the higher the rate of return, the sooner (presumably) we should expect the assault on our position by outsider capital. Probably we should also wish something less than full employment in the rest of the economy on the assumption that depression or recession will hamper the efforts of would-be rivals to acquire the necessary financial backing.

As ambitious cartel managers should we seek an industry characterized by a rapid, moderate, or negligible rate of technological change? Offhand it seems advisable to eschew industries where changes in product design are frequent, for such changes make the detection of chiseling more difficult and require the revisions of price policies and the renegotiation of quotas which have hastened the downfall of so many restrictive agreements over the years. In general, the fewer the decisions our members are called upon to make, the better the chance of securing consensus on some common plan of action. There is the additional consideration that frequent changes in product design encourage firms to rely too much on their own ingenuity and luck, and hence to underestimate the advantages of mutual restraint.

Changes in production technique, however, when unaccompanied by changes in the nature of the product probably serve our interests. Innovations that affect only production costs, especially if covered by patents (preferably patents possessing little or no value when used in isolation), have the double merit of making the entry of outsiders more difficult and reminding our members of the virtues of co-operation. Even if the innovations are unpatentable—or, at any rate, incapable of supporting patents that can withstand litigation—their rapid appearance increases the risk which newcomers face in attempting to enter the field. Established firms, after all, have the greatest experience in assessing the commercial potentialities of alternative methods of production.

5. *The relevance of cartel theory*

So much for the industry "ideally" suited to combination.[6] We might note that our model cartel is by no means so far removed from "reality" as might appear at first sight; indeed the business combinations that

---

[6] Not that we have exhausted the subject. There seems no point in prolonging the discussion further into diminishing returns since the list of factors that influence cartel effectiveness could be extended ad infinitum. Thus a New York salt producers' association once foundered on the rock of its members' religious differences. A. S. Dewing, *Corporate Promotions and Reorganizations* 205 (1914). For this reason, I doubt the usefulness of any general theory of "coalitions" that seeks to do much more than elaborate the obvious. For a distinguished contrary opinion, see John von Neumann and Oskar Morgenstern, *Theory of Games and Economic Behavior* 14–15 (2d ed. 1947).

have figured in reported court cases over the last three hundred years have almost invariably enjoyed at least one of the desirable preconditions set forth above—and usually two or more. That is, it is no accident that so many of the famous cartel cases have involved the activities of such imperfect competitors as salt producers, stevedoring concerns, common carriers, anthracite-mining companies, and skilled workers in the building trades.

Perhaps instead of inquiring into the circumstances that favor attempts at combination we should ask, When are the prospects of success so slight that an effort at co-operation is not worth the trouble and expense involved in trying to promote it? The answer would seem to be that in the absence of harassment by the law, such an attempt is always worth while unless the industry is located at one end or the other of the competition-monopoly spectrum. It is doomed to failure under conditions approximating pure competition, e.g., in staple agriculture. It is unnecessary, if one firm controls the output of a product so differentiated that the producer has no discernable community of interest with other enterprises, e.g., power and light companies. But for most sectors of the economy other than staple agriculture and public utilities, the urge to co-operate is as enduring and ubiquitious as the single firm's temptation to expand production so long as marginal revenue promises to remain above marginal cost. One must really look a long way to uncover a business enterprise so negligible or differentiated that it does not maintain membership in at least one trade association. (The British rubber industry in 1956 even boasted a Football Bladder Association.)

6. *Cartel management as an art*

Finally, our analysis of cartel behavior even within the limits of the "static" assumptions employed above serves to emphasize a point too often neglected, namely that the successful management of cartels is art, not science, and that nothing short of intervention by the State can guarantee the success of an industry's effort to turn the law of diminishing demand to its own account, however much the environment favors restraint. If the workings of business combinations were exposed to the light, we should expect that the successful cartel, even more often than the successful firm, would emerge as the product of exceptional management.

24

Chapter IV

THE THEORY OF CONSOLIDATION

1. *Consolidation as an alternative to co-operation and its limits*

We have seen that although the wish to form cartels is endemic in most industries, it is unlikely to produce full monopoly pricing or even alliances that endure for very long. Hence many authorities contend that cartels have little in common with large firms capable of appreciably influencing market price without outside assistance. According to one popular view, federal agencies spend much time and energy harassing trade associations whose activities are relatively innocuous; yet mergers which represent a more serious threat to competition go unsupervised, and large firms already in possession of a substantial part of the market are left alone. Let us, therefore, consider the circumstances in which temporary business coalitions are likely to give way to more permanent unions via mergers.[1]

If we assume static conditions of supply and demand—that is, no changes in technology, factor prices, or consumer tastes—the promotion of a consolidation clearly differs from the formation of a cartel in two important respects. (1) It requires the prospect that any monopoly power achieved by the consolidation will endure for some time; otherwise the consolidation is not worth promoting. (2) It poses a major problem of finance since some owners of established firms must be bought out. Conceivably all established producers might trustingly surrender control over their properties to the promoter in return for a non-marketable equity in his new venture, but this has never happened in an important merger. At least one skeptic, discounting the prospects of

---

[1] For an excellent older comparison of the origins of cartels and close combinations, see D. H. Macgregor, *Industrial Combination* 115–68 (1906).

the promotion, can be relied upon to demand payment for his co-operation in cash or gilt-edged bonds.[2]

A cartel may be said to function successfully so long as its policy of restricting output does not provoke a stampede on new capital into the industry. When so threatened, its members can pocket their earnings, revert to a policy of competition, and mark time before events once more favor a return to co-operation. The "rational" merging of rival firms, however, requires that the promoter must be able to pay something more than the sum of their discounted future earnings as competing or imperfectly co-ordinated enterprises. If consolidation can guarantee permanent protection against outsider capital, the promoter stands to realize a capital gain by buying out the established producers for anything less than their capitalized earning power when operated as a fully rationalized monopoly. If complete protection against new-comers is not assured, the merger value of the separate properties is correspondingly reduced.

Nevertheless, even on a premise of *ceteris paribus* and in the absence of a threat from outsider capital, complete monopoly is not likely to be achieved unless it can be executed in one fell swoop; for a consolidation which is merely partial reduces the promoter's incentive to press on to complete control of the market in at least two ways. (1) It raises the nuisance value of firms not acquired, thereby encouraging the remaining independents to hold out for a higher price. (2) By reducing the number of firms in the industry, it makes possible more effective action within the framework of a cartel. However, in so far as static conditions are approximated in the business world—and power to exclude newcomers is present—competition will most probably degenerate into some form of oligopoly. One may, for example, safely predict that any town which limits the number of taxicab permits while allowing them to be bought and sold in a free market will shortly witness a rapid consolidation of firms.[3]

Let us again rule out the easy case where government policies by

---

[2] The classic case of one man's skepticism was Andrew Carnegie's refusal to accept payment for his personal property in the common stock of the United States Steel Corporation when he sold out to the Morgan combine in 1901. F. L. Allen, *The Great Pierpont Morgan* 174–76 (1949).

[3] On this truth see United States v. Yellow Cab Co., 332 U.S. 218 (1947). In the ten years after 1929 one Morris Markin and associates cornered the following proportion of authorized cab franchises in the following cities: 100 per cent in Pittsburgh, 58 per cent in Minneapolis, 15 per cent in New York City and 77 per cent in Chicago. Showing a practical mastery of the principle of inelastic demand, Markin in 1937 even persuaded Chicago to allow him to surrender 1,071 out of the 4,085 franchises that he had purchased.

design or oversight fall in with the plans of aspiring monopolists. A merger for control of the market is obviously ill-advised if newcomers enjoy ease of entry. We must therefore ask, Does consolidation per se augment the power of established firms to exclude newcomers?

To some extent consolidation undoubtedly serves this end by imparting a flexibility to price and output policy that is not possible—or at any rate not probable—in the cartel. The cartel is a cumbersome device for combating rivals; indeed, when faced with the challenge of outsider capital, the cartel is likely to buy off newcomers with a share of the market or simply disintegrate. The consolidated enterprise, however, can fight back with any number of weapons, e.g., the patent infringement suit, the higher advertising budget, easier credit to customers, secret rebates and, if seriously pressed, even lower list prices.

Consolidation may make for flexibility in price and output policies in yet another way. In order to discourage cheating by its members, the cartel must adopt rules that discourage deviation from published prices and encourage the standardization of products.[4] Hence it cannot fully exploit price discrimination as a source of profit nor readily develop new markets by adapting products to the needs of individual customers. This disadvantage is eliminated by consolidation.

Nevertheless, to the extent that static conditions are approximated, it is improbable that an industry capable of supporting a fair number of firms will ever be monopolized completely unless the State lends a hand. The difficulty involved in securing control of the "last independent," together with uncertainty about the strength of the dike against outsider capital, means that total control is seldom worth its cost to the "rational" promoter. Even the original oil[5] and tobacco[6] trusts—

---

[4] Thus in Britain the association of metal window manufacturers from 1936 to 1939 reached an agreement on a standard range comprising 400 types of window suitable for housing. The standardization program was openly based on the principle that "the standard specification must be such that all members' windows appeared to be exactly alike from the point of view of the purchaser" and "must not allow deviations which could become effective selling points." Monopolies and Restrictive Practices Commission, Report on the Supply of Standard Metal Windows and Doors 12 (1956).

[5] By 1904 the rivals of the Standard Oil Company accounted for about 21 per cent of the oil refined in the United States. Commissioner of Corporations, Report on the Petroleum Industry 265 (1907). The strenuous efforts of Rockefeller before 1890 to corner refining capacity are described in 1 Allan Nevins, John D. Rockefeller 338–574 (1940).

[6] The tobacco trust concluded that all producers of handmade cigarettes could not profitably be excluded from the market, and that roughly 15 per cent of cigarette production could wisely be left to numerous small firms with only local

MONOPOLY IN ECONOMICS AND LAW

two of the most ruthless and aggressive combinations ever formed—eventually decided to settle for something less than total control of the market.

The striving for complete monopoly may be irrational, but mergers which seek it are not, for this reason, unknown. Before World War I numerous attempts were made to secure control of the market by purchase, and many of these mergers were successful in the sense that they created enclaves of monopoly power that have endured to the present (United Shoe Machinery Corporation) or would probably have endured had not the State intervened (original Standard Oil Company of New Jersey). Moreover, the history of combination strongly suggests that in the absence of an antitrust policy, promoters would still occasionally try to put together the One Big Firm. In accounting for these efforts to monopolize "in practice" we would seem to have a choice of four explanations.

1. Considerations of profit and loss are secondary; the promoters are actuated mainly by the hope of increasing their own personal prestige and power or the wish to associate themselves with something Big.

2. The promoters are gambling that consolidation will create an effective barrier to entry. The achievement of this end does not, of course, guarantee the profitability of the venture since a promoter may pay too much for his whistle. Yet if one assumes—as did some early students of the trust movement—that mergers are generated by foolish optimism,[7] a "trend to monopoly" is possible even though it neither increases economic efficiency nor enriches its promoters. The importance of chronic miscalculation in fostering industrial concentration should not be overemphasized; still, a number of large corporations that survive originated in promotional mergers that sadly disappointed their backers.

---

followings. R. B. Tennant, *The American Cigarette Industry* 40–43 (1950).

[7] The optimism exuded by the promoters of combination prior to 1904 was certainly excessive. (Whether they wholly believed their own claims is another matter.) After studying the promotional prospectuses, capitalization, and earnings records of thirty-five industrial mergers formed before 1904, A. S. Dewing concluded that "the estimated earnings were half again as large as the actual earnings of the first year after the union, and nearly twice as great (175%) as the average earnings during the ten-year period following consolidation." "A Statistical Test of the Success of Consolidations," 36 Q. J. Econ. 84, 91–92 (1922). For contemporary accounts of the "mania" of speculation that prevailed during the heyday of the Corporate Revolution, see A. D. Noyes, "The Recent Economic History of the United States," 19 Q. J. Econ. 167 (1905); and A. A. Osborne, *Speculation on the New York Stock Exchange, September, 1904–March, 1907* (1913).

3. Control of the market is a by-product of financial manipulation. The promoters expect to make their profits through (a) a capital gain arising out of a general increase in the demand for the industry's product or (b) a short-term capital gain made possible by the imperfection of the securities market. The role of financial chicanery in the age of the great mergers—roughly 1890 to 1910—has been noted by almost all students of the period;[8] and, indeed, not a few of the early promoters of mergers who preached the possibility of getting rich through monopoly often seem mainly to have been interested in selling watered stock to unwary investors.

4. Control of the market is a by-product of the striving for profit through improved efficiency; the combination of rival firms *really* is the product of an intelligently assessed prospect that economies of scale can be achieved through merger.

Given the willingness of some people to risk their capital in profitable fields that are not closed to them by law, complete monopoly is likely to be of short duration unless it is rooted in something more substantial than managerial empire building, promoter optimism, or sharp financial practice. And the pattern of competition that will emerge is perforce conditioned by the legal framework of the business world. If cartel agreements are legally enforceable, most industries most of the time will operate under a restrictive arrangement.[9] (Inevitably cartel monopoly will produce its own parasites, *i.e.*, small firms outside the cartel that are permitted to operate without molestation provided they stay small, and the cartel itself will occasionally disintegrate.) If cartel agreements are not legally enforceable, the uncertainty thereby imparted to business relationships will encourage consolidation, so that *ceterus paribus* the willingness of the courts to enforce restrictive arrangements will preserve some firms that would otherwise disappear by merger.[10] The refusal of American courts to enforce German-type cartel arrangements has doubtless encouraged corporate consolidations

---

[8] See, for example, E. S. Mead, *Trust Finance* (1903); A. S. Dewing, *Corporate Promotions and Reorganizations* (1914); or Eliot Jones, *The Trust Problem in the United States* (1922).

[9] A classic study of cartel operations under the protection of enforceable contracts is still Francis Walker, "Monopolistic Combinations in the German Coal Industry," 5 *Publications Am. Econ. Ass'n* (3d ser. 1904).

[10] In Anglo-American law the distinction between a "firm" and a cartel "composed" of member firms is reasonably clear. A firm generally exists as a legal entity or it does not. If it exists, it is either independent or a subsidiary of some larger organization. Under German law, which accords wider scope to freedom of contract in business matters, the dividing line between firm and cartel is often indistinct. Thus the *interessengemeinschaften* or community of interest achieved

designed to replace workable competition and unsatisfactory gentle-man's agreements with oligopoly. This point is easily made. It is more difficult to estimate the proximate importance of monopoly power as an incentive to merge. What of the venerable "economies of large-scale production?"

2. *Consolidation and economies of scale*

Although the importance of economies of scale as a stimulus to combi-nation has been discussed and debated for many years, economists do not yet agree on how this question should be answered. Nor, unfortu-nately, are they making much progress toward consensus; most of the arguments currently employed to minimize or exalt economies of scale as a factor promoting combination were common currency as early as 1905.[11] Given the passions engendered by the subject matter, we can-not hope to resolve an issue of sixty years' standing. But we can aspire to state the problem as clearly as possible and, perhaps, distinguish questions which are inherently unanswerable from those which cannot profitably be discussed without further study.

Now the term "economies of scale" itself is a source of confusion since over the years it has acquired three distinct meanings. The term is regularly employed to describe:

1. The existence of overhead costs in the shop or factory that yield the U-shaped curve of average manufacturing or "production"

---

when formerly independent firms pooled profits, exchanged shares, and agreed upon a common dividend policy under agreements running for many years does not closely correspond to any form of business organization known in common-law countries. See Hermann Levy, *Industrial Germany* 136–86 (1935), or Herbert von Beckerath, *Modern Industrial Organizations* 239–48 (1933). It is therefore somewhat misleading to say that a legal code which enforces cartel agreements tends to preserve "firms." There is the additional consideration that in such cir-cumstances production quotas become valuable property rights, so that efficient firms are tempted to buy or lease the facilities of their less efficient associates. This type of concentration seems to have been common in many German industries before 1939. See Karl Pribram, *Cartel Problems* 79 (1935).

[11] The discussion of scale economies as a factor encouraging mergers has progressed very little beyond C. J. Bullock, "Trust Literature: a Survey and a Criticism," 15 *Q. J. Econ.* 167 (1901). Its subsequent drift can be traced in E. S. Meade, "The Economies of Combination," 20 *J. Pol. Econ.* 358 (1912); Eliot Jones, *The Trust Problem in the United States* 499–541 (1922); J. M. Clark, *The Economics of Overhead Costs* 104–48 (1923); 2 A. S. Dewing, *Financial Policy of Corporations* 921–83 (4th ed. 1941); and Fritz Machlup, *The Political Economy of Monopoly* 51–53 (1952).

cost, *i.e.*, average total cost minus the sum of average delivery and average selling costs.

2. The saving that could be secured by ultimately replacing an existing plant with a larger one that would yield a lower total average cost of production if operated at its most efficient rate.

3. The economies which result from consolidation because the larger firm can obtain manpower and capital on more favorable terms.

3. *Overhead costs and optimum size of the firm*

Nobody doubts the existence of overhead costs The problem is rather, Do many firms so habitually operate below the rate of output at which average cost of production is lowest that consolidation will increase efficiency by enabling operations to be concentrated into a smaller number of larger plants? This question is really more difficult than appears at first glance.

Most businessmen believe that an increase in the rate of output would lower average cost of production in their firms. Case studies on how costs behave in particular industries support this belief.[12] And whenever marketing costs are present—as they are in most industries— it is probable that the firm produces at a rate of output at which average cost of production is falling. The case for this conclusion is presented in the Appendix to Chapter VIII. For the present, it will suffice to note that marketing costs so limit the extent of the market that the firm is unable to exploit profitably the economies of scale implicit in overhead costs.

Production cost, however, is not total cost, and evidence which purports to show that most firms operate where total average cost is falling is inherently suspect, since accurate statistics on the total cost of manufacturing and marketing an article are virtually unobtainable. In some trades cost of delivery is nominally borne by the producer and enters into his bookkeeping. In some trades cost of delivery is ostensibly assessed against the consumer and hence is overlooked by any study of the producer's costs, so that studies of how "total" cost behaves almost certainly overweight the importance of production costs.

We may conclude that (a) many—probably most—industries have excess capacity in the sense that the representative firm could reduce its average cost of production by increasing output but (b) given mar-

---

[12] Consult, for example, W. J. Eiteman and G. E. Guthrie, "The Shape of the Average Cost Curve," 42 *Am. Econ. Rev.* 832 (1952).

keting costs, it does not follow that total average cost would also fall if the firm's output were increased. As we shall note in Chapter VIII, technical efficiency in production is not affected by the fact that marketing costs have made the market imperfect. If freedom of contract and "rational" behavior are assumed, imperfect competition as well as perfect competition will yield an equilibrium in which firms are of optimum size. Case studies may reveal that in a given industry most plants are of less than optimum size in the sense that some larger plant, operated in the most efficient manner, would have a lower average cost of production. But without information on marketing cost we can say nothing about total cost and, hence, should not conclude that the industry is inefficient.

4. *Selling cost and excess capacity*

Two other versions of the argument that monopoly makes it possible to realize economies of scale by eliminating excess capacity may be noted. The first contends that excess capacity results from "socially wasteful" product differentiation based upon "standoff" advertising expenditures, *i.e.*, outlays that serve neither to "inform" the consumer nor increase the demand for the industry's product. Such outlays, so the argument runs, are made only because the rival firms cannot agree to eliminate them. Any one firm will suffer grievously if it reduces its advertising budget and the others do not follow suit; a monopolist who consolidates an industry plagued by this type of economic waste achieves an economy of scale simply by eliminating it. This argument is, of course, true to the extent that there exist economies of scale in "bad" advertising which an industry has not realized. Most probably the cost of producing cigarettes in the United States would be reduced if a monopolist ever succeeded in gaining control of the industry and "rationalizing" its advertising budget. There is no reason to disbelieve that the prospect of achieving this economy influenced the promoters of the original tobacco trust.[13]

---

[13] In fact, the advertising effort of the tobacco trust seems to have declined as its share of the market rose. Thus, by one estimate the trust prior to 1900 accounted for roughly one-half of the output of "little cigars" and spent on advertising about 10 per cent of its net receipts less tax from little cigars, whereas from 1905 to 1908 it controlled approximately 85 per cent of small cigar output and spent only about 1 per cent of the net receipts of this product on advertising. Likewise the advertising budget of the tobacco industry increased by more than one-third within three years after the breakup of the trust in 1911. 3 Commissioner of Corporations, *Report on the Tobacco Industry* 5–18 (1915).

Second, one may argue that when consumers are not "professional buyers" consumer sovereignty is a textbook fiction. Consumers want what they are conditioned to want by skillful sales promotion, and a monopolist is better situated than suspicious rivals to persuade people to want what the industry can most profitably produce. This is tantamount to saying that co-ordinated exploitation of consumer ignorance is more profitable to the exploiters than unco-ordinated exploitation. Unhappily, there is an element of truth in this depressing supposition— witness for example, the tactics of owners of theater chains who control enough houses to dominate the market. Consumer choice is drastically reduced by simultaneously releasing the same film in many theaters, and low rental films are played on days of the week when attendance is normally greatest.[14] We may conclude, then, that whenever selling costs are present, the possibility of "rationalizing" the industry's sales effort affords the prospect of an economy of scale that encourages consolidation.

5. Consolidation and factor costs

Economies may result from consolidation because the larger firm by virtue of its greater assets is able to obtain capital and manpower on more favorable terms than the formerly independent units. These savings may materialize because uncertainty is somehow reduced or because the elimination of competition confers monopsony power on the industry. In the first instance, consolidation yields a clear gain in economic efficiency; in the second, it merely changes the distribution of resources.

Unfortunately, the benefits of monopsony are not easily separated from those arising out of the reduction of uncertainty. To the degree that the gains are "real" in the sense of making possible a greater national income from a given quantity of resources, they arise in two ways: (a) by making possible a more efficient production of the factors themselves and (b) by reducing transport and other marketing expenses which in turn permits a more efficient use of plant capacity in industries where average production cost in the firm is not yet minimized.

Whatever the source of such gains, they would seem to be real enough to the single firm. Yet even these private economies have been

---

[14] For examples of this sort of market exploitation see United States v. Paramount Pictures, 334 U.S. 131 (1948), or the cinema guide of any London newspaper.

called into question as regards the capital market. One economist advances the following argument in private conversation. Since the interest charge can be resolved into payment for the use of capital ("pure" interest) and payment for uncertainty bearing, the lower interest rates open to the large firm for bonds and commercial paper may merely reflect the fact that equity capital bears a greater part of uncertainty in the large firm. This argument implies that the managers of large firms obtain their lower interest rates by giving tacit surety that, in contrast to small entrepreneurs, they will not so readily cut their own losses by a speedy liquidation or resort to bankruptcy. So far as long-term debt is concerned, this assumption may have some foundation in fact. It has, however, no relevance to the market for short-term secured loans, and even in this market size seems to entitle the large firm to more favorable terms for every type of loan.[15]

There are, of course, more obvious and plausible reasons why the large firm enjoys an advantage in the capital market even though it can offer no better collateral than that posted by a small firm. Bankers realize some economies by making loans in large amounts, so that *pari passu* large firms obtain lower interest rates than their small rivals because they borrow in larger amounts. Again, bankers fear that small firms are more likely to default, thereby putting them to the expense of foreclosure; hence, even though the loan is secured by good collateral, a premium is exacted from the small borrower to cover the risk of inconvenient litigation. In short, lenders believe that large firms by virtue of size alone are in a better position to ride out the squalls of the market that suffice to sink smaller rivals who can furnish comparable security.[16]

Let us accept, then, that corporate size per se enhances the power of the firm to survive, and that the advantage of the large firm in the capital market can at least partly be ascribed to this fact. A more difficult question remains. Does the staying power of the large firm represent its innate superiority as a way of organizing production in the

---

[15] The competitive edge of large firms in all sectors of the capital market is documented in "The Cost and Availability of Credit and Capital to Small Business," *Staff Report of the Board of Governors of the Federal Reserve System Submitted to the Subcommittee on Monopoly of the Senate Select Committee on Small Business*, 82nd Cong., 2d Sess., Subcommittee Print No. 8 (1952).

[16] For evidence that "in general, regardless of the year or the line of industry, small corporations experience greater variability in their rates of return than large corporations," see W. L. Crum, *Corporate Size and Earning Power* 331–35 (1939); see also "The Effect of Size on Corporate Earnings and Condition," Harvard Business Research Study No. 8 (1934).

face of uncertainty? Or does this power merely signify that after enough citizens have tied their fortunes to the large firm the State will always intervene to save it from destruction or undue distress? Intervention may take the form of temporary subsidy, legislation to protect the firm from rivals, or outright purchase at an inflated value.

No doubt public utilities enjoy some advantage in the capital market by virtue of their importance to the State.[17] Nevertheless, it is difficult to believe that the advantage conferred by size in the capital market is nothing more than the shadow of the State looming behind it. The more obvious explanation is simply that size increases the power of the firm to survive sudden reverses by diversifying products, lines of credit, sources of supply, and centers of decision-making. The importance of these considerations in fostering concentration is well illustrated by the history of banking.

In this field, the economies of scale that relate to the "plant" are slight; yet a striking decline in the number of banks has occurred over the last century in every commercially advanced country[18] where the safety of bank deposits has not been underwritten by the State and banks have been allowed to merge at will. In the United Kingdom, for example, freedom of contract has transformed several hundred banks into the "Big Five."[19] No doubt the usual reasons cited by bankers when explaining combination—the need to make loans in larger amounts, greater opportunity for specialization, etc.—have some validity, but the big bank's power to survive hard knocks by diversifying assets is certainly the main incentive to combination. In the United States, legislation hostile to branch banking long impeded, though it did not wholly check, growing concentration in banking; and until the 1930's the cost of preserving dispersion was paid in the heavy incidence of bank failures.[20] In recent years the federal government's commitment to insure deposits up to $10,000 has removed the need to exercise one's

---

[17] For numerous examples of this solicitude for corporate size in the depression relief work of the Reconstruction Finance Corporation, see the autobiography of its head, Jesse Jones, *Fifty Billion Dollars* (1951).

[18] In young industrial countries which allow branch banking a network of small independent banks does not develop. Thus Canada never had more than thirty-nine banks, this figure being reached in 1892. The number of banks was down to ten in 1936 with the four largest accounting for 80.26 per cent of total bank assets. James Holladay, *The Canadian Banking System* 96–97 (1938).

[19] An account of the merger movement in British banking is given in Joseph Sykes, *The Amalgamation Movement in English Banking, 1825–1924* (1926).

[20] The melancholy details of this policy are given in C. D. Bremer, *American Bank Failures* (1935).

judgment in selecting a bank, while at the same time, Federal Reserve policy guarantees that no banker shall be permitted to fail as a consequence of rashness or plain stupidity. Hence, in the United States size is no longer the main road to survival in banking.

Still another argument that many apparent economies of scale are not what they seem runs as follows. The large firm's success in buying more cheaply than its smaller rivals derives from its power to obtain "discounts not justified by a savings in cost to the supplier." These discounts allegedly represent, so to speak, the fruits of business blackmail. The supplier will suffer a serious loss if the custom of the big buyer is suddenly withdrawn and will pay anything less than this loss in rebates to keep it.

The "discount not justified by a savings in cost," however, has no more claim to the serious attention of economists than the "scientific tariff" or the "fair markup." The "unfair" bargaining tactics which big buyers allegedly employ are generally nothing more than efforts to secure a discount in return for a contract to purchase in quantity. If their suppliers, in the absence of legislation against price "discrimination," willingly grant quantity discounts in order to obtain the larger orders, the presumption is that they are justified in doing so by a savings in the cost of handling large orders.[21] The legal history of price discrimination is considered in Chapter XIV.

6. *The obstacles to corporate growth*

The economies associated with size have so impressed many writers that they have been moved to consider why consolidation ever stops short of monopoly or even the conglomerate firm that monopolizes several industries. Earlier authorities with a faith in freedom of contract as a bulwark of decentralization were not much troubled on this score. It was enough for them that the eye of a master seeking the most profitable employment of his own capital could not be everywhere in the large firm; hence the force of the profit motive—the mainspring of efficiency and innovation—inevitably ebbs as size increases.

---

[21] For a different view of the matter, see J. B. Dirlam and A. E. Kahn, *Fair Competition* 202–56 (1954). I cannot accept what I take to be the major inarticulate premise of these authorities—that accounting data of business firms are exact enough to warrant generalizations about the "fairness" of particular price policies. The main concern of Dirlam and Kahn, however, is to emphasize a truth often neglected by economists, *i.e.*, that certain types of price discrimination are so grossly unfair to particular parties that they should be discouraged without reference to their cost justification or effect on competition. (The example of discounts obtained by bribing a supplier's employees comes readily to mind.)

More recently, a limit to size has been found in "the principle of increasing risk." The larger firm can secure resources, especially capital, on more favorable terms than its smaller rivals, but the more capital employed, the smaller the relative share of the original owner's equity in the enterprise and the more vulnerable he is to a change in its fortunes.[22] To borrow an example:

> Suppose, for instance, that there is a chance that a firm might lose 10% of its total assets. If it had a net worth of $100,000 and borrowed no capital, it might find—if it was unlucky—that its total capital was reduced to $90,000. If, however, it borrowed $400,000, so that its total assets were $500,000, and the loss of 10% of its assets occurred, it would lose $50,000, representing half of its net worth. If it borrowed $900,000 and lost 10% of its total assets of $1,000,000, its net worth would be wiped out altogether. It is clear, therefore, that with a given chance of losing a given proportion of total assets there will be some point at which the firm will cease borrowing in order to expand its operations simply because of the increasing risk of loss of its own capital.[23]

This thesis has perhaps some relevance to the behavior of the small businessman who may fear that a heavy burden of debt in time of falling demand or rising costs will force him into bankruptcy or cause him to lose control of his firm in a court-imposed reorganization. (It recalls Henry Ford's pathological fear of investment bankers.) But the large company which has already divorced ownership and control is unlikely to be deterred from expanding by such considerations; indeed the weakness of the lender's position in a floundering company is a standard topic in textbooks on corporation finance.[24] In fine, there is little to be said about the limits to expansion that cannot be subsumed under a weakening of the profit motive as the size of the firm increases.

7. *Coexistence of small and large rivals*

Some writers have drawn attention to the persisting coexistence of small and large firms in many industries, and by tacitly assuming that

---

[22] M. Kalecki, "The Principle of Increasing Risk," 4 *Economica* (n.s.) 440 (1937), and K. E. Boulding, *A Reconstruction of Economics* 126–30 (1950).

[23] Boulding, *A Reconstruction of Economics* 126. Reprinted by permission of John Wiley & Sons, Inc.

[24] See, for example, 2 A. S. Dewing, *Financial Policy of Corporations* 1400–38 (4th ed. 1941).

there must be some unique optimum size of the firm in each industry, they have inferred that all significant economies of scale are realized by the smallest firm that is able to survive.[25] This argument overlooks the truth that the best size for a firm depends in large measure on the kind of management that it can command.[26] So long as managerial talent is both scarce and of different types, there is no reason to expect that successful firms in an industry will be of nearly equal size.

Moreover, as Professor Weston has pointed out, the apparent continued coexistence of large and small firms can be explained on still other grounds.[27] (1) The large firm may consent to hold a price umbrella over the heads of smaller firms either because it does not wish to incur the expense of driving them out or because it fears the antitrust laws. (2) The small firm does not really produce the same product as its larger rival; for example, it may survive by providing additional service or a product more carefully tailored to the customer's requirements.[28] (This is tantamount to saying that the large and small firm are not really in the same "industry.") (3) Small firms offset the economies enjoyed by large firms through the willingness of their owners to accept less than the "prevailing" rate of return on capital or the willingness of their managers to sacrifice leisure and the incomes available elsewhere in order to obtain responsibility. (4) Variations in rates of return on resources in firms of different sizes may have been obscured by the capitalization process. By this last reason, Weston apparently means that with capitalization at work, accounting data afford no good basis for drawing conclusions about the relative per-

---

[25] G. J. Stigler, "Monopoly and Oligopoly by Merger," 40 *Am. Econ. Rev. Proceedings* 23, 26 (1950).

[26] For the thesis that "it can only be in the managerial sphere that a business's costs of production will offer an obstacle for growth," see P. W. S. Andrews, *Manufacturing Business* 126 (1949). Andrews tacitly assumes that management is the only unique factor of production that most firms hire. Actually if the other resources which two rival firms use are not identical in every respect, they may coexist indefinitely although of different size; the firm with the lower unit costs simply has the greater output. On this truth see Milton Friedman's remarks on "Economies of Scale," in *Business Concentration and Public Policy* 230 (National Bureau of Economic Research, 1955).

[27] J. F. Weston, *The Role of Mergers in the Growth of Large Firms* 62–66 (1953).

[28] The tendency of large and small firms in the same industry to coexist by producing differentiated products has been stressed in one of the few case studies available, S. H. Wellisz, "The Coexistence of Large and Small Firms: A Study of the Italian Mechanical Industries," 71 *Q. J. Econ.* 116 (1957).

formances of small and large firms. The income consequences of mistakes and successes are capitalized in the valuation of assets and so undermine the validity of balance sheets and current income statements as a basis for comparing the efficiencies of rival firms.

We might make one addition to Weston's catalogue. In the present day, a major cost of size is the vulnerability of the large firm to collective bargaining pressures; so that in an industry composed mainly of small firms (*e.g.*, southern textiles), the large firm's ability to survive and expand even though saddled with higher wages than its smaller rivals indicates that, *ceteris paribus*, it is more efficient.[29]

8. *Research, size, and market power*

Finally, we may note the view which asserts that, however the case for economics of scale is assessed on static assumptions, concentration in an industry makes possible a more rapid rate of innovation than competition or loose association of firms would support; hence, small firms must inevitably give way to large firms through merger or survival of the fittest. This view was urged without much success in academic economics by defenders of the trusts even before 1900, but since the view so admirably rationalizes the growth of big business, it has become a conspicuous tenet in the folklore of capitalism. Recently its re-entry in academic circles has been sponsored by Joseph Schumpeter and J. K. Galbraith.

Schumpeter affirmed without going into details:

> As soon as we go into details and inquire into the individual items in which progress was most conspicuous, the trail leads not to the doors of those firms that work under conditions of comparatively free competition but precisely to the doors of the large concerns—which, as in the case of agricultural machinery, also account for much of the progress in the competi-

---

[29] An interesting and neglected problem is why, even in the absence of unionization, large firms tend to pay higher wages than small firms in the same industry. For fragmentary statistics relevant to this point see *Hourly Earnings of Employees in Large and Small Enterprises* (TNEC Monograph No. 14, 1941). A possible answer is that in a world of joint production good management, labor, and equipment cluster together for mutual benefit; that, for example, it does not pay to foist a $3,000-a-year secretary on a $30,000-a-year executive. To the extent that this hypothesis is valid, the higher wages paid by the large firm are evidence that size is associated with economies of scale.

tive sector—and a shocking suspicion dawns upon us that big business may have had more to do with creating that standard of life than with keeping it down.[30]

Galbraith offers a deductive proof for the tie between size and rate of innovation.

There is no more pleasant fiction than that technical change is the product of the matchless ingenuity of the small man forced by competition to employ his wits to better his neighbor. Unhappily, it is a fiction. Technical development has long since become the preserve of the scientist and the engineer. Most of the cheap and simple inventions have, to put it bluntly, been made. Not only is development now sophisticated and costly but it must be on a sufficient scale so that successes and failures will in some measure average out. Few can afford it if they must expect all projects to pay off.[31]

Or again:

Because development is costly, it follows that it can be carried on only by a firm that has the resources associated with considerable size. Moreover, unless a firm has a substantial share of the market it has no strong incentive to undertake a large expenditure on development. There are, in practice, very few innovations which cannot be imitated. . . . The net result of all this is that there must be some element of monopoly in an industry if it is to be progressive.[32]

Like most broad generalizations that seek to explain economic progress, the Schumpeter-Galbraith thesis is true "up to a point." One can cite industries, notably steel, radio, and chemicals, which appear to confirm the assertion that most of the cheap and simple inventions have been made.[33] One can cite other industries, notably textiles and

---

[30] *Capitalism, Socialism, and Democracy* 82 (3d ed. 1950). Reprinted by permission of Harper & Brothers. The vigor of Schumpeter's defense of bigness probably reflects the zeal of a convert. He had earlier held that the "process of incessant rise and decay of firms and industries" is the central fact about the "capitalist machine" 1 *Business Cycles* 94–97 (1939).

[31] *American Capitalism* 91 (1952). Reprinted by permission of Houghton Mifflin Company.

[32] *Ibid.*, pp. 92–93.

[33] The Schumpeter-Galbraith thesis almost perfectly describes the declining research importance of the small firm in the radio industry. See W. R. Maclaurin, *Invention and Innovation in the Radio Industry* 153–224 (1949).

garment manufacture, where this proposition is patently false. And finally, of course, there are industries, exemplified by the application of atomic energy, where inventions never were simple or cheap when measured against the technical skill and capital required to get the Wright brothers' machine into the air. The important truth is that the progress of technology has created some opportunities for profitable production which small firms cannot exploit. There are economies of scale in research that did not exist sixty years ago, and the appearance of these economies has *pari passu* promoted industrial concentration. The importance of this new impetus to industrial concentration, however, is another matter. That the large firm accounts for "some" technological progress is obviously and tritely true. The implication of the Schumpeter-Galbraith thesis that it accounts for "most" technological progress is practically impossible to prove or disprove, but given the innumerable variables that influence economic development, the reasonable man need not bow down in worship before the research laboratories of the large firm.[34]

9. *Recapitulation*

To sum up, the competitive advantage that the large firm enjoys over its smaller rival because it can borrow capital on more favorable terms and secure discounts by purchasing materials in greater quantity is a "true" economy of scale. These savings reflect not the exercise of

---

[34] For a statistical test of the Schumpeter-Galbraith thesis see Almarin Phillips, "Concentration, Scale and Technological Change in Selected Manufacturing Industries 1899–1939," 4 *J. Ind. Econ.* 179 (1956).

Phillips took capital per manufacturing establishment as an index of scale, the output accounted for by the industry's twenty largest establishments as an index of concentration, and the ratio of wage earners to product value as an index of productivity. Information was available for twenty-eight industries in both 1899 and 1939. Using rank correlation, Phillips found that "of the industries studied, those which were highly concentrated and had large-scale producing units in 1904 had significantly greater rates of decrease in the number of wage earners per unit of output between 1899 and 1939 than did the other industries." P. 192. As Phillips points out, his study does not so much support the Schumpeter-Galbraith thesis as fail to confirm "an inverse relationship between technological change and production concentrated in a relatively small number of large producing units." P. 193.

See also, Jacob Schmookler, "Inventors Past and Present," 39 *Rev. Econ. Stat.* 321 (1957). Schmookler's analysis of patent data indicates that "prevailing notions about the character of modern inventions are radically wrong." Not only are most patented inventions not made by a small, highly trained elite; as yet, more than half of the patents issued probably go to part-time inventors, and more to non-college graduates than to college graduates.

monopsony power but the elimination of uncertainty. We therefore discount the view that the only economies of scale worth bothering about relate to the plant—not to the firm—and, hence, that if consolidation merely transfers existing-size plants to common ownership, it is motivated mainly by the attractions of monopoly. The Schumpeter-Galbraith thesis that technological progress is the special preserve of the large corporation possessing appreciable market power we set down as unproved and implausible. The importance of scale economies in research in certain industries is readily endorsed.

One possible circumstance working against the persistence of competition or cartels we have not considered. Conceivably, a trend to concentration is the fortuitous by-product of technological change because, on balance, innovations enlarge the optimum scale of factory or shop (as measured by the capital commitment required) more rapidly than they raise the national income. If so, the source of innovation is immaterial, *i.e.*, one need not assume with Schumpeter and Galbraith that large firms have "caused" the improvements that have made possible their growth. Even if innovation is mainly the work of small firms, it promotes concentration to the extent that optimum plant size increases more rapidly than total output. So far as manufacturing industries are concerned, this view is supported by evidence. We shall reserve its examination for the next chapter.

Chapter V

MONOPOLY IN THE LIGHT OF EMPIRICAL STUDIES: 1

1. *The direct approach and its limitations*

The impatient reader may object that our roundabout way of inferring the existence of economies of scale unrelated to static technology at the plant level is unnecessary; that if the aim is to assess the relative importance of scale economies as opposed to monopoly in fostering concentration we would do better to examine the relevant data on the American economy with a view to answering the following questions.

1. Over the last sixty years, has the fraction of the national income accounted for by the largest 100, 200, or 1,000 corporations increased?
2. If so, have mergers played a conspicuous part in this increase?
3. If question 2 also receives an affirmative answer, were mergers mainly motivated by the hope of monopoly power, the prospect of achieving scale economies, or something else—tax pressure, personal prestige, gains at the expense of minority stockholders, etc.[1]

---

[1] Actually the only one of these other incentives that merits attention is the pressure to consolidate implicit in the tax laws. This pressure operates in two ways. (1) Given heavy corporate income taxation, firms which make profits can purchase firms which have made losses in recent years and apply the tax saving represented by the carry-over of these losses against the purchase price. (2) Given heavy death duties, many small businesses upon the death of the owner must be sold to pay these levies, and the heirs find a ready market among established firms, *e.g.*, the parties most interested in purchasing a textile firm are other textile firms. An inquiry sponsored by the Harvard Business School, however, has led to the conclusion that "the tax structure of recent years has tended to increase levels of concentration within the corporate sector of the economy and among all business firms, but that these tax effects have been of relatively moderate proportions." John Lintner and J. K. Butters, "Effects of Taxes on Concentration," *Business Concentration and Price Policy* 239, 274 (National Bureau of Economic Research, 1955).

The first two questions are easily disposed of. Over the last sixty years, the percentage of the national income accounted for by the largest corporations has greatly increased;[2] the increase was mainly accounted for by mergers. The remaining question is not susceptible to statistical treatment and cannot be answered so confidently. On one point, however, we can be emphatic. Much the greater part of this merger activity involved railroads and public utilities not in direct competition with one another;[3] hence the desire for monopoly power was a negligible factor in promoting the concomitant concentration. The author (at the risk of viewing Samuel Insul as a tool of historical necessity) believes that scale economies—notably the scale economy of finance—provided the main impetus behind utility and railroad combinations. But the spectacular chicanery associated with the consolidations over the years has encouraged the notion that they were undertaken mainly for the purpose of manufacturing the paper securities needed for a great national swindle.[4]

The ease with which the above questions can be answered suggests that the direct approach is not without its limitations, and two, in fact, are particularly serious. First, although one may talk meaningfully about a trend to or away from monopoly in a particular industry—or even in a particular sector of the economy—broad generalizations about the fate of competition for the whole economy are at best ambiguous and at worst devoid of any real content. Second, the number of firms comprising an industry—and the distribution of its output among them —is only one of many factors that governs its degree of monopoly. Let us explore these difficulties.

---

[2] Using mainly data gathered by the Temporary National Economic Committee, M. A. Adelman concluded that "the share of total corporate assets held by the 200 largest nonfinancial corporations was 33% in 1909, 48% in 1929, and 55% in 1933. Their share of total corporate income was 33% in 1920 and 43% in 1929. The share of total income received by the largest 5% of nonfinancial corporations was 79% in 1918, 88% in 1932, and 84% in 1942." "Effective Competition and the Antitrust Laws," 61 *Harv. L. Rev.* 1289, 1293 (1948).

For another examination of data that reaches substantially the same conclusions, see the statement of W. I. King in *Corporate Mergers and Acquisitions: Hearings Before a Subcommittee of the Senate Committee on the Judiciary,* 81st Cong., 2d Sess., 225–50 (1950).

[3] Thus assetwise at least four-fifths of the mergers recorded by G. C. Means from 1922–29 involved railroads and public utilities. "The Growth in the Relative Importance of the Large Corporation in American Life," 21 *Am. Econ. Rev.* 10, 30–36 (1931).

[4] See, for example, J. C. Bonbright and G. C. Means, *The Holding Company* (1932), or W. Z. Ripley, *Main Street and Wall Street* (1927).

2. *The "decline of competition": possible meanings*

The essence of monopoly is a comparative advantage of one party over another in power to restrict output. Someone succeeds in erecting a barrier to entry which forces or encourages manpower and capital to seek employment elsewhere. Yet what one firm may do, all cannot do; a power to restrict output that is shared equally by all firms is a contradiction in terms. Hence, writers who assert that "the economy is becoming increasingly monopolistic" generally mean one of three things.

1. The monopoly power enjoyed by some broad class of firms is increasing relative to the monopoly power enjoyed by some other broad class of firms; that is, the economy is becoming increasingly polarized into "monopolistic" and "competitive" industries.[5]

2. New firms find it increasingly difficult to enter the business world, so that an ever increasing share of the national income is accounted for by the "old" firms. This may be because the increasing complexity of technology and marketing enhances the competitive advantage of experience—the established producer's main defensive weapon—or because, in a world of high income taxes, new firms experience greater difficulty in obtaining their initial investment stake.

3. Wage and price rigidities are becoming more widespread in the factor markets. This means that, in the best of times, some resources are "misallocated" because they cannot secure employment in industries where they have their highest marginal revenue products; while in time of a decline in national spending, some resources are unable to secure employment in any industry.

The "polarization" of the economy into monopolistic and competitive industries turns mainly upon whether monopoly has increased in the manufacturing sector of the economy. This follows since distribution, the service trades, and agriculture now, as in the past, are highly competitive; public utilities are generally written off as "natural" monopolies; and in transport and finance the public policy commitment is

---

[5] An instance of this usage is G. J. Stigler, "Competition in the United States," *Five Lectures on Economic Problems* 46 (1949). Stigler holds that competition probably declined until around 1920 and has increased since that time. The decline of competition before 1920 is traced to the rise of manufacturing and the decline of agriculture. Its recovery after 1920 is traced to the more rapid development of trade and services.

now to the control of rates, service, and numbers rather than to competition. The fate of competition in manufacturing we shall consider presently.

Whether the role of new firms in the economy is viewed as declining or holding its own depends upon how a new firm is defined. The share of the national income originating in firms less than forty years old is undoubtedly declining and the share of the national income originating in firms less than twenty years old may be declining.[6] Economic progress, however, serves to increase the fraction of the economy's output that takes the form of services and quasi-luxuries—the stronghold of very small firms, so that it is most unlikely that the share of the national income originating in business units less than five years old has gone down in recent years.[7]

What of the third assertion, that the structure of factor costs is becoming ossified? To the extent that the growing power of labor unions does not affect all sectors of the economy equally—and it does not—this charge is true. Clearly, also, the rise of labor unions and the spread of minimum wage legislation have made it more difficult for money wages to fall in response to a decline in the demand for labor. Unemployment by definition exists to the extent that "real" wage rates are too high, so that the elimination of unemployment necessarily requires the reduction of "real" wage rates.[8] This can be done by cutting

[6] For estimates of median firm age of incorporated enterprise in different industries in 1946, see W. L. Crum, *The Age Structure of the Corporate System* 83–82 (1953).

[7] While the statistical data do not allow the testing of this supposition, it gains support from the steady increase in the business population since 1900—war and depression excepted. Thus government estimates place the number of firms at roughly 1.2 million in 1900, 1.6 million in 1913, 1.7 million in 1919, 3 million in 1929, 2.9 million in 1944, and 4.3 million in December, 1956. *Problems of Small Business* 66 (TNEC Monograph No. 17, 1941), and United States Department of Commerce, *Business Statistics* 23 (1957).

[8] We might note for the record that minimum wage legislation and the power of labor unions had virtually nothing to do with mass unemployment in the early years of the Great Depression in the United States. Both were then of negligible importance. The usual explanations given for the stickiness of money wage rates between 1929 and 1933 are (a) the employers' unwillingness to risk public censure by cutting wages too much, (b) the employers' conviction that mass unemployment would not last and hence, their unwillingness to risk a bad name among workers by cutting too much, and (c) the probability that in time of mass unemployment "excessive" wage reductions would touch off strikes and related worker disturbances. The pattern of wage rigidity from 1929 through 1933 in the United States is examined in Albert Rees, "Wage Determination and Involuntary Unemployment," 59 *J. Pol. Econ.* 143 (1951).

money wage rates or reducing the purchasing power of the money wage rate by raising the prices of consumer goods, *i.e.*, by inflation. Hence, the economy's commitment to collective bargaining and minimum wage legislation may only signify that the State will meet unemployment with corrective inflation. Or it may mean that the economy is prepared to "keep faith" with social reforms even though the price exacted is unemployment. The economic consequences of deciding never to cut money wage rates must remain a matter of conjecture until it has been put to the test of a major recession. In the meantime, our concern in this chapter is with the fate of competition in particular industries only.

3. *Concentration ratios and degree of monopoly*

As many writers have warned, considerable care must be exercised in inferring a trend to or away from competition from a change in an industry's concentration ratio. *Ceteris paribus,* an increase in some concentration ratio—say the share of an industry's output accounted for by its top four firms—is perforce a "trend to monopoly"; and concentration ratios thus register a change in degree of monopoly to the extent that other things do remain the same. In practice, this means that a change in the ownership structure of an industry which occurred eighteen months ago is more likely to have left some visible mark on competition than a change that occurred eighteen years ago. In the short run one has a better basis for assuming the relative constancy of the other major factors that influence degree of monopoly—elasticity of demand for the industry's output, nature of the product itself, the extent of the market, and the definitions of "product" and "industry" employed by the Bureau of the Census. Nevertheless, the worth of studies which seek to discern long-term trends in market structures by constructing concentration ratios for widely separated years should not be depreciated. If precise measurements are not insisted upon, such studies can register the direction of the trend in market structure over time. For example, if we accept that market areas have increased and the elasticity of demand for major products is greater than formerly,[9] then the

---

The interesting—and as yet unanswered—question is whether these impediments to wage cutting were any greater in 1930 than in, say, 1890. One may also speculate on what would have happened to money wage rates—and employment—after 1933 in the United States if the federal government had not intervened to discourage wage cutting.

[9] For a convincing exposition of these assumptions see M. A. Adelman, "Effective Competition and the Antitrust Laws," 1295–97.

failure of an industry's concentration ratio to rise over a period of thirty years is convincing evidence that competition has increased in the industry. Likewise, a small increase in the concentration ratio would indicate the absence of any significant decline in competition over the years.

4. *The coming of the Corporate Revolution*

For purposes of organization we may examine the evidence relating to concentration trends separately for the years before and after World War I. We may tentatively invoke the conventional justification for this division, namely that the mergers before World War I, especially in the years 1897–1904, "set" the present pattern of big business in the United States. We shall also conform to tradition by limiting our attention to changes in the ownership structure of manufacturing industries. This is not because, as is sometimes asserted, the relevant data is lacking for the rest of the economy. In fact, published statistics on transportation and public utilities are better adapted to appraising changes in concentration ratios than those relating to manufacturing. Rather this limitation is accepted because one does not really need to speculate about the fate of competition in industries other than manufacturing. Public regulation of rates and service—the negation of competition—has long been taken for granted in public utilities and railroad transportation—at least in principle. (What regulated industries do to consumers "in practice" is another matter.) Banking and insurance are so vulnerable to concentration that dispersion can be maintained in these fields only by the most solicitous legislation. As yet, the monopoly problems in distribution and the service trades are almost wholly those of cartels. The apprehension sometimes expressed over the rise of the chain stores can usually be written off as special pleading for high-cost small business.

We should, of course, like to have better data, especially data that would allow us to estimate the distribution of output among manufacturing firms at various dates.[10] Such information is not now avail-

---

[10] Some difficult problems of interpreting data would remain in the best tabulated of worlds. For example, we should like to have the wealth of statistics that would enable us to trace changes in the percentage of total manufactured output accounted for by the largest 10, 20, or 30 per cent of manufacturing firms from 1611 onward. Yet an increase in the number of very small firms that did not affect the percentage of output controlled by, say, the economy's four hundred largest firms would superficially indicate greater concentration. That is, because

able, nor is it likely to become available until a monumental research project is given access to all surviving federal, state, and local tax records. But the need for such a study is not great. The Census of Manufactures, hundreds of government reports, countless books, monographs, and articles, and the bound volumes of trade publications contain far more information on the progress of industrial concentration than we can comfortably digest.

The most cursory examination of this mass of evidence[11] suffices to establish two points. In the twenty-five years between 1885 and 1910, the percentage of total manufactured output accounted for by the top one, two, or three hundred firms greatly increased. The principal reason for this increase was merger activity rather than bankruptcy, the liquidation of enterprises, or the internal growth of successful firms.

At present no precise estimate can be formed of the magnitude of the rise in concentration during these years since we have only a rough idea of what the ownership structure of manufacturing was like in 1885 or 1910. By one generally accepted estimate, no more than 318 corporations had come into possession of at least 40 per cent of all manufacturing assets by 1904.[12] It is known that industrial mergers between 1887 and 1904 involved at least 15 per cent of the manufacturing establishments reported by the Census of Manufactures in 1900,[13] and since the consolidations of that day dealt in relatively large plants, the percentage of manufacturing assets affected was undoubtedly greater.

Probably the extent of this early merger movement is best con-

---

the *number* of firms had risen, the percentage of output contributed by each percentile of firms ranked by size would have increased. For an appraisal of statistical techniques used in expressing concentration, see J. M. Blair, "Statistical Measures of Concentration in Business," 18 *Bulletin of the Oxford University Institute of Statistics* 351 (1956).

[11] The definitive critique of mergers statistics is a study—not yet published —prepared by Ralph L. Nelson for the National Bureau of Economic Research, *Merger Movements in American Industry, 1895–1956*. An excellent introduction is J. W. Markham, "Survey of the Evidence and Findings on Mergers," in *Business Concentration and Price Policy* 141 (National Bureau of Economic Research, 1955). Valuable older works are Luther Conant, "Industrial Consolidations in the United States," 7 *Publications of Am. Stat. Ass'n* 207 (1901); John Moody, *The Truth About the Trusts* (1904); M. W. Watkins, *Industrial Combinations and Public Policy* (1927); and Shaw Livermore, "The Success of Industrial Mergers," 50 *Q. J. Econ.* 68 (1935).

[12] H. R. Seager and C. A. Gulick, *Trust and Corporation Problems* 60–61 (1929). The estimate of these writers is based on the data given in John Moody, *The Truth About the Trusts* (1904).

[13] Markham, "Survey of the Evidence and Findings on Mergers" 157.

veyed by absolute figures. According to one authority, prior to February, 1904, 318 industrial combinations produced security issues of over $7 billion and involved about 5,300 distinct plants.[14] Most of this activity was concentrated in the seven years between 1897 and 1904. By a conservative estimate, mergers produced new companies with authorized capitalizations totaling $1.89 billion in 1899 and $1.63 billion in 1901.[15] Combination on this scale has never been closely approximated in any subsequent year, even when the later merger activity is estimated in terms of depreciated currency.[16] But while the "fact" of the Corporate Revolution can scarcely be doubted, its causes—and more particularly its timing—have inspired a number of different explanations.

5. *Economies of plant scale as a factor promoting combination*

In discussions of the great merger movement, the undoubted growth of large-scale manufacturing after the Civil War is invariably cited as a major causal factor.[17] But what is a "scale increase" in manufacturing and how does one measure it? There is no point in dividing total value of manufactures by the number of manufacturing establishments ("plants"). This number fluctuates greatly from one census to the next; yet the combined output of the smallest 20,000 plants is never more than one per cent of the total.

A possible method of expressing scale increase is suggested by the

---

[14] Moody, *The Truth About the Trusts* 486.

[15] M. W. Watkins, *Industrial Combinations and Public Policy* 321–22.

[16] While this view is held by most authorities, it is not possible to be more specific given our inadequate information. In the earlier years, when big new firms were being constructed from many small ones, the sum total of assets involved was the measure of concentration. Since, however, mergers now usually occur when an established big firm buys out a small firm, merger activity should be expressed in terms of the assets of the "acquired" concerns. Unfortunately, the best data relates merely to the *number* of firms acquired in mining and manufacturing. By this test the peak year between 1919 and 1954 was easily 1929 when 1,245 mergers were reported. In contrast, only 419 mergers were reported for 1946—the greatest number in any year since 1931. Federal Trade Commission, *Report on Corporate Mergers and Acquisitions* 32–33 (1955).

[17] The most important single factor contributing to this increase was the completion of the railroad net in the United States. According to Markham, "it can be crudely estimated that the area served by the average manufacturing establishment in 1900 was about 3.24 times as large as it was in 1882." "Survey of the Evidence and Findings on Mergers" 156.

work of G. W. Nutter.[18] His analysis of the data for every Census of Manufactures year from 1899 through 1939 has shown that 92,000 plants have always accounted for at least 95 per cent of all output reported. Further, the distribution of output among these 92,000 plants has been remarkably constant with the largest 18,400 always contributing about 75 per cent of total product.[19]

An inspection of the Census of Manufactures for the thirty years before 1899 indicates that the same pattern held then, though one cannot be sure. In any event, we will not go far wrong if we assume that since the Civil War, no more than 92,000 plants have accounted for 95 per cent of all manufactured output, and hence that the average value of the output of these plants is a meaningful index of efficient manufacturing scale.

These assumptions yield an impressive increase in plant size between 1869 and 1909. If manufactured output is valued in 1913 prices, the increase was 595 per cent.[20] Two features of this forty-year growth are worth nothing. First, roughly one-helf of it came in the twenty years after 1869—that is, before the age of the great mergers. Second, even in 1909 average plant size was not astounding. Average gross output of the top 92,000 plants was only $219,000, while average gross output of the top 18,400 was $866,000. The increase in the average gross output of the top 100 or 200 industrial firms between 1869 and 1909 was, of course, much greater than 595 per cent. Clearly the need to merge in order to achieve manufacturing plants of optimum size *was not* the paramount cause of the Corporate Revolution. What of the other scale economies open to the firm?

6. *Scale economies external to the plant*

The possibility that a striving for economies external to the plant was a major cause of the Corporate Revolution was exhaustively explored between 1900 and 1920.[21] With one or two exceptions,[22] the investigators

---

[18] *The Extent of Enterprise Monopoly in the United States, 1889–1939* (1951).

[19] *Ibid.*, pp. 33–34.

[20] Using the Snyder-Tucker index of general prices and Census of Manufactures data. *Historical Statistics of the United States, 1789–1945*, 179, 231–32 (1946).

[21] During this period, the Industrial Commission, the Commissioner of Corporations, the Federal Trade Commission, and the Justice Department examined mergers in industries that included oil, tobacco, farm equipment, shoe ma-

found against scale economies as the major causal factor, and Henry Simons was, in effect, summarizing their findings when he wrote:

> Few of our gigantic corporations can be defended on the ground that their present size is necessary to reasonably full exploitation of production economies: their existence is to be explained in terms of opportunities for promoter profits, personal ambitions of industrial and financial "Napoleons," and the advantages of monopoly power.[23]

This view of the Corporate Revolution was long accepted by most American economists. Indeed, the ability to demolish the case for bigness presented by the uncritical defenders of large corporations was long regarded as a mark of professional sophistication. Recently this earlier interpretation of the Corporate Revolution has been called into question. Its harsher critics, epitomized by Schumpeter and Galbraith, contend that the original trust investigations were carried out by men who were inclined to resolve all doubts in favor of the efficiency of small business and unable to take the "long view." More temperate critics are disposed to return a verdict of not proven on the older theory of the Corporate Revolution. They maintain that, because the case studies of some early mergers indicate that the promoters were mainly impelled by desire for monopoly power or insider profits, it does not follow that most early mergers were so motivated; hence one should not ascribe "a single motivation to a large number of firms and persons in a highly diverse set of circumstances where numerous influences were possible."[24] Caution in scholarship, however, can be carried too far. If early trust investigators correctly discerned the causes of the mergers they did study, it is improbable that they should have failed to recognize the impetus behind the combination movement generally.[25]

---

chinery, iron and steel, asphalt, cordage, distilling, matches, meat packing, glucose and starch, can making, explosives, cash registers, and anthracite.

[22] Thus Jeremiah Jenks, sometime chief economist of the United States Industrial Commission, always considered that the monopoly aspect of the great merger movement was overrated. See his *The Trust Problem* (1903). A. S. Dewing, perhaps the most erudite of the trust investigators, while stressing the role of intent to monopolize in promoting combination, felt that it had generally been frustrated. "The doom of the inefficient waits on no legislative regulation. It is rather delayed thereby." *Corporate Promotions and Reorganizations* viii (1914).

[23] *Economic Policy for a Free Society* 59–60 (1948).

[24] J. F. Weston, *The Role of Mergers in the Growth of Large Firms* 32.

[25] We might note that the most recent inquiry into "economies of scale external to the plant" appears to bear out the conclusions of the trust investiga-

7. *The older theory of the Corporate Revolution: an estimate*

In any event, let us respect the findings of the trust investigations as embodying the hard work of able men. But let us ask with the wisdom of hindsight, What errors of theory or mistakes of emphasis did they commit? (At this late date it is all but impossible to revise their statement of the "facts," *e.g.*, the amount of water in the stock of the United States Steel Corporation in 1901.) The author submits that what we may call the Ripley-Fetter[26] theory of the Corporate Revolution after two of its most influential proponents especially needs revisions in three particulars.

First, it erred in inferring the existence of diseconomies of scale from the fact that many of the corporate combinations of the day had poor earnings records and not a few ended in receivership. The preoccupation of the Ripley-Fetter thesis with corporation financial statements caused its supporters to exaggerate the vulnerability of the large firm to the winds of competition and hence to overrate the part played by "predatory" or "unfair" business tactics in the Corporate Revolution.

Second, the earlier theory of mergers overemphasized the importance of a changing legal framework as a factor promoting combination. The law was held to have encouraged the Corporate Revolution in two ways. Before the New Jersey laws of general incorporation were passed in 1888,[27] corporate combinations allegedly were extremely difficult to execute because one company could not hold the stock of another. With the removal of this restriction, many combinations which might otherwise have never come into being made their appearance as New Jersey holding companies. This explanation of the timing of the merger movement is not convincing. Even before 1888 several states

---

tions. J. S. Bain, "Economies of Scale, Concentration, and the Condition of Entry in Twenty Manufacturing Industries," 44 *Am. Econ. Rev.* 15 (1954). On the basis of managerial and engineering estimates obtained from firms in twenty industries Bain concluded: "The economies of large multiplant firms are left in doubt by this investigation. In half the cases in which definite estimates were received, such economies were felt to be negligible or absent, whereas in most of the remainder of cases they seemed slight or small. Perhaps the frequently expressed suspicion that such economies generally are unimportant after all is supported . . . ." (P. 39.)

[26] For eloquent statements of the thesis see W. Z. Ripley, *Main Street and Wall Street;* and F. A. Fetter, *The Masquerade of Monopoly* (1931). A totally unvarnished version is presented in Fetter's memorandum, "The Fundamental Principle of Efficiency in Mass Production," in *Relative Efficiency of Large, Medium-Sized, and Small Business* 398 (TNEC Monograph No. 13, 1941).

[27] *Laws of New Jersey*, ch. 269, ch. 295 (1888).

had adopted general laws of incorporation that conferred the stock-holding privilege,[28] and many others had granted special charters that eliminated the traditional curbs on corporate activity. Moreover, it seems probable that in the nineteenth century—as in the twentieth—state legislatures were at all times prepared to supply charters tailored to the applicants' desires, and that they would earlier have gladly, and with alacrity, eliminated any objectionable restraints had a demand arisen.[29]

Again, the turn taken by antitrust policy around 1900 is alleged to have encouraged the Corporate Revolution. At this time, the federal courts first took a strong line against cartels but showed little inclination to disturb monopoly power in the single firm; hence, it is argued that monopolists took the obvious course and transformed cartels into close combinations. This contention has its grain of truth. The condemnation of a cartel in the *Addyston Pipe* case by the circuit court of appeals in February, 1898,[30] coincided with the start of the eighteen-month period that saw merger activity reach its peak, and at least two major consolidations—the mergers creating the United States Pipe and Foundry Company[31] and the United Shoe Machinery Company[32]—

---

[28] As early as 1888 one writer noted: "The fact that in New York and some other States a corporation cannot own shares of stock in other corporations presents no difficulty . . . There are States where a corporation may be formed for the purpose of owning shares of stock in other corporations. The wide-awake corporation lawyer who formerly incorporated his companies in Maine, Connecticut, or New Jersey now finds that the snug harbor of roaming and piratical corporations is in the little State of West Virginia." W. W. Cook, *Trusts: The Recent Combinations in Trade* 6 (2d ed. 1888).

Even in New York, from 1866 onward manufacturing corporations were subject to few serious limitations on their use of the holding company device. Fred Freedland, "History of Holding Company Legislation in New York State: Some Doubts as to the 'New Jersey First' Tradition," 24 *Fordham L. Rev.* 369 (1955).

[29] The preference of the trusts for incorporation in New Jersey was explored at length by the Industrial Commission. By its findings the main reasons were lower corporate taxation, unlimited capitalization, and less stockholder and director liability. New Jersey law provided that when stock was issued in exchange for property it became "fully paid up" stock, the judgment of the directors being conclusive in law as to the value of the property received. "Trusts and Industrial Combinations," 1 *Reports of the Industrial Commission* 11–13, 1077–1138 (1900).

[30] United States v. Addyston Pipe & Steel Co., 85 Fed. 271 (6th Cir.).

[31] In fact, three of the eight companies that combined to form the United States Pipe & Foundry Company in March, 1899, had been defendants in the cartel whose dissolution was upheld by the Supreme Court in December, 1899. *Moody's Manual of Corporation Securities* 710–11 (1901); Addyston Pipe & Steel Co. v. United States, 175 U.S. 211 (1899).

were precipitated by this decision, the promoters having previously inclined to some less irrevocable arrangement. Nevertheless, the role of the *Addyston Pipe* case in the Corporate Revolution has probably been exaggerated; the difficulty of financing the ambitious merger precludes it from being a close substitute for the cartel.

Finally, the Ripley-Fetter thesis failed to accord proper respect to the advantage conferred by corporate size in the capital market. When this competitive edge was not ignored, it was dismissed as signifying merely that the large corporations had superior contacts in Wall Street, *e.g.*, that bankers had friends, relatives, and investments in these firms. This neglect of finance is somewhat surprising given that the Ripley-Fetter thesis makes the Corporate Revolution a by-product of the striving after monopoly profits and the capital gains to be made out of new security issues. (While these two methods of turning an antisocial dollar are formally distinct, we will not fall into serious error by treating them together.)

The early trust investigations perceived that corporate combinations often produced a deluge of new securities, but they did not connect the Corporate Revolution with the rise of industrial securities on the national stock exchanges.[33] Yet a corporate revolution was scarcely conceivable without a highly organized capital market, and one could plausibly argue that industrial mergers before 1914 were largely a by-product of the rise of a nationwide capital market. As late as the first three months of 1894, the stocks of only sixteen mining and manufacturing companies were actively traded on the New York Stock Exchange.[34] By January, 1910, over a hundred active mining and industrials stocks had appeared,[35] most of which were the securities of companies mentioned by Moody in *The Truth About the Trusts*.[36]

---

[32] The *Addyston Pipe* decision strengthened the hand of the promoters of the United Shoe Machinery Company who faced the opposition of colleagues in the industry that wished to settle for a gentleman's agreement in 1899. *Brief for the United States* 59, 18 Records and Briefs in the Justice Department library (1918).

[33] Much miscellaneous information on the financial aspect of the Corporate Revolution is set forth in a memorandum on the securities of industrial combinations and railroads prepared under the direction of Jeremiah Jenks in 13 *Reports of the Industrial Commission* 913–45 (1901). This study was mainly undertaken to determine the presence or absence of inside manipulation of stock values. (Some abuses were found.)

[34] *Commercial & Financial Chronicle* 541 (March 31, 1894).

[35] *Commercial & Financial Chronicle* 32–34 (January 1, 1910).

[36] Much interesting information on the growth of the capital market is presented in T. R. Navin and M. V. Sears, "The Rise of a Market for Industrial Securities 1887–1902," 29 *Business History Rev.* 105 (1955).

This is not to say that mergers were usually—or even frequently—arranged for the express purpose of getting a security listed on the New York exchanges (although such a listing was sometimes necessary before established producers would consent to the combination because it more easily enabled them to unload securities that they knew or thought to be watered).[37] This is to say, however, that the rise of industrial securities on the stock market and promotional mergers were the means by which the liquidity of claims against capital was both achieved and put to use.

In any event, we can safely say that the improvement of the capital market after the Civil War made possible the large-scale merger, and that such a merger often served simultaneously to give the firm access to economies of marketing, economies of finance, and market power. The fact that early investigators overemphasized this last goal does not mean that it was unimportant or that their evidence is of little weight. Their work showed that, in many instances, mergers before 1905 created firms accounting for over one-half of the total output of their respective industries. Moody's survey indicates that this result was achieved in 78 out of 92 large-scale mergers described. Moreover, many of the new companies went to highly unprofitable lengths to rid themselves of competitors by intimidation or purchase. If more direct evidence is desired, some trust promoters can be convicted of seeking a monopoly on their own testimony since they openly proclaimed their aim.[38] In short, the Corporate Revolution produced a host of firms possessing appreciable market power, and the creation of this power was a major object of the combinations that made this revolution. This conclusion does not imply that the great merger movement was in any sense "unnatural." Given the rise of the national securities market, the unwillingness of the courts to enforce cartel agreements, and the absence of any federal agency that could contest these mergers, the Corporate Revolution was very nearly a matter of "manifest destiny."

---

[37] The listing of securities on the New York Exchange served this purpose, for example, in the formation of the cordage, leather, starch, and malt trusts. See Dewing, *Corporate Promotions and Reorganizations* 23–24, 67–71, 124–45, 278–89. Most of the common stock issued by these combinations for the properties acquired seems to have been dumped by the original recipients within a few years after consolidation.

[38] Thus the avowed purpose of the unsuccessful National Salt Company formed in 1899 was the creation of a company having 90 per cent of salt-making capacity in New York and control of "the product of other salt companies in the states of Ohio and Michigan." Its plan of organization dated March 11, 1899, is reproduced in 13 *Reports of the Industrial Commission* 250 (1901).

8. *Cutthroat competition as an incentive to combination*

What of the argument that the Corporate Revolution had its origins in unprofitable cutthroat competition? Many authorities have drawn attention to the "economic warfare" that prevailed in many industries around 1900 prior to the appearance of the trusts, but the apparent connection between the two phenomena has been made to support two seemingly incompatible hypotheses. Advocates of the Ripley-Fetter view have either (incorrectly) equated the price wars that often preceded mergers with workable competition or viewed them as a manifestation of the "unfair" competition by which aspiring monopolists sought to organize their industries. Critics of the Ripley-Fetter view have inferred from such crude business rivalry the existence of unrealized economies of scale that dictated a reduction in the number of firms in the interest of efficiency.

Actually these hypotheses are not wholly irreconcilable since "economic warfare" is a phrase with at least two distinct meanings. It may denote a temporary market situation in which most firms incur losses and, hence, indicate the presence of "excess capacity." If it does, any elimination of this excess by merger or unrestrained competition will be accompanied by a lowering of total average cost. Alternatively, the phrase "economic warfare" may describe the occasional breakdown of co-operation among the few in an oligopoly market—that is, "irrational" behavior. In this circumstance the consolidation of irritated or frightened oligopolists promises no lowering of total average cost in either the short run or the long run.

Which species of economic warfare was most important in the early years of the Corporate Revolution? The rapid expansion of market areas that came with the improvement of transport in the nineteenth century points to excess capacity as the main cause of entrepreneurial edginess and so supports the view which regards the great merger movement as a co-operation with the inevitable. Nevertheless, some cutthroat competition in this period occurred because businessmen had not yet acquired the mental attitudes appropriate to extensive oligopoly markets. This cultural lag, for example, most plausibly explains the bad relations between Andrew Carnegie and his rivals that moved J. P. Morgan to seek a consolidation of the steel industry in defense of his own steel interests.[39]

---

[39] In 1900 the Carnegie Steel Company of Andrew Carnegie and the Illinois Steel Company of "Bet-a-Million" Gates each had about 26 per cent of the country's output of steel rails; yet the two men proved unable to negotiate a

9. *A perspective on the Corporate Revolution*

The reader may object that we have been talking in dull generalities; that our conclusion is merely that, while the Ripley-Fetter thesis under-estimated the role of scale economies in the Corporate Revolution, the Schumpeter-Galbraith thesis has exaggerated it. Unfortunately, this is about all we can conclude from an examination of the evidence.[40] Perhaps the best way to order our thinking about the causes of the Corporate Revolution is by speculating on the unanswerable question: What would the economy be like today if the great combinations of the 1885–1910 era had never taken place?

If one really believes that the prospect of achieving economies of scale was the only significant cause behind these mergers, then only one answer is possible. The economy would be much the same. The present concentration ratios would have been brought about by a painful elimination contest instead of a civilized accommodation to the inevitable.[41] The author doubts that many authorities who know their

---

cartel agreement that they would respect. 2 *Brief for the United States* 266–67, 14 Records and Briefs in the Justice Department library (1919). The only "rational" element in the aggressive rivalry of the steel men before 1900 seems to have been a fear that monopoly of the industry was the prize which awaited him who first secured a completely integrated company; hence the industry's consternation when, in 1896, Carnegie secured a fifty-year lease on some of the best ore properties on the Mesabi range. 1 Commissioner of Corporations, *Report on the Steel Industry* 70–80 (1911).

[40] The difficulties of separating scale economies from monopoly as incentives to merger are nicely illustrated by the following exchange that occurred when the Industrial Commission was examining one Samuel Dodd, President of the International Silver Company, which in 1899 had lately combined sixteen manufacturers of silverware and related items.

Q. What was the purpose of your combination—to repress this competition, or to make economies in manufacturing?

A. That was just what we were trying to do; both.

Q. Both?

A. To make economies and put the thing under one administration, just as I said before. That is about all there is to it. 1 *Reports of the Industrial Commission* 1055 (1900).

[41] Generally speaking, a merger achieves no scale economy unless competition would have produced the same result. There are two exceptions to this rule. The first occurs when businessmen are so irrational or committed to independence that they will not leave or stay out of an unprofitable industry. The second occurs when competition has already so reduced the numbers in an industry that the survivors, being reasonable men who trust one another, decline to engage in a gladiatorial fight to the finish. For example, *if* the cost of producing automobiles could be reduced by placing the industry in the hands of one firm, the road to

business history would give this answer. Most would probably hazard the guess that, in the absence of the great combinations, the cutthroat competition that may prevail when scale economies in an industry are not fully exploited would have carried concentration beyond the 1890 level—but not to its present level. It is unlikely that they could closely agree on *how much* difference the Corporate Revolution has made to the ownership structure of American manufacturing.

---

efficiency would have to lie through consolidation; the Big Three would sensibly refuse to wage the warfare necessary to crown the victor and monopolist.

Chapter VI

MONOPOLY IN THE LIGHT OF
EMPIRICAL STUDIES: 2

1. *The permanent impact of the Corporate Revolution*

Let us accept that while earlier students of the Corporate Revolution too summarily dismissed economies of scale as a causal factor, they had good and sufficient reasons for emphasizing the parts played by the quest for monopoly and short-term capital gains in the stock market. Does it follow, as many authorities contend, that the present pattern of big business was largely set by mergers in the period 1885–1910?

The research of A. D. H. Kaplan is directly relevant to this question.[1] Kaplan found that of the 100 largest industrial corporations in 1909 (size being measured by capitalization) only 36 remained in this class in 1948. (Actually the number should be at least 46; Kaplan counted as additions to the list those firms that received an independent existence as a result of the breaking up of the oil and tobacco trusts by court order in 1911.) He concludes that, in view of these changes in rank, the rigidity of the big business sector of the economy has been overemphasized. Kaplan's data, however, do not indisputably support his conclusion. An examination of his lists of the 100 largest industrial firms in 1909, 1919, and 1948 indicates that the giants do not change their rankings with startling rapidity.

Consider the 35 largest firms in 1948. Of these, 22 were already among the top 100 in 1909[2] and 32 were in this class by 1919. More-

---

[1] *Big Enterprise in a Competitive System* (1954).

[2] By Kaplan's tabulation of the 35 largest firms in 1948, only 17 had ranked among the hundred largest in 1909. Five of the 35 largest firms in 1935, however, originated in the breakup of the oil and tobacco trusts in 1911. Kaplan does not include them among the top hundred in 1909, yet these five firms would seem to belong on the list. The oil trust was the second largest firm in 1909 and the tobacco trust the third largest.

over, almost without exception, every company which rose rapidly between 1919 and 1948 did so by merger or with the aid of bountiful government loans, orders, and gifts in wartime. The only firms which fell precipitously in the rankings were those which inexplicably persisted in tying their fortunes to coal mining and steam railroading long after the advent of cheap petroleum, diesel engines, and automobiles, *e.g.*, the American Locomotive Company which stood thirty-second in 1909 and was not among the hundred largest in 1948. Consequently, Kaplan's findings would seem to underline the importance of the Corporate Revolution in setting the pattern of industrial concentration in the American economy. Certainly they suggest that no large firm is likely to sink from view in the foreseeable future unless it selects and retains uncommonly inept management.

Nor has the pattern of big business changed much since Kaplan completed his survey. *Fortune* magazine has prepared estimates of the assets of the 500 largest industrial firms and the 50 largest merchandising firms and utilities for 1957.[3] If one retains Kaplan's definition of an industrial firm,[4] then of the 35 largest industrial firms in 1957, 20 had stood among the top 100 in 1909 and 30 had stood among the top 100 in 1919. Two companies which were not among the top 100 in 1919 ranked among the 35 largest industrial firms for the first time in 1957—International Business Machines and Olin Mathieson Chemical Corporation. The rapid rise of International Business Machines in recent years can be traced to defense expenditures on computing equipment. Olin Mathieson is the end product of widespread merger activity that culminated in the combination of the Mathieson Chemical Corporation and Olin Industries Incorporated in 1954.

2. *Industrial concentration since 1910*

We accept, therefore, that the present concentration ratios in manufacturing industries largely reflect the merger activity of the Corporate Revolution. This is not to deny that some undetermined but probably large number of mergers in the period 1885–1910 were not motivated mainly by the desire for market power.

---

[3] Industrial firms are listed in the July, 1958, issue of *Fortune*; merchandising firms and utilities in the August, 1958, issue.

[4] Kaplan and *Fortune* did not use identical criteria in selecting "industrial" firms. The *Fortune* list of industrials includes two quasi-utilities (Radio Corporation of America and Cities Service) excluded by Kaplan, and the *Fortune* list excludes five merchandising firms (Sears, Roebuck, F. W. Woolworth, J. C. Penney, S. S. Kresge, and Allied Stores) which Kaplan deemed industrial.

After 1910 the volume of mergers in manufacturing abruptly subsides, albeit for reasons that are not entirely clear. Among the factors which are generally thought to have produced this decline were (a) the appearance of an antitrust policy, (b) the poor earnings records of many combinations, (c) the fact of diminishing returns in merger activity—the best opportunities having already been pre-empted, and (d) the rise of the management dominated corporation whose officers have a vested interest in preserving its independence. Yet while merger activity never again approached the level reached at the high tide of the Corporate Revolution in 1901, it has not ceased, and its persistence has been conspicuous enough to inspire warnings that mergers are whittling away the foundations of workable competition in manufacturing industries.[5]

Several studies have recently appeared which enable us to assess the role of mergers in promoting concentration with more confidence than was possible in an age of poorer statistics. Most investigators beginning with G. C. Means[6] have attempted the difficult task of measuring changes in industrial concentration by using as their index the percentage of output, assets, or employment accounted for by the 100 or 200 largest firms.[7] The gravamen of their findings is that concentration so expressed has not much increased since 1910. (Admittedly this is an incautious generalization given the variety of indices used to express changes in concentration and the limitations of the relevant raw data.) More specifically, (a) mergers may have increased industrial concentration between 1910 and 1925, (b) the mergers of the late twenties and the high mortality of small firms in the early years of the Great Depression almost certainly increased industrial concentration between 1925 and 1935, and (c) industrial concentration changed hardly at all between 1935 and 1950. By a Federal Trade Commission estimate, the share of manufactured output accounted for

---

[5] For an expression of this concern see Federal Trade Commission, *Report on Corporate Mergers and Acquisitions* (1955).

[6] "The Growth in the Relative Importance of the Large Corporation in American Economic Life," 21 *Am. Econ. Rev.* 10 (1931).

[7] See, for example, J. W. Markham, "Survey of the Evidence and Findings on Mergers," in *Business Concentration and Price Policy* 141 (National Bureau of Economic Research, 1955); M. A. Adelman, "The Measurement of Industrial Concentration," 33 *Rev. Econ. Stat.* 269 (1951); and J. K. Butters, John Lintner, and W. L. Cary, *Effects of Taxation: Corporate Mergers* (1951). The title of this last work is misleading; it is more a treatise on mergers than a discussion of the effects of taxation on mergers.

by the 100 largest firms was 32.4 per cent in 1935; the comparable figure in 1950 was 33.3 per cent.[8]

A different approach to detecting changes in industrial concentration has been made by Professor G. W. Nutter. In his invaluable study on monopoly[9] the economy was divided into competitive and monopolistic industries, and an industry was deemed monopolistic if the four largest firms in the industry as defined by the Bureau of the Census accounted for 50 per cent or more of the industry's output. Nutter then examined the available data for 1899 and 1937–39 for the light that they could shed on the progress of industrial concentration— as yet the only variable governing degree of monopoly capable of measurement. By Nutter's findings, 32 per cent of manufactured output originated in monopolistic industries in 1899. In 1937 the comparable figure was 28 per cent.[10]

This change was not taken by Nutter as conclusive evidence of a decline of monopoly in manufacturing industries. He applied a second test for identifying monopolistic industries to the 1937 data which could not be used on the 1899 statistics. By this second test an industry was deemed monopolistic if (a) the four largest firms in the industry as defined by the Bureau of the Census accounted for 50 per cent or more of the industry's output, (b) the four largest producers of any census product of major value accounted for 75 per cent or more of the product, or (c) the industry had been labeled monopolistic in the most relevant study of the Temporary National Economic Committee.[11] When these criteria are employed, Nutter found that in 1937, 38.3 per

---

[8] *Report of the Federal Trade Commission on Changes in Concentration in Manufacturing 1935 to 1947 and 1950*, 17 (1954).

If the index of concentration is taken as the share of manufactured output of the two hundred largest firms, a more perceptible increase is registered. By the commission's estimate the top two hundred had 37.7 per cent of manufactured output in 1935 and 40.5 per cent in 1950.

But if the index chosen is the share of the assets of all manufacturing corporations held by the largest 139 firms, concentration apparently decreased from 1931 to 1947. By one estimate, the largest 139 firms had 49.6 per cent of total assets in 1931 and only 45.0 per cent in 1947. Adelman, "The Measurement of Industrial Concentration" 289.

[9] *The Extent of Enterprise Monopoly in the United States, 1899–1939* (1951).

[10] *Ibid.*, p. 40.

[11] Clair Wilcox, *Competition and Monopoly in American Industry* (TNEC Monograph No. 21, 1940).

cent of manufactured output had originated in monopolistic industries.[12] Therefore he did not rule out the possibility that monopoly *may* have increased in the manufacturing sector of the economy between 1899 and 1937.

One other finding of Nutter is relevant here. His study showed that, while 184,230 manufacturing establishments accounted for practically all manufactured output in both 1904 and 1939, the fraction of total output contributed by the largest 18,423 increased in the interval from 75.5 per cent to 78.2 per cent.[13] Hence, even though monopoly may have increased between 1899 and 1937 by some undetermined but probably small amount, not all of the increase can be ascribed to mergers.

Whatever their limitations, the studies briefly noted above suffice to discredit the wilder charges that a handful of large corporations are assiduously gobbling up their smaller rivals or driving them to the wall. But, of course, these studies do not prove that mergers are a policy problem of negligible dimensions. Two relevant considerations may be noted here.

First, most studies of concentration have aimed at discerning the place of the very large corporations in the American economy at various dates; yet it is probable that in recent years, mergers have been more important to the growth of medium-size corporations than large corporations. Thus, from 1939 through 1947, mergers accounted for roughly 4 per cent of the asset growth of the 100 largest manufacturing firms (growth being measured from a 1939 asset base), but 25.8 per cent of the growth of the next largest 150 firms.[14] A preoccupation with the fortunes of the largest corporations may, therefore, cause the progress of industrial concentration to be underestimated.

Second, while merger activity may not have produced substantially higher concentration ratios over the years, it may nevertheless have prevented or retarded declines that would otherwise have taken place. This available evidence indicates that this supposition is correct, and one study bears directly on the problem.

3. *Weston on mergers*

Professor Fred Weston undertook to measure the relative importance of mergers as against "internal" growth in the expansion of large firms

---

[12] Nutter, *Extent of Enterprise Monopoly* 40.

[13] *Ibid.*, p. 34.

[14] Butters, *Corporate Mergers* 266.

from the early 1900's through 1948.[15] Weston managed to obtain detailed information on 74 manufacturing firms, most of which rank among the country's largest 200 non-financial corporations when size is measured by volume of assets. His examination of the data indicates:

1. When company assets in the earlier period (mainly 1895 through 1910) are viewed as the product of "external growth"—*i.e.*, mergers—one-third of the growth in the assets of the 74 firms came about through combination.

2. When company assets in the earlier period are viewed as the product of internal growth, one-fourth of the subsequent growth in the total assets of these firms is registered as external growth.[16]

3. Growth by merger was more important in the earlier years of the century. Perhaps as much as 50 per cent of the asset growth of these 74 firms between the early 1900's and 1940 was accounted for by mergers.[17]

4. Considerable variation exists from one firm to the next among the 74 studied—and probably in their respective industries as well—as regards the importance of external growth. Thus mergers accounted for roughly two-thirds of the asset growth of the Republic Steel Corporation and less than three per cent of the asset growth of the R. J. Reynolds Tobacco Company.[18]

We might note that Weston did not allow for changes in the price level. The values of the assets acquired by merger were set down at their transfer price so that any increase in asset values due to inflation shows up as internal growth. Moreover, mergers and capital formation through the construction of new facilities probably were not uniformly distributed through time; indeed, it is likely that mergers clustered in the years before 1929 while internal growth has been more important since then. Hence, Weston's figures almost certainly understate the percentage of "real" corporate growth that one should ascribe to mergers. In any event, Weston's work establishes that, to date, mergers have been an important—probably the most important—source of growth in the large industrial corporation.

---

[15] *The Role of Mergers in the Growth of Large Firms* (1953); see also Weston's testimony on mergers given in *A Study of the Antitrust Laws: Hearings before the Senate Subcommittee on Antitrust and Monopoly*, 84th Cong., 1st Sess., Pt. 1, 406–10 (1955).

[16] Weston, *Role of Mergers* 13–14.

[17] *Study of the Antitrust Laws: Hearings* 408. This estimate of 50 per cent is an impression and does not appear in Weston's monograph.

[18] Weston, *Role of Mergers* 132–33.

4. *The consequence of banning mergers*

Would the large manufacturing firms have grown so rapidly in the last fifty years if public policy had categorically forbidden expansion by merger? Most authorities would return a negative answer to this question, although not necessarily for the same reasons. In the business world mergers may be said to serve two important purposes besides the creation of monopoly power.

1. Mergers transfer assets from falling to rising firms as some go down and others go up. The larger economic significance of mergers of this sort is negligible when (a) the rise and fall of firms can be traced to differences in the qualities of the managements that they command and (b) entry into the industry is relatively easy for newcomers. With these conditions present, it is a fair presumption that mergers will have no lasting effect on the ownership structure of the industry; the aggressive qualities that enable the industrious retailer, wholesaler, or textile manufacturer to develop a modest empire are not likely to withstand the corrosive influences of age, success, and nepotism.

2. Mergers make possible a less painful co-operation with technology in industries where the economies of scale are not fully realized. If average cost of production really can be cut by concentrating production in fewer and larger firms, mergers can bring about this rearrangement, thereby obviating the need for a gruesome fight to the finish. Nor is it certain economic warfare will bring about firms of optimum size. So long as the number of firms in the decreasing cost industry is large enough to make cartel co-operation difficult, competition will force price below total average cost because the competitors can devise no effective brake on output; hence the exit of capital will be encouraged. But once the process of elimination has concentrated production in a handful of firms, it may well stop, for now, even though victory in a fight to the finish may bring an assured monopoly, the remaining rivals may not feel that the prize is worth the danger of defeat. It follows that a merger may be the only way of taking the final step toward efficient production in oligopoly.

A ban on mergers would simultaneously retard expansion for the purpose of achieving market power, eliminate direct negotiations between rising and falling firms for the transfer of the latter's capital, and prevent competitors in decreasing-cost industries from achieving the optimum-size firm in one fell swoop; hence such a ban, whatever its other consequences, would certainly slow the growth of large firms.

Would an inflexible ban on mergers from 1910 onward have impeded economic development in the following years? The answer to this question depends upon the reasons behind the mergers, and here again, the evidence is inconclusive.

Since 1910 the ideals of antitrust policy have commanded sufficient respect that no promoter of a corporate consolidation has openly proclaimed that his object was monopoly power. Moreover, it is difficult—though not impossible—to find examples of post-1910 mergers in manufacturing that compel the inference that market power was the paramount object of the promoters. The "typical" merger now results when a successful firm which (a) wishes to expand and (b) can expand either by constructing its own facilities or buying out an established concern (c) chooses to expand by this latter route. Provided that the merger is "horizontal"—and the industry is not purely competitive—combination *pari passu* brings into existence market power. Since market power is useful to the firm, the presumption is that the prospect of achieving it was one factor which caused the firm to prefer external growth to internal growth. The decision, of course, was almost certainly influenced by other considerations as well, *e.g.*, tax laws, the possibility of forestalling patent litigation, the need for haste in expansion, and the outlay needed to obtain "working" control of the acquired concern.[19]

Nevertheless, the correlation between the persistence of concentration and merger activity in manufacturing industries strongly suggests that the hope of additional monopoly power is not yet a negligible consideration when the firm weighs the relative advantages of external and internal growth.[20] The problem of devising a policy toward mergers is reserved for Chapter XV. Suffice it to say that such a policy must necessarily be based upon presumptions, the most important being that any merger which promises an increase in market power should not be allowed.

---

[19] For a discussion of the advantages and disadvantages of merger growth from the firm's viewpoint, see Butters, *Corporate Mergers* 123–200; and Weston, *Role of Mergers* 70–75.

[20] One writer, who has grouped twenty-seven of the firms studied by Weston into eight industries, points out that "for every industry except rubber tires and possibly meat packing, relatively low proportional growth by merger is associated with declines in share of the market. For every industry except possibly meat packing and cigarettes (one firm only), relatively high proportional growth by merger is associated with increases in share of the market." G. W. Nutter, "Growth by Merger," 49 *J. Am. Stat. Ass'n* 448, 459 (1954).

5. *Bain on the profits of monopoly*

Finally, we might ask, Is there any direct evidence which suggests that monopoly "pays"? Is there any significant correlation between industrial concentration and average rate of profit in manufacturing industries?[21] If so, how much? These questions were explored by Professor Joe Bain in an excellent article which analyzed the relevant statistics on firms in forty-two census industries for the years 1936 through 1940.[22] (The profit rate for the firm was made the ratio of corporate net worth to earning before tax.) By Bain's findings:

> In the selected sample, the simple average of 22 industry average profit rates for industries wherein 70 per cent or more of value product was controlled by eight firms was 12.1 per cent; for 20 industries below the 70 per cent line it was 6.9 per cent.[23]
>
> In fine, it apparently pays to have monopoly power provided that

one has enough of it. Bain's results are especially valuable because he did not neglect to probe for other variables that might influence profitability. No significant correlation was found between average profit rate and size of firm, ratio of capital to total assets, ratio of overhead to total costs, ratio of net worth to sales, composition of purchasers as between producers and consumers, and durability of output.[24]

6. *Recapitulation*

In summary, we may say that the great mergers of the 1885–1910 era played a conspicuous part in producing the present level of concentration in the manufacturing sector of the economy, and that the importance of scale economies in bringing them about has probably been underestimated. We cannot, however, accept that scale economies were the only important incentive to combination around 1900. The evidence of the early trust investigations too plainly reveals that the advantages of monopoly were clearly and distinctly perceived by the early trust promoters.

Since 1910 the progress of industrial concentration has proceeded

---

[21] For some comments on the difficulties involved in getting a meaningful answer to this question, see A. Silberston and D. Solomons, "Monopoly Investigation and the Rate of Return on Capital Employed," 62 *Econ. J.* 781 (1952).

[22] "Relation of Profit Rate to Industry Concentration: American Manufacturing, 1936–1940," 65 *Q. J. Econ.* 293 (1951).

[23] *Ibid.*, p. 314.

[24] *Ibid.*, pp. 322–23.

at a slower and declining rate; indeed it has now either ceased or de-accelerated to the pace of a glacial drift.[25] Likewise, the importance of monopoly as an incentive to merge has declined steadily in importance during this period. Nevertheless, mergers have continued to account for a very substantial part of the growth of large firms, so that if mergers since 1910 have not increased the levels of concentration attained during the Corporate Revolution, they may still have helped to perpetuate them. The concentration ratio, however, is but one variable governing "degree of monopoly." Given that the other variables—the transportation barrier especially—have moved in the direction of more competitive markets, one may deduce that monopoly has certainly not increased—and has probably decreased—in the manufacturing sector of the economy since 1910.

---

[25] The simile is borrowed from Adelman, "The Measurement of Industrial Concentration" 295.

Chapter VII

THE REFINEMENTS OF
MONOPOLY THEORY: 1

1. *The simple case against monopoly*

In the preceding chapters we have assumed, as a matter of course, that in so far as monopoly power does not rest upon the economies of size, it results in a higher price to consumers of the product than would obtain under competitive conditions. We have assumed, that is, that monopoly power serves to change the distribution of income in favor of those who possess it. Underlying this view is the concealed premise that workable competition is the "normal" way of organizing production in most sectors of economy, and, hence, that the possession of monopoly power confers an unjust advantage in the contest for income.

In popular thought the unfairness of this advantage has always been the principal objection levied against it, and this condemnation still carries the most weight with judges and juries in antitrust cases. Over the years, however, the simple case against monopoly has been both called into question and bolstered by other indictments. In the two chapters that follow we shall examine these refinements of monopoly theory at some length.

2. *Further counts in the case against monopoly*

In the vast literature on the alleged evils of monopoly four charges regularly appear in a multitude of guises.

1. Monopoly by producing, *pari passu*, the concentration of control in industry is inimical to the interests of liberal democracy.
2. Monopoly encourages the waste of manpower and raw materials.
3. Monopoly reduces the rate of economic progress.

4. Monopoly "misallocates" resources and so produces the "wrong" composition of national income.

There is little that one can say about the first charge save that it cannot be substantiated by an appeal to the "facts" and is probably inherently incapable of demonstration. The inability of liberal democracy to survive the rise of "monopoly capitalism" has long been a cardinal tenet of most varieties of Marxist doctrine for reasons that need not concern us here; and many non-Marxist critics of the social order, appalled at the ease with which large enterprises once purchased judges and legislators, have concluded that progress toward the good society requires the elimination of the sources of corruption.[1] More recently writers who fear for the prospects of liberal democracy have contended that the strife which must accompany the emergence of close-knit economic power blocks in the economy will transfer economic decision-making to the only agency powerful enough to keep the peace—the State. Worse, the ensuing squabbles over the "just" price for steel and the "fair" wage for hod carriers will ultimately dissolve the consensus on values indispensable to the successful functioning of the democratic process. In the incisive prose of Henry Simons:

> Political determination of relative prices, of relative returns from investment in different industries, and of relative wages in different occupations implies settlement by peaceful negotiation of conflicts too bitter and too irreconcilable for deliberate adjudication and compromise. The petty warfare of competition within groups can be kept on such a level that it protects and actually promotes the general welfare. The warfare among organized economic groups, on the other hand, is unlikely to be more controllable or less destructive than warfare among nations. Indeed, democratic government would have hardly so good a chance of arbitrating these conflicts tolerably as have the League of Nations and World Court in their field.[2]

---

[1] The classic statement of the view that large corporations must either be closely regulated or destroyed if bribery was to be eliminated from politics is Henry Carter Adams, *Relation of the State to Industrial Action* (1887). Notwithstanding the passing of the railroad barons, the baleful influence of Big Business on politics is still urged as a reason for breaking it up. See, for example, Walter Adams, "Competition, Monopoly, and Countervailing Power," 67 *Q. J. Econ.* 469 (1953).

[2] *Economic Policy for a Free Society* 44. Copyright 1948 by the University of Chicago.

We shall not pause to probe the truth of the thesis that the mortal enemy of liberal democracy is monopoly in all its forms, since it must be accepted or rejected mostly on faith. Suffice it to say that the thesis rests upon a theory of political action much too simple to explain either the rise or fall of good societies.

3. *Monopoly and waste*

The less sweeping charge that monopoly causes economic waste has four main variations. First and foremost is the contention that monopoly, to the extent that it rests upon some artificial barrier to entry, ensures that potentially more efficient producers never get a chance to prove themselves. This contention is true *pro tanto* just as it is incontrovertible that the illiterate farm hand might have rivalled Henry or William James had he enjoyed comparable opportunities.

The second version of the charge that monopoly is wasteful presumes that actual diseconomies of scale characterize the operations of many large firms. The evidence that is usually cited in support of this notion is too fragmentary and defective to constitute an acceptable proof. Direct evidence consists of the results of a few case studies which seem to show that the largest company in an industry is sometimes less efficient than its medium-size rivals.[3] (The competitive difficulties of the United States Steel Corporation are often placed in evidence.) Indirect support for the charge sometimes takes the form of a fallacious inference from the "fact" that no obvious economies of scale justify the great size of many corporations. There are no economies of scale, *ergo* there must be diseconomies of scale. Yet *a priori* we have no good reason to suppose that within wide limits—and after an efficient production unit has been secured—substantial economies or diseconomies result when the production units under a common ownership are multiplied. (That an increase in the number of units under common ownership will eventually produce an unwieldy and inefficient giant is another matter.)

A third thread in the indictment that makes monopoly economically wasteful asserts that managements which lack the stimuli of competition go "soft." This contention neglects the truism that monopolists do not receive monopoly profits—or, in Frank Knight's phrase, that all profit and loss arise through changes in the capital account.[4] The bene-

---

[3] A much cited example of this sort of work is *Relative Efficiency of Large, Medium-Sized, and Small Business* (TNEC Monograph No. 13, 1941).

[4] *Risk, Uncertainty, and Profit* xxxviii (7th imp. 1948).

ficiaries of any successful attempt at monopoly are those managers, stockholders, and employees who realized capital gains or windfall wage increases as a consequence of the venture. The legal monopoly of a public utility clearly confers no additional boon on the Johnny-come-latelies in the organization; they must scramble for their gains in the same way as their opposite numbers in competitive industry. The only exceptions to this generalization are those cases where the original promoters lose interest in further aggrandizement after success (no example comes to mind) or where the employees of a protected concern are able to bequeath their positions to friends and relatives who would not find equally profitable employment outside the family firm. Nepotism of this sort is fairly common at all levels on some American railroads and in the building trades, but of course, an indictment of nepotism is, in last analysis, an indictment of the right of bequest itself.

Finally, it may be argued that monopoly produces economic waste by allowing the price and wage rigidities that subvert full employment. So far as the markets for final products are concerned, it has never been conclusively shown that industries characterized by high concentration ratios have more rigid prices than industries that are workably competitive;[5] and it can be demonstrated that an industry when monopolized can have more or less or the same degree of flexibility in prices depending upon the respective elasticities of its supply and demand curves.[6] As regards the market for labor and raw materials, however, the connection between monopoly power, price or wage rigidity, and unemployment is clear enough; that is, the fact that the number of man-hours worked on American railroads fell by 50 per cent between 1929 and 1933[7] was due in large measure to the inability of the railroads to enforce cuts in hourly wages against the powerful labor unions of the industry.

In discussing the tie between monopoly power in the factor market and the wastes of unemployment, we must guard against the fallacy of composition. So long as factor prices remain flexible in some industries, labor and materials made unemployed by the rigidities that are

---

[5] This problem is explored in Richard Ruggles, "The Nature of Price Flexibility and the Determinants of Relative Price Changes in the Economy," in *Business Concentration and Price Policy* 441 (National Bureau of Economic Research, 1955). Ruggles concludes that industrial concentration has no visible effect on price flexibility, but rather that industries with highly flexible prices are those whose costs are heavily weighted with outlays on farm products.

[6] J. R. Moore and L. S. Levy, "Price Flexibility and Industrial Concentration," 21 *S. Econ. J.* 435 (1955).

[7] Harold Barger, *The Transportation Industries: 1889–1946* 97–98 (1951).

maintained elsewhere will presumably be squeezed into this uncontrolled sector of the economy. Nevertheless, a narrowing of the sector of the economy in which flexible factor costs prevail contributes to unemployment in the sense that it impedes the movement of labor and so raises the volume of "frictional" unemployment. Whether the inflexible wage rates in strongly organized industries cause enough frictional unemployment to justify an attempt to weaken the power of labor unions is another matter.

4. *Monopoly and progress*

In one sense monopoly is clearly inimical to a rapid rate of innovation. A plant will presumably remain in production so long as its total revenue covers variable expenses, and variable expenses perforce increase with plant obsolescence. *Ceteris paribus,* the achievement of monopoly power lengthens the profitable life of equipment by causing plant to be used less intensively; that is, it reduces the rate at which unit variable cost rises over time.[8] Likewise, when demand increases, monopoly delays the construction of new facilities. When the firm must choose between building new plants and expanding the rate of output in existing plants, it will expand production by using existing facilities so long as the total cost of producing the additional output in old plants is less than the total cost of producing the additional output in a new plant.[9] Since monopoly reduces the increase in output that will be called forth by an increase in demand, the construction of new plants is thereby delayed.

But generally when writers contend that monopoly discourages progress, they do not have the above technical considerations in mind. Rather they mean that a monopolist by virtue of his protected position

---

[8] This idea is by no means new. As early as 1903 Henry Carter Adams alleged (albeit incorrectly) that "the fundamental explanation of the tendency towards the consolidation of manufacturing plants . . . is the desire on the part of proprietors of inferior plants to shield their capital from the competition of more perfect methods of production." "Trusts," 5 *Publications Am. Econ. Ass'n* 335, 344 (3d ser. 1904).

[9] For an interesting variation on this thesis, see E. D. Domar, "Investment, Losses, and Monopoly," in *Income, Employment and Public Policy: Essays in Honor of Alvin H. Hansen* (1948). Domar attaches particular importance to the new firm as a leader in the introduction of innovations because, not having any investment of a given type, it can immediately introduce the best modern equipment. The established firm must wait until its excess capacity has been eliminated by depreciation or a rise in demand.

does not fear that a rival will pioneer new products and new production methods and, hence, is not driven to do the pioneering himself.

So far as the introduction of the superior machine or production method goes, this criticism of monopoly is valid—witness the long life of equipment in the telephone industry regardless of whether it is conducted as a public or private monopoly. As regards invention itself—the process of establishing the superiority of the new machine or production method—the case against monopoly is not so clear. Indeed, as we noted in Chapter IV, no study has yet conclusively established a connection between technological development and market structure, and we have good grounds for believing that no significant tie exists.

5. *Monopoly and resource allocation*

In recent years the assertion that monopoly is obnoxious because it "misallocates" resources has formed the basis of the professional economist's case against monopoly.[10] Economists early perceived that monopoly does something more than transfer income from consumers to monopolist through higher prices. The monopolist's restriction of output causes some manpower and materials to seek employment elsewhere and so forces down the prices of goods produced in competitive industries. This forced shift of resources causes consumers to suffer yet again. They are not only poorer because the monopolist is richer. The distortion of resource allocation means that after consumers have paid tribute to the monopolist through higher prices, the "satisfaction" or "utility" of the goods that can be bought with the money remaining to them is reduced. Consumers must bear this indirect cost of monopoly because the market value of the output of an increment of "real" resources is greater in the monopolized industry than the market value of a comparable resource increment in a competitive industry. This conclusion follows since the progress of monopoly serves to widen the gap between the price at which a good is sold and its marginal cost of production.

Another conclusion—the fundamental theorem of "welfare" economics—also follows. If people could choose their manner of suffering exploitation—and if they chose intelligently—they would elect to pay

---

[10] The proofs advanced in support of this assertion are often elaborate and sometimes scarcely intelligible. Among the more lucid introductions to "welfare" economics are Tibor Scitovsky, *Welfare and Competition* (1951); I. D. M. Little, *A Critique of Welfare Economics* (2d ed. 1957); and J. de V. Graaff, *Theoretical Welfare Economics* (1957).

the monopolist his profit as a lump sum rather than through higher prices for the monopolist's product. That is, economic welfare would be increased if the monopolist could be bribed by his victims not to exercise the monopoly power that he possesses.

In so far as welfare can be given a money measure, people can be made "better off" if some portion of the economy's resources is diverted from competitive to monopolistic industries. The hard problem is, How far should this transfer be carried? Older authorities building on Benthamite foundations put forward a clear and definite rule of action.[11] Resources should be shifted from competitive to monopolistic industries until the market value of the product obtainable from an increment of resources was equal in both sectors of the economy,[12] i.e., until the price of a good was equal to its marginal cost of production. This recommendation may seem reasonable enough to the reader, but the assumptions on which it rests have not, for this reason, gone unchallenged. Most frequently disputed are the concealed premises that (a) the composition of the national income should be governed largely by consumer expenditures in the market place, (b) the pleasure, happiness, or utility that one man gets from spending his income may be compared with that realized by his neighbor—that is, that "interpersonal comparisons" are valid, and (c) persons who benefit from the exercise of monopoly power have no right to do so.

No believing Marxist will grant the first premise since he places no great value on "consumer sovereignty," and admittedly, in many situations, "the individual will not do when he is active what he agrees to be desirable when he is reflective."[13] Even liberal economists who

---

[11] The author's favorite Benthamite was the nineteenth-century lawyer who could confidently assume that "it is allowed by every writer on political economy that the great object of all rational politics is to produce the greatest quantity of happiness in a given tract of country." Joseph Chitty, *A Practical Treatise on the Law Relating to Apprentices and Journeymen and to Exercising Trade* 1 (1812).

[12] This "rule" is elaborately qualified in the finest statement of the older utilitarian position—A. C. Pigou, *The Economics of Welfare* (4th ed. 1932). *Inter alia*, Pigou explores the possibility that market prices cannot be trusted to guide the allocation of resources so as to increase economic welfare; for example, that the private expense incurred by a tenant farmer in marketing a crop may be more or less than the "true" cost of producing his output depending upon the system of land tenure in force.

The unreliability of market prices as a guide to "ideal" output that bothered Pigou has not much troubled later writers who have been more interested in the technique of devising a plan for securing the right distribution of resources. See, for example, A. P. Lerner, *The Economics of Control* (1944), or K. J. Arrow, *Social Choice and Individual Values* (1951).

[13] R. L. Hall, *The Economic System in a Socialist State* 56 (1937).

contemplate no radical substitution of politics for pricing in economic decision-making object that it is "unscientific," if not manifestly immoral, to compare the capacities for pleasure of different individuals. According to this argument the rich monopolist also has feelings. Indeed he may be a more sensitive individual than some of his boorish victims, so that one should not go about blithely eliminating monopoly at the monopolist's expense. Some writers who object to the making of interpersonal comparisons therefore assert the desirability of compensation. They contend that no change in production should be undertaken unless the reorganization can be carried through without making any consumer or producer worse off. That is, it must be possible for those persons who benefit from the elimination of monopoly to pay compensation to those persons who lose by the change and still "feel" themselves better off.[14]

The possibility of a compensated elimination of monopoly that makes somebody better off without making anybody worse off is held to derive from the willingness of most people to pay some premium above current market price in order not to be deprived of some part of a commodity that they consume. For example, assume that a man buys ten packs of cigarettes a week when the price is twenty cents a pack. He might be willing to pay, say, twenty-five cents a pack for ten packs a week rather than see his consumption restricted to five packs a week. Thus if state intervention reduces the price of a commodity in a monopolized industry, a consumer would pay something not to have the price raised to its former level. Conceivably the aggregate sums which could be collected from consumers—if everybody told the truth about how he "really" felt about the things he bought—would enable the State to compensate both the monopolist for his loss of profit and those consumers who felt themselves injured by the diversion of resources into the monopolistic sector of the economy.[15] This last category would,

---

[14] Some economists adopt the singular position that no compensation need actually be paid to persons who would lose through an increase in the output of monopolistic industries; that such an expansion is justified if the beneficiaries *could* compensate the losers out of their gains. The reasoning by which this conclusion was reached is not wholly clear. One advocate seems to imply that insistence upon the possibility of paying compensation is one way of getting reformers to think twice about the proposals that they bring forward. J. R. Hicks, "The Foundations of Welfare Economics," 49 *Econ. J.* 696, 711–12 (1939).

[15] The probability that a buyer will pay something more than the current price of a commodity rather than be deprived of some part of it is closely akin to the notion of "consumer surplus" favored by some writers. The most influential definition of consumer surplus makes it "the excess of the price which he (the consumer) would be willing to pay rather than go without the thing, over that

presumably, include individuals who had a highly developed taste for the products of competitive industries, notably food, clothing, and shelter.

One aspect of the charge that monopoly misallocates resources deserves particular emphasis. The layman's case against monopoly always equates monopoly power with some sort of objectionable and removable restriction of output, notably collusion and the ruthless determination of a monopolist to maintain his position against all comers. The economist's case equates monopoly power with the ability of a firm to influence the price of whatever it buys or sells, and this power may exist simply because the market in which the firm operates is made imperfect by the presence of transport costs. The economist who objects that monopoly misallocates resources is thus largely indifferent to the cause of the market imperfection. His main concern is with the magnitude of the loss that it imposes on "economic welfare"—"that part of social welfare that can be brought directly or indirectly into relation with the measuring-rod of money."[16]

That monopoly may reduce economic welfare because it distorts the distribution of resources and so yields the wrong composition of the national income is clear enough. But is an increase in economic welfare as the term is variously defined by economists a goal worth pursuing? Earlier authorities did not hesitate to answer this question in the affirmative. They assumed that any increase in economic welfare was tantamount to an increase in happiness, and in a poorer age this presumption was quite plausible. Any change in relative prices that permitted poor men to keep their families in greater health and comfort did increase happiness in a very real sense.

In a rich society the case for concerning ourselves with economic welfare is not so self-evident. One's preference for some minimum amount of food, clothing, shelter, and medical care is no doubt something more than an acquired taste, and it will not be much affected by a change in the relative prices of these items. The same cannot be said

---

which he actually does pay." Alfred Marshall, *Principles of Economics* 124 (8th ed. 1920). This measure works well enough when applied to expenditures on relatively unimportant goods and services but, of course, it makes no sense when applied to such necessities as water or medical care. If the consumer is faced with the prospect of losing only some portion of a commodity, how much he would pay to keep the portion depends upon its size. For a commentary on the possible uses of consumer surplus, see J. R. Hicks, "The Rehabilitation of Consumer Surplus," *Rev. Econ. Stud.* 108 (1941), or K. E. Boulding, "The Concept of Economic Surplus," 35 *Am. Econ. Rev.* 851 (1945).

[16] Pigou, *The Economics of Welfare* 11.

of a taste for luxuries and quasi-luxuries. The things we like are the things that we have come to like because, *inter alia*, they have for some time been low in price relative to other goods and services.[17] Hence if wealth abounds, the striving for an increase in welfare would become nothing more than a jaded search for ever more "pleasant states of consciousness." The ordering of consumer preferences that originally justified intervention against monopoly would be altered by the intervention itself and dictate yet another change.

But then no really rich society—rich in the sense that the same low infant mortality rate and expectancy of long life are found among rich and poor sections of the population—has yet appeared, so that an increase in economic welfare is a goal worth pursuing. "The goal of economic betterment is not a mere illusion."[18] Nevertheless, for reasons that require little elaboration, the welfare case against monopoly has had no impact on public policy, nor has it ever received a serious hearing in the seats of power. The problem of assessing the welfare gains and losses of monopoly[19]—not to mention the difficulty of establishing a system of prices, taxes, and subsidies that would yield a better distribution of resources—is formidable, and the indirect cost of monopoly is so widely diffused over the economy that it is incapable of generating much political passion.

We might also note that the welfare case against monopoly does not always lend support to the traditional policies designed to promote

---

[17] For one of the few inquiries into "how standards change and develop," see Hazel Kyrk, *A Theory of Consumption* (1923), especially 234–78.

[18] Pigou, *The Economics of Welfare* 84.

[19] Only one writer seems ever to have attempted an estimate of the welfare cost of monopoly. By his finding, the cost of monopoly in all manufacturing industries for the period 1924–28 amounted to "less than a tenth of a per cent of the national income." A. C. Harberger, "Monopoly and Resource Allocation," 44 *Am. Econ. Rev.* 77, 86 (1954).

As one critic has justly remarked, "If this estimate is correct, economists might serve a more useful purpose if they fought fires or termites instead of monopoly." G. J. Stigler, "The Statistics of Monopoly and Merger," 64 *J. Pol. Econ.* 33, 34 (1956). In fact, Harberger's estimate is based on the doubtful assumptions that (a) all firms have unitary elasticity of demand—that is, that the production and sale of an additional unit of product will neither increase nor decrease the firm's total revenue, (b) all firms have constant average manufacturing costs, and (c) the replacement cost of assets can be estimated from accounting data. But if a firm has unitary elasticity of demand, it will restrict output until *total cost*—not, we might emphasize, total average cost—is minimized. If a firm has constant average costs, the distinction between fixed and variable expenses is meaningless, and if the gains of monopoly are not at least partly capitalized into the book value of assets, accountants do not know their job.

competition—the suppression of collusion, trust busting, control of mergers, elimination of predatory competition, etc. So long as most industries were viewed as close approximations to "pure" competition—and economists had no qualms about making interpersonal comparisons—these measures promised an increase in economic welfare *pari passu*.[20] That is, if an indefensible barrier to entry were removed resources would move from more perfect to less perfect markets.

Some authorities gloomily affirm that we live in a "world of monopolies" and so imply that almost any trade restraint may be justified by welfare criteria if it diverts resources from more perfect to less perfect markets. By this reasoning the practice of a bricklayers' union in limiting the number of apprentices is neither good nor bad per se. It is good if the young man denied training takes up photoengraving or some other trade where the labor market is highly imperfect. It is bad if he is forced into agriculture or window washing. But of course we do not live in a world composed mainly of highly imperfect markets, so that while a restrictive practice *can* increase economic welfare, the presumption is against it serving this good end. The young man denied training as a bricklayer may secure entry into another skilled trade. He is more likely to be forced into some unskilled occupation whose members have no way of keeping him out.

The development of the welfare case against monopoly is further evidence (if any is needed) that the progressive refinement of economic theory, like most undertakings in this world, is subject to diminishing returns. In the hands of older writers it showed how and why restraint of trade was inimical to the consumer interest. In the hands of later writers it was milled away to the unhelpful conclusion that one can never be sure how intervention by the State will affect economic welfare. In a world where tastes are constantly altered by changes in prices, income, family size, advertising, and innumerable other influences in a wonderfully involved process of action and interaction, this truth is painfully self-evident.

Of what use, then, is the welfare case against monopoly? Provided that one shares the preferences and prejudices of nineteenth-century utilitarians—notably faith in the validity of interpersonal comparisons and the capacity of individuals to advance their own ends intelligently—the case strengthens the presumption in favor of impersonal price making as a way of organizing economic life. This pre-

---

[20] See, for example, the chapter on price making and welfare in M. W. Watkins, *Industrial Combinations and Public Policy* 84–111 (1927).

sumption can, of course, be set aside by a showing that the cost of maintaining competition as measured by the sacrifice of other values is too great. But then the restrictive practice will never lack for able and dedicated advocates. The welfare case for the free market is worth urging if only to remind statesmen that there really is a presumption in favor of impersonal price making.

Chapter VIII

THE REFINEMENTS OF
MONOPOLY THEORY: 2

1. Market imperfections and economic analysis

So far we have considered the simple and elaborate cases against monopoly. Let us now turn to the work of authorities whose desire to influence policy has been subordinate to their interest in exploring the nature of imperfect markets.

Schumpeter once complained that his distinguished predecessors, notably Wicksell and Marshall, constructed the model of a purely competitive market in order to understand the business world better and then fell prey to the error of confusing their abstraction with the reality that it was meant to illuminate.[1] Earlier economists were hardly so unsophisticated as this observation implies; but it is true that their most distinguished representatives usually chose to describe economic adjustments—movement toward "equilibrium"—on assumptions that imply pure competition in the market place, and that the limited usefulness of these assumptions for explaining price making in imperfect markets was not made clear.

It is also fair to say that earlier economists with an analytical bent were so preoccupied with the study of highly competitive markets that they were slow to perceive the significance of the Corporate Revolution. This delay resulted partly from their failure to make explicit the premises underlying their own work which would have shown the inevitability of departures from pure competition, but also it occurred because their interest lay more in understanding the business world of their own day than in discerning the direction of organizational change.[2] (One easily forgets that as late as 1890 the representative firm

---

[1] *Capitalism, Socialism, and Democracy* 75–79 (3d ed. 1950).

[2] These remarks do not apply to the most influential of the American economists of the late nineteenth century, the German-trained proponents of the "historical" method who founded the American Economic Association. But then they

in almost all industries really was the private partnership "which in the course of one or two generations had attained a goodly reputation of a personal and individual character."[3]) Thus, for some years after the progress of corporate concentration was generally thought to call for some sort of policy, the type of economic theory that could be brought to bear on the problem was defective in several important respects.

In retrospect, we can see that the development of "correct" economic theory was especially impeded by two shortcomings of economists. The first was their slowness in making explicit the various costs and revenues that govern the formation of price and output in the industry and the single firm; the second their delay in recognizing that transport and selling costs condemn most industries to imperfect competition.

2. *The clarification of cost and revenue functions*

As early as 1891, when the first edition of Marshall's *Principles of Economics* appeared, most authorities accepted that in the short run the expenses of the firm could usefully be divided into those that are independent of the rate of output and those that rise or fall with it. Over the years, the former have been variously termed "fixed," "overhead," "indirect," or "supplementary" costs while the latter have been designated "variable," "special," "prime," or "out-of-pocket" costs. The distinction between these two types of cost implied the definitions of average fixed cost, average variable cost, average total cost, and marginal cost that are now found in every textbook; yet for reasons which are not clear—and may well have been fortuitous—these definitions were not clearly formulated until the late 1920's.[4] The explicit recognition of "marginal revenue" was equally slow in coming,[5] although,

---

were so wedded to a crude social Darwinism that the Corporate Revolution struck them as an easily explained manifestation of social progress. The initial reaction of economists to the Corporate Revolution is examined in William Letwin, "Congress and the Sherman Antitrust Law: 1887–1890," 23 *U. Chi. L. Rev.* 221, 235–40 (1956), and H. B. Thorelli, *The Federal Antitrust Policy* 108–27 (1954).

[3] Alfred Marshall, *Industry and Trade* 314 (3d ed. 1920).

[4] Modern cost analysis may be said to have arrived with the appearance of Jacob Viner, "Cost Curves and Supply Curves," 3 *Zeitschrift für Nationalökonomie* 23 (1932), reprinted in *Readings in Price Theory* 198 (Stigler and Boulding eds. 1952).

[5] The marginal revenue curve in its modern guise seems to have made its first appearance in print in R. F. Harrod, "Notes on Supply," 40 *Econ. J.* 232, 238 (1930). A mathematical description of "the marginal movement in gross revenue"

again, economists as well as businessmen had long been familiar with the truth that an industry or firm may "spoil its market" by producing too much.

Until the requisite cost and revenue definitions were brought into sharp focus, economists could not derive the supply curve of an industry from the cost and revenue functions of its member firms. Hence, for several years there persisted in professional journals the confused—and in retrospect patently false—controversy over the question: (a) If output increases in a manufacturing industry, will total average cost rise or fall? (Since Ricardo's day most writers have accepted that farm products were produced under conditions of increasing cost.) (b) If output increases in the "representative" firm—that is, the firm that earns an "average" rate of return on its capital—will total average cost rise or fall? The controversy produced an answer to the first question, but it faded away before the second was resolved as professional interests strayed to new topics.

3. *Frank Knight on cost*

Many writers early perceived that decreasing average cost encouraged industrial concentration. Their work, however, was marred by a confusion of decreasing average cost in the industry with both economic progress and the decreasing average "production" cost for low rates of output that is implied by the existence of overhead costs in the single firm.[6] In the course of a famous essay[7] that dispelled this confusion, Frank Knight proved two important propositions. While decreasing-cost industries are conceivable, they are most improbable. If the firms in an industry really can reduce total average cost per unit by expanding output, then competition must give way to monopoly, the quest for profit ultimately concentrating production in the hands of a single efficient producer.

---

came two years earlier. T. O. Yntema, "The Influence of Dumping on Monopoly Price," 36 *J. Pol. Econ.* 686 (1928).

[6] As early as 1887 Henry Carter Adams had distinguished constant, diminishing, and increasing-return industries and concluded that "where the law of increasing returns works with any degree of intensity, the principle of free competition is powerless to exercise a healthy regulating influence." *Relation of the State to Industrial Action* 60 (1887). But Adams gives as his example of increasing returns the ability of an established railroad to appropriate the additional custom produced by economic development.

[7] "Some Fallacies in the Interpretation of Social Cost," 38 *Q. J. Econ.* 582 (1924), reprinted in *The Ethics of Competition* 217 (1935).

Building upon the definition which makes cost "the sacrifice of alternatives," Knight pointed out that an industry's total average cost will generally rise with an increase in output for two reasons. (1) All resources are not equally suited to the production of all commodities; additional units of one commodity can only be secured by using resources whose transfer involves the sacrifice of increasing amounts of other commodities. (This phenomenon is represented by "the transformation curve" in modern textbooks.) (2) The "fact" of diminishing demand ensures that as resources are diverted from one use to another, product price must rise for the contracting industry and fall in the expanding industry; so that even if all resources are equally suited to the production of both commodities, resources can only be enticed to move by the offer of higher prices.

If an industry really does have decreasing average cost, then its output must eventually pass to one firm.

> When the output of a commodity is increased, the cost of the productive services used to produce it will be higher; but this increase in their cost per unit may, it is held, be more than offset by economies in utilization, made possible by larger-scale operations, which increase the amount of product obtained from given quantities of materials and resources consumed. But technological economies arise from increasing the size of the productive unit, not from increasing the output of the industry as a whole. The possibility of realizing such economies—by the distribution of "overhead," or more elaborate division of labor or use of machinery—tends to bring about an increase in the *scale* of production, but this may happen independently of any change in the output of the industry. If competition is effective, the size of the productive unit will tend to grow until *either* no further economies are obtainable, *or* there is only one establishment left and the industry is a monopoly. When all establishments have been brought to the most efficient size, variation in total output is a matter of changing their *number,* in which no technical economies are involved.[8]

Only a brief addendum need be made to Knight's demonstration that in a true decreasing-cost industry production must pass into the hands of one firm or "productive unit." Knight argues that concentra-

---

[8] Knight, *The Ethics of Competition* 228–29. Reprinted by permission of Harper & Brothers.

tion will result from the action of "effective" competition, *i.e.*, by the withdrawal of some inefficiently small firms as all firms strive to cut total average cost by expanding output. But when only a few firms are left competition will no longer be effective. The survivors can tacitly agree among themselves to keep price high enough to cover total average cost, and providing price is not set too high, no outsider will be tempted to found a firm of optimum size since its advent will make the industry unprofitable for all.

Nevertheless, if the State does not intervene, the final step toward monopoly and efficient production will be taken even without the pressure of effective competition. The capitalized value of a single firm that produces a given output efficiently is greater than the sum of the capitalized values of firms that produce the same output inefficiently. Therefore, it will always pay the surviving firms to combine, or if these inefficiently small firms will not join forces, it will pay someone to acquire them at their capitalized values and reap a capital gain by concentrating production in a larger and more efficient firm.

Knight's analysis clearly implies that (a) the absence of monopoly in an industry is presumptive evidence that the industry operates under conditions of increasing average cost and (b) since technological progress cannot alter the "fact" that scarce resources can be used to produce different products, it cannot be said to make monopoly "inevitable."

Knight's analysis also suggests two conclusions that are not so apparent. Whether an industry is viewed as having increasing or decreasing average cost as output increases depends upon how narrowly the industry is defined. Few firms produce one product only; firms that produce identical products need not sell them in the same "market"; and firms that compete in the same market may offer wares that, in the customer's eyes, are not identical. Therefore, any grouping of "firms" into "industries" must, to some extent, be arbitrary. If enough firms—or sufficiently important firms—are placed in the same classification so that the "industry" makes a perceptible claim against the economy's resources, then this industry has increasing average cost. Conversely, if every firm that sells a differentiated product in a limited market is made a separate "industry," then we do indeed live in a "world of monopolies" and, therefore, in a world of decreasing-cost "industries."

This brings us to the other conclusion implicit in Knight's work. Since the firms that comprise an industry sell differentiated products in different markets, a firm may incur decreasing average cost while serving some customers and increasing average cost while serving others. Thus he "monopolizes" part of his custom and "competes" for the rest. A small machine shop, for example, might be able to reduce the total average cost of serving a nearby customer if only he would buy in larger quantities, whereas total average cost would rise if the firm increased its rate of delivery to a distant customer who already buys in large amounts.

4. Marketing costs in economic analysis

Unfortunately, Knight's essay on the nature of cost was little noted during the least cost controversy, mainly, we may suspect, because his exposition is not easily followed. A more influential clarification came when Piero Sraffa redirected attention to Marshall's suggestion that the representative firm may refrain from expanding production not because its average manufacturing cost is increasing but rather because it fears to spoil the market by unduly depressing price.[9] Sraffa, however, had freed himself sufficiently from the economist's preoccupation with pure competition to perceive that in a world of advertising outlays and delivery expenses, "cost" and "revenue" cannot be treated solely as functions of the rate of output. The gross receipts which a producer can realize from the sale of a given quantity of output are affected by the selling cost and delivery cost that he incurs to sell it. But Sraffa did not directly consider whether an increase in the output of the representative firm causes its total average cost to rise or fall.

The interdependence of cost and revenue for a firm that must incur selling and transport costs to market its product is so plain and obvious that one hesitates to make much of it. The explicit recognition of this interdependence, however, introduces a major complication into economic analysis. Economists commonly describe the behavior of the firm on the assumption that its costs and revenues are solely a function of the rate of output—a premise which makes possible the cost and revenue curves of the textbooks. This approach, of course, is ruled out once the firm is presumed to spend something to market its product in the most profitable manner.

For better or worse, the challenge to economic theory that came with the explicit recognition of transport and selling costs was not accepted, the reactions of economists being well illustrated by the two famous treatises on imperfect markets. In *The Economics of Imperfect Competition* (1933) Mrs. Robinson cryptically declined battle. "The fact that in the real world the demand curve and the cost curve of indi-

---

[9] "The Laws of Returns Under Competitive Conditions," 36 *Econ. J.* 535 (1926).

vidual firms are not independent presents a very formidable problem to economic analysis and no attempt is made to solve it here."[10] Price making in the firm was analyzed on the assumption that transport or selling costs could be ignored;[11] the firm was given a U-shaped curve of total average cost and a negatively sloped demand curve. This decision may be blamed for the origin and propagation of an article of false doctrine in economic theory, namely, the assertion that in imperfect competition a policy of *laissez faire* must lead to a no-profit-no-loss equilibrium in which each firm is of less than optimum size. By Mrs. Robinson's geometry the truth of this proposition follows *pari passu* from the impossibility of having the average revenue curve tangent to the U-shaped cost curve save at a point where the latter is falling.[12]

In fact, such an equilibrium can only be temporary on the assumptions introduced by Mrs. Robinson. If selling and transport costs are assumed away, competition can be imperfect for one reason only. Demand for the industry's product is so limited relative to scale of efficient production that it cannot support the number of firms needed for impersonal price making. But if this is true, then the industry's curve of long-run average cost is falling, and, as Knight had earlier shown, the elimination of firms must continue until either firms are no longer of less than optimum size or production has passed into the hands of one producer. (This truth is considered in the Appendix to this chapter.) Actually it would seem that Mrs. Robinson's great work is misnamed since her disregard of selling and transport costs implies monopoly rather than imperfect competition. It is because these marketing expenses check the expansion of a firm's output before all manufacturing economies have been realized that we can meaningfully distinguish imperfect competition from monopoly and pure competition.

Chamberlin's *The Theory of Monopolistic Competition* (1st ed. 1933) represents a more courageous attempt to deal with the problem of price making in imperfect markets. The methodological complications introduced by selling and transport costs are not evaded. Selling costs are made the heart of "monopolistic competition," and Chamberlin explicitly warns against putting too much faith in diagrams since cost and revenue do not exist independently of one another;[13] yet as the

---

[10] *The Economics of Imperfect Competition* 90 (1933).

[11] *Ibid.*

[12] *Ibid.*, pp. 98–99.

[13] "In summary, the 'competitive' cost curve which includes selling costs is inconsistent with itself, it is useless, it is misleading, and it is of very limited meaning." *The Theory of Monopolistic Competition* 175 (7th ed. 1956).

early builders of steamships declined to forgo the use of sail entirely, so Chamberlin retained the conventional diagrams, notwithstanding his insistence on their limitations. Here again the use of geometry led to the erroneous conclusion that imperfect competition produces an equilibrium where firms are of less than optimum size. "The impossibility of production under the most efficient conditions is settled once and for all by the shape of the demand curve."[14]

5. *Transport costs and imperfect competition*

While Chamberlin mainly emphasized selling costs as a source of market imperfection, other writers examined transport costs as an obstacle to pure competition. From Adam Smith onward, economists have known that impersonal price making required markets of considerable extent, and that transport charges, more than anything else, limit the extent of the market and, hence, the force of competition. Earlier writers were, of course, familiar with the role of arbitrage in organized markets. A systematic study of the tie between transport cost and pricing, however, had to wait upon the debate on the ethics of delivered pricing that began with the Federal Trade Commission's attack on Pittsburgh Plus in 1921.[15]

Frank Albert Fetter—the archfoe of delivered pricing—was apparently the first writer to set forth explicitly the price relationships that will prevail over a geographical area characterized both by impersonal price making and by delivery costs.[16] Fetter reiterated that in such an area—which he treated as a single market—arbitrage will insure that the price of a commodity at two points cannot differ by more than the cost of delivery between them; but he carefully corrected the popular notion that the world price of wheat was "set" in Liverpool in the sense that the price of wheat in Kansas or California was equal to the Liverpool price minus the shipping cost to that port. Rather, as he pointed out, the pattern of wheat prices throughout the world depended (in the absence of tariffs) on the distribution of wheat surplus and deficit areas.

It is a tribute to Fetter's sophistication that he did not make the

---

[14] *Ibid.*, p. 98.

[15] For the Federal Trade Commission's hostility to delivered pricing in steel see Fritz Machlup, *The Basing-point System* 45–47, 61–73 (1949), or G. W. Stocking, *Basing Point Pricing and Regional Development* 52–59 (1954).

[16] "The Economic Law of Market Areas," 38 *Q. J. Econ.* 520 (1924); *The Masquerade of Monopoly* 278–99 (1931).

common mistake of equating the marketing of wheat with "pure" competition. He claimed only that wheat was marketed under conditions of "effective" competition, and that "the local prices in the places from which wheat comes are less than the price in the purchasing market, and tend to be regularly less by the cost of shipment to that market."[17] This choice of words allows for some haggling over price between wheat farmers and millers outside the organized exchange. Fetter did not, however, emphasize the inevitable imperfection of the wheat market imposed by transport costs since his object was to show its superiority over the type of delivered pricing then practised in the steel industry.

Once the inquiry into the effect of transport costs on price making was broadened to include commodities not traded on organized exchanges, the incompatibility of transport costs and pure competition became unmistakable.[18] This truth was first underlined in the work of H. W. Singer, A. P. Lerner,[19] and W. A. Lewis.[20] The model used by these writers is of the simplest sort. By their assumptions, all firms have identical cost functions, the freight rate is uniform per unit of distance, and firms are at liberty to enter and leave the industry and to change their locations. With these conditions given, long-run or stable equilibrium requires three things. (1) All firms must be located at equal intervals from their nearest rivals. (2) Each firm has an exclusive market area that describes a hexagon. (3) The equilibrium firm operates at a rate of output at which average manufacturing cost is falling. If this last condition is not met, a new firm can insert itself between two established producers and profitably market a smaller output. (In the complete absence of overhead costs, the industry would presumably have as many sellers as buyers.) The study of the simplest model of spatial competition thus reveals that when a premise of "rationality" is wedded to the given condition of a delivery charge, the model dissolves into a collection of monopolies. Competition occurs only on the

---

[17] Fetter, *The Masquerade of Monopoly* 298.

[18] There appear to be only two situations in which the model of a perfectly competitive market can survive the introduction of a transport cost. The first is where buyers and producers cluster at two different points in space, so that the transport cost per unit of product is constant, unavoidable, and beyond bargaining. The second is where all transactions take place on organized exchanges. In all other cases, the presence of a transport cost for the product provides a range of prices that can be bargained over.

[19] "Some Notes on Duopoly and Spatial Competition," 45 *J. Pol. Econ.* 145 (1937).

[20] "Competition in Retail Trade," in *Overhead Costs: Some Essays in Economic Analysis* 116 (1949).

frontier that separates the otherwise exclusive territories of producers.

A close attention to the role of transport costs in price making also suggests that the firm in imperfect competition will attempt price discrimination, *i.e.*, that it will seek to enforce prices in two markets separated by a transport cost that differ by more or less than this cost. The firm maximizes profit by equating marginal cost to marginal revenue in each market, and at any rate of output the marginal cost of serving the more distant market exceeds the marginal cost of serving the nearer market by the unit cost of delivery between them. Since price is not the same as marginal revenue for the firm in imperfect competition, the prices which equate marginal cost with marginal revenue in both markets are unlikely to differ by exactly the unit cost of transport between the two markets.

6. *Chamberlin on monopolistic competition*

No sketch of how the study of monopoly has developed should end without mention of two contributions which claim to afford perspectives on the business world superior to those favored by most non-Marxist economists. The first is Chamberlin's concept of "monopolistic competition" as something different from "imperfect competition"; the second is "the theory of games."

Chamberlin contends that one may distinguish a type of business behavior—monopolistic competition—that cannot meaningfully be discussed within the economist's conventional frame of reference. Monopolistic competition is viewed as the product of so many forces tending both to competition and monopoly that it cannot be regarded as the intermediate section of a spectrum bounded at one end by pure competition and at the other by total monopoly. Chief among these forces is product differentiation. Chamberlin maintains that monopolistic competition resembles monopoly in that the firm does not face an infinitely elastic demand for its output and competition in that the uniqueness of its product discourages the firm from combining with others to restrict output. That is, the ceiling on the firm's rate of output is imposed not by the knowledge that other firms would retaliate by expanding production themselves, but rather by the firm's perception that even a unilateral expansion of output will raise its marginal cost above its marginal revenue. Given monopolistic competition, demand can only be increased by an investment in selling costs or an improvement in the product, and the impact of these moves on demand will not be felt immediately—hence the inutility of price cutting in most circumstances. In short, "monopolistic competition is a challenge to the traditional viewpoint of economics that competition and monopoly are alternatives and that individual prices are to be explained in terms of either the one or the other."[21]

The crux of the difference between monopolistic and imperfect competition lies in the interpretation of non-price competition. Most authorities regard non-price competition as the substitute method of seeking additional custom that rival firms devise in order to avoid price cutting.[22] In their view, non-price competition is ordinarily more serviceable to rival firms than price cutting because it is not so likely to touch off a price war that may prove mutually unprofitable. Likewise non-price competition is thought to have the merit of channeling business rivalry into restrained contests that are unlikely to bankrupt any contestant. Consumers will react to a price cut immediately whereas they will respond more slowly to advertising, style changes, better service, or even a genuine improvement in the product; thus rivals are not rudely taken by surprise and enjoy a breathing space in which to revise their own strategies. By this view, non-price competition has the additional virtue of channeling trade rivalry into strivings for lower costs. Cost reductions will also take time and afford competitors the chance to react.

We may note that these two explanations of non-price competition need not be mutually exclusive. The firm may refrain from expanding production because it both fears to spoil its own market by unilateral action and anticipates retaliation by producers of substitute products. The problem is rather one of weighting the importance of these considerations in innumerable cases.

Doubtless some firms that produce sharply differentiated products for limited markets forgo price cutting for the reasons urged by Chamberlin, *e.g.*, publishers of textbooks, tax reports, and investors' guides. Nevertheless, for the business world generally, the author believes that the weight of evidence points to imperfect competition rather that monopolistic competition as the "representative" type of imperfect market; that is, in industries where selling costs are high relative to other expenses, price competition is mainly forsworn not be-

---

[21] Chamberlin, *The Theory of Monopolistic Competition* 204.

[22] The popularity of this view of non-price competition probably explains why many economists have wrongly disputed Chamberlin's claim that monopolistic competition really does differ from imperfect competition. See, for example, Nicholas Kaldor, "Professor Chamberlin on Monopolistic and Imperfect Competition," 52 *Q. J. Econ.* 513 (1938).

cause the firm sees no advantage in reducing price assuming rivals will not follow suit, but because it fears that they will match any price cut.

In any event, the use of the competition-monopoly spectrum, to which Chamberlin objects, is not precluded because product differentiation contributes both to monopoly and competition. For example, differences in trade-marked soap flakes and detergents may discourage collusion among producers while simultaneously giving the single firm more power to vary its own price. But it does not follow that a rough assessment of the net impact of product differentiation on competition in the industry is impossible. We may still ask, If the community of interest among these producers is enough to warrant our grouping them as competitors, is the industry's rate of output raised or lowered by resort to product differentiation? As suggested above, the evidence derived from industry case studies known to the author indicates that product differentiation is cultivated mainly as a cushion against price competition.[23]

7. The theory of games

The original exposition of the theory of games we owe to John von Neumann and Oskar Morgenstern who maintain, like Chamberlin, that their work offers a perspective on the business world that is in many ways superior to that favored by most economists.[24] The theory of games is accepted by mathematicians as an intellectual achievement of the highest order—possibly "one of the major scientific achievements of the first half of the twentieth century."[25] That it should have first been put forward as an organon for analyzing the conduct of businessmen was probably fortuitous; indeed the application of game theory to economic problems forms but a very small part of the von Neumann-Morgenstern work.

Game theory depicts behavior on the assumption that players (a) take account of one another's strategies, (b) may themselves choose from among a number of alternative strategies entailing different degrees of risk of loss, and (c) seek given goals. The particular

---

[23] This is true, for example, of the case studies of non-price competition in A. R. Burns, *The Decline of Competition* (1935).

[24] *Theory of Games and Economic Behavior* (2d ed. 1947). Easier introductions to game theory are Leonid Hurwicz, "The Theory of Economic Behavior," 35 *Am. Econ. Rev.* 909 (1945); and J. D. Williams, *The Compleat Strategyst* (1954).

[25] 51 *Bulletin Am. Math. Soc.* 498 (1945).

game that is played depends upon the rules which the players must observe. They may, for example, be compelled to play their hands in isolation as in poker; they may be permitted to form alliances as in diplomacy; or they may be allowed to strive for the joint maximization of gains as in a cartel that divides profits and "rationalizes" production. Again, the game may be so arranged that what one player wins, the others must lose, or the aggregate gains of all players may vary according to the moves made—as when elasticity of demand for an industry's product is not unity. Once the rules are given, however, game theory, in the first instance, requires that each player select the strategy that promises the "maximum minimum gain." Let strategy A promise as much as 100 and as little as 2, whereas strategy B promises as much as 5 and as little as 3. The player must choose strategy B.

The prestige gained by game theory as an acknowledged contribution to mathematics has probably caused its potential usefulness as a way of looking at the business world to be much exaggerated.[26] (Economists are lamentably unsophisticated in their borrowing of ideas from the natural sciences.[27]) The main obstacle to the profitable use of game theory in economic analysis lies in the number and complexity of the equations that must be solved when the number of players and their possible strategies is expanded beyond three or four.[28] Consider the problem of describing price formation in a market where three rival shoe manufacturers can vary their respective outputs (strategies) from a thousand pairs a day to none at all. A description can be fashioned with the aid of game theory—but not without an inordinate amount of computation. Nor is any good purpose served by using game theory on this problem. Conventional calculus will yield the maximum monopoly profit that the firms could earn if conducted

---

[26] For other doubts about the promise of game theory in economic analysis, see Carl Kaysen, "A Revolution in Economic Theory?" 14 *Rev. Econ. Stud.* 1 (1946–47). Game theory has nevertheless found a place in a standard work on the public regulation of business. A. G. Papandreou and J. T. Wheeler, *Competition and its Regulation* (1954).

[27] Game theory has even been used to prove that "since under the present economic background of the automobile industry we must expect that there will be no wide divergence in pricing policies, so-called conscious parallelism or implicit collusion must take place on the price fronts regardless of the non-co-operation of the directors of the firms." Martin Shubik, "A Game Theorist Looks at the Antitrust Laws and the Automobile Industry," 8 *Stan. L. Rev.* 594, 624 (1956).

[28] One reviewer has computed that if ten persons play and they are allowed to form alliances, 115,975 combinations are possible. J. R. N. Stone, "The Theory of Games," 58 *Econ. J.* 184, 196 (1948).

as the co-ordinated parts of rationalized monopoly. How closely the firms approach this limit—and the manner in which they divide the fruits of collusion—depends upon the additional assumptions that one introduces. There is the additional consideration that game theory postulates a businessman who is both timid and ignorant; a policy of selecting the strategy that promises the highest minimum gain will not commend itself to the merchant who has some knowledge of how his rivals will react to his own moves and does not fear to act on this information.

8. *The uses of economic theory*

In summary we may say that the refinements of economic analysis serve two useful purposes in the study of monopoly. First, by delineating the marginal cost and marginal revenue functions of the firm and the industry, they make possible the theory of monopoly set forth in chapters II and III. Admittedly, this theory is an intellectual achievement of modest dimensions. Still, without it the discussion of monopoly never gets beyond the loose assertion that a monopolist will charge an "extortionate" price because he is not restrained by "competition" or, alternatively, that monopoly cannot exist because "the product of one firm is in competition with the products of all other firms." Second, by directing attention to the importance of selling costs, transport costs, and product differences, the refinements of economic analysis underline the truth that monopoly and economic activity are, to some degree, inseparable, and the recognition of this truth is the first step in discovering the possible in public policy.

Appendix to Chapter VIII

IMPERFECT COMPETITION NO BAR
TO EFFICIENT PRODUCTION

1. *The limitations of geometry as a source of confusion*

This appendix examines a proposition now developed in most textbook
treatments of imperfect or monopolistic competition. The proposition:
If producers enjoy free entry into imperfect markets, a no-profit-no-loss
equilibrium will be reached in which each firm is of less than optimum
size. That is, not only is the industry's equilibrium output too small
when judged by almost any welfare criteria, production is technically
inefficient in the sense that if the industry's organization were rationalized, the equilibrium output itself could be produced more cheaply by
distributing it among fewer and larger producing units.[1]

This thesis is generally expounded with the aid of conventional
graphical analysis. The imperfect competitor is given a U-shaped curve
depicting total average cost and a negatively sloped demand curve.
Since the demand curve cannot be tangent to the U-shaped cost curve
save at a point where the latter is falling, the inefficiency of the firm in
a no-profit-no-loss equilibrium in imperfect competition is held to
follow *pari passu.*

The use of geometry to analyze price making in imperfect markets, however, is a very doubtful expedient. If the market is made imperfect by the existence of selling costs and transport expenses, the
conventional graphical analysis has no validity. It depicts cost and
revenue on the assumption that each is solely a function of the rate of
output; yet any change in marketing outlay will change the total average cost of any output and it will probably change the firm's collection
of demand curves as well.

---

[1] See, for example, M. W. Reder, *The Theory of Welfare Economics* 54–55
(1947); J. E. Meade, *Economic Analysis and Policy* 154–55 (1936); W. J. Baumol
and L. V. Chandler, *Economic Processes and Policies* 428–29 (1954); or K. E.
Boulding, *Economic Analysis* 628–30 (3d ed. 1955).

Now if the graphical analysis is insisted upon, there would seem to be three legitimate ways of dealing with marketing expenses.

1. The U-shaped cost curve can be made to stand for average manufacturing ("production") cost only, while the firm's demand curve can be drawn on the assumption that it depicts the maximum revenue that can be realized from any quantity of output after all marketing costs have been deducted. If this approach is favored, nothing can be said about the optimum size of the firm since the diagram gives no information about total average cost; but a priori it is improbable that total average cost would be minimized by having the firm operate at the rate of output at which average manufacturing cost is lowest.

2. Average cost and revenue curves can be drawn on the premise that they describe the most profitable—or least unprofitable—combination of production, selling, and transport costs that obtain for each rate of output.[2] If this approach is chosen, it does not follow that the firm achieves a no-profit-no-loss equilibrium where total average cost is falling. Such an equilibrium would be possible where both total average revenue and total average cost were rising but total average cost was rising faster. No inferences about inefficiency could be drawn from an analysis based upon these "true" total cost and revenue curves. For example, a true decreasing average cost for the equilibrium firm would merely signify that *if* it were compelled to produce and market an additional unit of product, the ensuing loss would be minimized by a relatively small increase in total selling and transport costs.

3. The study of imperfect competition can proceed on Mrs. Robinson's assumption that selling and transport costs have nothing to do with the imperfection, that is, these inconvenient expenses can be assumed away.[3] This popular approach, alas, invites error. The only other source of market imperfection is the existence of overhead manufacturing costs in the firm, which, when joined to limited demand, make it impossible for the industry to support the number of firms needed for impersonal price making.

---

[2] No one seems ever to have drawn cost and revenue curves on this assumption. The method of construction that it implies, however, was obliquely suggested by R. F. Harrod many years ago. "The Laws of Decreasing Costs," 41 *Econ. J.* 563, 571 (1931).

[3] In *The Economics of Imperfect Competition* (1933) transport and selling costs are assumed away. In an earlier article Mrs. Robinson applied the graphical analysis to a case where the "imperfection of the market is due to differential transport costs." See "Imperfect Competition and Falling Supply Price," 42 *Econ. J.* 544 (1932). The error involved in this application was pointed out in a comment by G. F. Shove. "The Imperfection of the Market: a Further Note," 43 *Econ. J.* 113, 115–16 (1933).

2. *Product differentiation and the alleged wastes of imperfect competition*

The reader may object that any discussion of the elleged wastes of imperfect competition must make some mention of the economic consequences of "product differentiation." The author will confess to holding the conviction that economists *qua* economic theorists—as distinct from moral philosophers—have nothing to say about the social disutility of product differentiation.

Suppose that two "functionally identical" ten-ounce bottles of fluid sell for different prices while standing side by side. (The "functional identity" has been established by an "independent body composed of reputable chemists, psychologists, and economists.") What inferences are possible?

FIGURE 6
Alleged Equilibrium of the Firm in Imperfect Competition

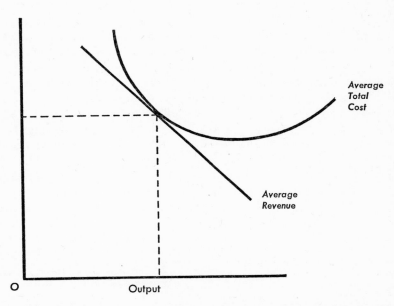

Clearly buyers are (a) uninformed or (b) misinformed or (c) both. (We assume that our independent body of experts did not err in its findings.) If buyers are deceived by advertising, no doubt the advertisers should be ashamed of themselves. No doubt, also, the resources employed to perpetuate the deception are, in a very real sense, "wasted." But what action—if any—should be taken to suppress "bad" sales promotion depends on many things—and not least on one's larger political philosophy. If buyers are uninformed because they are not experts, it may pay the State to invest in a program of consumer education. Then again, it may not. Even consumer education has its cost.

Suppose, however, that the two ten-ounce bottles of fluid that sell side by side for different prices are not functionally identical. Now, so far as the author can see, the two bottles "really" are different products. The fact that the difference can be traced to entrepreneurial ingenuity rather than innate differences in consumer tastes is immaterial. And "real" differences in products raise no analytical difficulties for the economist. Production is not inefficiently organized unless the cost of producing the present output of some particular product could be cut. It is the thesis of this appendix that there will be no technically inefficient provision of the "product" even though the market is imperfect.

The author would cast a parting stone by submitting that textbook treatments of product differentiation show the danger of mixing one's positive and welfare economics. That some product differentiation is bad is a proposition accepted by most people. Economists would do well to confine their remarks on the subject to the obvious truth that product differentiation is bad to the extent that it represents someone's exploitation of the gullibility and ignorance of his fellow men.

No good purpose is served by attempting to show that "rational" exploitation of consumer "irrationality" leads not only to the production of the wrong commodities in the wrong amounts but to their production in firms of less than optimum size as well. To do this successfully, one would have to show that the exploiters do not know their business, that is, that existing quantities of the wrong products could be produced and marketed more cheaply if production were rationalized. The ineptness of the producers of bad products in victimizing the public has never been demonstrated. If our thesis is correct, it cannot be demonstrated.

In any event, writers who inveigh against the wastes of product differentiation really do not mean to suggest that the cost of producing the existing quantities of the wrong products could be cut by a State-imposed rationalization scheme. Rather they would economize resources either by persuading people to want the right goods or by restricting consumer choice to the extent that consumers choose unwisely.

In short, the concept of "an industry producing differentiated products" has no place in any economic analysis that takes tastes and resources as "given." If two functionally identical ten-ounce bottles of fluid sell side by side for different prices they are, for purposes of supply-and-demand analysis, separate products, and the availability of substitutes for a product is taken into account when a demand function is assigned to it. These observations are not meant to imply that economists should abandon the study of the phenomenon of product differentiation by producers as a substitute for price cutting. They are only meant to establish that static analysis has no contribution to make to the study of this phenomenon.

3. *Efficiency and equilibrium in a market made imperfect by a transport cost*

If each firm in no-profit-no-loss equilibrium operates where total average cost is falling, the industry is, of course, inefficiently conducted; the cost of what it produces could be reduced by concentrating production in fewer, larger, and more fully utilized plants. But if we assume producer rationality and freedom of contract, no permanent equilibrium has yet been reached, nor will it be reached until a monopoly has emerged that (a) maintains a rate of output high enough to discourage the entry of new firms and (b) produces this output in the cheapest way. This argument is developed below.

We have seen that a definition of imperfect competition that rules out selling and transport costs has no significance. Let us therefore examine the problem of efficient output in imperfect markets on the explicit premise that a marketing cost is present, but while forswearing the temptations of geometry, let us keep our model as simple as possible. We shall assume:

1. The only marketing expense is a cost of transport from factory to market.
2. Markets are located at equal intervals along an endless road.
3. Each market has the same demand curve; this demand curve has an elasticity of unity at all points.
4. The freight rate is uniform per unit of distance.
5. The rate of output at which average manufacturing cost is minimized in each plant depends upon how the plant is designed, so that the long-run curve of total average manufacturing cost has the traditional envelope shape.
6. A plant can be located in any market along the road.

Let us also in the first instance—and for the purposes of exposition only—assume that the industry is organized by a monopolist legally protected from competition. Since elasticity of demand is unity in all markets, his objective is clear. He must design and locate his plants so as to sell one unit of product in each market at the lowest possible total average delivered cost. It will not profit him to deliver more than one unit of product to each market, for the injection of a second unit would merely reduce price by one-half and leave the total revenue yielded by the market unchanged. The monopolist knows his production possibilities; hence, the solution of this problem is a simple exercise in calculus.

We can write:

t = unit cost of transport between adjoining markets

x = the rate of output

$ax^2 + b$ = total manufacturing cost where $a < 1 < b$

r = the revenue obtainable in each market subject to the restriction that $\dfrac{r}{\sqrt{\dfrac{b}{a}}} < \dfrac{ax^2 + b}{x}$. (As we shall presently note, this restriction is necessary to ensure that the whole output of a plant is not sold in the plant's "home" market and all transport cost thereby evaded; $\sqrt{\dfrac{b}{a}}$ is the minimum value of $\dfrac{ax^2 + b}{x}$.)

xr = the revenue obtainable for selling in x different markets.

Total average cost is the sum of average manufacturing cost y and average delivery cost u. Average manufacturing cost is given by

$$y = \frac{ax^2 + b}{x}$$

or

$$y = ax + bx^{-1}$$

Average manufacturing cost is minimized when

$$\frac{dy}{dx} = 0$$

or when

$$x = \sqrt{\frac{b}{a}}$$

The construction of an equation which gives average delivery cost as a function of the rate of output presents a problem, since the average cost of delivering a given quantity of output depends on where it goes. Here the premise of unitary elasticity of demand in each market comes to our rescue. The monopolist will not sell more than one unit in each market. For one unit of output only there is no transport cost; it can be sold for r in the "home" market. The cost of transporting a unit to one of the 2 markets located nearest to the home market is t. The total cost of delivering 3 units to the 3 most profitable markets is $2t$.

The cost of transporting a unit of product to one of the two nth markets served by a plant is nt, and the total transport cost incurred in marketing x units of output in x different markets is therefore:

$$2t + 4t + 6t + \ldots \frac{2(x-1)t}{2} \tag{2}$$

or

$$\frac{x^2 t - t}{4}$$

Average cost of delivery u is given by:

$$u = \frac{\dfrac{x^2 t -}{4}}{x} \tag{3}$$

or

$$u = \frac{tx}{4} - \frac{tx^{-1}}{4}$$

Average total cost is:

$$y + u \tag{4}$$

or

$$\left(a + \frac{t}{4}\right)x + \left(b - \frac{t}{4}\right)x^{-1}$$

Profit per unit of distance is maximized when the average total cost of selling one unit in every market is minimized, that is, when

$$\frac{d(y + u)}{dx} = 0$$

or when

$$x = \frac{b - \dfrac{t}{4}}{a + \dfrac{t}{4}}$$

Average manufacturing cost, as we noted above, is minimized when $x = \sqrt{\dfrac{b}{a}}$. Consequently, when a transport cost is present, the rate of output which minimizes average total cost is less than the rate of output which minimizes average manufacturing cost, so that the monopolist's equilibrium output is distributed among plants in which average manufacturing cost is falling. Nevertheless, he provides one unit of output to each market in the most efficient manner.

Let us now open the industry—that is, our endless road of many markets—to anyone who wishes to intrude. Suppose, for simplicity's sake, that the entrenched monopolist has a total cost equal to one-half the maximum revenue obtainable per unit of distance. It follows that, given our assumption of unitary elasticity of demand in each market, an intruder by exactly duplicating the monopolist's effort—that is, by himself selling one unit in every market at the lowest possible cost— could capture one-half the maximum revenue obtainable per unit of distance. The entry of an intruder on this scale would eliminate profit from the industry but leave the average total cost unchanged. It also follows that the industry is now inefficiently organized since the monopolist could have cut average total cost by increasing the number of units sold in each market.

We can compute the optimum output per plant when the object is to sell 2 units in every market. Average manufacturing cost y remains

$$\frac{ax^2 + b}{x}.$$

We must, however, construct a new equation which will yield u_2 —average delivery cost expressed as a function of the output when 2 units are sold in every market. For 2 units only there are no transport costs; they can be sold in the home market. The total cost of transporting 2 units to one of the 2 markets located nearest the home market is $2t$. And the total cost of transporting 6 units in a way that (a) minimizes transport cost while (b) placing 2 units in every market is $4t$. It follows that the total cost of transporting x units so as to place 2 units in every market is one-half the total cost of transporting x units so as to place one unit in every market. (See equation 2). The average cost of transporting 2 units to every market can now be written:

$$u_2 = \frac{1}{2}\frac{(x^2 t - t)}{4x} \tag{5}$$

or

$$u_2 = \frac{x^2 t - t}{8x}$$

When 2 units are delivered to every market average total cost is:

$$y + u_2 = \frac{ax^2 + b}{x} + \frac{x^2 t - t}{8x} \tag{6}$$

or

$$y + u_2 = \left(a + \frac{t}{8}\right)x + \left(b - \frac{t}{8}\right)x^{-1}$$

The average total cost of sending 2 units to every market is minimized when

$$\frac{d(y + u_2)}{dx} = 0$$

or when[4]

$$x = \sqrt{\frac{b - \dfrac{t}{8}}{a + \dfrac{t}{8}}}$$

The capitalized value of an industry that sells 2 units in every market when each plant has an output of $\sqrt{\dfrac{b - \dfrac{t}{4}}{a + \dfrac{t}{4}}}$ is less than an industry which sells 2 units in every market by having each plant produce an output of $\sqrt{\dfrac{b - \dfrac{t}{8}}{a + \dfrac{t}{8}}}$. Assuming (a) rational business behavior and (b) freedom of contract, the original monopolist and intruder will either combine and rationalize production or sell out to a third party who will do the job.

If free entry into the industry is allowed, the rationalized monopolist must necessarily "overproduce" and sacrifice some part of his profit to ensure that a potential rival does not become an actual rival.[5] It only remains for us to show that he can avail himself of this protection.

---

[4] This expression can, of course, be generalized. The average total cost of selling g units in every market is minimized when $x = \sqrt{\dfrac{b - \dfrac{t}{4g}}{a + \dfrac{t}{4g}}}$.

[5] The objection may be raised that when the rational monopolist is faced with competition, he might react by bribing potential competitors to stay out or let them in "up to a point." If the offer of a bribe is accepted, the monopolist is poorer but the industry rate of output, spatial distribution of output, and average total cost of output are unchanged. This sort of business blackmail is not unknown to patent attorneys. It is, however, excluded by our assumption of free entry—the monopolist will still face aspiring competitors after his monopoly profit has been

Suppose that an exceptionally cautious monopolist were to sacrifice completely his monopoly profit in order to secure a quiet life; that he can do this by selling g units $(g > 1)$ in each market; and that he has minimized the average total cost of selling g units in every market. The average total cost of selling g units in every market is minimized by producing $\sqrt{\dfrac{b - \dfrac{t}{4g}}{a + \dfrac{t}{4g}}}$ units in every plant; and this output is less than the $\sqrt{\dfrac{b}{a}}$ units needed to minimize average manufacturing cost.

When the monopolist adopts the extreme course of forgoing all profit while producing efficiently, the rational intruder is effectively barred from entering the market. He cannot get an average total cost as low as the monopolist's without himself selling g units in every market. This is obviously unprofitable. If he sells less than g units in every market his average total cost exceeds average revenue. When a rationalized monopoly just breaks even, no intruder can profitably sell in any market. Hence, any spatial distribution of output from the plants of a rationalized monopoly that just suffices to discourage the entry of an intruder will afford the rationalized monopoly some profit.

We might note parenthetically that our industry has decreasing average cost only so long as some part of a plant's output is sold beyond the market in which the plant is located—so long, that is, as a transport cost is incurred. If the transport cost is made zero, our endless road of many markets is *pari passu* transformed into a perfectly competitive industry; the markets formerly kept separate by the transport cost disappear into one big market and the demand for the output of any single plant becomes infinitely elastic. Alternatively, one can retain the postulate of a transport cost but assign a value to r so that:

$$\frac{r}{\sqrt{\dfrac{b}{a}}} \lesseqgtr \frac{ax^2 + b}{x}$$

---

paid out in Danegeld.

There is no reason why a rational monopolist should not yield to competitors so long as the profit sacrificed by letting them in is no greater than the profit that must be lost by the overproduction necessary to keep them out. It is of no consequence to him that the first course of action has a social cost because it leads to output being distributed among plants of less than optimum size, but for the reasons noted above, this inefficiency cannot persist. A single firm producing a given output efficiently is always worth more than two firms producing the same output inefficiently; hence, it will pay somebody to acquire the inefficient firms at their capitalized value and reap a capital gain by rationalizing their production.

When this condition holds, a plant can cover its total cost by selling $\sqrt{\dfrac{b}{a}}$ units—the output which minimizes average manufacturing cost—in the home market. Hence, when it does not pay to transport goods, the industry's output has constant average cost; any additional increment will be provided by increasing the number of plants which produce $\sqrt{\dfrac{b}{a}}$ units.

In short, the assumptions which permit imperfect competition imply either efficient monopoly or efficient competition. So long as some part of a plant's output is sold beyond its home market, each plant has an exclusive sales territory and produces and distributes its output in the most efficient manner. The fact that a plant could cut average total cost by selling a greater output in its exclusive territory (or changing its spatial distribution of output) is not material. No market will contain more than one plant unless a plant can break even by selling, in that market, an output which minimizes its long-run average manufacturing cost.

Nor is maximum efficiency achieved in our market made imperfect by a transport cost only because we assume that the industry is dominated by a single monopolist. If each plant is individually owned, the burden of discouraging the entry of new firms is more widely distributed, but each plant owner has a stake in his own particular monopoly, and he can make it unprofitable for anyone to invade his market area by the necessary "overproduction." Having decided upon the rate and distribution of his output, the plant owner will minimize his loss of profit by selecting the location and design of plant that minimize his average total cost.

Admittedly, an industry composed of many small monopolists would have a co-ordination problem. Nevertheless, independent firms in our model will either learn to behave as if they were the co-ordinated units of a single big monopoly, or they will sell out to a promoter for a price that is greater than the industry's capitalized value as an incompetently managed collection of firms but less than its capitalized value as a rationalized monopoly. If one assumes that production is guided by the prospect of profit—and that this prospect can be intelligently assessed and freely pursued—an equilibrium peopled by firms of less than optimum size is a contradiction in terms.

It also follows, contrary to the conclusion advanced in most treatments of spatial competition, that free entry cannot eliminate all monopoly profit when a transport cost is the source of market imperfection. The portion of the monopolist's gain that remains after he has cut price low enough to make the entry of newcomers unprofitable is best viewed as a variety of economic rent that accrues to him who first organizes production efficiently.

In summary, then, stable long-run equilibrium requires efficient production. If the market is so limited that it can profitably be served only by a firm of less than optimum size, that firm is perforce a decreasing cost "industry" and it monopolizes the industry in which it sells.

4. *The wastes of imperfect competition as a product of irrationality and ignorance*

Has the proposition that imperfect competition produces a no-profit-no-loss equilibrium in which firms are of less than optimum size no validity? The answer would seem to be that inefficiency may characterize markets made imperfect by transport and selling costs for reasons that have nothing to do with these sources of imperfection.

If an industry is inefficiently conducted, it will always profit the established firms to combine for the purpose of rationalizing production. In practice, rationalization through combination may be extremely difficult to achieve, especially if the industry has considerable excess capacity. Some firms may irrationally prefer to retain their autonomy, and even though the desire to rationalize in the interests of higher profits is universally present, negotiators may lack the requisite skills to bring it off. So long as the excess capacity engendered by inefficiency persists, the construction of larger and more efficient plants may not pay. It is only in a purely competitive industry that the ability of an established inefficient firm to break even is proof positive that an efficient producer can profitably enter the field.

Again, imperfect competition may be associated with inefficiency because established producers and aspiring producers habitually overestimate their prospects and so give the industry an output that could be more cheaply produced if it were planned for in advance. Economic waste of this sort, however, is rooted in investor psychology, and it is more likely to characterize a purely competitive industry where, almost axiomatically, entry is even easier.

We may conclude, therefore, that the textbook demonstration that imperfect competition gives rise to a no-profit-no-loss equilibrium in which firms are of less than optimum size should be discarded. In "static" analysis the case against a laissez-faire policy toward imperfect competition must stand or fall on the possibility of demonstrating that "welfare" would be enhanced by an increase in the output of imperfectly competitive industries.

Chapter *IX*

MONOPOLY AT COMMON LAW: 1

1. *Antitrust policy and the common law*

During the debates on the Sherman bill, its backers repeatedly assured the floor that their object was to provide for federal enforcement of the common-law prohibitions of combinations, contracts, and conspiracies in restraint of trade.[1] The questions directed to them during the discussion period did not seek a clarification of this point, but were rather designed to place the legislators' opposition to corporate sin in the *Congressional Record*. One may doubt that the bill's advocates had any very clear notion of what policy their assurances implied. In any event, the position of restraints of trade at common law (and equity) has long posed a number of interesting and difficult questions for judges and historians alike.

In the early years of the Sherman Act, two issues especially troubled the courts. The first was whether an agreement by rival merchants to inhibit competition among themselves in order to obtain a higher rate of return on their invested capital constituted a criminal conspiracy to restrain trade or merely a contract which was contrary to public policy and hence unenforceable. Assuming that such a contract was not an indictable offense, the issue then became, Was an agreement imposing a direct restraint on trade unlawful per se or merely unenforceable when the restraint imposed was unreasonable?

By one popular view, often incorporated into dicta in both English and American opinions, all contracts in restraint of trade—that is, all agreements wherein the parties pledge themselves not to compete with one another—were originally unlawful in the sense of being unenforceable. Moreover, by this view, "conspiracy to monopolize" constituted an indictable offense. With the progress of commerce and a

---

[1] See, for example, the remarks of Senators Edmunds and Hoar, 21 *Cong. Rec.* 3151–52 (1890).

supposed widening of the freedom of contract, the conspiracy indictment fell into disuse and courts began, in effect, to distinguish between "direct" and "ancillary" restraints. The former were always void, but the latter were enforceable provided that they conformed to the standard of reasonableness declared in *Mitchel v. Reynolds*.[2] The consideration of this famous case is reserved for Chapter X. We might note that the distinction between direct and ancillary restraints must be read into the earlier decisions, for it was not explicitly framed until the Sherman Act reached the courts.[3]

If this thesis has a certain plausibility, it is mainly because the law reports before 1800 contain so few cases involving restraints on trade that are unmistakably direct. After this date, the reported cases indicate that both English and American courts began with increasing frequency to use "reasonableness" as a test for the enforceability of contracts made with the obvious intent to maintain prices, divide markets, and otherwise restrict competition. Nevertheless, throughout the nineteenth century some judges continued to deny the validity of all such contracts either because they were in "general" restraint of trade and hence unlawful or because they were inherently unreasonable. Legal historians and reflective judges have advanced several theories to account for this apparent inconsistency—none of them wholly convincing.

Some authorities hold that although the rule of reason was employed in the English courts by 1890 to decide the enforceability of contracts directly restraining trade, it was never accepted in the United States. By another view, contracts in restraint of trade were more favorably regarded in equity than at law, but we have it on high authority that notwithstanding the vehement dicta of some common-law judges when they voided these agreements, there was little, if any, real difference of opinion between equity and law on this score.[4]

The apparently inconsistent treatment of contracts restricting competition has also been explained on the ground that different jurisdictions had different common-law traditions.[5] An examination of the

---

[2] 10 Mod. 27, 88 Eng. Rep. 610 (1712); 10 Mod. 85, 88 Eng. Rep. 637; 10 Mod. 130, 88 Eng. Rep. 660 (Q.B. 1713).

[3] For one of the earliest statements of this distinction, see the opinion of William Howard Taft as a circuit court judge in United States v. Addyston Pipe & Steel Co., 85 Fed. 271, 278 (6th Cir. 1898).

[4] Nordenfelt v. Maxim Nordenfelt Guns & Ammunition Co. (1894) A.C. 535 (P.C.).

[5] Milton Handler, *A Study of the Construction and Enforcement of the Federal Antitrust Laws* 4 (TNEC Monograph No. 38, 1941).

reported cases does not bear out this thesis. It does not appear that American state courts were aware that any variants of the common law as it related to restraint of trade existed in the United States. Certainly they accorded virtual equality to one another's decisions. Nor does it appear that judges perceived any notable divergence of English and American law until the 1890's, when England received *Mogul Steamship Co. v. McGregor, Gow, & Co.*[6] and the United States the Sherman Act. After having read a fair number of restraint of trade decisions, one comes to doubt that the common law afforded any predictable treatment of litigation arising out of attempts to suppress competition.

There is, however, no good reason for expecting that the law in the past should have reflected a more consistent policy toward monopoly than it does today—or that it should exemplify a process of continuous evolution. It is, or should be, a commonplace truth that policies which represent a compromise negotiated by conflicting interests or philosophies usually contain a number of incongruous features. Likewise, given that only twelve years separated the *Appalachian Coals* decision,[7] refusing the dissolution of a joint sales agency, from Learned Hand's decision against a "good" trust in the *Alcoa* case,[8] we should know that judicial loyalty to competition is not a dogmatic thing.

We might also remember that since "monopoly" was not an offence known to earlier courts, the "common law of monopoly" was compounded out of several distinct legal traditions dealing with the efforts of merchants and workmen to influence price; and that the resulting confusion and inconsistency was further complicated by limited court reporting, little guidance from legislation, and the occasional lack of rapport between law and equity. Thus it is not really surprising that within twenty years after 1798 various English courts upheld the validity of a contract between two rival businessmen limiting competition,[9] ferociously fined a hop merchant for the ancient offense of engrossing,[10] and declared an agreement between several merchants rigging the price of imported fruit in London to be unenforceable while mildly suggesting that it was also indictable.[11] We may distinguish

---

[6] (1892) A.C. 25 (H.L.).

[7] Appalachian Coals, Inc. v. United States, 288 U.S. 344 (1933).

[8] United States v. Aluminum Co. of America, 148 F.2d 416 (2d Cir. 1945).

[9] Hearn v. Griffen, 2 Chit. 407 (K.B. 1815).

[10] The King v. Waddington, 1 East 143, 167, 102 Eng. Rep. 56, 65 (K.B. 1800).

[11] Cousins v. Smith, 13 Ves. Jr. 542, 33 Eng. Rep. 397 (Ch. 1807).

three main lines of precedents that have played some part in shaping the modern law of monopoly:

1. prohibitions against "interference with markets,"
2. the application of the law of criminal conspiracy to combinations in restraint of trade,
3. cases turning on the enforceability of "contracts in restraint of trade."

2. *Interference with markets*

The first tradition holds little interest for anyone save the legal antiquarian. It deserves mention only because reference to the venerable offense of interference with markets throughout the nineteenth century fostered the view that the common law once had a marked bias in favor of impersonal pricing. Interference with markets seems to have been a rather hazy offense, but it is generally understood to have covered the closely related acts of forestalling, regrating, and engrossing.[12] According to a statute of 1552,[13] forestalling was the buying of goods on their way to market or otherwise interfering with their entrance into the market; regrating was the purchase of goods in a market with intent to resell them in the same market or within four miles of the place of the market; and engrossing lay in buying in bulk with the object of enhancing the market price. At common law, interference with the markets apparently also covered "badgering" and "forbarring." "Badgering" was the act of buying corn victuals in one place and reselling them elsewhere at a profit, and "forbarring" was the purchase of goods outside the market with intent to sell them in the market at a higher price.

In view of the temptations to arbitragers in the highly imperfect markets of the prerailroad age, one may confidently doubt that the possibility of a prosecution for interference with markets ever made much difference to everyday business activities. The difficulty of producing admissible evidence,[14] together with the necessity of basing cases on information supplied by common informers seeking a share of

---

[12] On the technicalities of interference with markets see Wendell Herbruck, "Forestalling, Regrating, and Engrossing," 27 *Mich. L. Rev.* 365 (1929).

[13] Forestallers Act, 1552, 5 & 6 Edw. 6, c. 14.

[14] Thus, in one of the two reported engrossing cases in modern English law, King's Bench threw out the indictment on the technicality that "it includes several things, as fish, geese, and ducks, without ascertaining the quantity of each." The King v. Gilbert, 1 East 583, 584, 102 Eng. Rep. 226 (K.B. 1801).

the fines,[15] also worked against such prosecutions; yet the greatest economist of the age apparently felt otherwise. Commenting upon a statute of Charles II[16] which permitted the engrossing of corn so long as the price of wheat should not exceed forty-eight shillings the quarter of nine bushels, Adam Smith holds that this act

> . . . with all its imperfections, has perhaps contributed more both to the plentiful supply of the home market, and to the increase of tillage, than any other law in the statute book.[17]

Smith implies that prosecutions for forestalling and regrating were not unknown in his day and ridicules the fears which inspired them.

> The popular fear of engrossing and forestalling may be compared to the popular terrors and suspicions of witchcraft. The unfortunate wretches accused of this latter crime were not more innocent of the misfortunes imputed to them, than those who have been accused of the former. The law which put an end to all prosecutions against witchcraft, which put it out of any man's power to gratify his own malice by accusing his neighbour of that imaginary crime, seems effectually to have put an end to those fears and suspicions, by taking away the great cause which encouraged and supported them. The law which should restore entire freedom to the inland trade of corn, would probably prove as effectual to put an end to the popular fears of engrossing and forestalling.[18]

Since the Parliamentary Acts which defined interference with markets were repealed in 1772[19]—four years before the *Wealth of Nations* appeared—it is possible that the best of economists was not above beating a dead horse for literary effect. Nevertheless, the inflation of the Napoleonic era led to a recrudescence of prosecuting zeal on the doubtful technicality that the repeal of the declaratory statutes

---

[15] Most of the cases involving interference with markets, briefly described by an early authority, appear to have been brought on information supplied by common informers. See William Illingworth, *An Inquiry into the Laws, Antient and Modern, Respecting Forestalling, Regrating, and Ingrossing* (1800).

[16] Encouragement of Trade Act, 1663, 15 Car. 2, c 7.

[17] Adam Smith, *The Wealth of Nations* 501 (Mod. Lib. ed. 1937).

[18] *Ibid.*, pp. 500–01.

[19] 12 Geo. 3, c. 71 (1772).

did not touch interference with markets as a common-law crime.[20] The last reported cases involving the offense date from this time.[21] In 1844 Parliament explicitly removed the possibility of a prosecution for badgering, forestalling, regrating, and engrossing,[22] though one authority writing in 1836 describes the law on these subjects as "nearly obsolete."[23]

Professor William Letwin has argued that the common-law hostility to interference with markets is best viewed as a part of the con-

---

[20] For an account of one man's crusade to revive the punishments for interfering with markets, see J. S. Girdler, *Observations on the Pernicious Consequences of Forestalling, Regrating, and Ingrossing* (1800). Girdler offered rewards out of his own pocket for the conviction of forestallers and regraters, but on attending market at Henley, he was for his pains "accosted in the most violent and gross manner by a great number of Farmers, Mealmen, and others, who exclaimed, that he was not fit to live, and ought to be dispatched; and who followed him from the Corn-market to the door of Mr. Cox, where he took refuge." (P. 210.) Girdler found the local justices generally un-co-operative, though he recounts a few successes.

[21] The King v. Gilbert, 1 East 583, 102 Eng. Rep. 226 (K.B. 1801); The King v. Waddington, 1 East 143, 167, 102 Eng. Rep. 56, 65 (K.B. 1800); Rex v. Rusby, Pea. Add. Cas. 189, 170 Eng. Rep. 241 (N.P. 1800).

In the last case, Rusby was apparently convicted of buying and selling thirty quarters of oats in the London Corn Exchange on the same day—that is, of regrating. In his charge to the jury, Chief Justice Kenyon had denounced the views of Adam Smith on the regulation of the corn trade. The reports agree that an appeal to the King's Bench succeeded in staying sentence but differ as to the reasons. According to one version, the court divided equally on the issue, Was regrating per se an offense at common law? According to another, the justices held that regrating was still indictable, but in the absence of statutory guidance could find no appropriate penalty. 1 J. P. Bishop, *New Commentaries on the Criminal Law* 528 (8th ed. 1892). One historian reports that Rusby barely escaped lynching at the hands of a mob incited by Kenyon's remarks. D. G. Barnes, *A History of the English Corn Laws* 81–82 (1930).

In *The King v. Waddington*, King's Bench upheld the defendant's conviction on a charge of engrossing hops and circulating "false" rumors with the object of enhancing the commodity's price. According to the reporter: "The principal part of the evidence related to the forehand bargains made by the defendant with different planters for their growing crops of hops; a practice however which appeared to have prevailed for a considerable period of time in Kent, and without which some of the witnesses stated that in their judgment the cultivation of this plant, the expense of which was exceedingly heavy, could not be generally carried on." The King v. Waddington, 1 East 167, 169–70, 102 Eng. Rep. 56, 66–67 (K.B. 1800). The defense also argued that engrossing contracts had often been enforced by the courts. Nevertheless Waddington was fined £500 and sentenced to prison for three months.

[22] 7 & 8 Vict., c. 24 (1844).

[23] Archer Ryland, *The Crown Circuit Companion* 224 (10th ed. 1836).

tinuing attempt before 1800 to keep the price of foodstuff low by public regulation, a policy which in turn reflected a paternalistic state's fear of free trade; and that prosecutions for forestalling, regrating, and engrossing persisted so long because the stake of favored individuals and corporations in proprietary markets coincided with the popular prejudice against middlemen.[24] While Letwin makes a plausible case for this thesis out of the scanty materials available, he imputes more coherence to public policies than they really had. Thus in the two reported cases involving interference with markets,[25] Rusby was apparently convicted of an act of simple arbitrage or speculation; yet Waddington was clearly trying to run a corner on the Kent hop market. Even today a preference for impersonal pricing is commonly associated with a dislike of arbitrage and speculation and an abiding suspicion of any sudden departure from the "customary" price. Interference with markets was never successfully incorporated as a misdemeanor into the commercial law of the American colonies, though before 1660 legislation existed in Virginia and Massachusetts condemning it, and the inflation of the Revolutionary period produced at least one statute denouncing forestallers and engrossers.[26]

3. *Conspiracy to monopolize*

The sketchiness of court reporting before 1800 makes it nearly as difficult to assess judicial attitudes toward conspiracy indictments brought against combinations in restraint of trade.[27] Originally "conspiracy" had a narrow meaning at common law denoting the offense of knowingly causing an innocent person to suffer indictment for a crime.[28] In the seventeenth century the doctrine of criminal conspiracy was considerably broadened, although its exact scope has long been a matter for debate among historians of the law. It is reasonably clear that by 1700 it was an indictable offense for workmen or masters to com-

---

[24] William Letwin, "The English Common Law Concerning Monopolies," 21 *U. Chi. L. Rev.* 355, 367–73 (1954).

[25] Note 21 *supra*.

[26] F. D. Jones, "Historical Development of the Law of Business Competition," 36 *Yale L. J.* 42, 43–46, 54 (1926).

[27] For the treatment of trade restraints in the law of conspiracy see R. S. Wright, *The Law of Criminal Conspiracies and Agreements* (1887); H. L. Carson, *The Law of Criminal Conspiracies and Agreements as Found in American Cases* (1887); J. W. Bryan, *The Development of the English Law of Conspiracy* (1909).

[28] Wright, *Law of Criminal Conspiracies* 17–18.

bine for the purpose of advancing their ends by acts which were themselves indictable, notably by the intimidation of persons or the destruction of property. Likewise it was apparently settled law by this date that concerted action to bring about the commission of unlawful acts would support a conspiracy charge, even though no crime had actually been committed.[29] Hence, since Parliament repeatedly outlawed attempts to exact unjust or unreasonable wages and prices by statutes seldom enforced, most business and labor combinations were distinctly suspect in legal theory until the repeal of the combination laws in 1824.

The reports of the few conspiracy cases brought in England before the repeal of these acts, however, are so garbled and inadequate that they provide no very clear picture of how the conspiracy doctrine was actually applied. Prosecutions were mostly brought against working men who had attempted to achieve their ends by means which are still legally suspect, e.g., threats against persons and property. Indeed, one nineteenth-century judge expressed doubt that an agreement to seek higher wages or prices when unaccompanied by unlawful means was ever an offense under the common law;[30] and the only case reported in detail that can be cited against this estimate is *The King v. Journeymen-Taylors of Cambridge*[31] where King's Bench upheld the defendants' conviction on a conspiracy charge while conceding that their demands might not be unreasonable and the means employed to advance them were not unlawful per se.[32]

The author's desultory searches in the Public Record Office have not succeeded in throwing much additional light on how far the activities of organized workers really were treated as trade conspiracies. The court rolls contain at least one unreported case where the rule of the *Taylors'* case was applied against hapless journeymen.[33] In 1798 two shoemakers of Kingston-upon-Hull were sentenced to nine months

---

[29] *Ibid.*, pp. 8–9.

[30] *Ibid.*, p. 44.

[31] 8 Mod. *10, 88 Eng. Rep. 9 (K.B. 1721).

[32] Wright cast doubt on the accuracy of the report in this case, pointing out that the Cambridge tailors were made guilty of violating a statute which applied only to London. *Law of Criminal Conspiracies* 42.

[33] The rule of the *Taylors'* case may also have been applied in Rex v. Hammond and Webb, 2 Esp. 719, 170 Eng. Rep. 508 (N.P. 1799). The fragmentary report of this case merely says that several shoemakers were found guilty of conspiring to press for higher wages; it makes no mention of violence or intimidation. The rolls, however, show that they were also charged with implementing their conspiracy "with force and arms." Crown Roll 30 in King's Bench, Hilary term, 39 Geo. 3 (1799).

in Newgate prison because they did "unjustly, unlawfully, and oppressively conspire, combine, confederate and agree not to work for any master or person whatsoever at their then used and accustomed wages" and, consequently, did "quit and refuse the making of shoes for their then respective masters at their then used and accustomed wages to the evil example of all others in the like case offending and against the peace of our said Lord the King, His Crown and Dignity."[34] But then the court rolls also show that, as late as 1793, a group of striking tannery workers—"curriers"—successfully defended themselves against a conspiracy charge that specified no palpably illegal acts by pleading that there was no case to answer.[35] The moral is probably that Bentham's complaints about the uncertainty of the common law were well founded.

Nevertheless, the Parliaments which repeatedly legislated against combination and conspiracy in various trades during the eighteenth century no doubt believed that they were declaring *the* common law and revising its penalties.[36] Even the better known combination laws passed in 1799[37] and 1800[38] were thought to incorporate no new legal principle but were rather designed to improve the cumbersome enforcement procedure which largely nullified the usefulness of a conspiracy prosecution. (A conspiracy indictment entitled the defendant to a trial in a common-law court and, hence, to full use of the delays

---

[34] King v. Francis Willerton, William Thompson, and William Smith, Crown Roll 11 in King's Bench, Michaelmas term, 39 Geo. 3 (1798). The jury found Willerton not guilty.

[35] King v. Richard Miller and 30 other curriers, Roll 14 in King's Bench, Hilary term, 33 Geo. 3 (1793).

The gravamen of the charge was that the defendants struck for higher wages and raised and administered a strike fund. *Inter alia,* they replied that "they do not think that our said Lord the King will or ought further to molest them by reason of the premises aforesaid because they say that the said indictment and the matter therein contained are not sufficient in law and that they need not nor are they bound by the law of the land in any manner to answer thereto wherefore the insufficiency thereof they pray judgment and that they may be dismissed and discharged."

The case does not seem to have been prosecuted with much vigor. For referring to the defendants, the roll says that "no one cometh on behalf of our said Lord the King further to inform the Court here in the premise or to join in demurrer in law with them."

[36] A number of the many eighteenth-century statutes applicable to special industries are summarized in W. S. Holdsworth, "Industrial Combinations and the Law in the Eighteenth Century," 18 *Minn. L. Rev.* 369, 381–88 (1934).

[37] 39 Geo. 3, c. 81 (1799).

[38] 39 & 40 Geo. 3, c. 106 (1800).

and technicalities afforded by common-law procedure.) By the combination acts local justices of the peace could impose prison terms of up to three months, and a workman summarily sentenced could secure a jury trial in a common-law court only by posting a bond of twenty pounds.

By the conventional estimate, the last combination acts

> . . . were intended to render criminal all combinations of workmen, whether ephemeral or permanent, which were formed with the object of securing any improvement in the conditions of labour or of promoting anything which it was in the workmen's interest to obtain.[39]

But this judgment is contradicted by the language of the acts themselves, or, more accurately, the English combination acts, in common with so much later legislation dealing with restraint of trade, were not internally consistent. Thus the act of 1800 begins by unambiguously condemning all co-ordinated efforts upon the part of workmen to secure improved conditions and provides that any person who takes part in such action shall be guilty of a misdemeanor; but the act ends by prescribing a primitive system of arbitration to be followed in the event that workers acting together are unable to reach an agreement with their employers. Actually it is probable that this inconsistency was merely a belated recognition by Parliament of existing practice, since local magistrates, in purporting to enforce various statutes dealing with working conditions and combinations in particular trades, had often informally mediated between masters and journeymen.[40] The recently published extracts from the Home Office correspondence on labor troubles in the later Napoleonic period convey that

---

[39] R. Y. Hedges and Allan Winterbottom, *The Legal History of Trade Unionism* 20 (1930).

[40] Considerable light on the role of local justices in labor relations in eighteenth-century England is cast by the records of the Court of Quarter and General Sessions preserved in the Middlesex county archives. They indicate that (a) journeymen workers in the skilled trades, notably weavers, tailors, curriers and bakers, were fairly well organized, (b) their efforts at collective bargaining were technically illegal, but (c) when masters complained, the magistrates were more inclined to seek a reconciliation than inflict penalties. Thus, in 1763 the master tailors complained that their journeymen rejected the terms of employment prescribed by the magistrates, whereas one year later the magistrates, with the masters' consent, granted a wage increase and a shorter work day. Middlesex Sessions Book 1193 at 51; 1197 at 35. The records also indicate, as one would expect, that once tempers had cooled, the convictions of journeymen for unlawful combination were usually quashed.

Whitehall was reluctant to interfere in such disputes unless the public peace was thought to be endangered,[41] so that it is an exaggeration to say the systematic suppression of labor combinations was ever Parliamentary policy in England. Not that there is any reason to doubt that many journeymen had legitimate grievances against capricious local magistrates who took it into their heads to enforce the acts.

In any event, after the repeal of the combination laws in 1824 labor unions were but seldom harassed by criminal prosecutions, though the courts remained exceedingly hostile to the idea of collective bargaining.[42] As late as 1872, several workingmen were imprisoned for twelve months because they conspired to induce "breach of contract" by striking in protest against the dismissal of a fellow employee.[43] The subsequent indictments, however, turned mostly on controversial issues of long standing—the sympathy strike, closed shop, and the responsibility of union officers for disorder arising out of a labor dispute.

So far as merchants were concerned, prosecutions for conspiracy to monopolize or restrain trade were virtually unknown. We have the detailed report of not one case of this sort and English law books mention only three decisions which seem to involve "normal" combinations among businessmen to maintain prices to divide the market. Of these, the most frequently cited is *The King v. Norris*[44] in which King's

---

[41] Arthur Aspinall, *The Early English Trade Unions: Documents from the Home Office Papers in the Public Record Office* (1949).

For the view that the combination acts of 1799 and 1800 were virtually dead letters and have received attention far beyond their historical importance, see M. D. George, "The Combination Laws," 6 *Econ. Hist. Rev.* 172 (1936).

[42] This hostility to union officials pervades Justice Erle's treatise, *The Law Relating to Trade Unions* (1869), and it is manifest in his conduct of Reg. v. Duffield, 5 Cox Cr. C. 404 (1851) and Reg. v. Rowlands, 5 Cox Cr. C. 436 (1851). These cases were both spite prosecutions against officers of a national union who had organized a strike in the tin-plate industry that had been accompanied by considerable disorder.

[43] Reg. v. Bunn, 12 Cox Cr. C. 316 (1872). This is one of the few "pure" conspiracy cases involving a labor combination in the law reports. We have it on the authority of the trial judge that "there was no violence of demeanor, nor threatening of any sort by any of the men," 346.

[44] 2 Keny 300, 96 Eng. Rep. 1189 (K.B. 1758).

Two other conspiracy cases often cited are The King v. Eccles, 1 Leach 274, 168 Eng. Rep. 240 (K.B. 1783) and Le-Roy v. Starling, 1 Sid. 174, 82 Eng. Rep. 1039 (K.B. 1665).

In the latter case, Starling and other London brewers were apparently convicted of scheming to avoid making payment to persons who had purchased the right to collect the Crown's taxes on beer. Most writers believe this case to be the

Bench upheld a motion for leave to file an information against several salt manufacturers of Droitwich charging conspiracy to raise the price of their product, the defendants having bound themselves on penalty of a £200 forfeiture not to sell below an agreed-upon price.

In ruling for the Crown, the Chief Justice is reported to have held that an agreement to fix the price of salt or "any other necessary of life" is criminal and "at what rate soever the price was fixed, high or low, made no difference, for all such agreements were of bad consequence, and ought to be discountenanced."[45] This case is the only reported instance where a contract to suppress competition caused the parties to suffer a criminal prosecution, notwithstanding the many occasions on which the courts implied that such contracts were indictable. Judgment appears to have been given against Norris and his associates by default.[46]

An examination of the court rolls might turn up a fair number of

---

untraced *Tubwomen v. The Brewers of London* mentioned in a number of early decisions as holding that what one man may lawfully do alone may become conspiracy when done in concert with others. For an appraisal of the materials, see W. A. Purrington, "The Tubwomen v. The Brewers of London," 3 *Colum. L. Rev.* 447 (1903).

In *The King v. Eccles* King's Bench upheld the indictment of several persons, apparently master tailors, who were charged with conspiring to "impoverish" a rival by preventing him from trading. While the means employed were not described in the indictment, the Chief Justice is reported as saying: "The illegal combination is the *git* of the offense . . . persons in possession of any articles of trade may sell them at such prices as they individually may please, but if they confederate and agree not to sell them under certain prices, it is conspiracy; so every man may work at what price he pleases, but a combination not to work under certain prices is an indictable offence." The King v. Eccles, 1 Leach 274, 276ff, 168 Eng. Rep. 240, 241.

Rex v. De Berenger, 3 M. & S. 67, 105 Eng. Rep. 536 (K.B. 1814), is sometimes cited as a conspiracy case where the court evidenced a free-market bias. The defendants, however, were actually convicted of conspiring to raise the price of public funds—that is, drive up the price of government bonds—by circulating false rumors that Napoleon was dead and peace would soon be concluded.

[45] The King v. Norris, 2 Keny. 300, 96 Eng. Rep. 1189 (K.B. 1758).

[46] The Great Dogget Book of King's Bench records a plea of not guilty for Norris and the other saltmakers in Hilary term, 32 Geo. 2 (1758). The fact that the outcome of the case is not entered on the Crown Roll for this term indicates that the case was never tried. This silence may mean either that judgment was entered by default or that charges were dismissed. The former inference is more plausible since the court's *Rule Book* shows that in this term the prosecutor asked for a special jury and that in the following term the defendants applied to dispense with a personal appearance. Mr. A. W. Mabbs of the Public Record Office has kindly furnished this information.

conspiracy cases involving businessmen. For example, it is recorded that in 1791 nine London coal merchants were found not guilty of conspiring to engross coals by refusing to deal with shippers who sold any part of their cargoes to two coal merchants that the combination had black-listed.[47] But the fact remains that prior to 1890 no important case in England ever turned directly on the question, Could it be unlawful for masters and workmen to combine in order to advance ends that could lawfully be pursued by individuals acting alone? Consequently, as late as 1889 a dissenting judge in a civil case can still assert that conspiracy to restrain trade is a common-law crime.[48]

In the early years of the nineteenth century the ambiguity of the common-law treatment of conspiracy particularly troubled American courts since state legislatures, unlike Parliament, were extremely loath to deal with any aspect of the monopoly problem by statute; yet even in this country, the question of whether concerted action to affect prices or wages untainted by the use of criminal means is an indictable offense was never decided. In a number of early cases involving journeymen shoemakers and tailors[49] the courts reaffirmed that what is lawful for the individual acting alone is not necessarily permissible for individuals acting in concert, but in each of these prosecutions, the defendants were also charged with having threatened the injury of persons or the destruction of property. Eventually American judges in the nineteenth century found it more convenient to use the legal fiction that

---

[47] King v. Benjamin Kennett and eight others, Crown Roll 22 in King's Bench, Trinity term, 31 Geo. 3 (1791).

[48] Opinion of Lord Esher in Mogul Steamship Co. v. McGregor, Gow & Co., 23 Q.B.D. 598, 601–611 (1889).

In the mid-nineteenth century the view that price fixing was indictable had been re-enforced by a misreading of Lord Campbell's remarks in a private opinion. In 1852, while arbitrating differences between publishers and booksellers, he had described the booksellers' resale price regulations as "indefensible and contrary to the freedom which ought to prevail in commercial transactions." But Campbell explicitly rejected the argument of one disgruntled member of the trade that collusive resale price maintenance was "illegal as well as impolitic." On this incident, see B. S. Yamey, "Trade Conspiracies. An Historical Footnote," 17 *Modern L. Rev.* 139 (1954).

[49] People v. Fisher, 14 Wend. 9 (N.Y. Sup. Ct. 1835); Commonwealth v. Moore (Mayor's Ct., Phila. 1827); Commonwealth v. Macky (Ct. Q.S. 1815); People v. Melvin (Ct. Gen. Sess. 1809); Commonwealth v. Pullis (Mayor's Ct., Phila. 1806).

The original reports of the last four cases have not been reprinted in easily accessible collections but are substantially reproduced in 3 and 4 *Documentary History of American Industrial Society* (Commons and Gilmore eds. 1910).

peaceable combination to secure improved working conditions was never criminal conspiracy under the common law.[50] As in England, the law of secondary boycott, mass picketing, and the closed shop was never satisfactorily settled by the courts. After 1880 the conspiracy prosecution as a means of maintaining public order was rendered obsolete by the appearance of the injunction in labor disputes.[51] As for business monopoly, American merchants at no time had cause to fear a conspiracy prosecution so long as they eschewed violence and fraud in obtaining or defending their market position, and given the primitive governmental machinery of most states in the nineteenth century, even clearly criminal acts in support of business aggrandizement were hardly ever prosecuted.

In short, when the Sherman Act was passed in 1890 there existed no settled common-law doctrine of conspiracy with respect to restraint of trade except for the acknowledged principle that an agreement to commit a palpable criminal act would support an indictment whether or not the act had been overtly attempted. Federal judges who received the task of construing the criminal provisions of the Sherman Act were on their own.

---

[50] See, for example, Commonwealth v. Hunt, 45 Mass. 111 (1842), where the Supreme Judicial Court of Massachusetts threw out an indictment of Boston journeymen shoemakers whose society had adopted a bylaw requiring the payment of a forfeiture by any member who should work in a shop that employed non-union men.

[51] See E. E. Witte, "Early American Labor Cases," 35 *Yale L. J.* 825, 832 (1926).

Chapter *X*

MONOPOLY AT COMMON LAW: 2

1. *Contracts in restraint of trade*

Before the Sherman Act, the law of combination was, for all practical purposes, private law turning upon the enforceability of the contract in restraint of trade. Unfortunately, this phrase early came to describe all arrangements whereby two or more parties agree to limit competition among themselves in some designated market. Hence it covers several species of contract which otherwise have not much in common, notably:

1. a contract between master and apprentice stipulating that the latter will not set up in competition with the former after completing his training;

2. an agreement whereby a workman who has access to trade secrets accepts a job on condition that he will not hire out to a rival of his employer upon leaving the latter's service;

3. a contract whereby the seller of a business agrees to remain out of competition with the buyer in order to safeguard the transfer of "goodwill";

4. an agreement in which one competitor sells out to another and promises not to re-enter the market;

5. an arrangement wherein rival firms agree to pursue a co-ordinated marketing policy.

The first three varieties of restraint have only a remote bearing on monopoly except, perhaps, as evidence that the market is imperfect. They deserve mention only because they made an earlier appearance in court and so provided precedents that confused the courts' approach to monopoly in later cases.

Probably the courts have always been willing to enforce a contract in restraint of trade so long as it did not directly operate to suppress competition and represented a "reasonable" agreement between competent parties of comparable bargaining power.[1] The legality of such a contract is taken to have been unequivocably established in *Mitchel v. Reynolds* (1713),[2] the earliest relevant decision reported at length and one of the most frequently cited cases in commercial law.

Mitchel had leased a bakehouse from Reynolds in central London for a period of seven years on condition that the latter would not re-establish himself as a baker in the parish during the term of the lease. It was agreed that if Reynolds violated the agreement he should forfeit a bond to Mitchel. Reynolds failed to observe the bargain, but when payment was demanded his counsel, relying upon fragmentary dicta in a number of older cases,[3] pleaded that the contract was void by virtue of its being in restraint of trade. The court overruled this objection on the ground that a "reasonable" contract in restraint of trade was enforceable provided that it was made for "good and adequate consideration" and imposed a restraint which was "particular" rather than "general." The court went on to observe that a contract wherein a man pleaded not to follow his calling anywhere in England would be void since it could benefit no one, and that the disputed restraint commended itself because it was imposed for only seven years, the length of the lease. The confusion which subsequently followed from the distinction between partial and general restraints proclaimed in this case was prodigious.[4]

So far as monopoly is concerned, the important question in a restraint of trade case is not whether a restraint is partial or general but rather whether it further limits competition or merely protects an existing property value. For a century and a half after *Mitchel v. Reynolds* the courts wrestled with the task of distinguishing general from par-

---

[1] The very early cases in which contracts in restraint of trade were categorically condemned all involved conditions imposed by master craftsmen on adolescent apprentices. See, for example, The Dyer's Case, Y.B. 2 Henry V fo. 5 (1414), or Colgate v. Batchelor, Cro. Eliz. 872, 78 Eng. Rep. 1097 (K.B. 1578).

[2] 10 Mod. 27, 88 Eng. Rep. 610 (1712); 10 Mod. 85, 88 Eng. Rep. 637; 10 Mod. 130, 88 Eng. Rep. 660 (Q.B. 1713).

[3] Notably Rogers v. Parrey, 2 Bulstr. 136, 80 Eng. Rep. 1013 (K.B. 1614); Broad v. Jollyfe, Cro. Jac. 596, 79 Eng. Rep. 509 (K.B. 1620); Prugnell v. Gosse, Al. 67, 82 Eng. Rep. 919 (K.B. 1649).

[4] The finest review of the common-law treatment of contracts in restraint of trade that the author has found is in Davies v. Davies, 36 Ch. D. 359 (C.A. 1887). A list of all known restraint of trade cases described in England to 1946 is given in Frederick Pollock, *Principles of Contract* 328 (12th ed. 1946). For a collation of authorities on the subject, including a summary of American decisions to 1867, see Annot., 92 Am. Dec. 751 (1887).

ticular restraints until at length it was accepted that the period of time and geographical area over which the restraint extended were not the ultimate considerations; that the enforceability of the contract depended upon the reasonableness of the restraint imposed.[5] Not that this development was not much of an improvement since *Mitchel v. Reynolds* had implied two variants on the rule of reason: (a) the restraint should not unduly oppress the public, and (b) the restraint should be no more than was necessary to carry out the object of the contract. It is true that the decision had obliquely suggested that any contract executed primarily for the purpose of limiting competition was unenforceable, but given this paucity of reported cases involving price fixing in the seventeenth and eighteenth centuries we cannot be certain that this dictum was ever good law.

From an examination of the cases cited by several authorities,[6] it appears that the first reported decision involving the legality of a contract directly suppressing competition was not rendered until 1798. In that year the House of Lords, hearing *Smith v. Scott*[7] on appeal from Scotland, voided an agreement among six Edinburgh merchants in the business of supplying coaches for hire who had pledged themselves to charge higher uniform fares "owing to the rise of every article in the posting line for years back."[8] The case was not decided at common law, though the court remarked that had the combination been attempted in England, the defendants would have been liable to indictment for conspiracy (no precedents cited). A complaint was lodged with the local justices requesting that the defendants be fined and restrained from charging more than the customary rates. Although no fines were levied, the magistrates consented to order a return to the old fares. The appeal thus presented two issues. (1) Was the combination unlawful? (2) Did the justices have the price-fixing power in this trade?

The Lord Chancellor had no doubts on the first question. He is reported as ruling:

---

[5] Rousillon v. Rousillon, 14 Ch. D. 351 (1880) is usually cited as the case which established the ascendancy of the reasonableness test.

[6] T. C. Spelling, *A Treatise on Trusts and Monopolies* (1893); C. F. Beach, *A Treatise on the Law of Monopolies and Industrial Trusts* (1898); W. A. Sanderson, *Restraint of Trade in English Law* (1926); A. L. Haslam, *The Law Relating to Trade Combinations* (1931); R. Y. Hedges, *The Law Relating to Restraint of Trade* (1932); J. C. Peppin, "Price-Fixing Agreements under the Sherman Anti-Trust Law," 28 *Calif. L. Rev.* 297, 667 (1940).

[7] 4 Pat. 17 (H.L. 1798).

[8] *Ibid.* 18.

By this, your Lordships know, they were imposing a law to demand from the public, a certain and fixed rate for posting, which was illegal and unwarrantable. . . . The case is very different, whether an individual might or might not ask what rate for posting he thought fit, but he must not make a party business of it.[9]

On grounds of expediency, however, he denied the price-fixing power to the local justices. Although it might have been proper to fix the rates in a case of monopoly, "such as hackney coaches confined to a given number of persons," coaches for hire were another matter.

Experience shows that in this country, you have been well served on account of the failure of a measure which was attempted, of putting the *posts* into a mode of regulation similar to that on the continent. For this purpose, a bill was brought into Parliament, but the measure was opposed, and was not carried into effect.[10]

The Lord Chancellor's allegiance to free trade, however, was rather uncertain, for he advised that the justices should have dealt with the defendants by imposing fines to be waived on condition that they return to their former rates.

Only seventeen years later in *Hearn v. Griffin*[11] the Court of King's Bench upheld an agreement between two rival stagecoach lines made for the purpose of arranging schedules and fixing fares. With an uneven grasp of the theory of monopolistic competition, the Chief Justice stated:

How can you contend that it is in restraint of trade; they are left at liberty to charge what they like, though not more than each other? And by the agreement, particular days and times for each to run in the week are fixed. This is merely a convenient way of arranging two concerns that might otherwise ruin each other.[12]

Or again:

Each contracting party here has one day to work his particular coach. Nor is there any limitation as to the size of the coach;

---

[9] *Ibid.* 20.
[10] *Ibid.* 21.
[11] 2 Chit. 402 (K.B. 1815).
[12] *Ibid.* 403.

the defendant may have a long coach. This agreement does not preclude a third or more persons from starting in opposition to plaintiff and defendant.[13]

Meanwhile, in 1811, the Supreme Judicial Court of Massachusetts in *Pierce v. Fuller*[14] had sustained a contract patently executed for the purpose of suppressing nuisance competition. The operator of stage-coaches running between Boston and Providence paid $290 to the defendant, a rival, for "an old stage coach and one poor horse, both of the value of 190 dollars and no more,"[15] on condition that he withdraw from the route. The defendant agreed to forfeit $290 if he violated his promise. When sued for breach of contract, he both denied the charge and alleged the contract to be void. The court ruled against him on both counts, arguing that since he could run a stage on any other route, and third parties were not restrained from setting up in business on the Boston-Providence trip, the restraint was only "partial." Within the next fifteen years the same court three times affirmed the legality of a contractual restraint designed to suppress competition.[16]

In 1839 the New York Supreme Court in *Chappel v. Brockway*[17] upheld a contract by which the operator of a line of packet boats between Buffalo and Rochester on the Erie Canal bought out his rival for $12,500, on condition that the latter would forfeit a bond of $25,000 if he re-entered business on this run at any time. Indeed it was not until 1847 in *Hooker v. Vandewater*[18] that a contract suppressing competition was voided in a reported case on this side of the Atlantic. Here the court set aside the ruling of a referee in chancery which would have compelled the defendant to pay damages because he had failed to fulfill his part of a pooling agreement among bargemen on the Erie Canal. In this case the court relied not so much upon the unreasonableness of the restraint as upon an obscure and seldom enforced provision of a New York statute which condemned as a misdemeanor any conspiracy "to commit any act injurious . . . to trade or commerce. . . ."[19] One year later in *Stanton v. Allen*[20] the court reaffirmed the appli-

---

[13] *Ibid.*

[14] 8 Mass. 222 (1811).

[15] *Ibid.* 223.

[16] Perkins v. Lyman, 9 Mass. 521 (1813); Stearns v. Barrett, 18 Mass. 443 (1823); Palmer v. Stebbins, 20 Mass. 188 (1825).

[17] 21 Wend. 157 (N.Y. Sup. Ct. 1839).

[18] 4 Den. 349 (N.Y. Sup. Ct. 1847).

[19] 2 N.Y. Rev. Stat. 691, S.8 (1836).

[20] 5 Den. 434 (N.Y. Sup. Ct. 1848).

cability of this law to contracts in restraint of trade, but also stated that the questioned agreement would have been void at common law since the restraint imposed was unreasonable. The court's view was certainly plausible, for the case turned on the effort of an earnings-pool association which embraced all thirty-five companies operating boats on the Erie and Oswego canals to collect from a reneging member. (The association was held responsible for having raised freight charges on the canal from 40 to 50 per cent in the space of a few months.)

At present we can only guess whether the increasing frequency of reported litigation involving contracts suppressing competition after 1800 reflects mainly increasing judicial toleration of such agreements, better court reporting,[21] or the greater opportunities for profitable combination and co-operation that accompanied the quickening pace of industrialization. It would seem, however, that the rivalry, as touchstones of public policy, between the rule of reason and the doctrine that a direct restraint of trade is always unenforceable, began with the reported litigation on the subject. Nevertheless, while both principles were frequently proclaimed by the courts throughout the nineteenth century, the conflict was more apparent than real, for when one surveys the circumstances set forth in the more frequently cited cases that made the common law of combination, and provided that one ignores the intemperate dicta of judges, much of the apparent inconsistency disappears.

2. *The coming of the rule of reason*

Four problems especially plagued the courts in their efforts to pass upon the validity of restraints on competition. The first arose from a reluctance to acknowledge the existence of an unenforceable contract whose observance did not, at the same time, involve the commission of a tort or an indictable offense. The law, of course, has always recognized that private agreements could fall into this category but it has not regarded them favorably. The usual presumption is that when men in full possession of their faculties contract to do something which does not violate the criminal law, the public interest in fair dealing requires

---

[21] One economic historian has noted that while salt producers in western Virginia were permitted, perhaps even encouraged, by the courts to pool production and maintain prices for nearly fifty years before the Civil War, their arrangements produced very little reported litigation. T. S. Berry, *Western Prices Before 1861* 303–09 (1943).

that each party should keep his word. Indeed one judge has aptly described combination cases as:

> . . . the history of a protracted struggle between the principle of common honesty in private transactions, on the one hand, and the stern rule which forbade all restraints of trade on the other.[22]

Consider the most common dilemma confronting the court which had to pass upon the enforceability of a contract designed to implement collusion or suppress competition. In most cases litigation resulted because one party discovered that the other party was violating the agreement. When taken to court the defendant would either deny the charge or contend that the contract was unenforceable as being against public policy. On occasion, as in *Pierce v. Fuller*, he would deny violating the agreement and argue that even if the court found otherwise, the plaintiff had no remedy under the terms of the unlawful contract. Moreover, if the judge ruled the agreement unenforceable, the defendant stood to benefit both by his participation in the combination and by his violation of the agreement. Admittedly the law usually did not wish to encourage collusion in the market, but if collusion was not to be treated as criminal conspiracy, neither did it wish to place a premium on rank dishonesty. As Lord Mansfield early observed:

> The objection, that a contract is immoral or illegal as between plaintiff and defendant, sounds at all times very ill in the mouth of the defendant.[23]

A second problem facing the common-law judges arose out of the doubt that often intruded, especially in times of poor trade, that the end sought by the combination might not be a bad thing.[24] For example, if the plaintiff could make a plausible case that the restrictive agreement might help the contracting parties to stave off bankruptcy, a thoroughly objectionable way of transferring capital, his case was likely to receive a sympathetic hearing. Long before Keynes, it was popularly believed that in time of depression the public interest is better served by higher prices than by lower prices. Then again, courts

---

[22] Opinion of Lord Watson, Nordenfelt v. Maxim Nordenfelt Guns & Ammunition Co. (1894), A.C. 535, 555 (P.C.).

[23] Holman v. Johnson, 1 Cowp. 341, 343, 98 Eng. Rep. 1120, 1121 (K.B. 1775).

[24] See T. S. Berry, "The Effect of Business Conditions on Early Judicial Decisions Concerning Restraint of Trade," 10 *J. Econ. Hist.* 30 (1950).

MONOPOLY IN ECONOMICS AND LAW

were not unsympathetic to the view most recently elaborated by J. K. Galbraith[25] that private monopoly power is socially beneficial to the extent that it countervails somebody else's strong market position.[26] And finally, as early as 1829 in *Wickens v. Evans*[27] the court implied that combination was rendered less obnoxious to the extent that it made possible operating economies.

A third problem turned upon the practicability of "severance." The price-fixing feature of the contract might be vital for the attainment of a desirable as well as an undesirable end. Rival firms have often resorted to the device of a common selling agency which aims at the perfectly compatible goals of increasing demand by sales promotion while restricting output to make better use of whatever demand schedule currently prevails. Hence, when the court cannot divorce the legitimate purpose of the agreement from the illegitimate, the price-fixing feature must either be held enforceable or declared against public policy.

Finally, in the state courts of this country and the provincial courts of Canada, judges often sought to strike a balance between local and outside interests. Where a combination of local firms had executed an agreement to maintain prices in a regional or national market, it was by no means clear that the local interest would be served by declaring the contract void as against public policy; and even if the disputed arrangement adversely affected the interests of consumers within the court's jurisdiction, judges were likely to treat sympathetically the efforts of local merchants to act together for the purpose of meeting the inroads of "foreigners" in the local market.[28]

---

[25] *American Capitalism* (1952).

[26] See Commonwealth v. Carlisle, Brightly 36 (Pa. 1821). In this early labor case the Supreme Court of Pennsylvania denied the application for a writ of habeas corpus by several master shoemakers who had been taken into custody on a charge of conspiring to depress the wages of their journeymen, but observed: "The mere act of combining to change the price of labour is, perhaps, evidence of impropriety of intention, but not conclusive; for if the accused can show that the object was not to give an undue value to labour, but to foil their antagonists in an attempt to assign to it, by surreptitious means, a value which it would not otherwise have, they will make out a good defence," 42.

[27] 3 Y. & J. 318, 328, 148 Eng. Rep. 1201, 1205 (Ex. 1829). In this case the court upheld the validity of a contract executed by three box and trunk makers which had as its alleged object the elimination of wasteful competition.

[28] See, for example, Ontario Salt Co. v. The Merchants Salt Co., 18 Grant Ch. 540 (Ont. 1871). Here the Ontario Court of Chancery upheld an injunction which restrained violation of an agreement in which several salt manufacturers pledged themselves to employ a common selling agency on the ground that "the

In the face of the considerations noted above, nineteenth-century courts showed little disposition to dismiss actions seeking to enforce contracts suppressing competition without some examination of the circumstances in which they originated and the remedies sought. The agreements themselves show in their variety and ingenuity the power of the profit motive, but the type of accord which most frequently came before the courts was the ostensible "contract on bond" whereby the defendant pledged himself to forfeit some specified sum for every breach of the agreement.

Some courts observed the legal fiction that the forfeiture constituted "liquidated damages" on the ground that the authority of the law could not be used to enforce a privately established system of fines and punishments.[29] But after Lord Macclesfield in *Mitchel v. Reynolds* held that a reasonable penalty was tantamount to "liquidated damages" even though its punitive character was openly proclaimed, the distinction lost its meaning. In fact, although the alleged penalty feature of the contract on bond was often asserted, the author has found no combination case where an agreement was voided because the stipulated forfeiture was a penalty rather than liquidated damages.[30]

Contracts on bond affecting the market were mainly of two sorts. One merchant might buy out a rival on condition that the latter remain out of the market for some period of time—possibly life. Independent merchants might contract to impose a temporary limitation on compe-

---

object of the agreement was not unduly to enhance the price, but as it is expressly alleged in the bill, to enable the parties by concerted action to combat an attempt on the part of foreign producers and manufacturers (probably operating from Michigan) unduly to depreciate it," 544.

[29] By one estimate: "The essence of a penalty is a payment of money stipulated as in terrorem of the offending party; the essence of liquidated damages is a genuine covenanted pre-estimate of damage." Dunlop Pneumatic Tyre Co. v. New Garage & Motor Co., (1915) A.C. 79, 86 (H.L.).

Unfortunately, when as in most contracts restricting competition, an accurate pre-estimate of damage is not possible, this distinction ceases to have meaning. Forfeitures payable upon breach of contract are punishments intended to ensure that the contract will be observed. The ultimate absurdity came in Imperial Tobacco Co. v. Parsley, 52 Times L.R. 585 (1936), when the Court of Appeal declined to see the punitive character of a provision that required a retailer to forfeit £15 in liquidated damages for each and every pack of cigarettes sold below the retail price set by the manufacturer.

[30] In an early Massachusetts case, however, the Supreme Judicial Court allowed a transfer from law to equity on the ground that an $8,000 forfeiture owed by the petitioners for violating an agreement not to re-enter the market was not liquidated damages. Perkins v. Lyman, 11 Mass. 76 (1814). The final disposition of this case is not reported.

tition among themselves or to act together for the purpose of securing business from third-party competitors.

The contract stipulating withdrawal from the market presented a difficult problem to the courts since it concurrently served to transfer goodwill and suppress potential competition. By and large judges were inclined to order the payment of the forfeiture when such an agreement was violated on the premise, seldom explicitly stated, that the public's stake in honesty outweighed its interest in competitive pricing. Contracts on bond among merchants involving the suppression of competition were more carefully scrutinized by the courts, though not, as we have noted, with reference to any accepted "rule." The extremes in the treatment of combinations relying upon such agreements are well exemplified by the famous cases of *India Bagging Ass'n v. B. Kock & Co.*[31] and *Skrainka v. Sharringhausen.*[32]

In the *India Bagging* case—the earlier decision of the two which, unfortunately, was not well reported—eight importers of India cotton bagging in New Orleans found themselves with disturbingly high inventories. They therefore agreed in writing that for three months no importer should sell bagging except with the consent of the majority, and that for every bale of cotton bagging sold without permission, the offending importer would pay a penalty of $10 to the group. The combine brought suit against Kock for penalties totalling $7,400 whereupon Kock, though denying that he had violated the contract, filed a counterclaim for $3,000 allegedly paid to the other importers in accordance with the agreement. It is not clear from the report whether this latter sum had been paid in penalties or represented Kock's contribution to an earnings pool not mentioned in the written contract. The Louisiana court, however, sufficiently disgusted with the attempt to "enhance the price in the market of an article of primary necessity to cotton planters,"[33] dismissed both claim and counterclaim without any attempt to weigh the equities.

In *Skrainka v. Sharringhausen*, twenty-four operators of stone quarries, apparently in financial difficulties, agreed to divide the local market, sell only through a common agent for six months, and pay liquidated damages on any stone sold in violation of the agreement. An action was brought against Sharringhausen who acknowledged his breach of contract but pleaded that the plaintiff was entitled to no remedy since the contract was void by virtue of the restraint it im-

---

[31] 14 La. Ann. 164 (1859).

[32] 8 Mo. App. 522 (1880).

[33] 14 La. Ann. 164.

posed. The court, sympathetic to the plight of the quarrymen, ruled otherwise, holding:

> There is no evidence that it (the contract) works any public mischief, and the contract is not of such a nature that it is apparent from its terms that it tends to deprive men of employment, unduly raise prices, cause a monopoly, or put an end to competition.[34]

It is not clear whether the former popularity of the contract on bond in cartel operations reflected mainly the reluctance of the plaintiff to trust himself to the complexities of equity or the unwillingness of equity courts to compel specific performance of collusive contracts.

There is, so far as the author can discover, only one case in the British and American law reports in which the court allowed an injunction restraining the member of a cartel from charging less than the agreed-upon price[35] and only two cases in which a merchant was enjoined from re-entering the market after his business had been bought by a combination of rivals bent on eliminating competition.[36] It is unlikely that the infrequency of specific performance was due wholly to the unwillingness of judges to intervene so energetically in the suppression of competition. The absence of injunctive relief should prob-

---

[34] 8 Mo. App. 522, 527.

[35] Cade v. Daly, 1 Ir. R. 306 (1910). Here an Irish court ruled that a contract binding the members of the South of Ireland Mineral Water Manufacturers and Bottlers Trade Protection Association not to sell below agreed-upon prices was enforceable by injunction. But the court made it clear that injunctive relief was permissible only because the association had scant monopoly power; that, for example, while the agreement sought to maintain prices in the environs of Cork, it specifically exempted the towns of Middleton and Queenstown. The injunction was limited to six months.

[36] Oakdale Manufacturing Co. v. Garst, 18 R.I. 484, 28 Atl. 973 (1894); Nordenfelt v. Maxim Nordenfelt Guns & Ammunition Co. (1894) A.C. 535 (H.L.).

The first case involved a merger of three of the four firms producing oleomargarine in New England, the charter members of the combine agreeing not to set up independently for five years. One member unloaded properties valued at $28,000 upon the others for $60,000 and then failed to comply with his agreement. The court in granting an order restraining violation of the agreement was persuaded by the argument that the combine had not secured total control of oleomargarine in New England and had to face competition from firms located outside the region.

In the second case, the inventor Thorsten Nordenfelt had sold his interest in an armament firm for £287,500 to the plaintiff subject to the condition that he would take employment with no rival company for twenty-five years. The House of Lords upheld an injunction directing specific performance of the contract.

ably be ascribed in part to the primitive enforcement machinery at the disposal of the court in former times.

Toward the end of the nineteenth century courts were occasionally called upon to determine the legal status of restrictive agreements which provided for the pooling of earnings—a form of business cooperation that had to await improved techniques of record keeping and inspection. Judges apparently perceived that such contracts, by virtue of their elaborate enforcement provisions, were potentially more restrictive than straightforward accords to maintain prices and divide markets, for in most cases involving the pooling of earnings, they would neither order the contract observed nor enable a party to recover sums paid to others in accordance with its provisions. In fact, before 1890 the courts seem never to have upheld a pooling agreement among firms other than common carriers.[37]

In view of the popular hostility to rate wars and blatant discrimination, railroad pooling contracts presented a special problem for the courts, notwithstanding that the pooling of receipts on competing lines was forbidden by the Interstate Commerce Act of 1887[38] and a number of earlier state laws. But, although railroad pools were common in the seventies and eighties,[39] they produced surprisingly little reported litigation. In general, the language employed by the courts in refusing to uphold such agreements is not so uncomplimentary as that addressed to pooling contracts in other industries. Indeed, in every railroad case the courts imply that pooling would be lawful if its object were only the prevention of "ruinous" competition,[40] but in

---

[37] For a representative decision condemning the pooling of earnings see Emery v. Ohio Candle Co., 47 Ohio St. 320, 24 N.E. 660 (1890).

[38] 24 Stat. 379 (1887).

[39] For an examination of the origins of railroad pooling, see W. Z. Ripley, *Railroads: Finance and Organization* 573 (1920).

[40] See Chicago, M. & St. P. Ry. v. Wabash, St. L. & Pac. Ry., 61 Fed. 993 (8th Cir. 1894); *Ex Parte* Koehler, 23 Fed. 529 (C.C. Ore. 1885); Central Trust Co. v. Ohio Cent. Ry., 23 Fed. 306 (C.C.N.D. Ohio 1885), 133 U.S. 83 (1890); Nashua & L.R.R. v. Boston & L.R.R., 19 Fed. 804 (C.C. Mass. 1884), 136 U.S. 356 (1890); Cleveland, C.C. & I. Ry. v. Closser, 126 Ind. 348, 26 N.E. 159 (1890); Texas & Pac. Ry. v. Southern Pac. Ry., 41 La. Ann. 970, 6 So. 888 (1889), 137 U.S. 48 (1890). The first case is the most fully reported, and the court carefully reviews the judicial treatment of railroad pooling.

The application of the rule of reason to railroad pooling is sometimes thought to date from the English case Hare v. London & N. Ry., 2 J. & H. 80, 70 Eng. Rep. 978 (V.C. 1861). This case turned upon the right of a stockholder to enjoin the railroad management from fulfilling a pooling contract on the ground that it

only two cases did the court compel the defendant to fulfil a pooling contract that restricted competition.[41]

It will be noted that the law of competition before 1890 was almost wholly the work of English courts and American state courts. Federal precedents were virtually nonexistent, and no contract clearly involving the suppression of competition ever reached the Supreme Court.[42]

3. *Restraint of trade as a tort*

The law reports for the years before 1890 include few cases where third parties sought damages or relief for losses sustained or threatened by contracts in restraint of trade. In all cases that have come to the author's attention, no such application was successful unless the plaintiff had succeeded in convincing the court that the loss was inflicted by means which were, if not criminal, at least highly unorthodox. Common-law courts apparently treated the use of below cost sales, exclusive dealing contracts, and tying agreements employed for the express

---

was against public policy. The right was denied and the court also enthusiastically approved of pooling as an alternative to rate wars.

Actually, pooling contracts seem to have produced no reported litigation in England before 1890, although they were regularly employed. A possible exception is the fearfully complicated Shrewsbury & B. Ry. v. North-Western Ry., 6 Clark 113, 10 Eng. Rep. 1237 (H.L. 1857) in which the legality of an agreement to pool fares in perpetuity was one of many issues considered.

[41] Central Trust Co. v. Ohio Cent. Ry., 23 Fed. 306 (C.C.N.D. Ohio 1885), 133 U.S. 83 (1890); Nashua & L.R.R. v. Boston & L.R.R., 19 Fed. 804 (C.C. Mass. 1884), 136 U.S. 356 (1890).

[42] The closest approximation to a contract restricting competition to come before the Supreme Court before 1890 was Oregon Steam Nav. Co. v. Winsor, 87 U.S. (20 Wall.) 64 (1873). For a better statement of the facts giving rising to the case see Wright v. Ryder, 36 Cal. 342 (1868). The lower court decision that produced the appeal to the Supreme Court is Oregon Steam Nav. Co. v. Hale, 1 Wash. Terr. R. 283 (1870); but it is either incorrectly reported or the judge failed to grasp the issues in the California litigation.

The Supreme Court in a divided opinion upheld a provision in a contract of sale involving a steamship that stipulated the payment of $75,000 in liquidated damages should it be employed in California or on the Columbia River for ten years. While the ship had changed hands several times before the Supreme Court ruling, the provision had originally been inserted by the California Navigation Company which had secured a virtual monopoly on the passenger traffic of those waters. The opinion in this case is devoid of original thinking and left no visible mark on the development of common law in state jurisdictions.

purpose of eliminating a rival as legitimate business tactics irrespective of whether employed by the single firm or a combination.

The issue of predatory competition was squarely presented to the House of Lords in the leading case of *Mogul Steamship Co. v. McGregor, Gow & Co.*[43] Several shipping firms serving the port of Hankow took concerted action to eliminate a troublesome small rival by cutting rates, offering generous rebates to those shippers who would not deal with him, and refusing to employ as an agent any person who booked him cargoes. The small shipper sued for damages alleging malicious interference with his right to trade and fought the case in three different courts. In the Queen's Bench Division, Lord Coleridge rejected his claim, holding that "the line is in words difficult to draw, but I cannot see that these defendants have in fact passed the line which separates the reasonable and legitimate selfishness of traders from wrong and malice."[44]

In the Court of Appeal, Lord Esher contended that the plaintiff was entitled to damages since the defendants had entered into an indictable conspiracy to injure him.[45] A majority of this court, however, ruled for the defendants, one member remarking that "the combination, if in restraint of trade, is, prima facie, void only and not illegal."[46] This view of the case was unanimously affirmed by the House of Lords in seven opinions which agreed that "to draw a line between fair and unfair competition, between what is reasonable and unreasonable, passes the power of the courts."[47]

A few years later an American state court in reiterating that an injured party had no remedy against a combination of his rivals observed (correctly):

> No case can be found in which it was ever held that, at common law, a contract or agreement in general restraint of trade was actionable at the instance of third parties, or could constitute the foundation for such an action.[48]

The refusal of judges to afford relief to victims of "predatory" competition was hardly unreasonable in the nineteenth century in view

---

[43] 21 Q.B.D. 544 (1888), 23 Q.B.D. 598 (1889), (1892) A.C. 25.
[44] 21 Q.B.D. 544, 554 (1888).
[45] 23 Q.B.D. 598, 609–10 (1889).
[46] Opinion of Justice Fry, 23 Q.B.D. 598, 628 (1889).
[47] (1892) A.C. 25, 49.
[48] Bohn Mfg. Co. v. Hollis, 54 Minn. 223, 233–34, 55 N.W. 1119, 1121 (1893).

of the patent inadequacy of the court machinery to distinguish between "fair" and "unfair" prices. For that matter, it is by no means
clear that the present efforts of the Federal Trade Commission to suppress price discrimination "not justified by a saving in cost" do the consumer interest more good than harm, notwithstanding the agency's
vastly superior facilities for collecting and evaluating business
intelligence.

Efforts to eliminate rivals seem to have given rise to successful
actions only in three circumstances:

1. when third parties were "maliciously" enticed to break valid
contracts with the plaintiff;[49]

2. when pressures were employed against the plaintiff which were
not strictly "economic," e.g., threatening unwarranted patent infringement suits against the plaintiff or his customers;[50]

3. when they manifested a design to humble the plaintiff beyond
the needs of "rational" business aggrandizement.[51]

4. *The limits of the common law*

While the larger consequences of the Sherman Act and its amendments
will be debated for many years to come, the radical break with tradition represented by this legislation is clear enough. Our examination
of the common-law background of antitrust policy has sufficed to dispel
a number of misconceptions that persist because proponents of "posi-

---

[49] Murray v. McGarigle, 69 Wis. 483, 34 N.W. 522 (1887); Doremus v.
Hennessy, 176 Ill. 608, 52 N.E. 924 (1898).

[50] Buffalo Lubricating Oil Co. v. Standard Oil Co., 106 N.Y. 669, 12 N.E.
825 (1887). This decision of the New York Court of Appeals sustaining a civil
conspiracy suit against a corporate defendant is only briefly reported. Since the
case involved perhaps the most questionable episode in the history of the Standard
Oil Company, the facts have often been recounted. *Proceedings of the Committee on Manufacturers in Relation to Trusts,* H.R. Rep. No. 3112, 50th Cong.,
1st Sess. 424, 548 (1888); 2 Allan Nevins, *John D. Rockefeller* 76 (1940); 2
I. M. Tarbell, *The History of the Standard Oil Company* 88–100 (1904).

In both a civil and criminal case, the officers of a Standard Oil subsidiary in
Buffalo were found guilty of attempting to eliminate the plaintiff's competition
by harassing him with unfounded patent infringement suits, threatening his customers with similar actions, bribing his employees to leave his service, and sabo-
taging his plant. The fairness of the verdicts and awards has been questioned by
Nevins (and the evidence is certainly conflicting), but his dissatisfaction seems
to reduce to the complaint that the plaintiffs were not themselves men of particularly high probity.

[51] Delz v. Winfree, 80 Tex. 400, 16 S.W. 111 (1891).

tive" programs for *laissez faire* persist in seeking the aid and comfort of history.

Peaceable combinations were immune from legal harassment, however restrictive their practices. The enforcement of contracts imposing "direct" restraints on trade turned upon their "reasonableness." The tort action afforded no relief to victims of unfair competition no matter how blatant. The cases that we have noted indicate neither a hardening of judicial attitudes toward such agreements or tactics over the years nor any significant divergence between English and American doctrines during the nineteenth century. In the American cases before 1890 there is little to foreshadow the important federal decisions of the next twenty years. Rather the evidence suggests that, in the absence of statutory stimulus, the reasonableness tests of the common law would have passed, as a matter of course, into federal policy.

Chapter XI

THE ORIGINS OF
ANTITRUST POLICY

1. *Decline of the common-law faith in free entry*

In retrospect it is clear that the common-law attitude toward monopoly in the nineteenth century reflected the conviction that nothing very serious could happen to consumers so long as the law guaranteed freedom to trade. The rise of an antitrust policy resting upon statute registers the decline of this faith.

In the United States the inadequate character of the legal right to trade as a consumer safeguard first became apparent in the railroad age. In sparsely settled areas, the capital requirements of railroad construction precluded any close approach to workable competition in rate making, even assuming that every ambitious promoter could lay track. In practice, the right to build railroads—with or without the power of eminent domain—was not freely available to all comers even in those territories which could have supported a fair number of competing lines. Consequently, so long as railroad rates and service were largely free of government supervision, the industry was characterized by blatant discrimination among shippers and localities, traffic and earnings pools, and the consolidation of competing lines. Fortunately, the principle that railroads as a "business affected with a public interest" were subject to rate and service regulation was early established,[1] though its application was frustrated by adverse court rulings until after 1900.

If the limitations of the common-law faith in freedom to trade as a consumer safeguard first became apparent with the rise of the railroads, they were driven home forcefully by the success of the Standard Oil Company and the proliferation of the "trusts" in the

---

[1] Munn v. Illinois, 94 U.S. (4 Otto) 113 (1876).

1880's. The trust proper was an arrangement whereby the owners of stock in two or more companies transferred their securities to a set of trustees, receiving in return certificates which entitled them to share in the pooled earnings of the jointly managed companies. The label "trust," however, was soon applied to all forms of suspect business combination, many of which antedated the trust proper, e.g., pools and public utility monopolies.

The voting trust agreement in its origins was a legal innovation developed by the attorneys of the Standard Oil Company to meet an organizational problem.[2] Initially, the company held a charter from the State of Ohio which did not permit it to own property outside the state or the stock of another company. This limitation proved awkward as Rockefeller and his partners acquired properties elsewhere, though for a time it was circumvented by having the Standard Oil associates place the legal management of the acquired properties with an amenable "trustee." This arrangement worked well enough so long as the properties vested in this haphazard fashion were relatively few, but as the Standard Oil empire expanded, it was thought best to establish more formal arrangements for vesting the assets of the firm. In January, 1882, the properties and stocks of the multitude of companies that then comprised the organization were transferred by their owners to nine trustees, the owners accepting trust certificates in return.[3] The economic significance of this move, however, should not be exag-

---

[2] The trustee device popularized by the Standard Oil Company was immediately suggested by the stockholders' voting trust early employed to safeguard corporate control, especially in railroad reorganizations. The first such trust was apparently formed by certain shareholders in the Pacific Mail Steamship Company in 1864. J. A. Leavitt, *The Voting Trust* 20 (1941).

One author has traced the trust to the peculiar "cost-book" mining company that was formerly used to finance tin-mining ventures in certain counties of England. W. W. Cook, *Trusts: The Recent Combinations in Trade* 10–11 (2d ed. 1888). While the origin of this form of business organization is obscure, by 1850 it appears to have become essentially a partnership with transferable shares whose rights and liabilities were prescribed by local custom. The cost-book mining company is a legal curiosity that does bear some resemblance to the voting trust, but I have been unable to discover any connection between the two forms. The cost-book mining company is described in Thomas Tapping, *Readwin Prize Essay on the Cost Book: Its Principles and Practice* (2d ed. 1854). A brief description of the form is given in Kittow v. Liskeard Union, 10 Q.B. 7 (1874).

[3] This agreement is reproduced in 1 *Report of the Commissioner of Corporations on the Petroleum Industry* 361–70 (1907), also in Ernst von Halle, *Trusts or Industrial Combinations and Coalitions in the United States* 153–76 (1895).

gerated, since the restrictions placed by Ohio on the corporate privilege could have been evaded in any number of ways, *e.g.*, by vesting the Standard Oil properties in a corporation chartered under the laws of West Virginia. But the trust agreement proved serviceable to Rockefeller and his associates, and the use of this legal form by the most successful industrial company of the day called attention to its possibilities as a device for promoting combination.

The rapid rise of the Standard Oil Company undoubtedly served to dramatize an important structural change in the American economy. Nevertheless, its astounding success probably served to distract attention from the complexity of the early combination movement. In 1880, John D. Rockefeller and four partners held an equitable interest of at least 50 per cent in the properties controlled by the Standard Oil group and hence cannot be said to have employed the trustee device to combine rival firms in a promotional venture.[4] The trust agreement of January, 1882, was not particularly important in the history of the company but rather ratified monopoly as a *fait accompli*.

In this respect the Standard Oil trust materially differed from the other combinations of the day which received the same label.[5] Most so-called "trusts" were merely temporary cartels, though a few were promotional attempts to achieve monopoly by merger, notably the National Cordage Company organized in 1887.[6] Other combinations that came to light in the 1880's and 1890's defy classification as either cartels or close combinations and more closely resemble the modern British trade association than any form of business organization which survives in the United States.[7]

---

[4] The cumbersome legal structure of the Standard Oil group does not permit of a precise estimate. The key company—Standard Oil of Ohio—in 1882 had about 35,000 shares of stock outstanding of which 8,984 were held by Rockefeller, 3,000 by Henry Flagler, 2,925 by Stephen Harkness, 2,800 by Charles Pratt and 2,637 by Oliver H. Payne. 1 Allan Nevins, *John D. Rockefeller* 611–12 (1940).

[5] On this point see Alfred Marshall, *Industry and Trade* 512–15 (3d ed. 1920). Thirty years earlier Marshall had warned against generalizing about the future of trustee device combinations in the United States from the career of the Standard Oil Company—"the only Trust which can show a long record of undisputed success on a large scale." *Report of the Sixtieth Meeting of the British Association for the Advancement of Science* 898, 905 (1891).

[6] The disastrous history of this combination is recorded in A. S. Dewing, *Corporate Promotions and Reorganizations* 112–64 (1914).

[7] Such a halfway house between the loose cartel and the single firm exercising monopoly power is described in Pittsburg Carbon Co. v. McMillin, 60 N.Y. Supr. 67 (1889), 119 N.Y. 46 (C.A. 1890). Nine firms manufacturing electric-light carbons leased their properties for five years to a trustee who pro-

2. *The demand for regulation*

During the 1880's, Congress and the state legislatures were increasingly bombarded with petitions that the railroads, the Standard Oil Company, and the trusts in general be placed under some more stringent governmental control. The states readily responded with a host of laws which proved largely ineffectual, but it was not until 1887—one year after the Supreme Court had virtually killed regulation of railroad rates by the states in *Wabash Railway Co. v. Illinois*[8]—that Congress was moved to establish a federal regulatory commission.[9] Three years later, in 1890, the lawmakers passed the more general Sherman Act.[10]

By Section 1:

> Every contract, combination in the form of trust or otherwise, or conspiracy, in restraint of trade or commerce among the several States, or with foreign nations, is hereby declared to be illegal. Every person who shall make any such contract or engage in any such combination or conspiracy, shall be deemed guilty of a misdemeanor, and, on conviction thereof, shall be punished by fine not exceeding five thousand dollars, or by imprisonment not exceeding one year, or by both said punishments, in the discretion of the court.

By Section 2:

> Every person who shall monopolize, or attempt to monopolize, or combine or conspire with any other person or persons, to monopolize any part of the trade or commerce among the several States, or with foreign nations, shall be deemed guilty of a misdemeanor, and, on conviction thereof, shall be punished by fine not exceeding five thousand dollars, or by imprisonment not exceeding one year, or by both said punishments, in the discretion of the court.

> Given the vague bombast of the above provisions, generations of lawyers, judges, and economists have puzzled over what Congress "really" intended to accomplish by the Sherman Act. One cynical school

---

ceeded to set prices, apportion orders, and divide profits. Factory management remained with the individual firms. The combination came to light when the trustee became insolvent and a reneging member firm unsuccessfully sought to recover from the receiver for goods delivered while a party to the agreement.

[8] 118 U.S. 557 (1886).

[9] 24 *Stat.* 379.

[10] 26 *Stat.* 209.

of investigators has concluded that the lawmakers of 1890 were merely denouncing corporate sin in order to placate their more rustic constituents. According to one explanation favored by this school, the Republican majority while seeking to shove through the McKinley tariff bill in the session of 1890 became embarrassed by the charge that the tariff was "the mother of trusts" and sought to free itself from the odium of monopoly by passing the antitrust law. By another school of thought, the lawmakers were valiantly trying to stem the trend to concentration in the American economy and are not to be blamed if unfriendly attorney generals and judges sabotaged their efforts. The truth lies somewhere between these extreme interpretations of Congressional motives.[11] One has no reason to doubt that the railroads and Standard Oil were highly unpopular with many individual Congressmen, but then the backers of the antitrust bill with straight faces assured their colleagues that it was not going to "solve" the trust problem unless the states co-operated.[12]

There is really no point in trying to discern Congressional meaning in the amorphous phrases of sections 1 and 2 of the Sherman Act either by internal criticism or a search of the floor debates. The spokesman for the Senate Judiciary Committee defended its hazy language on two counts. The key phrases "combination" and "conspiracy," "restraint of trade" and "monopolize" had accepted meanings at common law. A more specific statute would have run the risk of being voided in the courts on the ground that "manufacturing" and "labor" were not commerce and hence beyond the power of the federal government to control.[13] The knowledge of the common law of monopoly manifested by the sponsors of the Sherman Act was imperfect to say the least, but

[11] The intentions of Congress in passing the Sherman Act have often been probed. Two excellent inquiries are William Letwin, "Congress and the Sherman Antitrust Law: 1887–1890," 23 *U. Chi. L. Rev.* 221 (1956), and H. B. Thorelli, *The Federal Antitrust Policy* 164–232 (1954).

[12] See, for example, *Protection of Trade and Commerce*, H.R. Rep. No. 1707, 51st Cong., 1st Sess. 1 (1890). "Whatever legislation Congress may enact on this subject, within the limits of its authority, will prove of little value unless the States shall supplement it by such auxiliary and proper legislation as may be within their legislative authority."

[13] This fear was not wholly fanciful. The courts before 1890 had often reiterated that "manufacturing is not commerce" and that interstate commerce begins only when goods were delivered to a common carrier for their "final journey" in interstate commerce and ends as soon as the "original package" in which they were shipped is broken. For an assessment of the extent of the federal commerce power when the Sherman Act was debated, see A. H. Wintersteen, "The Commerce Clause and the State," 28 (n.s.) *Am. L. Reg.* 733 (1889).

their case for confining the statute to acts which touched interstate commerce was well taken. (Indeed, given the hostile temper of the Supreme Court in its first antitrust case,[14] any statute which had presumed to forbid monopoly in manufacturing probably would have been condemned as unconstitutional.)

It is particularly unrewarding to probe the Congressional debates for evidence relevant to the questions concerning Congressional intent that have most bothered the courts. The debates provide no basis for discerning whether the Sherman Act was directed mainly at (a) the unfair methods employed by the Standard Oil Company to eliminate rivals—sales at prices below short-run marginal cost, commercial bribery, etc., (b) mergers which were causing small firms to give way to big firms in some manufacturing industries, or (c) cartel practices.[15] Nor do the debates throw light on how Congress intended that labor unions should fare under the act. The lawmakers of 1890 talked as if they believed that "unfair" competition was the main highroad by which size and market power were achieved; indeed, a curious feature of the Congressional debates is the absence of any prevalent assumption that size and concentration are the "inevitable" by-products of improving technology. On one occasion the Senate provisionally accepted an amendment which would have exempted combinations of workers "made with the view of lessening the number of hours of labor or of increasing their wages,"[16] but the amendment was lost in the deliberations of the Senate Judiciary Committee. Otherwise, labor unions were hardly mentioned.

3. *The enforcement provisions of the antitrust laws*

As finally passed, the Sherman Act contained both criminal penalties and civil remedies. A criminal conviction under the law carried a maxi-

---

[14] United States v. E. C. Knight Co., 156 U.S. 1 (1895).

[15] The *Congressional Record* indicates that the members of Congress in 1890 had not arrived at the distinction between cartels and "close" combinations that was soon to become popular. Thus the much abused Standard Oil Company figures in the debates as essentially a conspiracy against trade maintained by John D. Rockefeller and his partners. The specific condemnations of monopoly in the debates were mostly directed at the oil trust, but the existence of trusts (*i.e.*, some undesirable restraint of trade) was alleged—and by implication condemned—in the manufacture of steel rails, nails, iron nuts and washers, barbed wire, copper, lead, slate pencils, nickel, zinc, sugar, paper envelopes, gutta percha, oilcloth, cordage, jute bagging, castor oil, linseed oil, borax, ultramarine, matches, and pig iron.

[16] 21 *Cong. Rec.* 2611–12 (1890).

mum penalty of a $5,000 fine and one year in prison. (The maximum fine has lately been raised to $50,000.[17]) The Senate Judiciary Committee, which prepared the final draft of the antitrust law, manifested no enthusiasm for criminal provisions but accepted them because they had been added to Sherman's original bill during floor debate.[18] The committee did, however, scale the maximum fine down from $10,000 for each offense on the ground that severe penalties would increase the government's difficulty in securing convictions. While fines have been liberally levied over the years in criminal cases arising under the Sherman Act, prison sentences, mercifully, have not often been imposed. From July, 1890, to July, 1946, imprisonment was ordered in only thirty-one cases. Of these, fifteen involved business racketeering, thirteen labor racketeering, two wartime espionage, and one "normal" business. During this period, fines were imposed in about 250 cases, generally after pleas of *nolo contendere* had been accepted.[19]

In retrospect it seems clear enough that the Senate Judiciary Committee of 1890 was correct in viewing the criminal provisions of the Sherman Act as a mistake. A criminal conviction has no lasting consequences. It cannot produce dissolution or divestiture or even a permanent injunction against restrictive practices. The structure of the industry is unchanged, and if the malefactor returns to his evil ways he must be indicted, tried, and convicted all over again. Some authorities have argued that the criminal provisions of the Sherman Act are defective because they do not allow for a sufficiently heavy fine. The objection to this view is that no one really believes that a businessman who succumbs to the universal urge to restrict his output in the interest of a higher rate of return on his capital has committed a morally reprehensible act. In the language of older lawyers, while restraint of trade may be *mala prohibita,* it is certainly not *mala in se,* so that the use of a criminal indictment in a restraint of trade case merely introduces a note of simulated passion into litigation which obscures the important issues.

Another unfortunate provision of the Sherman Act is the section which permits private parties injured by a violation of the law to sue—and if successful—collect treble damages. The principal argument against the treble damage remedy follows from our objection to the imposition of criminal penalties. If there is nothing morally repre-

---

[17] 69 *Stat.* 282 (1955).

[18] 21 *Cong. Rec.* 2610–11 (1890).

[19] *United States versus Economic Concentration and Monopoly: a Staff Report to the Monopoly Sub-Committee of the House Committee on Small Business,* 79th Cong. 257–65 (1947).

hensible about restraint of trade when unaccompanied by palpably criminal acts, it is unjust that one company should be allowed to profit from the legal misfortunes of another.[20]

Two other objections to the treble damage suit derive from the manner in which it is employed in litigation. Since the plaintiff must establish proof of damage—and such proof is not easy—the remedy is of no use to unorganized consumers and small firms which keep few records and accounts. Further, since the courts insist upon a showing of the rough magnitude of probable damage, successful cases usually turn on issues of price discrimination where the plaintiff can show that if he could have had the defendant's wares on the best terms open to other buyers, his profits over some period would have been correspondingly greater. Yet in the thinking of most economists—if not in legal theory—the price discrimination complained of is more likely to promote workable competition than to subserve it.

Happily, the usefulness of the treble damage suit to litigious companies has, until recently at least, been largely nullified by strict judicial construction. Before 1914 the use of this remedy was virtually precluded by the difficulty of obtaining evidence that would establish both the defendant's violation of the Sherman Act and the amount of damage sustained by the plaintiff. By the Clayton Act, Congress provided that a final judgment or decree secured by the government against a defendant could be taken as prima facie evidence of his guilt in a private suit. In effect, the plaintiff was allowed to use for his own purposes evidence which had been collected and established by the federal authorities. But even this concession to private litigants was undermined by the qualification that guilt could not be assumed in a private damage suit if judgment against the defendant in the government criminal case had been entered after a plea of *nolo contendere* had been accepted by the court.[21] Nor could guilt be assumed if a civil

---

[20] For the widely held view that private damage awards are good because their prospect makes businessmen more responsive to the limited pressures that the antitrust agencies can apply, see the statement of Victor R. Hansen, head of the Antitrust Division, in *The Role of Private Antitrust Enforcement in Protecting Small Business—1958: Hearings before a Subcommittee of the Senate Select Committee on Small Business*, 85th Cong., 2d Sess. 140–46 (1958).

[21] The usefulness of a plea of *nolo contendere* in a government prosecution as a maneuver to bar private treble damage suits was somewhat weakened by Pfotzer v. Aqua Systems, 162 F.2d 779 (2d Cir. 1947). Here Learned Hand, after some hesitation, ruled that a plea of *nolo contendere* in a criminal case did not preclude the introduction of the record of the indictment in a treble damage suit when the object was to impeach the testimony of a defense witness.

case were settled by a consent decree before evidence had been taken, and up to June, 1946, well over half of all cases concluded by the government resulted in *nolo contendere* pleas or consent decrees.[22] Finally, use of the treble damage suit was for many years discouraged by the courts' insistence that the plaintiff show the extent of damages sustained as in an ordinary tort action, so that between 1890 and 1940, private suits for damages under the antitrust laws were successfully maintained in only thirteen reported cases.[23]

In recent years the courts have shown more inclination to award speculative damages in private antitrust suits with the result that litigation for treble damages has reached remarkable proportions.[24] The government antitrust suit against the major motion picture producers inspired private damage claims exceeding aggregate assets of the defendants.[25] It seems unlikely, however, that the courts will permit the treble damage award to become a standing threat to corporate profits in the American economy. Although on balance the drift of the law is in the direction of strengthening private antitrust remedies,[26] some recent decisions suggest that a judicial retreat to an earlier concept of

---

[22] *United States versus Economic Concentration* 262–70.

[23] W. J. Donovan and R. R. Irvine, "Proof of Damages under the Anti-trust Law," 88 *U. Pa. L. Rev.* 511, 525 (1940). The early treble damage cases are closely examined in P. E. Hadlick, *Treble Damages under the Anti–trust Laws* (1940).

[24] The developments are described in Homer Clark, "The Trebel Damage Bonanza: New Doctrines in Private Antitrust Suits," 52 *Mich. L. Rev.* 363 (1954). By one count, no less than 180 private antitrust suits were begun from 1944 through 1951, and in the 123 cases concluded, the plaintiff collected damages in 18 and obtained an injunction in 10. Note, "Antitrust Enforcement by Private Parties: Analysis of Developments in the Treble Damage Suit," 61 *Yale L.J.* 1010, 1064 (1952).

[25] The treble damage suits arising out of United States v. Paramount Pictures, 334 U.S. 131 (1948) are too numerous to list. The flood gates were opened two years earlier by the Supreme Court in Bigelow v. RKO Radio Pictures, 327 U.S. 251 (1946). In this case, Hollywood producers who owned theaters in competition with the plaintiff's single theater in south Chicago were compelled to pay treble damages to the plaintiff based on the profits he might have earned if they had not favored their own movie houses in the release of films.

[26] In addition to making treble damage suits easier to win, the courts have expanded the scope of private antitrust remedies in two other ways. In Fanchon & Marco, Inc. v. Paramount Pictures, 202 F.2d 731 (2d Cir. 1953), a group of stockholders were allowed to maintain a treble damage suit in the name of their corporation. In Schechtman v. Wolfson, 141 F. Supp. 453 (S.D.N.Y. 1956) a disgruntled stockholder was permitted to sue for the removal of certain corporation directors who were allegedly agents of a rival firm.

damage is probably under way in treble damage suits.[27]

The real teeth of the Sherman Act, viewed as an antimonopoly measure, lie in Section 4, which authorizes the Attorney General to restrain violations of the statute by proceedings in equity. The relevant clause says only that the government may "enjoin" unlawful acts, but the courts have construed this provision as entitling the federal government to the flexible remedies of equity including dissolution and divestiture. Legal proceedings against a company which do not ultimately produce equitable relief that alters market structure are generally a waste of time. (Criminal prosecution of a corporate defendant is often useful in laying the basis for a later civil case to be tried on the same facts, since the Attorney General is permitted a freer hand in collecting evidence in the criminal case.)

Writers favorable to the use of criminal prosecutions in antitrust cases often argue that an indictment or the threat of an indictment is a useful club to the Attorney General; that it enables him to persuade the defendant to comply with the wishes of the government in order to escape being put to the considerable expense of litigation, exposed to the possibility of being labelled a criminal in open court, and made vulnerable to subsequent private damage suits. No doubt the criminal provisions of the Sherman Act do serve this purpose. The larger usefulness of legal harassments as a means of maintaining and promoting competitive markets, however, is certainly open to question, and one may doubt that any policy which relies mainly upon the vigilance which federal officials exercise in supervising the use of market power has much to recommend it.

The problem of maintaining competition is the twofold one of ensuring that rival firms have no very solid basis for co-operation and removing uneconomic barriers to the "free flow of commerce." Once

---

[27] See, for example, Emich Motors Corp. v. General Motors Corp., 181 F.2d 70 (7th Cir. 1950), *modified*, 340 U.S. 558 (1951). In this case the circuit court of appeals in setting aside a treble damage award won by an automobile dealer for the cancellation of his Chevrolet franchise expressed itself as dissatisfied with the evidence introduced to show loss of profit; yet the evidence presented by Emich was much the same as that which won the plaintiff treble damages in the *Bigelow* case. See also Theatre Enterprises v. Paramount, 346 U.S. 537 (1954), a case where the suburban theater owner failed to secure treble damages even though he had suffered the same sort of discrimination at the hands of film distributors that enabled the plaintiff to collect in the *Bigelow* case. The discrimination was not quite so blatant in this later case. The complaining theater owner sought not merely equality of treatment with other suburban theaters but the rights of a downtown theater as well.

market power has come into existence, we may safely predict that its profitable use will not seriously be impeded by administrative discretion. So long, that is, as three manufacturers account for 90 per cent or more of the automobile output of the United States, it requires an inordinate confidence in the wisdom of civil servants to believe that their directives to the industry, even when backed by the threat of prosecution, make any difference to the prices or the quality of automobiles. In any event, criminal prosecutions under the antitrust laws are liable to the objection that when violation of the law is so widespread as to constitute "normal" conduct, it is unfair to penalize the few parties who are caught.

4. *Changes in the Sherman Act: the 1914 laws*

In the United States antitrust policy since its beginnings has been fashioned through litigation arising mainly under the Sherman Act. This reliance on case law is often deplored as allowing important economic issues to be resolved by wrangling over the vague phrases of sections 1 and 2 of the 1890 law. It is as often extolled as evidence of Congressional wisdom in leaving the details of policy to the courts. Actually, reliance upon case law in antitrust matters would seem to call for neither blame nor praise, nor even comment, since it is the usual form of lawmaking in common-law countries. The statute is, after all, an "extraordinary" remedy that is needed only when judge-made law proves unsatisfactory. The paucity of amendments to the Sherman Act is not necessarily evidence that the courts have accurately assessed the public temper or the intentions of Congress, but it does indicate that judicial errors relate to matters on which most congressmen have no decided opinions. Only four major amendments to the Sherman Act have been passed since 1890.

The two leading revisions came in 1914 with the passage of the Federal Trade Commission[28] and Clayton acts.[29] For better or worse, these statutes represent the only tangible return in Congress on twenty-four years of continuous and intensive debate on antitrust policy after 1890;[30] they were adopted after Congress had both refused a presi-

---

[28] 38 *Stat.* 717.

[29] 38 *Stat.* 730.

[30] The many efforts to amend the Sherman Act between 1890 and 1914 are recounted in O. W. Knauth, *The Policy of the United States Toward Industrial Monopoly* 43–65 (1914), and J. D. Clark, *The Federal Trust Policy* 79–164 (1931).

dential request to legalize cartel agreements approved by a federal agency[31] and declined to prescribe federal chartering for major corporations or further limit the area of judicial discretion in administering the Sherman Act.[32] The Federal Trade Commission Act established the regulatory commission of that name and charged it with the task of discouraging "unfair methods of competition" by cease-and-desist order. The Clayton Act amended the 1890 law in several particulars and divided responsibility for its enforcement between the Justice Department and the newly created commission. While the Clayton Act is nearly as amorphous as the law it purportedly clarified, it is generally thought to have had four main objects:

1. the granting to labor unions of some relief from the liability they risked by resorting to boycotts against firms involved in labor disputes,
2. the strengthening of the remedies open to private parties under the Sherman Act,
3. the categorical prohibition of certain business practices,
4. the imposition of more explicit restrictions on the use of corporate mergers.

The labor provisions of the Clayton Act and their fate at the hands of the courts we shall consider in Chapter XVIII. The remedies open to private parties were ostensibly strengthened in two respects. The plaintiff was permitted to petition for an injunction—an equitable remedy—restraining violations of the Sherman Act that were likely to injure him. The courts had earlier held that the act of 1890 did not authorize a suit in equity by a private party as an alternative to an action for treble damages.[33] This ruling did not wholly bar the use of injunctions in private Sherman Act cases, but it did mean that the ordinary federal rules of procedure applied and, hence, that no injunction would lie unless the plaintiff could show that he had no acceptable remedy at law.[34] By the Clayton Act the plaintiff was further allowed,

---

[31] Message of Theodore Roosevelt to Congress, 42 *Cong. Rec.* 3854 (1908).

[32] Thus Senator R. M. LaFollette unsuccessfully urged a bill which provided that a combination controlling more than 40 per cent of the national output of a "business" should be presumed to restrain trade unreasonably; the bill also provided that this assumption could be rebutted by the introduction of other relevant evidence. 47 *Cong. Rec.* 4183 (1911).

[33] Notably Blindell v. Hagan, 54 Fed. 40 (E.D. La., 1893); and Gulf, C. & S. F. Ry. v. Miami S. S. Co., 86 Fed. 407 (5th Cir. 1898).

[34] The act of 1789 which established the federal judiciary expressly provided that "suits in equity shall not be sustained in either of the courts of the United States, in any case where plain, adequate and complete remedy may be had at law." 1 Stat. 82.

in effect, to introduce as prima facie evidence of the defendant's misconduct a judgment or decree that had been entered for the Attorney General in a case involving the defendant; that is, he was allowed to use for his own purposes evidence which had been collected and established by the federal authorities.

Specifically prohibited by the Clayton Act were the following business practices where "the effect may be to substantially lessen competition or create a monopoly in any line of commerce": (a) contracts that bind the buyer not to purchase specified products from third parties as a condition of receiving the seller's product, (b) the interlocking directorate in rival corporations, and (c) discrimination in price "between different purchasers of commodities." The prohibition also extended to the acquisition of the stock of one company by another or the formation of a holding company which would hold the stock of both. For reasons we shall note at length in Chapter XV, the merger provision of the Clayton Act was long rendered a dead letter by the narrow interpretation placed upon it by the courts and the Federal Trade Commission. The clause was construed to mean that the commission had no power to block mergers executed by having one company purchase the physical assets of another, nor could it even order the divestiture of stock unlawfully acquired if the captured corporation were dissolved before the commission could act. These loopholes were finally removed by the Celler Amendment in 1950.[35]

The 1914 laws were thus responsible for the present jurisdictional overlap in antitrust law enforcement. Only the Justice Department can bring a case under the Sherman Act, while the Federal Trade Commission has the exclusive use of the act by which it was created. The Clayton Act is their common property. As one authority has pointed out, this administrative confusion appears to have no other basis than the rivalry of the Congressional committees on the Judiciary and Interstate Commerce.[36] Vying with one another for the credit of amending the Sherman Act in 1914, the Judiciary Committee reported the Clayton Act and the Interstate Commerce Committee countered with the Federal Trade Commission Act.

Still, a reading of the Congressional debates suggests that a larger role in antitrust work was envisaged for the Federal Trade Commission than it has yet attained. No doubt its failure to develop can be ascribed in part to the head start of the Justice Department in the field, but the main reasons for the enduring pre-eminence of this

---

[35] 64 Stat. 1125.
[36] Clark, The Federal Trust Policy 166–67.

older rival lie in the handicaps under which the commission labored in its formative years. Until the Wheeler-Lea Act (1938)[37] an order of the commission could be ignored with relative impunity, unlike a court judgment obtained by the Attorney General. A commission order was not binding until it was confirmed by a federal court, and the courts declined to accord the same respect to the commission's findings of fact that they had given to those of the Interstate Commerce Commission. More important, the Federal Trade Commission in the greater part of its activities early took on the character of a federal better business bureau which was at best indifferent to monopoly problems and at worst inclined to feel that "hard" competition was perforce "unfair" competition. Finally, as noted above, judicial hostility long ensured that the commission could not act against mergers even when it was so moved.

Under the 1914 laws, the Federal Trade Commission could enforce a cease-and-desist order only by applying to the circuit court of appeals for review and enforcement, and the onus of proving both the legality of the order and the fact of its violation rested on the commission. Since punishments could not be imposed until the culprit placed himself in contempt of court, the cost of compelling compliance with a disputed cease-and-desist order was high. (In fact, up to April, 1927, about one-third of the commission's orders seem to have been ignored.[38]) By the Wheeler-Lea Act an order issued under the Federal Trade Commission Act becomes final after sixty days unless the affected party petitions the circuit court of appeals to have it set aside. Violation of a commission order which has become final carries a fine of $5,000 for each offense. Commission orders issued under the Clayton Act, apparently through Congressional oversight, are still enforced in the older and more cumbersome manner.

5. Changes in the Sherman Act: post-1914 legislation

If one may draw an inference from inactivity, Congress since 1914 has been well pleased with the drift of case law in antitrust litigation. Indeed, the last forty years have produced only two major amendments to the Sherman Act.

By the Robinson-Patman Act (1936)[39] Congress ostensibly sought

---

[37] 52 *Stat.* 111.

[38] G. H. Montague, "Anti-trust Laws and the Federal Trade Commission, 1914–1927," 27 *Colum. L. Rev.* 650, 655–56 (1927).

[39] 49 *Stat.* 1526.

XI. ORIGINS OF ANTITRUST POLICY

to strengthen the provisions of the Clayton Act relating to price discrimination. The wording of the main sections of the later law is extremely obscure and has not been much clarified by litigation. The special-interest groups which prevailed upon Congress to pass the Robinson-Patman Act—notably the Wholesale Grocers' Association whose legal counsel drafted the bill on which it was based[40]—were not concerned with the effects of price discrimination on consumer welfare. Their undisguised purpose was to prevent chain stores and other large retailers from obtaining quantity discounts that contribute to the discomfort of smaller rivals. (The law was, in fact, aimed directly at the Great Atlantic & Pacific Tea Company and Sears, Roebuck and Company.) If the Robinson-Patman Act has not materially promoted this end by protecting inefficiency, the reasons lie in the limited resources of the Federal Trade Commission, the willingness of the courts to acquit discriminating defendants who can show that their low prices were "made in good faith to meet an equally low price of a competitor," and the difficulty of curtailing bargaining in a predominantly private-enterprise economy. The second amendment to the Sherman Act after 1914 came in the Miller-Tydings Act (1937)[41] which, as clarified by the McGuire Act (1952),[42] legalized a weak sort of resale price maintenance. These two developments are examined in Chapter XIV.

A number of other statutes have technically amended the Sherman Act by giving special dispensations to particular industries. Railroad and trucking mergers have been transferred to the jurisdiction of the Interstate Commerce Commission.[43] The antitrust laws apply to insurance companies only "to the extent that such business is not regulated by State law."[44] Co-operative marketing associations in agriculture and fishing have received the legislative blessing,[45] and the participation of American shipowners in cartels is lawful provided the United States Maritime Commission does not object.[46] The enforcement of the Clayton Act as regards commercial and savings banks is vested in the Federal Reserve Board rather than the Federal Trade Commis-

---

[40] *Business and the Robinson-Patman Law: A Symposium* 102–04 (Benjamin Werne ed. 1938).

[41] 50 *Stat.* 693.

[42] 66 *Stat.* 631.

[43] 41 *Stat.* 456 (1920); 49 *Stat.* 543 (1935).

[44] 59 *Stat.* 33 (1945).

[45] 42 *Stat.* 388 (1922).

[46] This exemption dates from the Shipping Act of 1916, 39 *Stat.* 728.

sion. The Justice Department may proceed against these institutions for violations of the Sherman Act, but it has seldom done so.

These diminutions of the authority of the two major antitrust agencies have found little favor with the friends of the Sherman Act, since regulatory agencies not unnaturally prefer regulation to competition. Nevertheless, in most cases the restrictions placed on the Justice Department and the Federal Trade Commission in areas which are the special preserve of other agencies have served to end or forestall an unseemly and confusing conflict of governmental policies. The regulation of transportation is a case in point.

In two early cases[47] the Justice Department with the aid of the Interstate Commerce Commission persuaded the courts that the activities of railroad rate-making associations violated the Sherman Act. As the powers of the commission increased, it found that conspiracy in rate making greatly simplified its own task of checking rate and service discrimination, so that rate-making associations flourished with its tacit approval for many years. When the Justice Department once more began to harry them,[48] Congress resolved the conflict in the Reed-Bulwinkle Act (1948)[49] by legalizing rate agreements among railroads and motor carriers which receive the approval of the Interstate Commerce Commission.

The Webb-Pomerene Act (1918)[50] is sometimes cited as a major revision of the antitrust laws. While it grants an ill-defined exemption to associations which are engaged solely in the export trade and provide the Federal Trade Commission with information on their activities, the economic consequences of this act have not been great. Only 149 export groups registered with the commission between 1918 and 1947 and of these only 52 still operated in the latter year.[51] Before 1945 the antitrust agencies did not trouble themselves about the activities of exporters. Since then, the courts, in upholding the government suits against Webb-Pomerene associations, have ruled that the act was largely declaratory of the earlier antitrust laws;[52] indeed, one judge has

[47] United States v. Trans-Missouri Freight Ass'n, 166 U.S. 290 (1897); United States v. Joint Traffic Ass'n, 171 U.S. 505 (1898).

[48] United States v. Association of Am. Railroads, 4 F.R.D. 510 (D. Neb. 1945); Georgia v. Pennsylvania R.R., 324 U.S. 439 (1945).

[49] 62 *Stat.* 472.

[50] 40 *Stat.* 516.

[51] S. C. Oppenheim, *Cases on Federal Anti-trust Laws* 796 (1948).

[52] United States v. United States Alkali Export Ass'n, 86 F. Supp. 59 (S.D.N.Y. 1949); United States v. Minnesota Mining & Mfg. Co., 92 F. Supp. 947 (D. Mass. 1950).

Actually the backers of the Webb-Pomerene Act almost certainly wished

held that a main object of the Webb-Pomerene Act was to extend the extraterritorial jurisdiction of the antitrust agencies in the interest of promoting competition.[53]

Perhaps the most execrable amendment to the antitrust laws came in the Motor Carriers Act of 1935,[54] which imposed the quasi-monopoly regulation appropriate to railroads on trucking despite the highly competitive nature of this industry. In the interest of "a co-ordinated national transportation policy," motor carriers were made subject to rate regulation and restrictions on entry. Scheduled or common carriers can begin service on new routes only after obtaining a certificate of convenience and necessity from the Interstate Commerce Commission which may also set their maximum and minimum rates. The non-scheduled trucker wishing to operate across state lines as a contract carrier must obtain a permit from the commission and abide by whatever minimum rates it prescribes. The very evident survival of competition in trucking can be ascribed to two beneficent operations of countervailing power when the Motor Carriers Act was drafted. Legislators apprehensive of States' rights explicitly denied the Interstate Commerce Commission the benefit of the *Shreveport* doctrine,[55] which allows it to regulate intrastate commerce whenever such regulation is necessary to make effective its regulation of interstate commerce; and the commission was given no power to regulate even the interstate activities of private carriers (those used only to haul the goods of their owners) except in matters of safety.

6. Reflections on the antitrust law enforcement

The reluctance of Congress to legislate in the general area of monopoly problems and the calculated vagueness of the laws enacted have dele-

---

to legalize the participation of American firms in cartels that functioned mainly in foreign markets but believed it politically inexpedient to say so. Hence the ambiguous urging of "co-operation to promote competition" that enabled the courts to construe away the intended effect of the statute with apposite quotations. For examples of the double talk in which the Webb-Pomerene Act was born, see Federal Trade Commission, *Report on Co-operation in American Export Trade* (1916). The Congressional history of the statute is given in H. A. Toulmin, *International Contracts and the Anti-trust Laws* 1–28 (1947).

[53] United States v. United States Alkali Export Ass'n, 86 F. Supp. 59, 66–67.

[54] 49 *Stat.* 543.

[55] The evolution of this doctrine can be traced in the Minnesota Rate Cases, 230 U.S. 352 (1913); Houston & Texas Ry. v. United States, 234 U.S. 342 (1914); and Wisconsin R.R. Comm. v. C. B. & Q. R.R., 257 U.S. 563 (1922).

gated the task of making the law of monopoly to the courts and the Federal Trade Commission. Before we proceed to consider how the relevant case law has developed, several caveats may be in order. First, the non-lawyer is warned that the courts and the Federal Trade Commission must abide by the rules of the game. Important issues must be decided by ostensible quibbling over the generalities and platitudes enshrined in federal statutes—the meaning of "combination," "conspiracy," "monopolize," "restraint of trade," or "to substantially lessen competition." And since judges must ordinarily respect *stare decisis,* lawyers endeavor to win cases by citing precedents rather than by attempting to prove or disprove injury to competition. Economists, especially, when they first encounter antitrust problems, are irritated both by the irrelevance of many issues which receive so much attention in court and the failure of the contending parties to make use of the best economic arguments at their disposal.

Critics of antitrust policy may properly question whether courts and regulatory commissions are the best agencies for making the law of monopoly. (The alternatives involve securing more explicit legislation from Congress or vesting more discretion in civil servants.) But so long as the present arrangements stand, judges and commissioners should not be criticized for behaving according to their natures.

Again we should not forget that the content of the law is always influenced by the machinery available to enforce it. This dependence means that what judges, legislators, and civil servants say must always be read against the background of what they can do; and that the less they can do, the more irresponsibly they are likely to talk. (Witness the violence of the language employed by impotent state legislators to denounce monopoly.) It also means that law is often obliquely made by changing the enforcement machinery; thus the five-fold increase in the Antitrust Division's appropriations between 1938 and 1942[56] was a more important contribution to an effective antitrust policy than all of the amendments to the Sherman Act ever passed.

We should also remember that the antitrust laws—the Sherman Act especially—are often employed to achieve ends which have little or nothing to do with the problems of monopoly. Given the marked disinclination of Congress to legislate on matters affecting the conduct of corporations, professional associations, and labor unions, the Attorney General has sometimes found the Sherman Act useful for attacking evils for which no specific statutory remedy exists. Thus over the years,

---

[56] C. D. Edwards, *Maintaining Competition* 297 (1949).

it has been invoked to send labor racketeers to prison,[57] induce the American Medical Association to grant hospital privileges to physicians who join group health insurance programs,[58] and compel the country's largest news agency to offer its facilities to all newspaper owners on equal terms.[59] In such cases, one should recognize what the Attorney General is about and disregard the peculiar—and frequently foolish— arguments by which he makes his case.

Finally, the young reader is cautioned against the naïveté of cynicism. Laws which reformers acclaim as good are passed with the indispensable assistance of organized groups bent on advancing the narrow interests of their members. Certain firms are regularly punished for their disinclination to "co-operate" with public officials. (The relatively small United Shoe Machinery Corporation has defended three costly suits in forty years.) The modest appropriations of the antitrust agencies have generally contrasted sharply with the Congressional denunciation of monopoly, and judges often hand down decisions which cause the teacher of law or economics to despair of his calling. But then life is neither possible nor palatable without the persistence born of avarice, the zeal of the self-righteous, and the errors inherent in the learning process. The important thing is that the problems of this world have better and worse solutions. Whatever its defects, antitrust policy represents the conscious striving for a better solution to a particularly difficult set of problems.

---

[57] See, for example, Boyle v. United States, 259 Fed. 803 (7th Cir. 1919).

[58] American Medical Ass'n v. United States, 317 U.S. 519 (1943).

[59] Associated Press v. United States, 326 U.S. 1 (1945).

Chapter XII

THE LAW OF CARTELS

1. *Alternatives in cartel policy*

Our brief examination of the Congressional history of the antitrust laws has indicated that not much is to be gained by probing for the legislators' intent, that the federal judges who received the task of construing these statutes were on their own. Moreover, in the beginning they had no significant body of empirical investigations to draw upon and were, of course, without experience in treating the economic issues thrust upon them.

The one foundation on which the courts could build was the common-law precedents in cartel cases, for, as we have seen, the legal problems raised by price fixing and market sharing were not new in 1890. As regards these practices, the main issue before the federal courts after 1890 was the relevance of the common-law tradition of Britain and the American state jurisdictions to the construction of the Sherman Act. In the absence of relevant legislation, respect for *stare decisis* would probably have sufficed to incorporate the common-law rule of reason into federal practice as the jurisdiction of the federal courts expanded under the pressure of events. When this transition was impeded by legislation, the problem became, How would the federal courts use common-law precedents to give meaning to the nebulous provisions of the law of 1890? In retrospect, it would appear that three alternatives were open to federal judges.

1. They could have construed away the Sherman Act by requiring a showing of intent to commit palpably criminal acts—arson, fraud, murder, etc.—before finding unlawful restraint of trade.

2. They could have interpreted the statute to mean that the suppression of competition constituted a misdemeanor whenever the public interest had been demonstrably injured. Had this version of the reasonableness test been affirmed, elaborate cartel arrangements for limiting output would probably have disappeared from the business

scene while less restrictive gentlemen's agreements and trade associations dedicated to discouraging "cutthroat competition" would have remained.

3. Federal judges could have liberally construed the phrase "combination in restraint of trade." The practical consequences of this course would not have differed greatly from those of the second course given the administrative task of policing the whole economy, but it would have served to strengthen the hands of federal officials seeking to check or eliminate objectionable trade practices.

2. *Decline of the reasonableness test in cartel cases*

From the beginning—and with little hesitation or vacillation—the federal courts chose this last course. In fact, so far as legal theory goes, federal policy toward cartels was set in two of the earliest cases decided under the Sherman Act.

The first case involved the efforts of the government to enjoin the price-fixing operations of the Nashville Coal Exchange in *United States v. Jellico Mountain Coal & Coke Co.* (1891).[1] The exchange was a close approximation to the "ideal type" of the non-pooling cartel. It comprised "several mining companies of Kentucky engaged in rising coal, and most of the coal dealers of Nashville, Tenn." that had contracted to observe minimum colliery and retail prices in marketing coal and to remit fines to the exchange for every violation of the agreement. In addition, the members of the exchange had pledged themselves not to deal with collieries or coal dealers who were not members of the association. As the court observed in granting the government's petition, "the purposes and intentions of the association could hardly have been more successfully framed to fall within the provisions of the act of July 2, 1890 had the object been to organize a combination, the business of which should subject it to the penalties of that statute."[2] Indeed, the court regarded the guilt of the company as so obvious as to make unnecessary a review of the common-law precedents. The defendants' effort to establish that the challenged restraint was lawful by virtue of being "reasonable" was brushed aside with the remark that "the attempt—the contract to do the thing prohibited—is enough to incur the penalties of this law."[3]

The second case involving price fixing by rival concerns produced

[1] 46 Fed. 432 (C.C.M.D. Tenn.).
[2] *Ibid.* 436.
[3] *Ibid.* 437.

a more careful examination of the common-law background. In *United States v. Trans-Missouri Freight Ass'n* (1897)[4] the Justice Department sought to dissolve a rate-making association wielding a complex system of fines and other punishments which had been formed by eighteen Midwestern railroads. (The association replaced an earlier traffic pool discontinued after the enactment of the Interstate Commerce Act of 1887.[5]) By the view of the trial court,[6] the case raised three issues. (1) Did the Sherman Act apply to the railroads given that they were forbidden by the act of 1887 to exact charges that were "unreasonable or unjust"? (2) Was the common-law rule of reason relevant to the case? (3) If so, were the rates set by the association unlawful by virtue of being unreasonable?

Without reviewing the relevant Congressional debates, the trial court concluded that the Sherman Act was not meant to cover the activities of railroads. After accurately tracing the rule of reason in cartel cases decided at common law, the court held it material to the interpretation of the federal statute and ruled that since the government had failed to show that the rates fixed by the association were unreasonable, the defendants were not acting unlawfully. In the circuit court of appeals, this decision was upheld and elaborated in the majority opinion.[7] One judge dissented, however, on the ground that although the rule of reason might apply to most contracts in restraint of trade, public utilities were not entitled to claim the same degree of freedom of contract allowed to competitive enterprises. When the case reached the Supreme Court, the majority opinion, in effect, reiterated the doctrine declared in the *Jellico* decision and so reversed the lower courts.

> The language of the act includes *every* contract, combination in the form of a trust or otherwise, or conspiracy, in restraint of trade or commerce among the several States or with foreign nations. So far as the very terms of statute go, they apply to any contract of the nature described.[8]

Following the *Jellico* decision, the majority opinion also declined to consider the relevance of common-law precedents. The notion that railroads were not covered by the Sherman Act was emphatically and

---

[4] 166 U.S. 290.
[5] 24 *Stat.* 379.
[6] 53 Fed. 440 (C.C.D. Kan. 1892).
[7] 58 Fed. 58 (8th Cir. 1893).
[8] 166 U.S. 290, 312.

properly rejected after attention to the Congressional debates. A dissenting opinion endorsed the reasoning employed by the lower courts.

It was *Addyston Pipe & Steel Co. v. United States* (1899),[9] however, which firmly established the illegality of the price-fixing cartel. In this suit the government, acting on evidence supplied by an informer,[10] sought to enjoin the activities of six manufacturers of cast-iron pipe who had formed the Associated Pipe Works for the purposes of rigging bids on municipal government contracts and pooling the receipts. The complicated agreement provided that when municipalities advertised for bids, the privilege of submitting the lowest bid was to go to the member which offered to pay the largest bonus into the common fund. The lowest court was unable to perceive the illegality of this arrangement, holding that (a) the Associated Pipe Works, like the sugar trust,[11] was a combination affecting manufacturing only and hence outside the Sherman Act, and (b) the government must prove the "unlawful" character of the restraint alleged since the defendants had asserted its legality.[12] The decision was reversed by the circuit court of appeals in an opinion delivered by William Howard Taft which is of interest in view of the attention it subsequently received.[13]

Unwilling to rely upon the language of sections 1 and 2 of the Sherman Act, Judge Taft felt obliged to reconcile his view that price fixing was unlawful per se with common-law precedents. By his reading of history, the use of the reasonableness test in cartel cases was merely the occasional deviation of the courts from the established principle that a "general" restraint on trade was always unenforceable, and he interpreted "general" restraint to mean a "direct" or intended restraint upon competition as against an "ancillary" or fortuitous restraint.[14] Previously a "general" restraint had described a provision that made the contract binding over a wider geographical area than was necessary to achieve the legitimate objects of the contract.

When the *Addyston* case reached the Supreme Court, Justice

---

[9] 175 U.S. 211.

[10] A secretary formerly employed by the cartel made public the evidence in order to obtain 25 per cent of the sums owing to municipal waterworks that had been overcharged through collusion in bidding on pipe contracts. *Transcript* 144–45, in Records and Briefs, Supreme Court library (1899).

[11] United States v. E. C. Knight Co., 156 U.S. 1 (1895).

[12] 78 Fed. 712 (C.C.E.D. Tenn. 1897).

[13] 85 Fed. 271 (6th Cir. 1898).

[14] Taft later reiterated this interpretation of the common law in *The Antitrust Act and the Supreme Court* (1914).

Peckham, speaking for the Court, declined to pass upon Taft's interpretation of history. Rather he was content to observe that "where the
direct and immediate effect of a contract or combination among particular dealers in a commodity is to destroy competition between them
and others, so that the parties to the contract or combination may obtain increased prices for themselves, such contract or combination
amounts to a restraint of trade in the commodity, even though contracts
to buy such commodity at the enhanced price are continually being
made."[15] But the tone of Peckham's decision plainly conveys that he
regarded the restraint imposed by the pipe combination as "unreasonable."

The legal ban on cartel price fixing was further strengthened by
Swift & Co. v. United States (1905).[16] Here the Supreme Court upheld
a decree enjoining concerted action by the major meat packers to
(a) bid up the price of livestock for short periods in order to entice
farmers to bring animals to market and so depress livestock prices below their "normal" level by distress sales, (b) divide livestock purchases among themselves in the major stockyards of the country, and
(c) secure rates from the railroads not open to smaller meat packers.
In this case, no "contract" in restraint of trade was established by the
government—only unlawful combination. The decision thus fore-
shadowed the liberal standard for proof that the courts have allowed
to the government in civil cases involving price fixing.

Explicit recognition of the principle that any concerted action by
rival producers to fix prices is unlawful per se is generally taken to have
been established in the *Trenton Potteries* case (1927).[17] The Justice
Department had indicted twenty-three manufacturers of sanitary pot-
tery, alleging a conspiracy to maintain prices and sell only to "legitimate" jobbers. The main issue before the Supreme Court was whether
the lower court had erred in refusing to charge the jury that

> the essence of the law is injury to the public. It is not every
> restraint of competition and not every restraint of trade that
> works an injury to the public; it is only an undue and unreason-
> able restraint of trade that has such an effect and is deemed to
> be unlawful.[18]

In a split decision, the high court found no error but did not

---

[15] 175 U.S. 211, 244.
[16] 196 U.S. 375.
[17] United States v. Trenton Potteries Co., 273 U.S. 392.
[18] *Ibid.* 395.

unambiguously declare what has come to be called the per se doctrine. Rather it held (debatably) that "the power to fix prices, whether reasonably exercised or not, involves power to control the market and to fix arbitrary and unreasonable prices"; and hence that "agreements which create such potential power may well be held to be in themselves unreasonable or unlawful restraints, without the necessity of minute inquiry whether a particular price is reasonable or unreasonable as fixed and without placing on the government in enforcing the Sherman Law the burden of ascertaining from day to day whether it has become unreasonable through the mere variation of economic conditions."[19]

In the *Socony-Vacuum* case (1940),[20] however, the Supreme Court unequivocally condemned all price-fixing agreements ruling that "under the Sherman Act, a combination formed for the purpose and with the effect of raising, depressing, fixing, pegging, or stabilizing the price of a commodity in interstate or foreign commerce is illegal *per se*."[21] Nor was the Court employing idle rhetoric. The restraint condemned in this case could have survived almost any reasonableness test it might have cared to impose. The Justice Department in a criminal suit had attacked a combination of major oil distributors and independent refineries which was endeavoring to regulate the flow of gasoline into the market for the purpose of "stabilizing prices." Gasoline prices were lowered by "hot oil" pumped and marketed during the depression in violation of various state laws, and the association had been formed at the instigation of a federal agency—the short-lived National Industrial Recovery Administration. Moreover, the major oil companies were not the sole beneficiaries of the challenged marketing program. Also aided were (a) independent refineries whose limited storage capacity compelled them to sell cheaply since a reduction of output by any one refiner would have caused them to lose retail outlets to rivals and (b) established retailers who found themselves in unprofitable gasoline wars. Nevertheless, the Court held to a literal interpretation of Section 1 of the Sherman Act and condemned the federally inspired restraint.[22]

---

[19] *Ibid.* 397–98.

[20] United States v. Socony-Vacuum Oil Co., 310 U.S. 150.

[21] *Ibid.* 223.

[22] In fairness, we should note that the Justice Department was actuated by something more than a legalistic loyalty to the per se doctrine when it prosecuted a depression-stricken industry's effort at self-help. The most active supporters of the state "conservation" laws restricting oil pumping and the petroleum code

The ultimate rigidity in the application of the per se rule came some years later in *Kiefer-Stewart Co. v. Seagram & Sons* (1951)[23] when the Supreme Court upheld an award of treble damages against two companies controlled by the same individuals. The defendant concerns had "conspired" with each other to deal only with wholesalers who, in the inflationary years after World War II, consented not to resell the defendants' products *above* their stipulated resale prices. The Court was on safe ground in affirming that "such agreements, no less than those to fix minimum prices, cripple the freedom of traders and thereby restrain their ability to sell in accordance with their own judgment."[24] But it adopted an unintelligible position when it held that "common ownership and control does not liberate corporations from the impact of the antitrust laws."[25]

The only important deviation from the per se rule in cartel cases came in the slough of depression and involved the sickest of industries. In 1932 the Justice Department sought to enjoin the activities of a common sales agency formed by 137 producers of bituminous coal in the Appalachian field for the twin objects of "regulating" the marketing of the product and promoting its use.[26] As a cartel, the association was of the weakest sort if, indeed, it deserves this name at all. It had no power to restrain the outputs of its members; scarcely one-half of the producers in the Appalachian region had taken out membership; any increase in the price of coal promised to reopen numerous mines previously shut down by low prices; and, although the members of the association controlled an estimated 73 per cent of Appalachian output, most of the product was sold outside of the region in competition with other fields.[27] In view of the industry's difficulties, the Supreme Court

---

of the National Industrial Recovery Administration were the major oil companies who had easier access to imported gasoline and crude oil than their smaller rivals. They wished to curtail the pumping of domestic crude oil, not only to keep up the prices of petroleum products, but also to check the expansion of smaller companies by keeping up the price of domestic crude oil. The so-called "independents" in the industry, for their part, wished to keep up the price of petroleum products by raising the tariff on oil imports. But then a perfect community of interests between business rivals is a contradiction in terms. The clash of interests in the struggle to limit petroleum production during the Great Depression is well described, though with a small business bias, in W. J. Kemnitzer, *Re-birth of Monopoly: a Critical Analysis of Economic Conduct in the Petroleum Industry of the United States* 122–52 (1938).

[23] 340 U.S. 211.
[24] *Ibid.* 213.
[25] *Ibid.* 215.
[26] Appalachian Coals, Inc. v. United States, 288 U.S. 344 (1933).
[27] *Ibid.* 375–76.

found the modest restraints sought by the combination to be eminently reasonable, *e.g.*, its effort to eliminate the practice of allowing different salesmen to sell the same load of coal in competition with one another.

The injunction restraining the activities of the association granted by the district court was therefore set aside. The Supreme Court, however, took the precaution of hedging its departure from the per se doctrine by providing that, "if in actual operation," the program of the Appalachian producers should unduly burden interstate commerce or impair fair competition, the Government could reopen the case without the necessity of reproducing the voluminous evidence already introduced. Given the innate weakness of the coal combination—the improbability that it could perceptibly influence the price of coal—the departure from the per se rule represented by the Appalachian decision is more apparent than real. The case is mainly important as a reminder that the rule of reason in American cartel law is not dead, only dormant.

3. *The per se doctrine as a fortuitous development*

In view of the popularity of the reasonableness test in price-fixing cases decided at common law, its rapid displacement by the per se rule after 1890 is rather surprising. Most probably the change was the unintended consequence of writing criminal penalties into the Sherman Act. In an age of extensive court reporting, the courts could not easily have retained the reasonableness test without, at the same time, construing away the first two sections of the law. Had the courts chosen to observe common-law precedents, they would have been required to distinguish (a) reasonable price-fixing agreements enforceable at law or equity, (b) unreasonable price-fixing agreements which were unenforceable but not criminal, and (c) agreements which were both unenforceable and indictable.

If the courts had assumed the burden of making these distinctions, they would have both vastly increased the volume and complexity of their own work and rendered the enforcement task of the Justice Department even more difficult. By ruling that price-fixing agreements were unlawful per se, the federal bench was able to give a "reasonable" interpretation of Congressional intent and at the same time escape the necessity of passing upon the enforceability of a multitude of contracts in restraint of trade that would otherwise have accompanied the expansion of federal jurisdiction.

Admittedly the administrative case for the per se rule in cartel litigation is a strong one. It saves the antitrust agencies much trouble and expense, and the experience of countries that have accepted the reasonableness test seems not to have been happy.[28] The economic case for making price fixing a per se offense, however, is extremely weak. In times of widespread unemployment, the State's economic policy is so patently bankrupt that it is presumptuous for public officials to harass firms which are trying to save themselves by price-maintenance schemes. In the case of a "sick" industry the plight of its masters and hands may well justify whatever good they can do for themselves by collective self-help,[29] and finally, of course, there is no equity in suppressing a particular cartel unless one can prevent the industry from being victimized by combinations of its customers and suppliers.

When a balance is struck, the author is prepared to accept that the administrator's case for treating cartel agreements as unenforceable per se outweighs the economist's case for using a rule of reason, but he would question whether the administrator's case is strong enough to warrant treating cartel agreements as criminal per se. This doubt derives from the impression that cartels are weak in the American economy mainly because they are powerless to enforce their understandings in court and not because their members fear criminal prosecution at the hands of vigilant and all-powerful antitrust agencies.

4. *Trade associations and the law*

Since the emergence of the per se doctrine in price-fixing cases, the courts have most frequently encountered cartel problems in cases involving the activities of trade associations. The task of passing judg-

---

[28] In Britain no restrictive agreement has been held unreasonable in a reported case since Hilton v. Eckersley, 6 El. & Bl. 47, 119 Eng. Rep. 781 (K.B. 1855). The introduction of the reasonableness test by the French courts has been made responsible for the nullification of a statute against collusive price fixing. Heinrich Kronstein and Gertrude Leighton, "Cartel Control: A Record of Failure," 55 *Yale L.J.* 297, 300–01 (1946).

[29] Thus, in 1926 J. M. Keynes criticized the hard pressed Lancashire cotton spinners not because they restricted shipments to overseas markets but rather because they did it in a way that he considered unnecessarily wasteful. The spinners could only agree among themselves to abide by a shorter work week; hence inefficiency resulted because production was too much curtailed in efficient mills and too little curtailed in inefficient mills. Keynes felt that somebody—preferably bankers supported by public opinion—should impose a tight cartel on the industry that would allow production quotas to be bought up by the more efficient firms. "The Position of the Lancashire Cotton Trade," 40 *The Nation & Athenaeum* 291 (1926–27); see, also, his address to the Master Cotton Spinners in Manchester as reported in 90 *Manufacturers Record* 83 (December 9, 1926).

ment in this area is complicated by the fact that intrigue among members of a trade group to limit output is perfectly compatible with any number of commendable works, notably research, sales promotion, lobbying, maintenance of product standards, and the provision of accurate market information.

Trade associations most commonly run afoul of the law in the course of their efforts to collect information on prices, costs, and output from their members and to advise them of the results. The crux of the legal problem is, of course, the use made by the trade association of the information in which it deals. As the Supreme Court observed on one occasion, if better intelligence serves to perfect the market, as "if like statistics were published in a trade journal or were published by the Department of Commerce,"[30] their collection and distribution is both laudable and lawful. Whereas, if the gathering of production data is an integral part of a policy of restriction, the statistical services of the trade association violate the Sherman Act. The following cases will serve to illustrate the evolution of the reasonableness test as it applies to reporting activities of trade associations.

The first of the suits against trade associations which sought, via open price plans, to cultivate the gentlemanly "new competition" advocated by Jerome Eddy reached the courts in 1920. In this case, the government sought to enjoin the intelligence activities of the American Hardwood Manufacturers' Association—a trade group then lately formed by three hundred-odd firms supplying rough hardwood lumber to local mill works and lumber yards.[31] At the time of the trial, the defendants were held to produce about one-third of the industry's national output. The burden of the government's charge was that the trade association, under the cloak of promoting the exchange of production statistics, brought about a reduction of output that materially raised the price of lumber. This restraint was allegedly achieved by an exchange of information that enabled member firms to co-ordinate their activities and was accompanied by the constant exhortation of the association's statistician not to spoil the market by increased production.

Given the large number of defendants and their relatively small share of the country's hardwood output, use of the reasonableness test would seem to have dictated dismissal of the suit. However, events and the engaging naïveté of the association's promoters ("co-operation, not competition, is the life blood of commerce") favored the federal attor-

---

[30] Maple Flooring Manufacturers Ass'n v. United States, 268 U.S. 563, 585 (1925).

[31] American Column & Lumber Co. v. United States, 257 U.S. 377 (1921).

neys. The first year of the association's missionary work happened to coincide with the general increase in the cost of building materials that occurred after World War I, and its officers, in justifying their salaries, did not scruple to hint that price increases were the tangible benefits of "open" pricing. In upholding the injunction granted by the district court, the majority opinion of the Supreme Court ruled:

> While it is true that 1919 was a year of high and increasing prices generally and that wet weather may have restricted production to some extent, we cannot but agree with members of the "Plan" themselves, as we have quoted them, and with the District Court in the conclusion that united action of this large and influential membership of dealers contributed greatly to this extraordinary price increase.[32]

It was left to Justice Brandeis in his dissenting opinion to doubt that the activities of a trade association so loosely organized could have greatly affected the price of lumber.[33]

The second open-price case to reach the Supreme Court afforded a better example of how the pooling of production data might qualify as a restrictive practice.[34] This suit arose when a professional promoter of trade associations sold twelve producers of linseed oil, cakes, and meal on the advantages of the "new competition." The defendants, according to the majority opinion, manufactured and distributed "a very substantial part" of the linseed products consumed in the country. That the purposes served by the statistical service they supported were not wholly innocent is clear enough. The articles of association provided, for example, that a member could forfeit a deposit of from $1,000 to $10,000 for failing to provide accurate information to association officers, and that a member could demand an audit of a rival's books if he had reason to believe that the rival was supplying false or incomplete data to the association.[35] The district court inexplicably found no collusion, but the Supreme Court, in a short opinion granting

---

[32] *Ibid.* 409.

[33] Some small manufacturers believed that they had obtained higher prices as a consequence of the Hardwood Association's activities and expressed their gratitude to its statistician in writing, but they probably deceived themselves. One investigator found that lumber prices rose so rapidly in the 1919 inflation that the one- to two-week-old figures furnished by the Association to its members were generally below the current market prices, and no uniformity in prices was achieved. M. N. Nelson, *Open Price Associations* 177–82 (1923).

[34] United States v. American Linseed Oil Co., 262 U.S. 371 (1923).

[35] *Ibid.* 382.

the government's request for an injunction, reaffirmed the *American Column* doctrine.

Two difficult cases that reached the Supreme Court in 1925 produced, for the first time, judicial sanction of a reasonable use of open pricing. In *Maple Flooring Ass'n v. United States*[36] the Court, with three justices dissenting, dissolved an injunction banning the intelligence activities of twenty-two producers of maple, beech, and birch flooring. The defendants, located mainly in Michigan, were found to have shipped roughly 70 per cent of these types of flooring marketed throughout the country in 1922. That the activities of these firms were not wholly free of collusion is suggested by two circumstances disregarded in the majority opinion. The trade association was a direct descendant of a cartel which had apportioned sales quotas certainly as late as January, 1916, and probably as late as March, 1920; and the defendants quoted delivered prices f.o.b. plus transport cost from Cadillac, Michigan. This suit is often cited as a basing-point case, but since sixteen of the seventeen maple flooring mills co-operating were located within a two-hundred-mile radius of Cadillac, the arrangement could more accurately be called collusive f.o.b. pricing.[37]

The above evidence notwithstanding, the majority opinion chose to emphasize the social usefulness of accurate market information. Citing J. A. Hobson and Irving Fisher, the Court found:

> It is the consensus of opinion of economists and of many of the most important agencies of Government that the public interest is served by the gathering and dissemination, in the widest possible manner, of information with respect to the production and distribution, cost and prices in actual sales, of market commodities, because the making available of such information tends to stabilize trade and industry, to produce fairer price levels and to avoid the waste which inevitably attends the unintelligent conduct of economic enterprise. . . . Competition does not become less free merely because the conduct of commercial operations becomes more intelligent through the free distribution of knowledge of all the essential factors entering into the commercial transaction.[38]

---

[36] 268 U.S. 563.

[37] A map showing the distribution of maple-flooring mills in the early 1920's is reproduced from court records in F. A. Fetter, *The Masquerade of Monopoly* 232 (1931).

[38] 268 U.S. 563, 582–83.

A similar respect for the collection of statistics was displayed in *Cement Manufacturers Protective Ass'n v. United States* (1925).[39] In this case a divided high court again dissolved an injunction barring the operation of an open-price plan covering nineteen cement producers in the middle Atlantic states. Here the two main issues turned upon (a) the use of a multiple basing-point system of pricing and (b) the concerted efforts of the defendants to stop contractors from accepting cement ordered in advance when the price was favorable and then cancelling such orders when the price was unfavorable.

Base pricing was held by the Court to have been an established trade practice in the cement industry before the formation of the trade association. Contractors' abuse of their right to cancel orders was viewed by the justices as unfair business behavior (analogous to not paying one's debts on time) which the cement manufacturers could legitimately confederate to check.

In retrospect, it would seem that the Supreme Court erred in applying the reasonableness test to open pricing in three of the first four cases decided, but given the novelty of the problem—and the genuine complexity of the economic issues involved—the economics of these decisions should not be judged harshly. In any event, both the district court and the Supreme Court revealed an enviable mastery of the open-price problem in *Sugar Institute v. United States* (1936).[40]

Here the government sought to dissolve a trade association maintained by fifteen companies then refining from 70 to 80 per cent of all sugar consumed in the country. (Nearly one-half of the defendants' total production was concentrated in two firms.) When the Sugar Institute was formed in 1927, the industry was generally unprofitable and its plight worsened by much secret rebating. The initiating members first considered the possibility of assigning production quotas, but on being advised by counsel that this expedient was no longer legal, they settled for an open-price plan and a program of cost-reducing assistance to high-cost producers. It was hoped that such aid would deliver marginal firms facing ruin from the temptation to seek additional revenue by price cutting.

The district court was not unsympathetic to the problems of the sugar trade and readily granted that any information that might help the institute members to make more intelligent decisions was a good thing; nevertheless, it drew the line at the use of trade statistics to implement a concerted policy of restraint. It therefore directed that the

---

[39] 268 U.S. 588.
[40] 297 U.S. 553.

institute should cease circulating information on the prices which its members planned to charge in the future, but permitted the continued distribution of data on transactions already concluded.[41] Given the small membership of the Sugar Institute, the district court probably erred in assuming that information on closed transactions would not help the members to co-ordinate their future price and output policies. But the court correctly perceived that such information was not so directly suited to this purpose as reports on future prices binding upon the members. The lower court's decree was affirmed without important modification by the Supreme Court.

In summary, then, no hard-and-fast dividing line separates "good" and "bad" trade statistics. Better intelligence both enables buyers and sellers to make more intelligent individual judgments—a development which presumably contributes to realizing the preconditions necessary for effective competition—and at the same time facilitates co-operation on the part of business rivals. One may fairly question the judgment of the courts in appraising the statistical activities of trade associations in particular cases, but short of outlawing trade associations completely, the reasonableness test is indispensable for evaluating their activities.[42]

5. *Cartels and patents*

At present, the only cartel arrangements that may be said to raise important and unresolved legal issues are those that involve the purchase and licensing of patents. In the United States, as in most countries, the inventor is entitled to treat his seventeen-year monopoly as a transferable property right. He may sell the exclusive rights to make, use, or vend his patented article, machine, or design, or he may retain ownership and license others to use his patent. The patent license may relate to (a) the production of a patented product, (b) the use of a patented machine to produce an unpatented product, (c) the use of a patented part in an unpatented machine, or even (d) the use of a patented idea to produce an unpatented product from unpatented materials. The owner of a patent may restrict the use of his patent to a certain time and place, and in some circumstances, he may establish product quotas and prices on an article made under license with the use of his patent.[43]

---

[41] 15 F. Supp. 817 (S.D.N.Y. 1934).

[42] For more searching comment on these issues see Comment, "Trade Association Statistics and the Anti-trust Laws," 18 *U. Chi. L. Rev.* 380 (1951).

[43] The most lucid and incisive evaluation of the American patent system is F. L. Vaughan, *The United States Patent System* (1956). Other useful works are G. A. Bloxam, "Letters Patent for Inventions: Their Use and Misuse," 5 *J. Ind.*

At first glance, there appears to be no inherent conflict between antitrust policy and the patent system. One might plausibly maintain that the patent monopoly is merely the temporary and occasional reward given by the State to the man who has disclosed a useful invention. At second glance, some possible points of conflict between the two bodies of law can be discerned, since a patent monopoly is not exercised in a vacuum. For example, the total value of competing patents held by rival firms is clearly less than the total value of the same patents held by one firm or placed under common management in a patent pool. Even under ideal conditions—and only patent lawyers can believe that the American patent system remotely approximates the ideal—the courts would face the difficult task of deciding precisely *how much* monopoly power was conferred by a particular patent grant.

In practice, the judicial duty is immensely complicated by two defects of the American patent system that are in no sense inevitable. The first is the doctrine long accepted by the courts that the patent owner may both suppress his invention and stop anyone else from using it during the period of his monopoly;[44] yet if the patentee may deny his discovery to the public as a matter of right, he is perforce a public benefactor when he allows his patent to be worked on almost any terms. (Conceivably his terms could be so onerous or dishonorable that the public would be better off without his invention for seventeen years, but this is most improbable.) Hence, it is illogical to charge the

---

Econ. 157 (1957); E. T. Penrose, *The Economics of the International Patent System* (1951); and W. B. Bennett, *The American Patent System* (1943).

[44] This doctrine was first endorsed by the Supreme Court in Continental Paper Bag Co. v. Eastern Paper Bag Co., 210 U.S. 405 (1908), though it had long been acted on by inferior courts. Nor did the Supreme Court qualify the right of patent suppression in any way. In this case, the patent holder had purchased the patented design of an improved bag-making machine for the express purpose of protecting his investment in older and inferior equipment. Nevertheless, the Court asked rhetorically, "Can it be said, as a matter of law, that a non-use was unreasonable which had for its motive the saving of the expense that would have been involved by changing the equipment of a factory from one set of machines to another?" 429.

For an earlier argument that "under a patent which gives a patentee a monopoly, he is bound either to use the patent himself or allow others to use it on reasonable or equitable terms," see Hoe v. Knap, 27 Fed. 204 (C.C.N.D. Ill. 1886). This case is especially interesting in that the issue before the court was non-use rather than suppression. The plaintiff held the patent on an accessory used with printing presses which he made to order and apparently had never received an order for a press with the patented device. The court declined to issue a temporary injunction restraining infringement but required the defendant to give bond to cover any damages which might ultimately be assessed against him. The outcome of the case is not reported.

patentee with unlawfully restraining trade which makes use of his patent when admittedly he may legally suppress such trade in its entirety.[45] Nevertheless, the courts have adopted this untenable position by endeavoring to distinguish between lawful and unlawful exploitation of a patent monopoly.[46] In these circumstances, it cannot possibly devise any consistent set of rules to assess how far a patent owner may go in exercising monopoly power under his grant; the attempt to reconcile antitrust policy and patent practice is foredoomed to produce a welter of conflicting precedents. Given, however, the cumulative encroachments of antitrust policy on the patent grant, we may expect that the courts will eventually dispel this confusion by repudiating the doctrine that the patentee is lawfully entitled to suppress his invention.[47]

The second remedial defect of the American patent system derives from the failure of judges and administrators to agree upon the standards of originality that an inventor must meet in order to gain a valid patent. The Patent Office conducts the initial investigation of an inventor's claim and, if satisfied, issues a patent. This grant merely entitles the fortunate party to sue others for the infringement of his monopoly rights. The suit is tried in a federal court which must then decide (a) whether the patent has, in fact, been infringed and (b) if so, is the patent valid or did the Patent Office err in issuing it? Since the Patent Office believes that patent applications should be encouraged, the standards of patentability that it sets are well below

---

[45] The classic statement of this philosophy is the decision in Heaton-Peninsular Button-Fastener Co. v. Eureka Specialty Co., 77 Fed. 228 (6th Cir. 1896). In upholding the right of a manufacturer of patented button-fastening machines to sell them subject to the restriction that unpatented metallic fasteners be bought only from him the court held: "If, then, the patentee has the exclusive right to the use of his invention or discovery, during the term of his patent, it would seem to follow that any use by another, unauthorized by the patentee, would be an infringement of his monopoly. If, therefore, he can find a purchaser for a machine subject only to certain specified uses, any violation of the privilege granted would be an infringement, for which the remedies granted patentees would be appropriate," 292.

[46] This attempt dates from Standard Sanitary Manufacturing Co. v. United States, 226 U.S. 20 (1912).

[47] In Special Equipment Co. v. Coe, 324 U.S. 370 (1945), three justices, in a dissenting opinion, called upon the Court to repudiate the patentee's absolute right to suppress his invention. Neither patent suppression nor non-use, however, was an issue in the case; it involved the efforts of the patentee to "fence" his patent on a machine by securing a patent covering a combination of parts used in the machine. Actually, the paper-bag patent case seems to have been the only occasion on which the Supreme Court has had to rule on the legality of patent suppression.

those insisted upon by the courts, so that each year thousands of patents are issued which would be voided if tested by litigation.

One might suppose that given the fearfully complicated engineering problems frequently raised in patent cases, the courts would be disposed to honor the decision of an expert body, provided that it was duly made, issued after notice and hearing and supported by evidence. The courts reason, however, that since a patent confers a monopoly which would otherwise be against public policy, the decisions of the Patent Office are not entitled to the same standing as those of other federal agencies. The right to hear argument de novo on the validity of a challenged patent is therefore jealously reserved; the courts accord a presumption of validity to a certification of the Patent Office, but nothing more.[48] We may also suspect that the courts' experience has given them a poor opinion of the expertness professed by patent examiners. Actually the budget of the Patent Office permits only a perfunctory glance at most applications received,[49] and the validity of a patent is often influenced by the particular court in which its fate is decided.[50] The trivial patents that have reached the Supreme Court before being thrown out include grants covering rubber caps placed on wood pencils, an oval rather than a cylindrical roll for toilet paper to facilitate tearing off strips, rubber grips on bicycle handlebars, and the substitution of flat cord in place of round cord for the loop at the end of suspenders.[51]

---

[48] By the Patent Act of 1952, 66 *Stat.* 792, the courts were expressly directed to presume the validity of a patent and place the burden of proving invalidity on him who asserts it. In actions for damages arising through infringement this rule has long been applied and was endorsed by the Supreme Court as early as Blanchard v. Putnam, 75 U.S. (8 Wall.) 420 (1869). In equity cases, however, the presumption of patent's validity was not always accepted without additional evidence. See 3 A. H. Walker, *Patents* 2085–87 (Deller's ed. 1937).

[49] The problems of the United States Patent Office have often been examined at length. For a recent survey see *American Patent System: Hearings before the Subcommittee on Patents, Trademarks, and Copyrights of the Senate Judiciary Committee,* 84th Cong., 1st Sess. (1956).

[50] A Commissioner of Patents once pleaded the difficulty of predicting how judges would rule on patents as justifying the Patent Office's liberal attitude toward applications. By his reasoning a patent should be issued so long as there was a reasonable probability that some court in the country would uphold it. Testimony of C. P. Coe, *Hearings before the Senate Committee on Patents on S. 475,* 75th Cong. 1st Sess. 117–18 (1937).

[51] These examples are taken from a longer list of Patent Office absurdities compiled by Justice Douglas. Great Atlantic & Pacific Tea Co. v. Supermarket Equipment Corp., 340 U.S. 147, 156–58 (1950).

In general, the suspicion of the patent grant varies directly with the rank of the court—a circumstance which suggests that the more closely a claim to exercise monopoly power is examined, the less likely it is to find favor in the eyes of the reasonable man. Thus from 1948 through 1954 the district courts ruled on 664 patents in reported cases. Of this number, 201 were found valid and infringed, 355 invalid, and 108 not infringed. In the same period, the courts of appeal considered 429 patents, finding 77 valid and infringed, 269 invalid, and 83 not infringed. The Supreme Court in these years threw out 5 of the 7 patents which came before it. From 1925 through 1954 the Supreme Court examined 87 patents; 13 were found valid and infringed, 57 invalid, and 17 not infringed.[52]

The predilection of the Patent Office for issuing grants of doubtful validity has two especially unfortunate consequences for antitrust policy. First, it often means that holders of patents must resort to pooling and cross licensing if their grants are to be worked at all. Otherwise they must either engage in interminable lawsuits to determine their rights or else watch others appropriate their inventions with impunity. Indeed, the proliferation of patents has led to the preposterous "standoff"—an impasse where one man's patent cannot be employed commercially except in conjunction with someone else's patent; therefore they must either co-operate in order to profit from their respective grants or else sell out to a third party.[53]

Second, the multiplication of doubtful patents creates a strong presumption that any elaborate pooling of patents violates the Sherman Act. The patents pooled may be invalid, or valid but commercially worthless, so that the patent pool merely cloaks a price-fixing or market-sharing agreement. More probably, the pooled patents are a mixed bag consisting of valid patents, spurious patents, questionable patents, valuable patents, worthless patents, and patents whose worth is anybody's guess.

In these circumstances, the efforts to bring patent pools under the

---

[52] Reckoned from Patent Office data in *Hearings on Patents* 177–83.

Judicial hostility to patent grants is by no means confined to the United States. British reports list 925 cases involving patents from 1887 through 1944. In 503 decisions, patents were declared invalid. From 1867 through 1944 the Supreme Court of Canada heard 43 patent cases and ruled against the patentee in 28. H. C. Fox, *Monopolies and Patents* 255–73 (1947).

[53] For a recent case lost by the government because the defendant established that a cross-licensing agreement with a competitor was necessary to resolve a patent standoff, see United States v. Birdsboro Steel Co., 139 F. Supp. 244 (W. D. Penn. 1956).

antitrust laws have necessarily produced curious, contradictory, and even humorous results. The considerations which seem to receive the courts' closest attention are (a) the nature of the restraint imposed by the licensor, (b) the number of participants in the agreement, and (c) the right of the patentee's opponent to question the validity of the patents involved in the suit. Generally speaking, the weaker the restraint imposed upon the patent's use and the fewer the firms involved, the greater the likelihood that the court will support the patentee.[54] As regards the right to impugn the validity of a patent, the present state of the law seems to be about as follows: Anyone sued for patent infringement may raise the issue provided he has not previously waived this right. (This qualification is important because patent licenses commonly contain a clause wherein the licensee acknowledges the validity of the patentee's grant.) Even if the licensee has agreed not to contest the validity of the patent which he uses, he may nevertheless do so when the agreement permits the licensor to set the price of any article that the licensee sells.[55] The assumption here is that such price fixing is clearly illegal unless it represents a legitimate exercise of the patent right; hence, the public has a stake in having the validity of the patent explored. In a civil case brought under the Sherman Act, the government may, at any time, attack the "asserted shield of patentability."[56] (The government seems never to have contested the validity of a patent in a criminal prosecution.)

As yet, patent law and antitrust law have directly collided in so few cases that it is difficult to say more than this, but the drift of judicial opinion in the direction of resolving conflicts in favor of antitrust policy is clear enough.[57] Although the Supreme Court early confirmed

---

[54] This problem is considered at length in Note, "Patent Pooling and the Sherman Act," 50 *Colum. L. Rev.* 1113 (1950).

[55] Sola Electric Co. v. Jefferson Electric Co., 317 U.S. 173 (1942).

In another case the Supreme Court permitted the defendant to attack the validity of a patent covered by a license that contained a price-fixing clause even though the clause had probably been inserted at the defendant's request. Edward Katzinger Co. v. Chicago Metallic Mfg. Co., 329 U.S. 394 (1947).

[56] United States v. United States Gypsum Co., 333 U.S. 364, 388 (1948).

[57] The opening skirmishes in the patent-antitrust clash are traced in the symposium on "Patents and Antitrust Laws" in *Lectures on Federal Antitrust Laws* 45–115 (University of Mich. Law School, 1953); "Patent-Antitrust Problems," in *Report of the Attorney General's National Committee to Study the Antitrust Laws* 223–59 (1955); and H. F. Furth, "Price-Restrictive Patent Licenses under the Sherman Act," 71 *Harv. L. Rev.* 815 (1958). Actually the first shot in this contest was fired as early as Edison Electric Light Co. v. Sawyer-Man Electric Co., 53 Fed. 592 (2d Cir. 1892) when the defendant in an infringement suit

the right of a patentee to set the price of a good made under license,[58] the right was drastically circumscribed in later cases;[59] indeed the circuit court of appeals has recently concluded that

> the patent laws were not intended to empower a patentee to grant a plurality of licenses, each containing provisions fixing the price at which the licensee might sell the product or process to the company, and that, if a plurality of licenses are granted, such provisions therein are prohibited by the anti-trust laws.[60]

It may be the manifest destiny of federal attorneys to carry through the revision of national patent policy—repeatedly refused by Congress—under the guise of enforcing the antitrust laws.

That the patent system is greatly in need of overhauling is a truth acknowledged by most students of the problem except, unhappily, the most influential, *i.e.*, patent attorneys and congressmen.[61] Until a reform radically reduces the number of patents issued each year, the conflict between patent law and antitrust policy must grow in magnitude and confusion. The economic significance of this clash, however, is difficult to assess. The fraction of the national income represented by patent royalties is insignificant, and one may doubt that the decisions affecting innovation made by most businessmen are much influenced

---

urged (unsuccessfully) that the plaintiff was not entitled to protection because he had unlawfully extended his patent monopoly. But until recently the courts have been extremely loath to further complicate patent cases by allowing the introduction of antitrust issues.

[58] Notably in United States v. General Electric Co., 272 U.S. 476 (1926). Bement v. National Harrow Co., 186 U.S. 70 (1902) is sometimes cited as sanctioning price fixing through a system of patent licenses. Here, however, the Supreme Court decided the case solely on the basis of a state court record involving a single contract and remarked that if the record had established (as it had not) that the licensor had executed too many price-fixing contracts, they would be illegal.

[59] Notably, United States v. Masonite Corp., 316 U.S. 265 (1942); and United States v. Line Material Co., 333 U.S. 287 (1948).

[60] Newburgh Moire Co. v. Superior Moire Co., 237 F.2d 283, 293–94 (3d Cir. 1956).

[61] Over the years many suggestions have been made for revising the patent system. For some thoughtful and original recommendations see Michael Polanyi, "Patent Reform," 11 *Rev. Econ. Stud.* 61 (1944). *Inter alia*, Polanyi proposes that in order better to reward inventors, promote the rapid exploitation of new ideas, and avoid litigation, the now scarcely used English "license of right" be substituted for the patent monopoly. That is, anyone would be entitled to employ the licensed invention upon payment of a royalty to the licensee based upon the value added to his output by its use.

by the danger of a patent infringement suit.[62] Nevertheless, in several major industries, notably electrical equipment and aircraft production, no firm can safely operate without paying royalties to—or participating in—a patent pool. The most we can say is that authorities who stress the wisdom of limiting—or at least clarifying—the patent privilege deserve a sympathetic hearing.

[62] For a forceful statement of the view that the defects of American patent law make it a major buttress to monopoly and brake on technological development, see A. E. Kahn, "Fundamental Deficiencies of the American Patent Law," 30 *Am. Econ. Rev.* 475 (1940). Kahn's illustrative material, however, is taken mostly from the electrical equipment industry—a notoriously fertile field for patent litigation.

Chapter *XIII*

THE LAW OF UNFAIR
COMPETITION: 1

1. *The common law and business ethics*

Since the beginning of antitrust litigation, the most difficult issues have been bound up with the activities of the large firm possessing appreciable market power in its own right. For purposes of exposition we may view these questions of law and economics as arising out of:

    a. the elimination of competition by "unfair" methods,

    b. the elimination of competition by voluntary mergers,

    c. the presence of monopoly or oligopoly as a consequence of the scale of production.

    Market power of this last sort may exist either because demand is insufficient to maintain more than a handful of producers or because the established producers command the resources which would enable them to initiate a price war against rash new rivals.

    From *Pierce v. Fuller* (1811)[1] onward, common-law judges have often depreciated the importance of "predatory" competition—this term was, of course, unknown to them—as a legal problem on the premise that freedom to engage in trade would shortly defeat the effort of any merchant to dominate his market by such methods. Palpably fraudulent practices were, then as now, actionable, though as we noted in Chapter X the standards of proof enforced by the courts in tort actions made it exceedingly difficult for parties injured by such practices to collect damages. In the case of consumers, recovery of damages was, for all practical purposes, impossible.

2. *Passing of the common-law rule: the Standard Oil case*

After 1890 the judicial indifference to the methods of competition rapidly disappeared in the United States in the face of the remarkable

---

[1] 8 Mass. 222.

success of the Standard Oil Company;[2] for John D. Rockefeller proved to the satisfaction of most observers that market power ruthlessly and intelligently employed in an industry where the capital investment required for entry is beyond the means of the industrious artisan can nullify "the right to trade" as a consumer safeguard against monopoly. The Standard Oil Company made this point quite conclusively by controlling 80 per cent or more of all refining capacity in the United States during the thirty years prior to its dissolution in 1911. If the Sherman Act was to command respect, it was inevitable that the Justice Department should challenge the oil trust. Finally, in November, 1906, the Justice Department moved to break up the organization and five years later its efforts were largely successful.

The precise roles in the rise of the Standard Oil Company played by luck, good management, and a determination to be rid of competitors that did not always respect the criminal code need not concern us here. But without depreciating the business genius of Rockefeller and his associates, one may doubt that the market position of their company in 1911 could have been acquired or long preserved without resort to business practices of the most questionable sort.

In 1906 the Standard Oil Company presented probably the most tempting target for a dissolution decree that has ever come before the courts. At one time or another it had employed nearly every unfair tactic denounced by economists, lawyers, and legislators—bribery of public officials, exclusive dealing, the secret railroad rebate, bogus independents, harassing lawsuits against competitors, local price cutting to eliminate small rivals, and possibly arson as well. Moreover, in 1906 the company still retained most of its ill-gotten gains and one-third of its securities was still held by the seven individuals who were the major architects of its power.[3] Any damage to stockholder interests that might result from dissolution would fall, in some measure, on the

---

[2] Actually, the federal courts seem never to have accepted the English doctrine that one may do anything to get rid of an un-co-operative rival provided that (a) the means employed are lawful and (b) one has nothing against him personally and so acts from "disinterested malevolence" rather than malice. But then the federal courts received no reported case raising the issue of unfair competition before 1890. An unheeded plea for the acceptance of this conception of *laissez faire* (at least in judging tort liability suits between private parties) was, however, entered by Joseph McKenna while a circuit judge in Continental Insurance Co. v. Board of Underwriters of the Pacific, 67 Fed. 310 (C.C.N.D.Cal. 1895).

[3] United States v. Standard Oil Co. of New Jersey, 173 Fed. 177, 183 (C.C.E.D.Mo. 1909).

guilty parties, though since the oil industry was rapidly expanding no serious losses were anticipated by the court. In a decree which for the amount of reorganization imposed upon a major industry has never been equalled, the circuit court ordered the Standard Oil Company to rearrange itself into thirty-odd companies,[4] and its decree was subsequently upheld, with minor changes, by the Supreme Court.[5] Unfortunately, neither court found it necessary to analyze in detail the economic issues presented by the case.

Curiously enough, the circuit court scarcely alludes to the nefarious deeds of the Standard Oil Company but rather treats it as the corporate cloak put on by John D. Rockefeller and a few associates to cover an unlawful conspiracy to restrain trade. In the Supreme Court, the majority opinion of Chief Justice White dwells on the unsavory past of the defendant but does not indicate whether the main reason for upholding dissolution was the unwisdom of (a) allowing so much power to continue in a company with so black a past or (b) permitting so large a share of the industry's productive capacity to remain in a firm that was not the product of "normal" growth.

The decision in the *Standard Oil* case is generally taken to have incorporated the rule of reason into antitrust policy as regards close combinations. As we noted in Chapter X, common-law judges, in passing upon the enforceability of cartel agreements, sometimes implied that the possession of monopoly power was not unlawful per se, but that it forfeited the protection of the law if acquired by disreputable means or was unreasonably exercised. The rule of reason was given this meaning in the *Standard Oil* case by Justice Harlan when, in his minority opinion, he spoke out against any softening of the Court's hostility to cartel agreements as earlier manifested in the *Trans-Missouri*[6] and *Addyston Pipe* cases.[7]

It is unlikely, however, that Chief Justice White in the majority opinion was using the term with its common-law connotations—though his logic is so tortuous and his sentence structure so involved that we cannot be sure what he did mean.[8] A close reading of the case suggests

---

[4] *Ibid.* 197–200.

[5] Standard Oil Co. of New Jersey v. United States, 221 U.S. 1 (1911).

[6] United States v. Trans-Missouri Freight Ass'n, 166 U.S. 290 (1897).

[7] Addyston Pipe & Steel Co. v. United States, 175 U.S. 211 (1899).

[8] The reader is invited to try his hand at construing the following sentence taken from Chief Justice White's opinion in the *Standard Oil* case. "The merely generic enumeration which the statute (the Sherman Act) makes of the acts to which it refers and the absence of any definition of restraint of trade as used in the statute leaves room for but one conclusion, which is, that it was expressly

that Justices White and Harlan were concerned with different problems and talked at cross-purposes. Thus, Chief Justice White is seemingly at great pains to point out the impossibility of taking the first two sections of the Sherman Act literally and, hence, the necessity of spelling out the meaning of the key phrases—"monopolize," "contract in restraint of trade," etc. Justice Harlan ignores his brother's argument and replies that any modification of the language previously used by the Court in condemning cartels would lead to judicial sanction of the unacceptable distinction between good and bad trusts.[9]

3. *The condemnation of "unfair" competition extended: the Corn Products case*

The infamous history and spectacular success of the Standard Oil Company made unnecessary any searching analysis of the meaning of "unfair" competition as a means of attaining and protecting monopoly power. Such an examination we owe to Learned Hand's opinion in the *Corn Products* case[10]—probably the finest discussion of the problem available in the law reports or elsewhere.

The Corn Products Refining Company was organized in 1906 through the merger of the leading manufacturer of glucose and the leading manufacturer of cornstarch. Several smaller concerns were also absorbed and the two major parties had themselves acquired numerous smaller companies during the previous ten years. At its formation, the Corn Products Company completely controlled the output of glucose

---

designed not to unduly limit the application of the act by precise definition, but while clearly fixing a standard, that is, by defining the ulterior boundaries which could not be transgressed with impunity, to leave it to be determined by the light of reason, guided by the principles of law and the duty to apply and enforce the public policy embodied in the statute, in every given case whether any particular act or contract was within the contemplation of the statute." 221 U.S. 1, 63–64.

[9] Justice Harlan is surely referring to cartels in the following passage: "When Congress prohibited *every* contract, combination or monopoly, in restraint of commerce, it prescribed a simple, definite rule that all could understand, and which could be easily applied by everyone wishing to obey the law, and not to conduct their business in violation of law. But now, it is to be feared, we are to have, in cases without number, the constantly recurring inquiry—difficult to solve by proof—whether the particular contract, combination or trust involved in each case is or is not an 'unreasonable' or 'undue' restraint of trade." 221 U.S. 1, 102–03.

[10] United States v. Corn Products Refining Co., 234 Fed. 964 (S.D.N.Y. 1916).

and commanded about two-thirds of cornstarch production.[11] The tactics employed by the promoters of the combine were not especially unethical; indeed, like many other aspiring monopolists in the Corporate Revolution, they paid far more than many of the acquired firms were worth as competing properties—a fact from which the court not unreasonably inferred an "intent to monopolize."

The Corn Products Company in its infancy appears to have enjoyed rather inefficient management.[12] Saddled with much high-cost capacity in an industry where rivals could acquire more modern plants with a modest outlay, it was soon challenged and reacted by manipulating prices with the object of discouraging the entry of new rivals and hastening the exit of old ones. To this end the company first adopted a "profit-sharing" scheme whereby customers were indiscriminately given rebates on condition that they had purchased glucose from no other firm. When this method of injuring competitors proved too costly, more selective pressures were applied to them, e.g., by local price wars carried on through a bogus independent and interference with their lines of credit. In the words of Judge Hand, the policy of the defendant amounted to "candy without profit, syrup without profit, jam and jelly without profit—all to increase or maintain the volume of business."[13]

The tactics of the company—mainly directed toward maintaining its precarious hold on the glucose and glucose products market—were moderately successful. According to the court's findings, at least 36 per cent of glucose syrup production had been captured by other firms between 1906 and 1913, but the Corn Products Company was apparently holding its own in the market at the time of the trial and remained much the biggest producer in the field.[14]

When the Justice Department brought suit for dissolution, the defense rested its case on two main arguments. (1) The Corn Products Refining Company had been formed in order to redeem the industry from "ruinous" competition. (2) The rise of rival glucose producers had made moot the issue of monopoly since it is not the task of equity to punish for unlawful deeds that are over and done with.

Both points were elegantly dispatched by Hand.

---

[11] *Ibid.* 973.

[12] A critical account of the management policies of the Corn Products Refining Company to 1914 is given in A. S. Dewing, *Corporate Promotions and Reorganizations* 49–112 (1914).

[13] 234 Fed. 964, 988.

[14] *Ibid.* 1008–09.

They say that they combined to prevent a ruinous competition, and this is true; but the immediate result of the combination was such a rise in price as attracted new capital into an industry whose producing capacity, on paper, was already more than the market would take.[15]

On the second point, he was moved to observe:

The national will has not declared against elimination of competitors when they fail from their inherent industrial weakness. On the contrary, it has declared with great emphasis against any methods by which such weakness might be concealed; in so doing it has assumed a positive purpose toward industry, has established a norm to which competition must conform. This purpose the Corn Products Refining Company has persistently and ingeniously endeavored to thwart from the outset. Its constant effort has been to prevent competitors from that test which would in the long run discover whether they could manufacture as well and as cheaply as itself. It has tried throughout, by its power temporarily to affect commercial conditions, so to obscure the actual industrial facts as to make impossible any test of relative strength. That it has failed does not change the past or make its continued existence in any sense less compromising to the future. There is every assurance that it will continue unfair trade methods, unless it be forcibly prevented.[16]

That an injunction against certain tactics of the company was in order Hand did not doubt. Dissolution, he felt, presented a more serious problem, since from his reading of Supreme Court opinions in Sherman Act cases, he was not certain whether the company's market power was unlawful per se or unlawful only because of its unreasonable exercise.[17] If the first interpretation was followed, dissolution would be mandatory. If the second was favored, it might prove unnecessary. Hand finally concluded that the record of the company was black enough to support the inference that any power it still possessed probably would be abused in the future; hence dissolution was ordered.

Hand's direction of dissolution in the *Corn Products* case is unique in one respect. It was probably the only experiment in trust

---

[15] *Ibid.* 1014.
[16] *Ibid.* 1015.
[17] *Ibid.*

busting decreed by a federal court that anticipated that a financial loss would fall upon stockholders. Hand granted that dissolution might cause some loss of foreign trade and some outlay for the remodelling of plants before they could support independent companies, but he was prepared to take the risk on the ground that "there is nothing in this evidence which indicates any serious demoraliation of the industry at large."[18]

In summary, the *Standard Oil* and *Corn Products* cases may be taken as affirming the doctrine that the use of monopoly power to deny the market to rivals is against public policy. It may be stressed, however, that the defendants in these suits were ordered dissolved for different reasons.

Standard Oil suffered this fate because its market control rested upon the use of obnoxious means largely abandoned before 1900. The Corn Products Refining Company was reduced to smaller units because, never having achieved the success of Standard Oil, it persisted in seeking market control with the use of illegitimate tactics. Probably one should not accept at face value the reasons advanced by a court to explain why it orders or denies dissolution. The action of a court is governed not so much by the tactics or market position of the defendant as by the possibility of breaking him up without unduly disturbing the interests of workers and stockholders. (This proposition is argued at length in Chapter XVII.)

Few authorities would quarrel with Hand's condemnation of business tactics designed "temporarily to affect commercial conditions so to obscure the actual industrial facts as to make impossible by test of relative strength." Likewise, the test of "fairness" implied in this dictum commands a ready assent, namely, Does the firm throw away short-run profits in order to eliminate or intimidate rivals? Nevertheless, no moral opprobrium attaches to the type of aggressive competition condemned in the *Corn Products* case. It is too much to expect that businessmen should be able, at all times, to distinguish the attractions of monopoly from those of "true" efficiency. The competition stigmatized by Hand as "predatory" is objectionable only because there exists a presumption that it injures the interests of consumers.

The Standard Oil Company, however, had resorted to a number of practices—notably commercial bribery and the use of violence—which were blatantly unethical. The probability that these tactics may also have injured consumers was really immaterial; indeed, they were

---

[18] *Ibid.* 1017.

objectionable even though they served to lower prices to consumers by exacerbating fear and distrust among business rivals. The *Standard Oil* decision contains no explicit condemnation of "unfair" competition that is not also "predatory" in the sense of being morally reprehensible. But the Court's disapproval of the milder forms of disinterested malevolence which, without being contemptible, do not respect the sensibilities of reasonable men is clearly implied. With the passage of the Federal Trade Commission Act[19] in 1914, "unfair methods of competition" became unlawful, and the task of making the law of unfair competition began in earnest.

4. *The condemnation of unfair competition as a source of confusion*

In the United States cases involving restraint of trade and business ethics have come to be decided under the same few vaguely worded statutes. This peculiar and unfortunate development is largely a matter of historical accident. Under the common law, cases falling into these two categories were decided by reference to different sets of precedents. "Unfair" competition had originally denoted the unlawful appropriation of another's trade-mark. By 1890 the term had also come to cover practices closely akin to trade-mark piracy, for example, simulating the trade name of a competitor, copying his manner of packaging his product, and using personal or geographical names that the public had come to identify with a particular firm. Further, in the United States at this date, "unfair" competition was not confined to practices that may be subsumed under the general heading of "passing off" one's product as somebody else's but denoted as well commercial bribery, interference with a competitor's contracts, any "malicious" interference with his business, and gross deception of the public.[20] Thus in 1890 "unfair" competition was different things to different men.

It is a revealing commentary on the business ethics of our forebears that while the use of merchants' marks and other business identifying symbols is very ancient, legal protection of trade-marks is of

---

[19] 38 *Stat.* 717.

[20] The expansion of the doctrine of unfair competition beyond trade-mark piracy can be traced in G. D. Cushing, "On Certain Cases Analogous to Trade Marks," 4 *Harv. L. Rev.* 321 (1891); O. R. Mitchell, "Unfair Competition," 10 *Harv. L. Rev.* 275 (1896); and C. G. Haines, "Efforts to Define Unfair Competition," 29 *Yale L.J.* 1 (1919).

recent origin,[21] and in the first reported case involving a trade-mark in 1742,[22] the court indignantly rejected the injured party's plea for injunctive relief as patently absurd.

> An objection has been made, that the defendant, in using this mark, prejudices the plaintiff by taking away his customers. But there is no more weight in this, than there would be in an objection to one innkeeper, setting up the same sign with another.[23]

Forty-one years later in deciding a dispute between two purveyors of "Dr. Johnson's Yellow Ointment," Lord Mansfield is reported as holding that "if the defendant had sold a medicine of his own under the plaintiff's name or mark, that would be fraud for which an action would lie."[24] In this case, however, the disputed mark had first been used by the plaintiff's father, and the court dismissed the action on the implied ground that an unpatented trade-mark was not a transferable property right deserving the law's protection. It was not until 1824 that King's Bench upheld a judgment for trade-mark infringement,[25] and the right to enjoy protection in a trade-mark acquired by inheritance was not confirmed in a reported decision until 1843.[26]

The first American case involving trade-mark infringement seems to have been *Thompson v. Winchester* (1837)[27] wherein the Supreme Judicial Court of Massachusetts rejected the argument that the manufacturer of an unpatented article had no property right whatsoever in his trade-mark. (In this case the plaintiff was endeavoring to protect his stake in "Thomsonian Medicines" which purported to incorporate his discoveries of "valuable medicinal properties in various vegetable substances and the best manner of compounding the same for medical purposes."[28]) A few years later the right to property in a trade-mark

---

[21] The faltering steps by which the merchant's mark became a property right that the law would protect are traced in F. I. Schechter, *The Historical Foundations of the Law Relating to Trade-Marks* (1925), especially 122–71.

[22] Blanchard v. Hill, 2 Atk. 484, 26 Eng. Rep. 692 (Ch.).

[23] *Ibid.* 487.

[24] Singleton v. Bolton, 3 Dougl. 293, 99 Eng. Rep. 661 (K.B. 1783).

[25] Sykes v. Sykes, 3 B & C 541, 107 Eng. Rep. 834 (1824).

[26] Croft v. Day, 7 Beav. 82, 49 Eng. Rep. 994 (Rolls Ct. 1843).

The early history of trade-mark protection in Britain is traced in F. M. Adams, *A Treatise on the Law of Trade Marks* (1874).

[27] 36 Mass. 214.

[28] *Ibid.* 214.

was confirmed in the federal courts.[29] The practical import of these early decisions favorable to trade-mark protection was, of course, largely nullified by uncertainty, expense, delay, and the high standards of proof of damage enforced at law and equity,[30] and in 1879 a Congressional attempt to make trade-mark infringement a violation of the criminal code was ruled an unconstitutional usurpation of States' rights.[31]

If the businessman injured by the unethical acts of a competitor had little hope of relief or redress, the unorganized public had none whatever, except for the occasional prosecution of the trader who gave short weight or adulterated his product with a poisonous substance. As business ethics improved during the nineteenth century[32]—and no cynic should maintain that they did not—the demand for governmental machinery to enforce a higher standard of business conduct could have been met in any number of ways, *e.g.*, through the creation of special courts, regulatory commissions, or officially sanctioned better business bureaus. Unfortunately, in the United States the supervision of business ethics was entrusted to the Federal Trade Commission and the Justice Department—the two agencies which also had the task of discouraging restraint of trade.

This dual responsibility came about mainly because of the supposed role of unfair competition in the rise of the trusts. The sponsors of the Federal Trade Commission bill no doubt exaggerated in 1914 when they asserted that "it is now generally recognized that the only effective means of establishing and maintaining monopoly, where there is no control of a natural resource as of transportation, is the use of unfair competition";[33] but in support of this view they could cite the

---

[29] Taylor v. Carpenter, 3 Story 458 (1st Cir. 1844), 2 Wood & M. 1 (1st Cir. 1846). The first case was in equity, the second at law.

[30] Thus, only sixty-two reported cases involving trade-mark infringement are known to have been decided in American courts prior to 1870. *Report of the Commissioners Appointed to Revise the Statutes Relating to Patents, Trade and Other Marks, and Trade and Commercial Names*, S. Doc. No. 20, 56 Cong., 2d Sess. 93 (1900).

[31] Trade-Mark Cases, 100 U.S. (10 Otto) 82 (1879).

[32] Alfred Marshall, for example, rightly made the improvement in business ethics a major factor of economic progress, pointing out, *inter alia*, that the separation of ownership and control in the modern large corporation is possible only because owners trust managers as they did in no previous age. *Industry and Trade* 311–16 (3d ed. 1920).

[33] Conference committee report on the Federal Trade Commission bill, H.R. Rep. No. 1142, 63 Cong., 2d Sess. 18–19 (1914).

writings of economists of the stature of John Bates Clark.[34] In any event, Congress chose to approach obliquely the problem of business ethics on the assumption that it is a facet of monopoly, and the antitrust agencies, armed with the 1914 legislation and the condemnation of predatory competition given in Sherman Act cases, proceeded to brand as unfair competition:

1. trade practices that deceive the public, notably false advertising and misbranding;
2. trade practices which corrupt the public, *e.g.*, the use of lotteries in sales promotion;
3. trade practices which are contemptible even though no injury to the public can be shown, *e.g.*, bribery of a rival's employees to betray his trust;
4. restraint of trade generally and predatory competition in particular;
5. trade practices by which large firms gain at the expense of smaller rivals.

The use of the antitrust laws to discourage business tactics that fall into the first three categories is praiseworthy (if illogical) and need not concern us here; yet it is only within narrow limits that the antitrust laws can simultaneously promote competition and protect particular businessmen from its consequences. In recent years the intervention of the antitrust agencies on behalf of small business has prompted the criticism that federal policy now aims at the substitution of "soft" competition for "hard" competition in the interest of protecting inefficient small firms. Since the assault on restrictive practices has mounted apace with the State's paternalistic concern for small business, this charge is not really fair. It is true, however, that the antitrust agencies have never evidenced any willingness to recognize that they have committed themselves to the pursuit of goals that are sometimes incompatible.

5. *Hard versus soft competition as a policy goal*

A bias in favor of soft competition was revealed by the Federal Trade Commission in one of its earliest cases and was provoked by a firm

---

[34] *The Control of Trusts: An Argument in Favor of Curbing the Power of Monopoly by a Natural Method* (1901). The natural method of John Bates Clark is competition purged of predatory practices. His faith in the method was somewhat weaker when, in 1912, he published a revision of the book called simply *The Control of Trusts*.

which, over the years, has consistently championed the cause of hard competition in retailing. In June, 1918, the commission ruled that the mail-order house Sears, Roebuck and Company had acted unfairly by (a) alleging that its expert buying of tea and sugar in large quantities enabled it to sell more cheaply than some rivals, (b) intimating that its rivals charged more than a fair price for the items, and (c) selling sugar "below cost" provided that some minimum amount of other products which yielded a profit on the total transaction was also purchased.[35] In fine, the commission accused Sears of using sugar as a loss leader and disguising this practice by exaggerating the economies obtained by purchasing sugar in large amounts.

The commission therefore ordered the company to cease its objectionable advertising and stop selling sugar "below cost." When Sears declined to change its price policy, the commission petitioned the circuit court of appeals for review and enforcement. The court readily endorsed the part of the commission's order relating to misleading advertising but, in effect, struck out the section which forbade the sale of sugar below cost. By the court's reasoning, so long as no question of trade restraint was involved, the defendant was entitled to price as he pleased. "We find in the statute no intent on the part of Congress, even if it has the power, to restrain an owner of property from selling it at any price that is acceptable to him or from giving it away."[36] The selling of sugar below cost was banned by the court only to the extent that it was an integral part of the condemned advertising scheme. One might wish that a more abrupt challenge had been offered to the notion of a sale "below cost" on the occasion of its first appearance in court as a central issue, but then, for reasons that we shall presently consider, the notion never has been vigorously attacked in court.

A more telling blow for soft competition was struck by the Attorney General in the unreported and neglected *United States v. Swift & Co.* (1920).[37] In this suit, the Justice Department challenged the right of the five largest meat packers to branch out beyond slaughtering. Two features of their expansion especially were viewed with suspicion

---

[35] Sears, Roebuck & Co., 1 F.T.C. 163 (1918).

[36] Sears, Roebuck & Co. v. Federal Trade Commission, 258 Fed. 307, 312 (7th Cir. 1919).

[37] The facts giving rise to this case and the arguments relied upon by both sides are available elsewhere. See Federal Trade Commission, *Report on the Meat-Packing Industry* (1920), especially Part IV, "The Five Larger Packers in Produce and Grocery Foods," also Swift & Co. v. United States, 276 U.S. 311 (1928), 286 U.S. 106 (1932).

—vertical integration in the form of transport facilities owned by the meat packers and the Big Five's success in wholesaling a multitude of finished food products in addition to meat and the by-products of meat packing. (In 1920 finished food products probably accounted for between 15 and 20 per cent of the total sales of the major meat packers.[38])

The government made no effort to show injury to consumers as a consequence of the ancillary activities of the meat packers. In fact, it conceded that the presence of the defendants in the wholesale market made for lower grocery prices, though warning that "certain advantages may be enjoyed which will enable the packer to sell cheaply, which are in no sense an indication of economic efficiency from the social point of view, and which do not fall within the legal prohibition against 'unfair competition.'"[39] Rather its case rested upon the debatable premise that the vertical integration and product diversification of the meat packers threatened the existence of some wholesale grocers whose preservation was in the consumer interest. By view of the Federal Trade Commission:

Hundreds of jobbers are willing to match their skill and their judgment under free market conditions against the skill and judgment of the packers. What they fear is the manipulation of market conditions through the large buying power which comes from large control of capital and credit, and through the speculative buying which often characterizes packer dealing; they fear the packers' control of storage facilities, the superior transportation service which they have been permitted to build up for themselves, the power which comes from numerous controlled outlets and markets reached by their peddler-car system, their branch-house organization and kindred selling agencies.[40]

The government therefore petitioned the court to divest the meat packers of their transportation facilities and order them to withdraw from the distribution of over a hundred different items ranging from canned oysters to structural steel.[41] In order to escape a worse fate,[42]

---

[38] IV *Report on the Meat Packing Industry* 27–38 (1920).

[39] *Ibid.* p. 32.

[40] *Ibid.* p. 29.

[41] *Transcript of Record* 121–22 in 10 Records and Briefs, Justice Department library (1927).

the meat packers accepted a consent decree that, incorporating most of the government's recommendations, ratified their withdrawal from the wholesale grocery trade. The *Swift* case may thus be taken as the first important suit in which the antitrust agencies confused the protection of competition as a consumer safeguard with the preservation of competitors as an end in itself. The difficulty subsequently experienced by the antitrust agencies in deciding whose interests are most deserving of protection is well illustrated by two cases that reached the circuit court of appeals in the early 1920's.

In the complicated *Federal Trade Commission v. Mennen Co.* (1923)[43] the commission, apparently in the interest of hard competition, ordered the Mennen Company—a purveyor of toilet articles—to cease discriminating against fifty-three chain drugstores and buying co-operatives representing independent drugstores. Discrimination allegedly occurred because the Mennen Company refused to classify these purchasers as "wholesalers" and thus allow them the lower prices which were granted to bona fide wholesalers who purchased in no greater quantities. The defendant had been induced to adopt this price policy by the National Wholesale Druggists' Association whose members had promised in return to favor Mennen products over those of its rivals who gave wholesaler discounts to chain stores and co-operatives.[44] The commission found, however, that the Mennen policy of discrimination violated the Clayton Act by restraining competition among the company's customers and directed that it should be abandoned.[45]

The circuit court of appeals understandably refused to enforce the commission's order. Citing the report of the House Judiciary Com-

---

[42] The major meat packers feared that they would be visited with unfriendly legislation unless they acted to placate the hostility of the organized wholesale grocers whom their competition had adversely affected. In the five years before 1920 Congressional hearings were held on several bills that would have compelled the meat packers to sell off their stockyards and private car lines, stop handling a wide range of food products, and cease "engaging in any unfair or unjustly discriminatory practice." For an analysis of the consent decree accepted in 1920 and the agitation leading up to it, see G. O. Virtue, "The Meat-Packing Investigation," 34 *Q. J. Econ.* 626 (1920).

[43] 288 Fed. 774 (2d Cir.)

[44] The evidence indicated, for example, that the Mennen Company regularly checked with the National Wholesale Druggists' Association on the acceptability of customers who sought the wholesaler's discount. Mennen Company, Docket No. 606, Vol. 1, pp. 58–60 (Federal Trade Commission library).

[45] The Mennen Co., 4 F.T.C. 258 (1922).

XIII. LAW OF UNFAIR COMPETITION: 1

mittee on the Clayton bill,[46] it held that the provisions making price discrimination suspect were directed at the excessively vigorous tactics by which the discriminator sought to eliminate rivals in the *Standard Oil* and *American Tobacco* cases and were not meant to apply to a firm's "normal" classification of its customers.

Given the calculated vagueness of legislators in antitrust matters, the court's interpretation of Congressional intent in the *Mennen* case was as plausible as the commission's. The real culprits in this case were, of course, the wholesale druggists who openly "conspired" against a rival and, in some respects, more efficient form of distribution. But then the commission had no authority to use the obvious remedy of a Sherman Act action against the wholesale druggists and could only proceed by indirection. The *Mennen* case is yet another instance of the difficulty of moving from word to deed through the complexities of administrative law.

Shortly after the *Mennen* decision, the commission reversed its field and intervened on behalf of soft competition, but with no greater success. In *National Biscuit Co. v. Federal Trade Commission* (1924)[47] the company allegedly violated the Clayton Act by granting discounts to chain stores which it refused to allow to buying co-operatives composed of independent grocers who purchased in "like amounts." According to the commission, this discrimination was unfair because the cost of selling like amounts to the two types of retailers was the same. According to the defendant, the unit cost of selling to independent grocers was higher.[48] In setting aside the commission's order

---

[46] According to the report: "Section 2 of the bill is designed to prevent unfair discriminations. It is expressly designed with the view of correcting and forbidding a common and widespread unfair trade practice whereby certain great corporations and also certain smaller concerns which seek to secure a monopoly in trade and commerce by aping the methods of the great corporations, have heretofore endeavored to destroy competition and render unprofitable the business of competitors by selling their goods, wares, and merchandise at a less price in the particular communities where their rivals are engaged in business than at other places throughout the country." *Antitrust Legislation,* H.R. Rep. No. 627, 63d Cong., 2d Sess. 8 (1914).

[47] 299 Fed. 733 (2d Cir.)

[48] It must be conceded that the defendant produced persuasive evidence to support its assertion that "in the long run" a given quantity of crackers could be sold more cheaply to chain stores than to independent grocers. In fact, the company had once experimented with a policy of granting cumulative discounts to a grocers' buying club in the Chicago area. The club had broken down because its agent, who had posted a deposit guaranteeing payment of its members' bills,

directing an end to the alleged discrimination, the court held:

> It may be that the cost of selling the chain is the same as the cost of selling to the owner of but one store; but that does not sustain the charge of price discrimination, for there is no provision in the Clayton Act, or elsewhere, that the price to two different purchasers must be the same if it cost the seller as much to sell one as it does to the other.[49]

For good measure the court also questioned the commission's finding of fact, pointing out, *inter alia,* that a buying co-op was not responsible for the debts of its members as was a chain store for the orders placed by its individual branches.

It was not until *Van Camp & Sons Co. v. American Can Co.* (1929)[50] that the Supreme Court encountered the issue of "hard" versus "soft" competition and then, unhappily, in a case that showed the judicial treatment of economic issues at its worst. Van Camp petitioned for an injunction to restrain the American Can Company from granting to another packing company a 20 per cent discount on cans purchased together with the "free" use of canning machines. The defendant did not bother to justify the discrimination on any grounds. He merely asserted that the petition should be dismissed for want of equity because the Clayton Act only forbade unlawful discriminations that unduly injured competition in the discriminating firm's industry, and the plaintiff did not charge that the discrimination complained of injured competition in can making. This argument was accepted by the district court.

On appeal, Van Camp argued plausibly that a monopoly in canned goods was as repugnant to the Clayton Act as a monopoly in cans, and, consequently, that the defendant's discrimination was unlawful if it contributed to either end.[51] A puzzled circuit court thereupon requested a ruling from the Supreme Court on two questions. (1) Does the Clayton Act forbid price discrimination which tends "to substan-

---

withdrew after he had experienced difficulty in getting them to pay up on time. *Official Report of the Proceedings before the Federal Trade Commission in the Matter of FTC v. National Biscuit Company,* Docket No. 836, pp. 2193–2202 (Federal Trade Commission library). The commission's case rested solely upon the company's admission that the bookkeeping cost of selling like amounts to chain stores and buying clubs was often the same.

[49] 299 Fed. 733, 739.

[50] 278 U.S. 245.

[51] *Brief for Appellant* 20–21 in 32 Records and Briefs, Supreme Court library (1928).

tially lessen competition" in the line of commerce in which the victim is engaged? Or only price discrimination which affects competition in the discriminating firm's industry? (2) Does a firm violate the Clayton Act when, without establishing a defense allowed by the law, it practices discrimination that substantially lessens competition? Note that these questions were purely hypothetical—no evidence had been produced to show that the discrimination attacked actually affected competition in the packing industry or even competition between Van Camp and the firm which received the preferential treatment. If the Supreme Court had confined itself to ruling on the questions on which it heard argument, it would not have touched on the issue of soft versus hard competition raised by the *Mennen* and *National Biscuit* decisions. Instead, in answering the two questions before it in the affirmative, it also held:

> The effect of the discrimination is to substantially lessen competition, and its tendency is to create a monopoly, in the line of interstate commerce in which complainant and the packing company are competitively engaged.[52]

Possibly the Court meant to say that, since Van Camp's contention that the discrimination of the American Can Company substantially lessened competition in the packing industry was unchallenged, it had made out a prima facie case for an injunction restraining the practice. The cryptic ambiguity of the decision, however, together with the highly competitive character of the packing industry permitted the inference that price discrimination is unfair if it (a) is not justified by differences in accounting costs, (b) is not made in good faith to meet competition, and (c) materially injures a given customer of the discriminating firm. Whatever the intention of the Supreme Court, the *Van Camp* decision appeared to sanction the soft competition advocated by government attorneys in the *Swift* and *National Biscuit* cases.

---

[52] 278 U.S. 245, 253.

Chapter *XIV*

THE LAW OF UNFAIR
COMPETITION: 2

1. *Congress approves soft competition:*
the Robinson-Patman Act

If legal status of price discrimination was not much clarified by the
Van Camp decision,[1] Congress in the singular Robinson-Patman Act
(1936)[2] seemingly declared in favor of soft competition with a vengeance. This amendment to the Clayton Act,[3] which is probably incom-
prehensible to anyone unacquainted with the subtleties of American
lawmaking, purports to declare unlawful two types of price discrimination: (1) price differences which (a) are not justified by a difference
in cost to the seller and (b) tend substantially to lessen competition
and (2) price differences which (a) are justified by a savings in cost
to the seller and (b) do not tend substantially to lessen competition
but (c) are nevertheless unjustly discriminatory because not enough
buyers can avail themselves of the lowest price.

Moreover, under the Robinson-Patman Act, liability for wrongdoing is not confined to the seller but extends also to anyone who
"knowingly" receives the benefits of unlawful price discrimination.
Should the Federal Trade Commission find that "available purchasers
in greater quantities are so few as to render differentials on account
thereof unjustly discriminatory or promotive of monopoly in any line
of commerce," it may "fix and establish quantity limits" thereby making unlawful "differentials based on differences in quantities greater
than those so fixed and established."

In short, the Robinson-Patman Act, on its face, outlaws all bargaining as the process is understood in the business world.[4] Congress,

---

[1] Van Camp & Sons Co. v. American Can Co., 278 U.S. 245 (1929).

[2] 49 *Stat.* 1526.

[3] 38 *Stat.* 730 (1914).

[4] The full absurdity of the Robinson-Patman Act becomes apparent when
one contemplates the difficulties involved in determining the legality of price

of course, contemplated no such quixotic crusade but merely intended to soften, in some measure, the competition waged by a few large firms that had injured politically influential retailers and wholesalers. (One can make a good case that the law was aimed specifically at three companies, Sears, Roebuck, Goodyear Tire & Rubber, and Atlantic & Pacific.[5]) This object could probably have been realized had Congress limited itself to giving the Federal Trade Commission small appropriations and broad hints as to the firms they should have been used against.

The legislators, however, took the additional precaution of providing that, while the accused must bear the burden of rebutting a prima facie case showing that he gives unlawful discounts, "nothing contained herein shall prevent a seller rebutting the prima-facie case thus made by showing that his lower price or the furnishing of services or facilities to any purchaser or purchasers *was made in good faith to meet an equally low price of a competitor, or the services or facilities furnished by a competitor,*" (italics supplied). No one can know by how much Congress intended that this "good faith" clause should restrict the application of the Robinson-Patman Act. In *Standard Oil Co. v. Federal Trade Commission* (1951)[6] the Supreme Court, with three members dissenting, gave the clause a literal construction and ruled that any price discrimination was permissible provided that it was practiced in good faith to meet competition. The dissenting justices argued that a successful rebutting of the prima facie case showing unlawful discrimination should merely transfer the burden of proof from the defendant to the commission.[7]

The sections of the Robinson-Patman Act which relate to buyers

---

discrimination involving differentiated products. See F. M. Rowe, "Price Differentials and Product Differentiation: the Issues under the Robinson-Patman Act," 66 *Yale L.J.* 1 (1956).

[5] These three firms were, on several occasions, investigated by congressional committees before 1936 and are explicitly named in the report of the House Judiciary Committee on the Robinson-Patman bill as its proper targets. H.R. Rep. No. 2287, 74th Cong., 2d Sess. (1936).

[6] 340 U.S. 231. The case involved Standard's grant of quantity discounts to four jobbers of gasoline in Detroit. A determined Federal Trade Commission then sought to ban these discounts on the grounds that they were not departures from Standard's price policy forced by competition but a part of the policy itself. This argument was also rejected by the Supreme Court with four members dissenting. 355 U.S. 396 (1958).

[7] The good faith defense was further strengthened in Standard Oil Co. v. Brown, 238 F.2d 54 (5th Cir. 1956). Here the court of appeals found that the trial court had erred in charging the jury that a discriminating firm must show that the discrimination was necessary in order to meet "lawful" competition.

who "knowingly" receive unlawful discounts and empower the commission to prescribe the discounts that a firm may allow are virtually dead letters.[8] Buyers can plead that they (a) have no knowledge of what their suppliers charge other customers and (b) cannot know whether any discounts they receive are justified by a savings in cost to the supplier.[9] Likewise the fixing of quantity discounts on any significant scale is out of the question, being beyond the means of the Federal Trade Commission or, indeed, any governmental agency that the country would tolerate in peacetime. Not that the commission has shown any enthusiasm for the task of setting quantity discounts. To date it has sought to exercise the power on only one occasion.[10]

Given the commission's limited resources and the ability of businessmen to shelter behind the good faith clause, the economic consequences of the Robinson-Patman Act have been slight.[11] Nevertheless, since it is an execrable concession to small business groups and an insult to the public intelligence, we may wonder that so few protests have been made against it. The reason probably lies in the difficulty of framing a convincing defense of price discrimination.

Let us suppose that a businessman who is accused of unlawful discrimination consults an economist in the preparation of his defense. He will probably receive assurances along the following lines. The major inarticulate premise of the Robinson-Patman Act is simply wrong; most prices in this world are not equal to the seller's average

---

[8] Up to November, 1953, the commission had decided only twelve cases involving buyer discriminations under the Robinson-Patman Act. Note, "Buyers' Liability for Price Discriminations Under Robinson-Patman," 63 *Yale L.J.* 260, 261 (1953).

[9] This defense was accepted in the only discrimination case against buyers to reach the Supreme Court. Automatic Canteen Co. of America v. Federal Trade Commission, 346 U.S. 61 (1953).

[10] The order of the Federal Trade Commission related to the range of discounts that rubber manufacturers might allow in the sale of replacement tires and tubes. In the district and circuit courts the order was set aside on a technicality. Federal Trade Commission v. B. F. Goodrich Co., 242 F.2d 31 (D.C. Cir. 1957).

The commission found that the tire companies were practicing unlawful discrimination by allowing the maximum quantity discounts to firms that purchased more than $600,000 worth of tires a year; it directed that the maximum discount should relate to the carload lot of 20,000 pounds of tires. The district and circuit courts held that the findings of the commission were insufficient to justify limiting the maximum discount to the carload lot.

[11] For a more serious view of the Robinson-Patman Act by an equally unfriendly critic, see M. A. Adelman, "The Consistency of the Robinson-Patman Act," 6 *Stan. L. Rev.* 3 (1953).

cost of production plus a "fair" markup. Assuming that the seller (a) acts rationally, (b) knows his costs and markets, and (c) does not quote exceptionally low prices for the express purpose of ruining some particular competitor, then he will seek to equate the marginal cost of delivered output with marginal revenue in every separate market in which he sells. (A customer is a "market" in so far as he can be kept separate from other customers.) Consequently, the seller's average cost of serving a customer is not relevant to the price which he quotes to that customer. The buyer who receives the best price may owe his good fortune to his location in a market where demand for the seller's product is weak or elastic, or he may enjoy it because the marginal cost of "selling" him is unusually low.

The economist's analysis of price discrimination is not easily made to support a defense of the practice. The price differential that occurs when the seller exploits different demand curves in different markets is, for all practical purposes, indefensible except, perhaps, on the ground that all doubts should be resolved in favor of freedom of contract. The defendant in an action for violating the Robinson-Patman Act will prefer a more specific defense. He is not likely to dispute that *if* the unit costs of selling to two customers are equal, then they are entitled to the same price, and that if these unit costs are different, the price differential should not exceed this cost differential. Having made this concession, he could conceivably argue that his price differences merely reflect proper cost differences.

Unfortunately, the businessman's own cost data can usually be used to show that this is not so. His economic consultant may tell him what he already perceives subconsciously—that accounting data are not accurate enough to allow him to dispense with his own hunches about "true" costs;[12] that, for example, they do not show the long-run savings in advertising outlays that come from dealing with buyers who regularly place large orders. The businessman, however, who expounds the limitations of his accounting system is not likely to receive a sympathetic hearing in court.[13] He is better advised to argue that, being

---

[12] For an elaboration of the idea that the overhead and variable costs of economics textbooks have "little or nothing in common with accounting concepts," see J. P. Miller, *Unfair Competition* 362–73 (1941).

[13] On one occasion the limitations of accounting data were successfully pleaded by the defendant. Goodyear Tire & Rubber Co. v. Federal Trade Commission, 101 F.2d 620 (6th Cir. 1939), *certiorari denied* 308 U.S. 557 (1939). Goodyear was accused of discriminating in favor of Sears, Roebuck and Co. Goodyear, however, impressed upon the court the value of a large assured sale to Sears "in removing hazard and insuring stability, the avoidance of profit fluctu-

at the mercy of the market, his challenged prices are perforce made in good faith to meet the equally low prices of competitors.

2. *Tying contracts and exclusive dealing*

Our discussion of fair competition should not end without notice of tying contracts and exclusive dealer arrangements—the much maligned contractual obligations that were banned by the Clayton Act where their effect was to substantially lessen competition.[14] The exclusive dealer arrangement practically describes itself. One firm is allowed to obtain the product of another on condition that it will not deal in the rival products of third parties. Sometimes the buyer, in return for consenting to such an agreement, receives the exclusive right to buy or sell the seller's product in some designated market, *i.e.*, he gets the dealer franchise. Exclusive dealing may also take the form of a requirements contract. Here the buyer—usually a manufacturer in his own right—promises to purchase all of some commodity from the seller in return for some consideration—a lower price, maintenance on his machinery, easy credit terms, etc.

The tying contract exists in more varieties but always involves the sale or lease of a good on condition that some other good be purchased with it. Sometimes the same result can be achieved by the negative injunction that certain products shall not be used with the seller's. The contract may tie the use of a patented and unpatented article, the

---

ation inevitable in its other business, and the casting upon Sears of the risk which Goodyear normally bore of raw material price decline and credit losses," 622. These advantages were alleged by the defendant to be real and substantial "even though they may not readily be measured in terms of dollars," and dismissed by the commission as "too speculative, intangible and remote to justify a price discrimination," 625. The circuit court of appeals decided that since the commission had no acceptable formula for determining cost, it had not shown that Goodyear's low price to Sears was not "reasonably based on quantity."

The above case involved price discrimination practiced before passage of the Robinson-Patman Act. Since 1936 sellers have generally failed in their efforts to make out a cost justification for price discrimination in FTC proceedings. See H. L. Shniderman, "Cost Justification under the Robinson-Patman Act: the FTC Advisory Committee's Report," 25 *U. Cin. L. Rev.* 389, 393–95 (1956).

[14] The language of the Clayton Act refers only to exclusive dealing—agreements or understandings which bind one party not buy or deal in the products of third parties—but the act was early construed to cover tying contracts on the ground that they could be made to serve the same purpose as exclusive dealing arrangements. United Shoe Machinery Corp. v. United States, 258 U.S. 451 (1922).

use of machines and materials, or require the joint use of the seller's different products. It may also take the form of "full line forcing" whereby the distributor in order to handle a popular product of the seller must take his less popular products as well. Tying contracts and exclusive dealer arrangements early became suspect by virtue of their popularity with a number of aggressive trusts, notably the American Tobacco, United Shoe Machinery, International Harvester, and Corn Products Refining companies.[15] While this suspicion was not unfounded, their serviceability as tools for fortifying a monopoly position has probably been much exaggerated.

Tying contracts and exclusive dealer arrangements are suspect because they increase the amount of capital that a firm must command before it can successfully market a product sold subject to such restrictions. Consequently, they constitute an additional barrier to entry in both manufacturing and distribution. For example, if canning machinery available on lease is restricted to use in connection with cans obtained from the lessor, the potential rival must be able to offer both cans and canning machines before he can offer competition. In the absence of a tying contract, he could begin business offering cans alone. Again, the aspiring manufacturer of farm equipment in the world of exclusive dealership must equip himself with a dealer organization before he can function.[16]

That tying contracts and exclusive dealer arrangements pose a barrier to entry is clear enough. The barrier may be artificial in that it is mainly designed to make the life of rivals more difficult; yet it may also make possible a bona fide economy of scale in manufacture and

---

[15] The tying contracts and exclusive dealer arrangements that incurred Congressional displeasure are examined in W. H. S. Stevens, *Unfair Competition* 54–96 (1917).

[16] In the days when the International Harvester Company—formed in 1902 by the merger of five leading manufacturers of farm equipment—was struggling to retain its dominant position, it marketed five different lines of implements through rival dealers with whom it had exclusive dealing contracts. This policy served to discourage the expansion of rival manufacturers by denying them access to a majority of dealers in the country, keeping the dealers of International Harvester on their toes, and making life hard for any dealer who sought to make a living by handling the equipment of the rivals of International Harvester.

In 1918 the company accepted a consent decree that limited it to one dealer in each town and so lost the services of almost five thousand dealers, many of whom were taken over by competitors. The government's attack on exclusive dealing as a barrier to entry in the farm equipment industry is recounted in United States v. International Harvester Co., 273 U.S. 693 (1927). In this case the Supreme Court denied the government's request for additional relief.

distribution. Tying contracts and exclusive dealer arrangements are, in fact, a rudimentary form of vertical integration in marketing and can be defended with the arguments that are commonly used to justify this form of combination.

Vertical integration ordinarily evolves as a way of reducing uncertainty by "regularizing" production. Communication is improved between production engineers and the sales force, inventories can be reduced, greater quantities of labor and materials contracted for in advance, and in times of strain, strong departments of the firm can subsidize weak ones. To a more limited extent, these ends are also served by tying contracts and exclusive dealer arrangements. Indeed, when one examines the most frequently cited cases where these contracts have been challenged, restraint of trade stands out as the obvious purpose only in a few suits involving the use of patents.[17] In most of these cases, the use of tying contracts and exclusive dealing arrangements can be explained in terms of the savings in cost that they achieve —as the defendant invariably points out.

We should also note that tying contracts can be employed to achieve ends that are not closely related to either the extension of monopoly or the reduction of costs.[18] In *Federal Trade Commission v. Gratz* (1920)[19]—the first case involving a tying contract to reach the Supreme Court under the 1914 revisions of the Sherman Act[20]—the

---

[17] A classic example of the attempted use of a tying clause to extend a patent monopoly is Motion Picture Patents Co. v. Universal Film Co., 243 U.S. 502 (1917). The plaintiff had once owned the basic patents upon which the motion picture industry was founded, notably the patents on the motion picture projector and the flexible film, but they had expired leaving the plaintiff with only an improvement patent covering a device for feeding the film into the projector. The device, however, was, according to the Court, "the only one with which motion picture films can be used successfully," 508. The plaintiff therefore sought to prolong his monopoly of film distribution by providing that his films alone could be used in a film projector containing the patented film feeder. The Supreme Court, with three justices dissenting, held the maneuver to constitute an unlawful extension of the patent right and dismissed the plaintiff's contributory infringement suit against a firm that had produced films for use in the plaintiff's projectors.

[18] An excellent analysis of the different purposes served by tying contracts is given in W. S. Bowman, "Tying Arrangements and the Leverage Problem," 67 *Yale L.J.* 19 (1957).

[19] 253 U.S. 421.

[20] The original complaint against Gratz charged that his use of a tying contract was both an unfair method of competition under the Federal Trade Commission Act and a violation of Section 3 of the Clayton Act. The commissioners accepted, however, that the evidence was insufficient to show a violation of the latter statute. 258 Fed. 314, 316. Their finding that this practice constituted unfair competition was subsequently rejected by the Court.

disputed restraint was designed by the defendant to protect his inventories in a time of rapidly rising prices. The defendant, a leading distributor of the steel ties used to bale cotton, required his customers to purchase bagging along with ties; his object was to discourage regular customers and professional speculators from hoarding steel ties in anticipation of a steel shortage and price rise during World War I.[21]

Again, a tying contract may be the means by which a firm that controls the output of one product turns its monopoly to more profitable account by discriminatory pricing. Suppose that a seller is in a position to lease a patented bottle-capping machine to customers who have different ideas as regards the value of the machine, and that, as a condition of the lease, he can require that only bottle caps supplied by himself shall be used in the machine. The monopolist could choose to remain out of the bottle cap field and simply rent his machine to all customers for a fixed sum per month. He can, however, increase the profits from his patent monopoly by (a) establishing a fixed rental on his machines, (b) requiring customers to buy bottle caps from him, and (c) pricing patented machines and bottle caps so as to discriminate against customers who place a higher value on his equipment. That is, such customers will be made to pay a larger sum for use of the machine and bottle caps taken together than if the seller had simply established a fixed rental on all machines and sold no bottle caps.

If the patented machine is worth more to customers who use it intensively, the monopolist will set a low rental on his machines and exact a high price for bottle caps with no discounts given for quantity purchases. If the patented machine is worth more to customers who use it less intensively, he will set a high rental on his machines and grant quantity discounts on bottle caps sold. In each case, the sale of bottle caps is the means of charging different "real" rentals on bottle-capping equipment. The tie-in requirement does not enable the seller to use his patent monopoly on machines to increase his profit by driving suppliers of bottle caps out of business; indeed the rational monopolist will buy bottle caps from anyone who can make them cheaper than himself for resale to his customers. Rather the tie-in requirement merely allows him to exploit more profitably his monopoly of the patented machine.

---

[21] "You must be very careful and not let people like Goyer pick you up on ties without a proportionate quantity of bagging. As to bagging, do not sell over one million yards without further instructions from us, as there is a strong probability of an early advance in both bagging and ties." Gratz to his Vicksburg agent on June 24, 1916. *Transcript of Record* 262, 36 Records and Briefs in the Justice Department library (1919).

Why should a firm go to the trouble of dealing in two commodities to exploit his monopoly of one? Why will it not simply sell the monopolized product to different customers at different prices? The advantages (and limitations) of a tying arrangement as a method of price discrimination are suggested by the circumstances of the noted *button-fastener* case[22] of patent lore.

Here the plaintiff sold a patented machine for stapling buttons to high button shoes—an operation formerly done by hand at higher cost. Some customers made only a few shoes per machine, while others made a great many. Assuming that the machine saved the user a fixed sum on each button stapled, it was worth more to the more intensive users than to the less intensive users. If the plaintiff sold his machines at different prices, he risked misjudging his customers' willingness to pay. Also, he might find that favored customers were reselling machines to other parties from whom he expected to exact higher prices. The plaintiff sought to circumvent these obstacles by selling his machines cheap —allegedly at "actual cost"—subject to the restriction that only his staples should be used in them. By charging a higher than competitive price on staples he stood to collect different sums in return for the use of identical machines. The plaintiff's appearance in court, however, indicates that not all customers were willing to abide by the tying agreement and purchase his high-priced staples when others were available.[23]

Discriminatory pricing is, of course, a suspect practice in the eyes of judges and civil servants. A priori it can be shown to increase or decrease the output of a monopolized product depending upon the nature of the seller's different markets, and one is tempted to say that price discrimination should be encouraged when it increases output and discouraged when it does not. Unfortunately, in actual business situations, it is virtually impossible to know enough about the seller's markets to say how price discrimination affects his output.[24]

A further possibility is that a tying arrangement serves a wholly trivial purpose. It may merely disguise the price of a commodity for promotional purposes as, for example, when the local sporting-goods

---

[22] Heaton-Peninsular Button-Fastener Co. v. Eureka Specialty Co., 65 Fed. 619 (C.C.W.D. Mich. 1895).

[23] The above analysis of the button-fastener case is taken, with minor modifications, from Bowman, "Tying Arrangements," note 18, 23–24.

[24] On the difficulty of discerning the effect of price discrimination on output even in the simplest market situation, see Joan Robinson, *The Economics of Imperfect Competition* 179–202 (1933).

shop offers a thousand cartridges at half price with every rifle purchased.

Finally, a firm may have more than one end in view when it elects to tie the sale of one product to that of another—as in *Times-Picayune Publishing Co. v. United States* (1953).[25] One morning newspaper and two evening newspapers were published daily in New Orleans. The morning paper and one of the evening papers were owned by the Times-Picayune Publishing Company which required certain advertisers to buy space in both papers at a combination rate. Since the same facilities were used to publish the company's two papers, the tying arrangement in some measure reduced the cost of publication by standardizing advertising displays and making the volume of advertising more predictable. (From the publication standpoint, the evening paper was only a late edition of the morning paper.) The use of tied ads also enabled the publisher to discriminate among his customers. Buyers who had no use for evening advertising had to pay for it in order to obtain a monopolized product—morning advertising, and the case arose because the Justice Department felt that Times-Picayune was using a monopoly of morning advertising to strengthen its afternoon paper at the expense of its only rival—indeed the defendant was charged with operating his evening paper at a loss. Only an exhaustive analysis of newspaper publishing in New Orleans, a project beyond the scope of this book, would reveal the "main" object of the tying arrangement in this case.[26]

3. *Legal status of tying contracts and exclusive dealing*

Although tying contracts and exclusive dealer arrangements generally serve purposes other than the extension of monopoly, the drift of case

---

[25] 105 F. Supp. 670 (E.D. La. 1952), *reversed* 345 U.S. 594 (1953).

[26] The district court's ruling in the *Times-Picayune* case that the defendant was using its monopoly of morning advertising to strengthen the position of its afternoon paper carefully examined the evidence and was closely reasoned. It did not, however, consider how far the requirement that advertisers purchase space in both papers was only a device for exploiting its monopoly of morning advertising. (This facet of the case was important because in many cities publishers demand that advertisements be run in both morning and evening newspapers even though they have a complete local monopoly.)

The majority opinion in the Supreme Court that reversed the lower court's ruling revealed no grasp of economics and not much attention to the trial proceedings. Justice Clark, speaking for the Court, was mainly concerned lest the Justice Department interfere with "freedom of the press" by depriving a newspaper of one source of advertising revenue.

law has still been against them over the years. Tying contracts have been made virtual per se violations of the antitrust laws on the assumption that they serve "hardly any purpose beyond the suppression of competition."[27] In the view of the Supreme Court, the presumption that a tying contract unlawfully restrains trade is so strong that, when the volume of business covered by such a contract is "substantial," its illegality is automatically established; that is, the antitrust agencies need not show that anyone—customer, consumer, or rival—is actually injured by the practice.[28] On one occasion the Supreme Court took the extreme position that a tying contract restricting the use of a patented machine was against public policy even though it was not shown to have violated the antitrust laws.[29]

The Supreme Court has expressly distinguished the type of exclusive dealing popularly known as requirements contracts from tying contracts generally and recognized their possible virtues. In the *Standard Stations* case (1949)[30] it could say:

In the case of the buyer, they may assure supply, afford pro-

---

[27] Standard Oil Co. of California v. United States, 337 U.S. 293, 305 (1949).

[28] International Salt Co. v. United States, 332 U.S. 392 (1947); Northern Pacific R.R. v. United States, 356 U.S. 1 (1958). It is a measure of the Court's suspicion of the tying contract in the *salt* case that the agreement there condemned does not really deserve this name. The company leased certain salt-processing machines to industrial customers on condition that they use only its salt in the machines; but the leases provided that the lessee could use other people's salt in the machines provided that it (a) met specified standards and (b) could be obtained at a price lower than the International Salt Company was prepared to quote. This method of leasing equipment was plausibly explained on the ground that the successful functioning of the machines, which the lessor undertook to repair and service, required salt of uniform quality. The Court, however, was not impressed: "The appellant had at all times a priority on the business at equal prices. A competitor would have to undercut appellant's price to have any hope of capturing the market, while the appellant could hold that market by merely meeting competition," 397. Since testimony, was not taken in this case, the court record does not reveal whether the condemned tying clause was mainly intended to cut the cost of maintaining leased equipment or frustrate the sales efforts of other salt processors. The protection afforded to the lessor was so weak that it is unlikely to have greatly promoted either end, so that consequences of the decision for the marketing of industrial salt were most likely negligible.

[29] Morton Salt Co. v. Suppiger Co., 314 U.S. 488 (1942). Morton leased a patented machine for depositing salt tablets in food being readied for canning on condition that only its salt be used. The Court refused to allow Morton to collect damages from the defendant who had sold salt to Morton's lessees knowing that it would be used in violation of their contracts.

[30] Standard Oil Co. of California v. United States, 337 U.S. 293.

tection against rises in price, enable long-term planning on the basis of known costs, and obviate the expense and risk of storage in the quantity necessary for a commodity having a fluctuating demand. From the seller's point of view, requirements contracts may make possible the substantial reduction of selling expenses, give protection against price fluctuations, and—of particular advantage to a newcomer to the field to whom it is important to know what capital expenditures are justified—offer the possibility of a predictable market.[31]

The Supreme Court, however, felt that the administrative complications that would ensue if the antitrust agencies were required to show injury to competition whenever a requirements contract was challenged were too great; hence, in this case it ruled that a violation of the Clayton Act is established by "proof that competition has been foreclosed in a substantial share of the line of commerce affected."[32] In short, the Court seems to argue that a tying contract violates the law because it probably was designed to suppress competition, whereas exclusive dealing—at least in the form of a requirements contract— violates the law because the administrative machinery of the State is unable to distinguish between good and bad methods of exclusive dealing.

4. *Resale price maintenance*

It would also be inappropriate to conclude our survey of the law of unfair competition without some mention of resale price maintenance —a business arrangement which, rightly or wrongly, many businessmen considered to be the essence of "fair trade." The history of resale price maintenance—that is, the control exercised by a manufacturer over the price at which his product sells after leaving his hands—is a fascinating study in the interaction of law, technology, and the profit motive.[33] In the days when trade-marks enjoyed scant legal protection, such control was seldom worth bothering about, so that, at first, resale price maintenance was attempted only on copyrighted and patented articles

---

[31] *Ibid.* 306–07.

[32] *Ibid.* 314.

[33] The development of resale price maintenance can be traced in C. T. Murchison, *Resale Price Maintenance* (1919); E. A. R. Seligman and R. A. Love, *Price Cutting and Price Maintenance* (1932); and E. T. Grether, *Price Control under Fair Trade Legislation* (1939).

and secret preparations—products which could not easily be duplicated in the consumer's eyes. Resale price maintenance seems to have been originally pressed by manufacturers of some protected products who felt that the haphazard pricing of their wares by distributors reflected upon their own reputations for fair dealing.[34] Later, as the protection of trade-marks improved and mass advertising media developed, other manufacturers concluded that advertising paid and would be rendered more effective if the product could be promoted at a uniform price and widely distributed. Concomitantly, certain distributors who dealt in the wares of different manufacturers perceived that custom could be attracted by offering highly advertised products for sale at less than the manufacturer's recommended price, and so was born the "loss leader."

Once the courts, prodded by legislation, conceded that a manufacturer's trade-mark should not be infringed, it was a short step to granting that, in some circumstances, any goodwill inherent in a uniform resale price might also be entitled to protection. How much protection the manufacturer's resale price deserved was another problem and one that has never been clearly resolved. The manufacturer's right to negotiate a contract stipulating resale price was at first conceded as a proper exercise of the contractual privilege,[35] but it was later withdrawn on the ground that it violated the Sherman Act by restraining competition among the manufacturer's distributors.[36] Nevertheless, the manufacturer's right to enforce his resale price by withholding supplies from price cutters[37] was often upheld by the courts, although, on balance, the drift of federal case law before 1937 was in the direction of discouraging resale price maintenance.

If the original pressure for resale price maintenance came from manufacturers who viewed it as a commercial asset, the battle was soon taken up by jobbers and retailers who did not wish to be undersold by their more enterprising rivals. When the Great Depression drove thou-

---

[34] Thus, in Britain resale price maintenance seems to have been pioneered by the better publishers led by Macmillan who felt that the haggling between booksellers and customers reflected upon reputable authors and publishers because it encouraged absurdly high nominal book prices. Frederic Macmillan, *The Net Book Agreement and the Book War: 1906–1908*, 2 (1924).

[35] A resale price maintenance contract governing the sale of a patent medicine ("Wistar's Balsam of Wild Cherry") was upheld by the Supreme Court as early as Fowle v. Park, 131 U.S. 88 (1889).

[36] Dr. Miles Medical Co. v. Park & Sons Co., 220 U.S. 373 (1911).

[37] See, for example, Great Atlantic & Pacific Tea Co. v. Cream of Wheat Co., 227 Fed. 46 (2d Cir. 1915); or United States v. Colgate & Co., 250 U.S. 300 (1919).

sands of small distributors to the edge of failure and beyond, the demand for a dampening of price competition reached irresistible proportions, and state after state passed a "fair trade" law which allows the manufacturer to compel all who deal in his product to observe his minimum resale price. The novelty of this legislation lay in the provision that the manufacturer could bind distributors to observe his suggested retail price by simply giving them notice of it, *i.e.*, the distributor's signature on a contract was unnecessary.[38]

Given the constitutional limitations on the power of the several states to regulate interstate commerce, the scope of state fair trade laws was most uncertain, but resale price maintenance was generally thought to have received federal approval in the Miller-Tydings Act (1937).[39] Most authorities accepted that, by this act, the manufacturer of a distinctive product sold in "free and open competition"[40]—whatever this might be—was permitted to enforce resale price maintenance by notice in all states which had enacted fair trade laws; yet in 1951 the Supreme Court ruled that Congress had meant to legalize resale price maintenance only to the extent that it was secured by a contract,[41] so that a retailer who could obtain a supply of the manufacturer's product without committing himself to respect the stipulated resale price could sell below it with impunity. A few months later, Congress made its policy perfectly clear by the McGuire Act.[42] This law explicitly provides that when state legislation authorizes resale price maintenance by notice, it may be used by any manufacturer whose business takes him into the state.

Nevertheless, the enthusiasm of Congress for this form of price control was distinctly qualified. The McGuire Act did not modify the legal rule that manufacturers may not join with one another or cus-

---

[38] Forty-six states have now enacted fair trade laws. In sixteen states, the provision making resale price maintenance binding on non-signers has been held to violate the state constitution. 1958 *CCH Trade Reg. Rep.* ¶3003.

[39] 50 *Stat.* 693.

[40] This limitation on resale price maintenance is of slight consequence and has figured in only one case. In Eastman Kodak Co. v. Federal Trade Commission, 158 F.2d 592 (2d Cir. 1946), the circuit court of appeals upheld a commission order directing Eastman to refrain from enforcing resale price maintenance on certain types of color film for which there were no close substitutes; the court accepted that the film was not sold in free and open competition. The commission subsequently rescinded part of its order when another firm began marketing color film. S. C. Oppenheim, *Cases on Federal Anti-trust Laws* 430–31 (1948).

[41] Schwegmann Brothers v. Calvert Distillers Corp., 341 U.S. 384 (1951).

[42] 66 *Stat.* 631 (1952).

tomers to detect and punish price chiselers.[43] (That there is some collective enforcement of resale price maintenance "in practice" is another matter.) So long as the burden of enforcement falls mainly upon the individual producer, resale price maintenance can profitably be applied only to the small fraction of the national income that consists of highly advertised products for which there is no well-organized secondhand market. In practice some manufacturers stipulate a resale price merely to humor their distributors and make no serious effort to enforce it.[44] When a manufacturer really wishes to control the pricing of his product by retailers, he will rely upon a written contract, an agency agreement, or the denial of further supplies to un-co-operative customers.

That resale price maintenance should not be employed to cloak price fixing by cartels or preserve inefficient distributors is generally acknowledged.[45] Its use to protect the prestige value of a product or the manufacturer's reputation for fairness poses a more difficult problem. The answer is dictated mainly by how one views the economic function of advertising. Most economists regard most sales promotion as an effort to exploit the consumer's ignorance and gullibility by filling him with misgivings about his social acceptability; hence, they see resale price maintenance as an unqualifiedly bad thing. A minority group in the profession defends advertising as an important means by which a progressive economy discovers and creates new wants and thus sympathizes with the manufacturer's efforts to preserve the fruits of advertising.[46] No doubt both views contain a measure of truth. Nevertheless,

---

[43] The Supreme Court found that collective resale price maintenance violated the Sherman Act in United States v. A. Schrader's Son, Inc., 252 U.S. 85 (1920), and the Federal Trade Commission Act in Federal Trade Commission v. Beech-Nut Packing Co., 257 U.S. 441 (1922).

[44] Sometimes only the large and conspicuous retailers can be made to observe resale price maintenance. On occasion the major New York department stores have attacked the practice because manufacturers of fair-traded products cannot— or will not—police their smaller retail outlets. See E. R. Corey, "Fair Trade Pricing: A Reappraisal," 30 *Harv. Bus. Rev.* 4–7 (September, 1952).

[45] The British experience confirms that when collective enforcement is allowed, resale price maintenance serves these purposes. For a view which makes collective resale price maintenance partly responsible for the "excessive" number of retail shops in Britain, see Margaret Hall, *Distributive Trading* 142–70 (1949). Its operation is described in detail in B. S. Yamey, *The Economics of Resale Price Maintenance* (1954), and Monopolies and Restrictive Practices Commission, *Collective Discrimination,* Cmd. No. 9504 (1955).

[46] The connection between advertising and resale price maintenance is by no means as direct and unsubtle as the above remarks suggest. Generally, only

the legal protection now accorded to resale price maintenance in the United States is hardly unreasonable, though it may be thought to err on the side of indulgence. The author would prefer to see the Mc-Guire Act repealed, the courts directed to refrain from enforcing resale price maintenance contracts, and the manufacturer given free rein to exercise as much control over resale price as he could obtain by threats, boycotts, and cajolery. A revision of the law in this direction would have the merit of withdrawing the patronage of the State from resale price maintenance while, at the same time, it would relieve the antitrust agencies of a difficult enforcement problem that is not worth solving.

5. *A perspective on unfair competition*

Since its common-law beginnings, the term "unfair competition" has acquired at least three distinct meanings. It now denotes (a) business tactics designed to eliminate or intimidate a rival, (b) morally suspect trade practices that may or may not injure the public as consumers, and (c) the means by which large firms profitably exploit economies of scale at the expense of small firms. Thus, a charge of unfair competition can be brandished by the antitrust agencies to restrain competition, foster competition, or achieve ends unrelated to the molding of market structures. In a number of cases where the fairness of the defendant's conduct was the main issue, the antitrust agencies have intervened on the behalf of soft competition.[47] Their vigilance has also been mainly responsible for the virtual disappearance of the aggressive price cutting by which large firms formerly dispatched and disciplined

---

advertised products are sold subject to resale price maintenance, but as one authority points out, resale price maintenance can also serve as a substitute for very heavy advertising outlays. "Price maintenance (if it is not practised by all competitors) may serve as a convenient inducement to some distributors to handle the brands of firms which do not command the resources necessary for heavy advertising." Yamey, *The Economics of Resale Price Maintenance* 33.

[47] Two notable examples of this bias are Federal Trade Commission v. Morton Salt Co., 334 U.S. 37 (1948) and Corn Products Refining Co. v. Federal Trade Commission, 324 U.S. 726 (1945). In both cases the Supreme Court sustained the commission in its wrongheaded efforts to interfere in buyer and seller bargaining in two highly competitive industries on behalf of high-cost small buyers. In the *Morton* case the company was held to have discriminated unlawfully by confining its lowest price to the five chain stores that bought more than 50,000 cases of salt a year. In the *Corn Products* case, the defendant offended by giving special treatment to the candy manufacturer who was his largest single customer for glucose.

smaller rivals.[48] Happily, the good sense of the courts has so far frustrated the more ambitious of their misguided efforts to protect competitors from the consequences of competition.

---

[48] Examples of sales at prices below short-run marginal cost for the obvious purpose of eliminating rivals are becoming increasingly difficult to uncover. The last instance of this practice that received widespread notoriety was E. B. Muller & Co. v. Federal Trade Commission, 142 F.2d 511 (6th Cir. 1944). Here the court found that the country's largest manufacturer of granulated chicory—a substance often added to coffee in the more backward areas of the South—had gone to unreasonable lengths to dispose of the only other producer of granulated chicory in the country. *Inter alia,* Muller was held to have violated the Federal Trade Commission and Robinson-Patman acts by selling below cost in his rival's home market. He had also circulated false rumors about his rival's product, made false claims for his own product, and defrauded the railroads in order to ship more cheaply into the rival's territory.

Chapter XV

THE LAW OF MERGERS

1. *The decline of common-law indifference*

The elimination of competition by mergers untainted by "predatory" or "unfair" business practices posed a difficult problem for courts in the early years of the Sherman Act. It could be approached neither by reference to common-law precedents nor by the reasonableness test that sufficed to justify the dissolution of the oil and tobacco trusts. In two nineteenth-century cases involving the whisky and sugar trusts, the courts implied that mergers freely negotiated by competent parties were not unlawful because they eliminated competition. The issue of competition, however, was central in neither case, the Justice Department being rebuffed on technicalities.

In *United States v. Greenhut* (1892)[1] a typing error caused an indictment of the officers of the whisky trust to be quashed because it failed to aver that the defendants in monopolizing the "manufacture and sale of distilled spirits" also unlawfully restrained interstate commerce.[2] In *United States v. E. C. Knight Co.* (1895)[3] the Attorney Gen-

---

[1] 50 Fed. 469 (D.Mass.)

[2] On May 19, 1892, three days after the opinion was delivered, the federal attorney in charge of the prosecution, Frank Allen, wrote to the Attorney General: "By an omission of the typewriter in the last line the indictment was invalidated, otherwise, the Judge has informed me, that he should have sustained it. The amount of work which we have to do in this office, with the really insufficient clerical force renders us at times liable to some slip of this kind, which I am very glad to say was only a slip and not the result of carelessness in the preparation of the indictment. A new indictment, containing (4) counts, has been carefully prepared and I have no doubt that it will pass muster." Correspondence of the Attorney General concerning *United States v. Greenhut,* National Archives.

The case, however, was dropped when federal courts in Ohio and New York refused to permit the detention of several defendants pending their removal to Massachusetts for trial. *In re* Corning, 51 Fed. 205 (N.D. Ohio); *In re* Terrell 51 Fed. 213 (C.C.S.D.N.Y.); *In re* Greene, 52 Fed. 104 (C.C.S.D.Ohio).

[3] 156 U.S. 1.

eral sought to stop the American Sugar Refining Company which already controlled two-thirds of the sugar-refining capacity of the country from acquiring four more companies that would have given it nearly complete control of the industry. But the majority of the Supreme Court, while conceding that the challenged merger would produce monopoly in manufacturing, invoked the hoary nineteenth-century rule that "manufacturing is not commerce." Since the sugar trust's monopoly of manufacturing only indirectly affected interstate commerce, the federal government was without jurisdiction; hence, the lower court was upheld in its refusal to block the merger.

These false starts notwithstanding, the principle that freedom of contract does not extend to the suppression of competition was established a few years later in *Northern Securities Co. v. United States* (1904).[4] The circumstances which provoked this suit are curiously absent in the reported decision, though they are set forth at length in the printed record.[5] A majority of the Supreme Court chose to treat the suit as involving the government's effort to stop J. P. Morgan and James Hill from employing a New Jersey holding company—the Northern Securities Company—to ensure working control over the Northern Pacific and Great Northern railroads. In fact, the case arose out of the contest between the Morgan-Hill interest and its archrival, Joseph Harriman. The two northern railroads which figured in the case were controlled by Morgan and Hill and had their eastern terminals at Duluth and St. Paul; the Union Pacific Railroad to the south was controlled by Harriman and reached only as far east as Omaha and Kansas City. The object of their rivalry was the Chicago, Burlington & Quincy Railroad which connected with both systems and had an entry into Chicago.

At first, victory apparently went to the Morgan-Hill interest when, through the Northern Pacific, it succeeded in gaining control of the Burlington; but in a memorable Wall Street battle, Harriman countered by surreptitiously bidding for control of the Northern Pacific itself. The plot discovered at the eleventh hour, Morgan countered by staggering stock purchases of his own. In the resulting scramble for shares, the price of Northern Pacific common rose in four days from

---

[4] 193 U.S. 197.

The case is discussed at length in B. H. Meyer, *A History of the Northern Securities Case* (1906).

[5] See, for example, *Oral Argument of the Attorney General* 20–21 in 10 Records and Briefs, Justice Department library (1903).

$144 to $1,000,[6] and bearish speculators stretched themselves to the point of promising delivery of more shares than they could possibly have secured.

When the battle ended, Harriman controlled a majority of the 1,550,000 shares of common and preferred stock taken together, while the Morgan-Hill interest was still in a position to vote 410,000 of the 800,000 shares of common stock outstanding.[7] Both classes of stock carried voting rights, but unfortunately for Harriman, a neglected provision in the charter of the Northern Pacific permitted its directors to retire the preferred stock on any first of January prior to 1917.

The elder Morgan, however, was never one to antagonize a rival when profitable co-operation was possible. Hence, before the legal complexities of the speculators' plight could be explored, the contending parties agreed to compose their differences by vesting their holdings of Northern Pacific stock in a New Jersey holding company. The Morgan-Hill interest also elected to place its holdings of Great Northern stock with the new company which it, of course, controlled. By this arrangement the Morgan-Hill interest both strengthened its hold on the Great Northern, Northern Pacific, and Burlington railroads and established a community of interest with Harriman's Union Pacific.

The real objections to the compromise devised by the railroad barons were two. First and foremost, it would have given two railroad empires an incentive to co-operate in the routing of traffic out of Chicago; second, it would have reduced the likelihood that the Great Northern and Northern Pacific railroads might again be operated as separate enterprises after Morgan and Hill had passed from the scene. The Supreme Court, however, ignored the rivalry between Harriman and the Morgan-Hill interest and chose to treat the two northern railroads of the latter as independent and competing lines. The New Jersey holding company was viewed as a device for restraining competition and ordered to disgorge its holdings of Northern Pacific and Great Northern stock.

In a dissent which cogently exposed the errors of the majority opinion, Justice Holmes was moved to reflect that great cases, like hard cases, make bad law. Nevertheless, in this instance, a poorly reasoned decision served a worthy end. *Northern Securities Co. v. United States* may not have compelled J. P. Morgan to compete

---

[6] F. L. Allen, *The Great Pierpont Morgan* 213 (1949).
[7] *Ibid.*, pp. 213–14.

with himself, but it may be taken to have established the all-important principle that the State need not show intent or power to exclude third parties from the market in order to set aside contracts executed for the purpose of reducing competition. Henceforth the problem became, How seriously must competition be threatened before the court will enjoin a merger or dissolve a *fait accompli?*

2. *The rise of the reasonableness test*

This question is more easily asked than answered. The difficulty of devising appropriate remedies in cases where market power has been achieved by reputable means was made clear when the Justice Department moved to dissolve the American Can Company and the Du Pont powder trust. Superficially these combinations had much in common. Each was palpably unlawful in its origins, having been formed by the rapid consolidation of a large number of rival firms executed for the undisguised purpose of eliminating competition. Neither succeeded in gaining complete control of the market; yet, when brought to trial, both combinations accounted for over one-half the outputs of their respective industries. Despite these similarities, the American Can Company emerged from the courts with its organization intact,[8] while the powder trust was broken up into three independent units.[9]

In the six years prior to July, 1907, the Du Pont Company directly or indirectly acquired sixty-four companies manufacturing explosives and so gained control of two-thirds or more of the output of every major variety of gunpowder produced in the country outside government arsenals.[10] No unseemly pressures were applied to rivals either before or after the combination was formed. Nevertheless, the circuit court consented to order dissolution on the ground that the combination merely continued in another guise and more effective manner an illegal cartel—the Gunpowder Association—which had embraced the leading producers of explosives for most of the years from 1872 to 1902.[11]

The American Can Company, formed in 1901, is perhaps the finest clinical specimen of the ambitious consolidation that flourished during the Corporate Revolution. It brought under common control "somewhere over 100" can-making plants and nearly as many firms

---

[8] 1 *Decrees and Judgments in Antitrust Cases* 535 (1916).

[9] *Ibid.*, p. 10.

[10] United States v. E. I. Du Pont de Nemours & Co., 188 Fed. 127, 145–46 (C.C.D. Del. 1911).

[11] *Ibid.* 151–52.

whose owners were persuaded to join the combination in response to generous offers and vague threats.[12] The carrot, however, seems to have been more freely brandished than the club, for while the new company made efforts to monopolize the supply of tin plate and secure patents covering the best can-making machinery, the court found that in the case of all properties acquired, "the amounts paid appear to have ranged all the way from 1½ to 25 times the sum which would have sufficed to have replaced the property sold with brand new articles of the same kind."[13] (The evidence also showed that the promoters did not even bother to appraise many of the plants that they purchased.)

The American Can Company began operations with nearly complete control of the output of cans manufactured for sale,[14] but through its inability to corner the tin-plate supply and the blunder of following a policy of high prices that made the industry attractive to new firms, its share of the market had fallen to about 50 per cent by 1913.[15] The district court accepted that, shortly after 1904, the company had despaired of achieving complete monopoly and abandoned aggression in favor of a policy of live and let live with its competitors. The industry thereupon developed the "dominant-firm" pattern of price leadership that has endured, with occasional reversions to cutthroat competition, until the present day.

The decision of the American Can Company to forswear the strenuous life of the aspiring monopolist for the comfortable existence of a respected oligopolist was commended by the court; indeed it was cited by the court as a good reason for denying the government's request for dissolution. In distinguishing this case from the earlier suits that had produced the "ultimate" remedy, the court observed:

> In most of the cases in which dissolution has been decreed, the defendants had, not long before proceedings against them were instituted, done things which evidenced their continued intent to dominate and restrain trade by the use of methods which interfered more or less seriously with the reasonable freedom of their customers or competitors. As has been shown,

---

[12] United States v. American Can Co., 230 Fed. 859, 868 (D. Md. 1916).

[13] *Ibid.* 870.

[14] The court accepted that the American Can Company when first formed "made in the neighborhood of 90 per cent of the cans manufactured for sale." Its percentage of can production was probably much lower since, as late as 1913, canners themselves made roughly one-third of the cans that they used. *Ibid.* 898–99.

[15] *Ibid.* 898.

defendant for a number of years past has done nothing of the sort.[16]

The district court's explanation of why it refused to break up the American Can Company is not wholly convincing. The Standard Oil Company at the time of its dissolution had an even longer record of good conduct than the can trust in 1916, and as we noted above, the powder trust was not found to have employed predatory tactics on any significant scale.

One explanation of the courts' failure to accord similar treatment to the can and powder trusts is that the two cases were heard before different judges. We can, however, distinguish two other considerations which may have influenced the courts in these decisions. First, the scale of efficient production was larger in powder manufacture. Prior to consolidation the industry had long supported a successful cartel, whereas can making seems to have known no such effective restraint. Thus the powder trust could plausibly be viewed as an effort to circumvent the condemnation of cartels set forth in the *Addyston Pipe* decision,[17] while the formation of the American Can Company permitted no such inference. This difference may also have led the court to conclude that ease of entry made dissolution of the can trust unnecessary.[18]

Second, the powder trust could better withstand the shock of dismemberment. Ably managed and with its stock closely held by the Du Pont family, it had had an exceptionally impressive earnings record during its short life. As the court correctly anticipated, the short-run consequences of dissolution for the employees and stockholders of the powder trust were negligible. It was by no means certain that any new firms that might be formed out of the limping American Can Company and could escape bankruptcy.[19]

---

[16] *Ibid.* 902.

[17] Addyston Pipe & Steel Co. v. United States, 175 U.S. 211 (1899).

[18] According to the court: "It does not even to-day take very much money to go into can making, and if one has industry, character, some little ability, and a fair average of luck, to stay in it. The instant defendant attempts to exert oppressively its great influence in the trade and what may be conceded to be its present domination over prices, these small shops would extend their output and many others would be opened." 230 Fed. 859, 900.

[19] The powder trust between 1903 and 1909 paid $11 million in dividends and in September, 1909, had a surplus in its treasury of "$12 or 13 million." 188 Fed. 127, 147. The can trust in 1916 was still in arrears on its cumulative preferred stock. 230 Fed. 859, 900–01.

3. *Mergers and the Clayton Act*

By the Clayton Act (1914)[20] Congress sought to give the Federal Trade Commission concurrent jurisdiction over mergers with the Justice Department. Whether Congress also intended to lower the standard of proof of possible damage to competition that the government must meet in order to block a merger is uncertain. The relevant passage of Section 7 of the law (since amended) says only:

> That no corporation engaged in commerce shall acquire directly or indirectly, the whole or any part of the stock or other share capital of another company engaged also in commerce, where the effect of such acquisition may be to substantially lessen competition between the corporation whose stock is so acquired and the corporation making the acquisition, or to restrain such commerce in any section or community, or tend to create a monopoly in any line of commerce.

While this passage could have meant much or little, not enough cases were brought by the antitrust agencies to secure clarification. Most of the cases that they did bring involved firms in sick industries, so that the courts were disposed to view sympathetically any merger that might help the acquirer or the acquired to avoid the shoals of bankruptcy. The government's lack of success with the merger provision of the Clayton Act can also be traced to the tactical blunder of requiring the courts to rule upon two thorny issues at the same time. Not only were the courts called upon to construe the ambiguous phrases of the provision itself, they were also asked to define the powers of the newly created Federal Trade Commission vis-à-vis their own equity jurisdiction. Since historically the courts have tended to regard the regulatory commission as a superfluous rival of doubtful competence, it would have been better had the early merger cases involving the Clayton Act been brought as equity proceedings by the Attorney General. They were allowed to arise, however, through the efforts of the Federal Trade Commission to establish its authority.[21]

These attempts were sharply rebuffed in *Thatcher Manufacturing*

---

[20] 38 *Stat.* 730.

[21] Probably no federal administrative tribunal has had a more hostile reception in court than the Federal Trade Commission. But then no agency began its career with a more ambiguous mandate. On these points see F. E. Cooper, *Administrative Agencies and the Courts* 360–70 (1951).

Co. v. Federal Trade Commission (1926)[22]—the first of the commission's hard cases to reach the Supreme Court. In this case the defendant corporation, a glass maker, had bought the stock of four rival firms, transferred title to their physical assets to itself, and then dissolved the acquired companies. The prize thereby secured was a virtual monopoly of the production of milk bottles in the United States fortified by exclusive licenses to use the best patented bottle-making equipment.[23] When the facts came to the attention of the commission, it sought to resurrect the expired concerns by directing Thatcher to divest itself of the assets formerly belonging to them. A divided lower court upheld the commission's order as it affected three of the four acquired companies,[24] but the Supreme Court, accepting the logic of the dissenting circuit judge, ruled that:

> The Act has no application to ownership of a competitor's property and business obtained prior to any action by the Commission, even though this was brought about through stock unlawfully held. The purpose of the Act was to prevent continued holding of stock and the peculiar evils incident thereto. If purchase of property has produced an unlawful status, a remedy is provided through the courts. . . . The Commission is without authority under such circumstances.[25]

In retrospect it would seem that a most important question was raised and left unanswered by this decision, namely the nature of the "remedy provided through the courts" to which it alluded. It is not clear whether the reference is to a suit in equity under the Clayton Act or under the Sherman Act. (The merger was so obviously for market control in this case that the Justice Department could probably have blocked it under either statute.) The *Thatcher* decision did, however, confirm that the commission was virtually powerless to act against mergers since the acquiring party could escape its jurisdiction by the simple expedient of buying the physical assets of a rival instead of the

---

[22] 272 U.S. 554.

[23] Thatcher Manufacturing Co., 6 F.T.C. 213, 240 (1923).

[24] The circuit court of appeals sanctioned the absorption of one company by Thatcher on the grounds that (a) the acquired firm's output of milk bottles was so inconsequential that the merger did not substantially lessen competition and (b) Thatcher was really interested in certain patent licenses held by the acquired firm which would aid it in breaking into the production of other types of glassware. Opinion of Judge Woolley, *Transcript* 298–99 in 11 Records and Briefs, Justice Department library (1926).

[25] 272 U.S. 554, 561.

securities of his firm.[26] The commission in an ill-considered conference ruling had earlier acknowledged the validity of this loophole.[27]

The Justice Department determinedly moved against a merger under the Clayton Act on only one occasion and then with no success.[28] In *United States v. Republic Steel Corp.* (1935)[29] it petitioned to enjoin the country's third largest steel firm from buying a controlling interest in a smaller steel company, but the district court in a rambling opinion influenced by the steel industry's sad plight in 1935 ruled, *inter alia*, that the lessening of competition inherent in the merger was not "substantial."[30] For good measure, the court also accepted that Republic sought to acquire the smaller firm in order to raise efficiency, and that since two larger firms already held 52 per cent of the country's steel-making capacity, competition might benefit from the strengthening of the third ranking company.[31] The government did not appeal. Thus, in the first thirty-six years after 1914, decisions under the Clayton Act appear to have blocked only two industrial mergers.[32]

So long as the Justice Department's efforts against mergers met with reasonable success under the Sherman Act, the fate of Section 7 of the Clayton Act excited no great interest; indeed the earnest and repeated recommendations of the Federal Trade Commission that it be revised fell on deaf ears in Congress for twenty years. The revision did not come until 1950 when Congress was moved to act by the failure of the Attorney General in *United States v. Columbia Steel Co.*

---

[26] A few years later, even the ceremonial vestige of power over mergers was stripped from the commission in Arrow-Hart & Hegeman Co. v. Federal Trade Commission, 291 U.S. 587 (1934). Here the commission, acting promptly, lodged a complaint against the defendant who had purchased the stock of a rival firm and before it could take title to its physical assets and bury the corporate corpse. The interment, however, was carried out before the complaint could be heard, and in a five-to-four decision, the Supreme Court held that the maneuver estopped the commission from ordering divestiture.

[27] F.T.C. 542 (1919).

[28] At least two other cases involving mergers in the distribution of motion pictures were begun by the Justice Department under Section 7 of the Clayton Act but never fought out. Milton Handler, "Industrial Mergers and the Anti-Trust Laws," 32 *Colum. L. Rev.* 179, 264–65 (1932).

[29] 11 F. Supp. 117 (N.D.Ohio).

[30] *Ibid.* 123.

[31] *Ibid.* 124–25.

[32] Aluminum Co. of America v. Federal Trade Commission, 284 Fed. 401 (3d Cir. 1922); Federal Trade Commission v. Western Meat Co., 272 U.S. 554 (1926).

In an early case the Attorney General relied upon both the Sherman and Clayton acts to have a merger set aside. United States v. New England Fish Exchange, 258 Fed. 732 (D.Mass. 1919).

(1948)[33] to stop a major steel company from acquiring a small Pacific Coast fabricator. (This case is considered below, see p. 224.) By the Celler Amendment,[34] Congress directed:

> That no corporation engaged in commerce shall acquire, directly or indirectly, the whole or any part of the stock or other share capital and no corporation subject to the jurisdiction of the Federal Trade Commission shall acquire the whole or any part of the assets of another corporation engaged also in commerce, where in any line of commerce in any section of the country, the effect of such acquisition may be substantially to lessen competition, or to tend to create a monopoly.

This revision of the Clayton Act overrules the *Thatcher* decision by empowering the commission to order the divestiture of physical assets. Possibly it also overrules the *Columbia Steel* decision by striking out the phrase in the 1914 law which required a showing that the effect of a merger "may be to substantially lessen competition between the corporation whose stock is so acquired and the corporation making the acquisition. . . ."[35]

The elimination of the phrase in the original act which forbade all mergers where the effect may be to restrain commerce "in any section or community" was, according to Congressional spokesmen, made "for the express purpose of avoiding the conception that Section 7 of the Clayton Act as amended is to apply to mergers and acquisitions between small local corporations which have minor significance."[36] The Federal Trade Commission had once sought to block the combination of two small coal companies in Pennsylvania that controlled a negli-

---

[33] 334 U.S. 495.

[34] 64 *Stat.* 1125.

[35] The backers of the Celler Amendment expressed themselves as dissatisfied with the Justice Department's inability to block the merger in the *Columbia Steel* case. Although this case was brought under the Sherman Act, it was lost because the Justice Department could not convince the Court that the acquirer and acquired were in substantial competition with each other. Congressional supporters of the Celler Amendment described its language as "less restrictive" than that of Section 7 of the original Clayton Act. H. R. Rep. No. 1191, 81st Cong., 1st Sess. 5–6, 11 (1949). The reasonable layman or lawyer, however, can be pardoned if he fails to see why the new phrasing is less restrictive than the old or establishes a test that would suffice to block a merger of the *Columbia Steel* type. Congressional reluctance to draft a more specific merger law is considered in Note, "Section 7 of the Clayton Act: a Legislative History," 52 *Colum. L. Rev.* 766 (1952).

[36] S. Rep. No. 1775, 81st Cong., 2d Sess. 4 (1950).

gible fraction of anthracite output; its effort was unsuccessful, but had been supported by one judge in a dissenting opinion.[37]

At present writing, the law of mergers would seem to be about as follows: The government could without great difficulty block the attempted union of two profitable oligopolists—say Ford and General Motors in the automobile industry. It could probably prevent an oligopolist from acquiring a rival if the acquisition was likely to appreciably increase his share of the market—and if the firms involved were financially "sound." Any effort to stop the merging of two small firms in a highly competitive industry—say, textile manufacturers in South Carolina—would most probably fail.

With the passing of the giant consolidations that flourished during the Corporate Revolution, the law of mergers has become increasingly difficult to apply. Even the small-scale merger that ratifies the capitulation of one competitor to another now seldom turns up in court, though it is not yet extinct.[38] Henceforth antitrust policy must deal mainly with mergers that manifest no obvious intent to restrict competition and, when viewed as isolated acts, do not even appreciably increase anybody's market power; yet since a large number of small mergers equals a big merger, many authorities argue for strict control of all mergers on the ground that it is better to crush eggs than wrestle with full-grown snakes.

This thesis is open to the objection that, after enough mergers have occurred in an industry, further consolidation will so obviously effect competition that it can be attacked under the Sherman Act. But if the object is to keep the leading firms in an industry on their respective toes, there is merit in a policy that preserves their small rivals since experienced competitors are more likely to innovate successfully than inexperienced newcomers. In any event, properly administered, a strict control of mergers can do no harm provided that a firm which is not allowed to grow by merger can expand by building new facilities. In a perfect capital market, the firm would indifferently regard "external" and "internal" growth provided that external growth conferred no monopoly power.[39] Since the "repre-

---

[37] Temple Anthracite Coal Co. v. Federal Trade Commission, 51 F.2d 656 (3d Cir. 1931).

[38] For examples of mergers involving blatant commercial intimidation see Schine Theatres v. United States, 334 U.S. 110 (1948); and United States v. Crescent Amusement Co., 323 U.S. 173 (1944).

[39] In fact, the imperfections of the capital market do affect the choice between external and internal growth. Thus immediately after World War II

sentative" merger now takes place when a big firm buys out a small firm, it is reasonable to assume that the big firm—if the merger were disallowed—could achieve comparable growth by expanding its own facilities. The hard questions are rather (a) would the large firm do so and (b) if not, would the small firm disappear anyway through failure or voluntary liquidation?

These questions were, in fact, the important economic issues in the *Columbia Steel* case[40] decided in the Supreme Court in 1948. (They were not so regarded by a majority of the Court.) The United States Steel Corporation, over the protest of the Justice Department, was permitted through its subsidiary, Columbia Steel, to acquire the largest independent fabricator serving the western market.[41] The merger was allowed by a five-to-four vote because the Court, after plowing through the statistical minutiae invariably submitted in an antitrust case, concluded that the acquirer and the acquired were not in substantial competition with each other and, hence, that their consolidation did not "unduly" restrain trade in steel pipe.[42]

What criteria should the Court have used in passing upon the legality of the *Columbia Steel* merger? The sponsors of the Celler Amendment were certainly not specific. But most economists who sympathize with the aims of the antitrust agencies would probably answer that the Court should have tried to discern the probable effect of the merger on the industry's rate of output in the near future. If the merger seemed likely to reduce output, the presumption is that it should not have been allowed. But how does one estimate the probable effect of a merger on output?

Many authorities favor the present case-by-case approach, that is, they would trust civil servants to devise and apply the criteria that

---

mergers were stimulated by the low market value of common stocks relative to company earnings, since it was often cheaper to acquire physical assets by merger than by the construction of comparable plant. J. F. Weston, *The Role of Mergers in the Growth of Large Firms* 84 (1953).

[40] United States v. Columbia Steel Co., 334 U.S. 495 (1948).

[41] The firm acquired by the United States Steel Corporation sold its products mainly in Texas, Louisiana, and the area west of the Rocky Mountains. In this market during 1946 the corporation accounted for roughly 13 per cent of the total sales of structural steel; the acquired concern was the next largest supplier with about 11 per cent of total sales. *Brief for the United States* 41 in 142 Records and Briefs, Justice Department library (1947).

[42] 334 U.S. 495, 530.

separate good and bad mergers. This approach is open to the objection that it is slow,[43] expensive, and calculated to introduce even more uncertainty into the body of antitrust law.[44] A simpler way would be to proceed on the assumption that if a market is already imperfect, any merger that reduces the number of firms that buy or sell in that market will make it more so and, hence, should not be allowed. The use of this presumption would, of course, virtually ban growth by merger in all but modest-size family firms—a result which could be achieved more cheaply and explicitly by legislation if concreteness were not so alien to the antitrust laws.

Admittedly the suppression of mergers involving large- and medium-size firms might block corporate consolidations that would increase competition by enabling two small firms to contend better with a still larger rival. It might also rule out mergers in decreasing-cost industries that simultaneously restrict competition and increase industrial efficiency. So long, however, as a firm is free to grow by building its own facilities, a tough merger policy is unlikely to do great harm. In any event, the antitrust agencies employing a case-by-case approach can be trusted to block a merger in a highly concentrated decreasing-cost industry, regardless of its probable effect on the industry's efficiency; for *if* the cost of producing automobiles could be cut by combining Ford and General Motors, government economists and lawyers would be the last people to accept the reality of this economy of scale.

The test for mergers suggested above implies, of course, that there is only one situation which justifies the approval of a merger involving firms that do not buy and sell in markets that closely approximate pure competition. The court or the Federal Trade Commission must believe that at least one of the parties will fail completely—that is,

---

[43] In the six years prior to January, 1957, the antitrust agencies, using the Celler Amendment, brought only twenty-six cases and concluded but seven. Two mergers were allowed by the courts. The Justice Department accepted three consent decrees and the Federal Trade Commission two consent orders. Ephraim Jacobs, "Consent Judgments in Merger Cases," 43 *Am. B.A.J.* 23 (January, 1957). The economics of the first twenty-eight cases begun under the Celler Amendment are examined in J. W. Markham, "Merger Policy Under the New Section 7: A Six-Year Appraisal," 43 *Va. L. Rev.* 489 (1957).

[44] The case-by-case approach is defended by a distinguished government economist in I. R. Barnes, "Markets, Competition, and Monopolistic Tendencies in Merger Cases," 40 *Marq. L. Rev.* 141 (1956). For the view that the discretion of civil servants in merger cases should be narrowly circumscribed, see G. J. Stigler, "Mergers and Preventive Antitrust Policy," 104 *U. Pa. L. Rev.* 176 (1955).

suspend production and not merely continue operations in receivership as a ward of the court—if combination is not allowed.[45] Thus the *Columbia Steel* merger should have been disallowed on the ground that no evidence was produced to show that it was needed to spare the owners and employees of the California fabricator the losses of a sheriff's sale.

While the rule that all mergers in significantly" imperfect markets are suspect unless they involve at least one firm on the edge of failure has not yet been accepted by the courts—or even urged by the antitrust agencies—the drift of case law is in the direction of a more careful screening of mergers. In part, this drift can be traced to the increasing number of suits involving mergers made possible by the new-found wealth of the antitrust agencies; in part it is another aspect of the courts' accommodation to the idea of administrative discretion in the United States. It is probable that the Celler Amendment will ultimately prove serviceable for blocking mergers that could not be enjoined under the Sherman Act as previously interpreted.[46] As yet no case raising the issue has reached the Supreme Court.

4. *Vertical and conglomerate mergers*

Some authorities argue that vertical and conglomerate mergers present a special problem in antitrust policy because they may serve to soften competition even though they do not statistically reduce the number of competitors in any given industry.[47] The argument most commonly advanced against allowing such mergers to go unsupervised is that by increasing the size of firms, they make possible the "leverage" which permits large firms to secure discounts from suppliers not open to

---

[45] This test was implied by Justice Stone in a dissenting opinion as early as International Shoe Co. v. Federal Trade Commission, 280 U.S. 291 (1930). The Court, over the objection of the Federal Trade Commission, allowed a flourishing shoe firm to acquire a smaller shoe firm in financial straits. Justice Stone dissented on the ground that the acquired concern "plainly had large value as a going concern, there was no evidence that it would have been worth more or as much as if dismantled, and there was evidence that the depression in the shoe trade in 1920–21 was then a passing phase of the business," 306.

[46] The Federal Trade Commission has held that in screening mergers under the Celler Amendment it is entitled to a lower standard of proof of injury to competition than the courts have used in Sherman Act cases. Pillsbury Mills, Inc., 50 F.T.C. 554, 566–67 (1953).

[47] Notably C. D. Edwards, *Big Business and the Policy of Competition* 123–24 (1956).

smaller rivals. The fallacy implicit in this contention we noted in Chapter IV.

Nevertheless, there are two good reasons for subjecting vertical and conglomerate mergers to federal scrutiny.[48] First, they *may* contain an element of common garden variety monopoly; for example, they may enable the acquiring concern to cut a rival off from important raw materials or customers—hence the objection to allowing Du Pont a voice in the management of General Motors.[49] Second, by increasing the assets of a single management, such combinations make it easier for firms to acquire and protect market positions where the scale of efficient production makes difficult the entry of new firms; that is, the increase in assets enhances the power of the firm to intimidate potential rivals by temporarily marketing some portion of its output at a price below short-run marginal cost. Sales at prices below short-run marginal cost are, of course, of no avail if entry is so easy that potential competitors refuse to be disciplined—they will merely bankrupt the firm that attempts them.

Vertical and conglomerate mergers by concentrating the control of corporate wealth in fewer hands may also increase the opportunities for the abuses of wealth inspired by malice, anger, and ostentatious display—that is, abuses which are not motivated by disinterested

---

[48] While the courts have not yet had to contend with conglomerate mergers, vertical integration has been encountered on many occasions. The courts have sometimes seemed to condemn vertical integration for the wrong reasons. On these occasions, however, the judicial speculation on the economic significance of vertical integration has generally been unnecessary. The courts were really condemning suspect trade practices, use of corporate size to intimidate smaller rivals, or a firm's effort to thwart rate regulation by padding the costs of its regulated subsidiaries in order to secure a higher rate base. On this matter see Robert Bork, "Vertical Integration and the Sherman Act: The Legal History of an Economic Misconception," 22 *U. Chi. L. Rev.* 157 (1954).

[49] United States v. E. I. Du Pont de Nemours & Co., 353 U.S. 586 (1957) requires Du Pont to dispose of its 23 per cent stock interest in General Motors. The Supreme Court reasoned that the proportion of stock gave Du Pont considerable power to influence General Motors policy, and that this power has been used to favor Du Pont in the placing of orders for chemical products to the substantial injury of Du Pont competitors. The economics of the *Du Pont* decision would seem to be unexceptionable. (If Du Pont did not use a 23 per cent stock interest in General Motors to encourage the purchase of Du Pont products, the most plausible inference is that non-interference was inspired by the fear of an antitrust suit.)

The law of the Du Pont decision is more debatable since it entails the use of the merger provision of the Clayton Act to set aside a merger consummated thirty-eight years before.

malevolence. To the extent that corporate combination serves this purpose, it is open to the same objections directed against great inequalities in the distribution of personal wealth and income. The merits of the case for equalizing power by equalizing wealth and income, however, is a subject too vast for tangential treatment in a book on monopoly.

Chapter *XVI*

THE LAW OF GOOD TRUSTS

1. *Market power in the large firm*

In the first forty years of the antitrust laws, the courts were not called upon to explore the issues posed by the existence of market power that was unequivocally the product of "natural" growth, *i.e.*, market power which had come into being unattended by wholesale mergers or the unethical elimination of rivals. Nor did the courts receive an important case involving parallel action among competitors untainted by overt conspiracy. Many authorities contend that market power in the large firm is scarcely ever the product of natural growth. The truth of this assertion is certainly debatable, but regardless of its merits, it is irrelevant to the modern problem of trust busting. When market power has long endured, its distant origins are a matter of antiquarian interest only, and property rights in "unnatural" market power like property rights in stolen goods are strengthened by the passing of time. Rather when the courts are requested to reduce market power in the large firm, the material questions are:

1. What will happen to the efficiency of the firm and its industry if trust busting is decreed?
2. How will trust busting affect the fortunes of the firm's stockholders and employees?
3. How much loss of efficiency should be risked in order to promote competition?
4. How much damage may be inflicted upon private parties to advance this end?

2. *"Natural" growth monopoly: the first shoe machinery case*

The legal status of natural growth monopoly was first explored in a case involving the United Shoe Machinery Company of New Jersey— an eminently successful concern that has since become a favorite target of the Antitrust Division. The company was formed in 1899 through a merger of seven manufacturers of shoemaking equipment.[1] This combination together with subsequent acquisitions gave the new firm nearly complete control of the shoe machinery trade in the country, so that, according to one estimate, the United Shoe Machinery Company in March, 1911, supplied all but 985 of the 28,657 shoe machines leased by shoe manufacturers.[2]

In December, 1911, the government brought suit seeking dissolution of the company and certain injunctive relief as well. Stripped of technicalities, the government's case rested mainly on three charges. (1) The company was formed for the express purpose of dominating the market. (2) The defendant had, on several occasions, sought to drive the few remaining producers of shoemaking equipment from the field by patent infringement suits and sales below cost. (3) The leases granted by the defendant covering the use of its equipment were designed to make it unprofitable for shoemakers to rent or buy equipment from any other firm, for they provided that the United machines could not be used in connection with those obtained from any rival manufacturer. Each of these charges was supported by evidence that would have sufficed to convince most impartial observers of their truth.

The defense, however, was prepared with a plausible rebuttal. It argued that before combination the key shoemaking machines were patented by separate companies; that these patented machines were complementary rather than competing products; and that the formation of the combination was designed to (a) achieve the economies of vertical integration and (b) remove the serious danger of costly patent litigation that hung over the industry. The use of predatory or unfair competitive tactics was, of course, stoutly denied, the defense averring that the castigated tying clauses were necessary to ensure that leased equipment was properly employed and that, in fact, the practice of leasing rather than selling machines antedated the formation of the United Shoe Machinery Company.

The trial court was thus required to choose between two copiously documented explanations of how the defendant had come into control of the shoe machinery industry. That the court should have decided against dissolution and divestiture is understandable, nor is it surprising that the court saw the evolution of a company that manufactured a complete line of shoe machinery as natural growth.[3] The

---

[1] United States v. United Shoe Machinery Co., 247 U.S. 32, 39 (1918).

[2] Eliot Jones, *The Trust Problem in the United States* 166 (1922).

[3] United States v. United Shoe Machinery Co., 222 Fed. 349 (D.Mass. 1915).

puzzling aspect of the case is that the trial court so swallowed the explanations of the defendant that it refused to attach any weight whatsoever to direct evidence of "intent to monopolize." The Supreme Court, speaking through Justice McKenna, upheld the dismissal of the suit with the remark:

> The testimony was conflicting, it is true, and different judgments might be formed upon it, but from an examination of the record we cannot pronounce that of the trial court to be wrong. Indeed, it seems to us to be supported by the better reason.[4]

The courts' handling of the first *shoe machinery* case was thus distinguished neither by a grasp of economic theory nor by a careful weighing of the evidence. Nevertheless, the courts' instinct that cautioned against breaking up the defendant corporation was eminently sound. The Justice Department grossly underestimated the importance of scale economies in the industry; indeed in the most recent antitrust suit against United Shoe Machinery, the court held dissolution to be impractical because production had become concentrated in a solitary plant.[5] That the importance of the tying contracts as a buttress to monopoly was much exaggerated is also most probable. These contracts were struck down in a later case brought under the Clayton Act in 1922,[6] yet only one small company has entered the field since that time.[7]

In retrospect, it would appear that the Justice Department erred in not recognizing the United Shoe Machinery Company for what it was—a child of the American patent system. The companies which went into the combination had been organized to exploit particular patents, and it was unlikely that many of them could—or should—survive the expiration of their patent protection. Indeed, the shoe machinery industry in 1899 was an excellent example of the wastes of "monopolistic" competition as described by Professor Chamberlin.[8] Firms were of less than optimum size, products were excessively differentiated, and rationalization was precluded by a barrier to entry—the patent laws. The determination with which the United Shoe Machinery

---

[4] 247 U.S. 32, 41.

[5] United States v. United Shoe Machinery Corp., 110 F. Supp. 295, 348 (D.Mass. 1953).

[6] United Shoe Machinery Corp. v. United States, 258 U.S. 451 (1922).

[7] For the more recent history of the United Shoe Machinery organization see H. L. Purdy, M. L. Lindahl, and W. A. Carter, *Corporate Concentration and Public Policy* 229–49 (2d ed. 1950), or Carl Kaysen, *United States v. United Shoe Machinery Corporation* (1956).

[8] *The Theory of Monopolistic Competition* (7th ed. 1956), especially 246–50.

Company sought complete monopoly has obscured the fact that the production of shoe machinery in 1899 was destined to pass from the many to the few. A "good" decision in the first *shoe machinery* case would have entailed an exhaustive analysis of the patent system in the light of the aims of antitrust policy. In 1918 the Court was neither asked nor equipped by experience to undertake this study.

3. *The courts meet oligopoly: the steel case*

The problem of how the law should treat market power in the single firm that stopped short of "domination of the market" was first raised in the suit against the United States Steel Corporation that remained in the courts from 1911 to 1920. Unhappily, the government's handling of the case was so inept that the main economic issues were not brought into focus. This faulty presentation may partly be ascribed to the government's decision to rely upon the kinds of evidence that had earlier sufficed to secure the dissolution of the oil and tobacco combinations; that is, the case was built around the "intent" of the original promoters of the United States Steel Corporation to "dominate" the market by buying up or intimidating independent steel producers. The weakness of the government case, however, must also be attributed to the inadequate character of the economic theory from which it sought guidance. The inevitability of "parallel action" or "tacit collusion" whenever competition is limited to a few firms was not then a common textbook notion, so that the government was unable to give the court an intelligible description of price leadership. Instead, during the trial it advanced three different explanations of the corporation's role as a price leader. The corporation was depicted as coercing other steel firms into observing its prices by the threat of price wars, conspiring with them to maintain prices, and so powerful that it could set steel prices regardless of how smaller rivals behaved. Further, the federal advisers so completely missed the significance of the basing-point system employed by the steel industry—"Pittsburgh Plus"—that it was not even cited as evidence of collusion.

The case produced four opinions during its progress through the courts that are worth examining in view of its importance as a precedent. In the district court, the case was argued before four judges who concluded that no dissolution or divestiture should be applied against the corporation since it (a) did not dominate the market, (b) could not dominate the market acting alone, (c) could "unlawfully" restrain competition only by conspiring with rivals, and (d) had so conspired in the past in the noted Gary dinners but had desisted shortly before the antitrust suit was instituted in 1911.[9]

The district court, however, could not agree on the motives behind the mergers that produced the United States Steel Corporation. According to the majority opinion, these mergers were intended to realize the economies of vertical integration and were, therefore, amply justified. The authors of the concurring opinion felt that consolidation had created a company that exceeded the size needed for efficient steel production; and this estimate, together with evidence indicating that the company's promoters had recklessly purchased many properties for the sole purpose of eliminating their competition, led them to conclude that the steel company was born in unlawful conspiracy. The concurring judges accepted that the promoters' designs had been frustrated by the tenacity of competition, and that since the law was no longer violated, the government could make no case for equitable relief. The district court would only offer to retain jurisdiction over the case to ensure that the defendant would not resurrect the Gary dinners.[10] The Justice Department declined this concession and carried an unsuccessful appeal to the Supreme Court.

Justice McKenna's majority opinion in the *steel* case is often cited as (a) reiterating the rule of reason which holds that the existence of market power alone is not unlawful, only its unreasonable exercise and (b) refusing dissolution on the ground that the defendant was a "good" trust.[11] This interpretation of McKenna's remarks is not wholly accurate. In declining to order trust busting, Justice McKenna relied upon the lower court's finding of fact that, whatever the original intent of the corporation's promoters, it no longer possessed market power that violated the law. "The opinions indicate that the evidence admits of different deductions as to the genesis of the Corporation and to the purpose of its organizers, but only of a single deduction as to the power it attained and could exercise."[12] Only after accepting the district court's finding of fact that no unlawful monopoly existed did McKenna, in the course of a rambling commentary, introduce his oft-cited dictum:

> The Corporation is undoubtedly of impressive size and it takes an effort of resolution not to be affected by it or to exaggerate its influence. But we must adhere to the law and the law does

---

[9] United States v. United States Steel Corp., 243 Fed. 55 (D.N.J. 1915).
[10] *Ibid.* 161.
[11] United States v. United States Steel Corp., 251 U.S. 417 (1920).
[12] *Ibid.* 442.

not make mere size an offense or the existence of unexerted power an offense. It, we repeat, requires overt acts and trusts to its prohibition of them and its power to repress or punish them. It does not compel competition nor require all that is possible.[13]

Since the above remarks are usually quoted as standing alone, we might digress to note the context in which they appear. McKenna's observations were inspired by his irritation at the major flaw in the government's case, namely its inability to decide upon the significance of the defendant's role of price leader in the steel industry. (In 1920 price leadership had not even been named.) The government first sought to show that the smaller steel companies were coerced into following the big company's prices by fear of cutthroat competition, but when officers of these smaller firms took the stand to deny that they feared the United States Steel Corporation, the government shifted its ground and charged that "the combination embodied in the Corporation unduly restrains competition by its *necessary effect* and therefore is unlawful regardless of purpose."[14]

By the italicized phrase the federal attorneys probably meant only to suggest the inhibitions on competitors that oligopoly imposes. If so, Justice McKenna failed to grasp their intent, for after noting this argument, he reproves the government for inconsistently demanding that the defendant should wage war on its rivals while standing ready to punish him if he should drive them from the field.[15]

> Competition consists of business activities and ability—they make its life; but there may be fatalities in it. Are the activities to be encouraged when militant, and suppressed or regulated when triumphant because of the dominance attained? To such paternalism the Government's contention, which regards power rather than its use the determining consideration, seems to conduct. Certainly conducts we may say, for it

---

[13] *Ibid.* 451.

[14] *Ibid.* 450.

[15] In fairness to Justice McKenna, it should be said that during oral argument he gave the government an opportunity to clarify its explanation of price leadership. At one point he inquired whether the independent steel firms had the power to force down prices. The government counsel blandly replied, "Oh yes, but their output would be used up so quickly that the Corporation could resume its price control." McKenna did not press the matter, although he properly doubted that this answer was satisfactory. *Oral Argument for the United States* 121–22 in 14 Records and Briefs, Justice Department library (1919).

is the inevitable logic of the Government's contention that competition must not only be free, but that it must not be pressed to the ascendency of a competitor, for in ascendency there is the menace of monopoly.[16]

The truth probably is that when McKenna wrote that the law "does not compel competition nor require all that is possible" he meant by "competition" the occasional outbursts of economic warfare that erupt when oligopolists so lose control of their tempers as to forget the advantages of live and let live. In a vigorous dissent, Justice Day argued that (a) the growth of the steel company was manifestly unnatural, (b) its 50 per cent share of the market in 1920 gave it the power to exterminate smaller rivals, (c) the defendants were entitled to no accolade for failing to make use of such power unlawfully acquired, and (d) hence the company should be broken up.

The decline of the percentage of steel output accounted for by the United States Steel Corporation has now rendered academic the merits of the 1920 decision.[17] The case, however, admirably illustrates the truth that economic theory as well as law is made by antitrust litigation. The fact that the minority opinion in the *steel* case was more carefully reasoned and cogently phrased has given it an unwarranted authority with later writers, for Justice Day's main finding of "fact"— that in 1920 the rest of the steel industry existed only on the big company's sufferance—was clearly wrong.[18] The majority opinion drew the correct conclusion from the wrong premises when it reasoned that the defendant was not acting unlawfully because (a) unlawful conduct entails "control" of an industry, the use of predatory tactics, or overt collusion and (b) the steel company in 1920 qualified as a monopolist by none of these tests.

The dissenting justices sensed that the tests of monopoly being applied by the Court were too narrow, but since in 1920 no one had yet

---

[16] 251 U.S. 417, 450.

[17] The Attorney General estimated that the fraction of the country's ingot capacity accounted for by the United States Steel Corporation had declined to 31.4 per cent in 1946. United States v. Columbia Steel Co., 334 U.S. 495, 505 (1948).

[18] This proposition embodies the wisdom of hindsight, *i.e.*, the knowledge that the United States Steel Corporation's share of the industry's output declined from 1901 through 1946. During the trial the officers of rival firms gave conflicting testimony as regards the power of the defendant to eliminate competition, though they mostly agreed that it would not pay him to seek complete monopoly through aggressive price cutting. See *Summary of Evidence* 850–70 in 14 Records and Briefs, Justice Department library (1919).

lucidly expounded the theory of oligopoly, they were forced to explain this uneasiness by asserting that by one or more of these tests the steel company really *was* an unlawful monopoly.

4. *The coming of the "new" Sherman Act*

Taken together, the government defeats in the *steel* and *shoe* cases indicated that the courts regarded the Corporate Revolution as a closed book; that, henceforth, nothing short of a showing of the most ruthless determination to "dominate" the market would move the court to order dissolution and divestiture on the scale imposed by the *oil, tobacco,* and *powder* trust decrees. The government therefore dismissed its more ambitious trust-busting suits then pending, and the task of shaping an economic policy relevant to "good" trusts that began in the *steel* case was postponed for nearly twenty years after 1920.[19]

When the antitrust agencies were recalled to life with greatly increased appropriations and staff shortly before World War II, the government obtained a series of decisions that seemingly gave judicial approval to the liberal economist's case against monopoly. We shall presently argue that the break with tradition represented by these decisions is much exaggerated; that although the government arguments were more sympathetically heard than formerly, the courts still declined to enter decrees that would seriously disturb monopoly power. The reasons for the conservatism of judges are considered in the next chapter. For the present, let us concentrate on the words rather than the deeds of the courts and consider the three decisions rendered between 1943 and 1948 which form the heart of the so-called "new" Sherman Act.

5. *Monopoly as a per se offense: the Alcoa case*

In 1937 the government brought a civil suit against the Aluminum Company of America (Alcoa) which, at this date, was the sole producer of virgin aluminum ingot in the United States, practically the sole supplier of the product to the country—imports being negligible—and an important fabricator of aluminum products as well. Independent fabricators in the industry (there were several hundred in 1937) were thus dependent upon Alcoa for virgin ingot, though they had an alternative

---

[19] The most important of the suits abandoned after the *steel* decision were United States v. American Can Co., 256 U.S. 706 (1921); and United States v. Quaker Oats Co., 253 U.S. 499 (1920).

source of supply in aluminum scrap which was bought and sold in a relatively free market.

The complaint alleged three main offenses. (1) At various times Alcoa had purchased patents and combined with foreign producers of aluminum in order to restrain competition in the American market, the most notable instance of such behavior being its purchase of the Aluminium Company of Canada (Alcan). (2) Alcoa regularly practiced a "cost squeeze" on independent fabricators; that is, the price of virgin aluminum ingot was deliberately kept high in order that the latter might not expand at the expense of Alcoa subsidiaries that produced competitive aluminum products. (3) Alcoa violated the law by virtue of its complete control of ingot production; the origin of this market power and the reasonableness of its exercise were alleged to be immaterial since Section 2 of the Sherman Act condemns "every person who shall monopolize." By way of remedies the government requested that Alcoa sever its international connections and transform itself into several smaller companies.

Alcoa replied that it neither interfered with anyone's right to enter upon the production of aluminum ingot nor sought to drive the small fabricators of aluminum products from the field. Any monopoly power that the company might possess was held to be the result of natural growth and reasonably exercised; consequently, the dissolution of Alcoa would jeopardize the present efficiency and future progress of the aluminum industry without conferring any benefit on the public.

In 1941 the district court in a 207-page decision accepted Alcoa's explanations at their face value and dismissed the government's complaint.[20] The Supreme Court, unable to muster a quorum to hear the appeal, sent it to the circuit court of appeals for final judgment. In the most famous of all antitrust opinions, Learned Hand, speaking for the court, upheld the government, after considering at length Alcoa's defense that it was a natural monopoly of good deportment and thus no offender against the antitrust laws.[21] In rejecting the plea Hand relied upon the following arguments:

1. Since price-fixing agreements among rival firms are unlawful per se, the courts cannot logically allow comparable monopoly power to be vested in a single firm. The objection that such power is not unlawfully held until it is "unreasonably" exer-

---

[20] United States v. Aluminum Co. of America, 44 F. Supp. 97 (S.D.N.Y.).
[21] United States v. Aluminum Co. of America, 148 F.2d 416 (2d Cir. 1945).

cised is relevant only so long as the firm does no business. As soon as the firm begins to sell at all, "it must sell at some price and the only price at which it could sell is a price which it itself fixed."[22]

2. Alcoa had actively discouraged the entry of new firms into ingot production by expanding its capacity more rapidly than the demand for its output warranted. This program of accelerated development together with the heavy capital requirement for entry into the field effectively reserved ingot aluminum production to Alcoa.

3. The possibility that efficiency and progress might suffer if the company were dissolved or divested of certain facilities could not bar the use of these remedies. In failing to distinguish between "good" and "bad" trusts, Congress was not necessarily actuated by economic motives alone. "It is possible, because of its indirect social or moral effect, to prefer a system of small producers, each dependent for his success upon his own skill and character, to one in which the great mass of those engaged must accept the direction of a few."[23]

That Alcoa's conduct—if not its very existence—offended against the antitrust laws Hand and his associates did not doubt. They declined, however, to prescribe remedies but instead directed that the framing of a decree be delayed until the court could discern what effect the sale of the aluminum capacity constructed by the government during World War II would have on the structure of the industry. Subsequently, government favors established two new firms as producers of aluminum ingot, so that in 1950 the district court to which the case was sent could conclude that the restoration of competitive conditions required nothing more than the severing of the connection between Alcoa and Alcan.[24] (Eleven individuals and trust funds held a controlling interest in both companies.[25])

Notwithstanding the force and elegance of Learned Hand's opinion, the law of the *Alcoa* case is ambiguous in one important particular. The decision is often interpreted as establishing that it is unlawful for a firm to possess power of the magnitude that discourages the entry of

---

[22] *Ibid.* 428.

[23] *Ibid.* 427.

[24] United States v. Aluminum Co. of America, 91 F. Supp. 333 (S.D.N.Y. 1950).

[25] *Ibid.* 394.

new competition and, hence, that the government need not show that the firm has actually flayed about with such power. As noted above, however, the court found an abuse of monopoly power in the maintenance of "excess capacity."[26]

In fact, the significance of this barrier to entry in the aluminum industry was probably overrated. The size of investment need to begin production together with the head start enjoyed by Alcoa were more important deterrents to prospective newcomers, though, strictly speaking, the nature of the barrier to entry that aids the monopolist would seem to be unimportant in the light of the *Alcoa* decision. If the monopolist responds to the threat of potential competition by keeping prices low in order to ensure that it does not materialize as actual competition, he violates the law. If, disdainful of anyone's ability to challenge his position, he charges what the traffic will bear, his monopoly power is presumably "unreasonably" exercised.

6. *Oligopoly as a per se offense: the second tobacco case*

The second, if somewhat shaky, foundation of the new Sherman Act was provided by the criminal conviction returned against the Big Three tobacco companies in 1941 and upheld by the Supreme Court in 1946.[27] At the time of the trial the defendants—American, Liggett & Myers, and R. J. Reynolds—accounted for roughly 70 per cent of domestic cigarette production. As in most criminal prosecutions brought under the Sherman Act, the arguments employed in this case were better calculated to inflame the jury than educate the court. This was particularly unfortunate since the important issues on which the decision turned related mainly to the interpretation of evidence. (The American practice of according to the right of trial by jury to corporations is a quaint bit of nonsense that reformers have not yet removed from the law.)

In effect, the government charged that the defendants between 1937 and 1940 had (a) conspired among themselves to influence the price of cigarettes and cigarette tobacco and (b) monopolized the cig-

---

[26] For another statement of the view that Judge Hand's *Alcoa* decision "is not as revolutionary as it seems," see A. E. Kahn, "A Legal and Economic Appraisal of the 'New' Sherman and Clayton Acts," 63 *Yale L. J.* 293, 296–305 (1954).

[27] American Tobacco Co. v. United States, 328 U.S. 781. This case is examined at length in W. H. Nicholls, *Price Policies in the Cigarette Industry* 352–403 (1951).

arette industry in that they had worked together to discourage the expansion of the smaller cigarette firms. Since the Big Three had been made wary by previous encounters with the antitrust laws, the Justice Department was unable to produce the sort of evidence showing collusion that would have made conviction automatic, *e.g.*, minutes of secret meetings or the testimony of witnesses describing incriminating conversations. The federal attorneys, however, could—and did—introduce voluminous exhibits to show that the Big Three refused to engage in price competition with one another—a fact taken for granted by most cigarette smokers. Circumstantial evidence was also produced to support the reasonable supposition that the advertising, tobacco-buying, and price policies of the defendants were influenced by the wish that the share of cigarette production accounted for the industry's smaller firms should not increase further. (The Big Three's share of the market had fallen from 90.7 per cent in 1931 to 68 per cent in 1939.[28])

The government's need to rely upon circumstantial evidence raised two main issues. (1) Did the evidence indicate that the defendants had actually conspired to suppress competition while successfully removing the traces of collusion? (2) Did the evidence indicate that the defendants, without articulate communication with one another, had devised a common plan of action that eliminated price competition among themselves and discouraged the growth of their small rivals? The tactics of opposing counsel did little to make these issues clear to the court. The defense argued that (a) the evidence did not show that the defendants had conspired to pursue a common policy but merely that, belonging to the same industry, they were buffeted by the same market pressures and (b) this parallel action was lawful so long as it was not the product of collusion. The government replied that (a) the circumstantial evidence could be explained by assuming that the defendants had secretly conspired to maintain prices and (b) even if they had not done so, they perforce violated the Sherman Act when, by the use of sign language, they achieved the same end. According to the government, what mattered was not how competition was suppressed but the fact that it was suppressed.

This involved argument on the proper way of interpreting evidence was largely lost on the court. The trial judge, as a matter of course, instructed the jury that circumstantial evidence could imply conspiracy. The jury, without going into details, found the defendants guilty on all counts, and the circuit court of appeals ruled that the

---

[28] 328 U.S. 781, 794.

jury's finding of fact was adequately supported by evidence.[29] The Supreme Court consented to hear argument on one issue only—"whether actual exclusion of competitors is necessary to the crime of monopolization under Section 2 of the Sherman Act." Relying upon Learned Hand's opinion in the *Alcoa* case, it held:

> Where the circumstances are such as to warrant a jury in finding that the conspirators had a unity of purpose or a common design and understanding, or a meeting of minds in an unlawful arrangement, the conclusion that a conspiracy is established is justified. Neither proof of the exertion of the power to exclude nor proof of actual exclusion of existing or potential competitors is essential to sustain a charge of monopolization under the Sherman Act.[30]

The Court probably did not intend that the above remarks should be taken literally. A close reading of the opinion indicates that by "actual exclusion of existing or potential competitors" it meant retaliatory action against firms that sought to enter the industry—not merely the pursuit of a policy calculated to ensure that no one is tempted to embark upon such an adventure. In the *Alcoa* case the defendant was held to have unlawfully discouraged competition by a policy of accelerated investment. In the *tobacco* case the defendants were found to have achieved this end by lavish expenditures on advertising, bidding up the price of the cheaper tobaccos much used by the smaller cigarette manufacturers, and refusing to deal with retailers who sold the brands of the small firms too cheaply.[31]

Some writers incautiously discerned in the *tobacco* decision the Court's acceptance of the view that oligopoly which does not rest upon obvious economies of scale is undesirable. They believed that the Court had jettisoned the legalistic approach to antitrust problems, so that henceforth federal attorneys would not have to win conspiracy cases by pouncing upon unsophisticated small businessmen who had never

---

[29] American Tobacco Co. v. United States, 147 F.2d 93 (6th Cir. 1944).

[30] 328 U.S. 781, 810.

[31] The Court was especially critical of the leaf-buying policies of the defendants. "At a time when the manufacturers of lower priced cigarettes were beginning to manufacture them in quantity, the petitioners commenced to make large purchases of the cheaper tobacco leaves used for the manufacture of such lower priced cigarettes. No explanation was offered as to how or where this tobacco was used by petitioners. The compositions of their respective brands of cigarettes calling for the use of more expensive tobaccos remained unchanged during this period of controversy and up to the end of the trial." 328 U.S. 781, 803.

heard of the Sherman Act or seek victory in monopoly cases by parading tearful bankrupts who would recount how they had been unfairly crushed by the trust.

Writing in 1947 an eminent authority gave thanks that

> the old preoccupation of the judges with evidence of business tactics they regarded as ruthless, predatory, and immoral has all but disappeared. We have come a long way towards assimilating the legal to the economic conception of monopoly. We are close to the point of regarding as illegal the kind of economic power which the economist regards as monopolistic.[32]

Our examination of the *tobacco* case indicates that the interpretation contains an element of wishful thinking. The most we can say is that, in this case, the government for the first time argued that oligopoly per se was unlawful and was not reproved by the Court.

7. *Size as a per se offense: the A & P case*

The finishing touch to the legal theory of the new Sherman Act came in 1949 when the circuit court of appeals upheld a criminal conviction returned against the Atlantic & Pacific Tea Company.[33] The case is noteworthy in that it could not have been won either under various rules of reason employed in the pre-1940 litigation or under the doctrines of the *Alcoa* and *tobacco* cases; for the company, though the largest single grocery chain in the country, had for many years accounted for no more than 10 per cent of national food sales,[34] and while in certain localities A & P's share of the market was considerably higher, the case presented no issue of "local monopoly."[35]

---

[32] E. V. Rostow, "The New Sherman Act: A Positive Instrument of Progress," 14 *U. Chi. L. Rev.* 567, 575 (1947).

[33] United States v. New York Great A & P Tea Co., 173 F.2d 79 (7th Cir. 1949).

[34] The court accepted A & P's estimate that in 1943 it accounted for 7.1 per cent of the total sales of "stores engaged primarily only in sale of food at retail." United States v. New York Great A & P Tea Co., 67 F. Supp. 626, 633 (E.D. Ill. 1946).

[35] The most that can be said is that the timing of A & P purchases in certain produce markets, notably Chicago, could—and occasionally did—affect day-to-day price quotations. J. B. Dirlam and A. E. Kahn, "Integration and Dissolution of the A & P Company," 29 *Ind. L. J.* 1, 14–15 (1953).

The conclusion of these authorities that A & P therefore enjoyed some monopsony power at the local level must, however, be questioned. The essence

Technically, the A & P Company was found guilty of violating the Sherman Act by systematically employing its bargaining power and skill for the purpose of securing from suppliers "discounts not justified by a saving in cost." Before passage of the Robinson-Patman Act (1936)[36] A & P had on many occasions brought pressure to bear on its suppliers to obtain prices lower than those quoted to other buyers.[37] Pressure had been applied mainly through the exaction of so-called "phantom brokerage"; that is, when dealing directly with a supplier who also sold through produce brokers and commission agents, A & P naturally demanded a price concession on the ground that it furnished the supplier with a service that he would otherwise pay for. When the Robinson-Patman Act's ban on phantom brokerage was upheld,[38] the company took evasive action by refusing to deal with some suppliers who used agents or brokers and hoped by this maneuver to avoid the charge of forcing them to discriminate against their other customers. Suppliers who chose to abandon their middleman contacts with small retailers often found themselves selling mainly to A & P. Having enticed them to put too many eggs in one basket, A & P thereupon proceeded to demand "unfairly" low prices on pain of transferring production to its own plants, or so the prosecution claimed. For good measure, it introduced the remarkable "recoupment theory" alleging that if food processors sold some items cheap to A & P, they could only survive by selling other items dear to A & P's rivals; and since these competitors did most of the grocery business in the country, the general level of food prices was perforce raised. While the court carefully refrained from endorsing this fallacious thesis—a jury trial was waived—the company was nevertheless convicted.[39]

---

of monopsony is the buyer's power to depress price by reducing purchases and so causing the seller's cost of production to fall as the seller cuts his output. Power to influence the output of food products the A & P Company most assuredly did not have.

[36] 49 *Stat.* 1526.

[37] The purchasing tactics of the A & P Company were extensively investigated in the 1930's. See, for example, Federal Trade Commission, *Final Report on the Chain-Store Investigation*, S. Doc. No. 4, 74th Cong., 1st Sess. 53–65 (1935).

[38] Great Atlantic & Pacific Tea Co. v. Federal Trade Commission, 106 F.2d 667 (3d Cir. 1939).

[39] The epitome of the A & P case offered above stresses the court's attention to the defendant's buying tactics and neglects several subsidiary issues, notably, the *raison d'être* of its policy of using certain stores to subsidize others in order to "meet competition." In defense of this emphasis, we may note that the trial judge made A & P's centralized purchasing the "rotten thread" in the "fabric"

Fortunately, the effort of the Justice Department to follow through with a civil suit that would have stripped the organization of its processing plants and broken the company into several regional chains came to naught.[40] In retrospect, the *A & P* decision is not easily appraised. It is atrocious as economics and obscure as law, and it leaves in doubt the firm's right to brandish about the alleged economies of vertical integration in its bargaining with suppliers.[41]

8. *The uses of the new Sherman Act*

The direct economic consequences of the *Alcoa, tobacco,* and *A & P* decisions were, of course, negligible, and the opinions rendered in these cases contained enough ambiguous phrases to make their significance as precedents uncertain. Indeed ambiguity is the distinguishing feature of the new Sherman Act. The courts' attitude to the arguments taken by the Justice Department from academic economics resembles that of the legendary African tribe which welcomed penicillin provided that it was fortified by the witch doctor's incantation. The courts are prepared to believe that corporate size, control of the market, and oligopoly are undesirable to the point of being illegal, but judges also cling to the old gods and find that Alcoa, A & P, and the tobacco companies protected their market positions by unreasonably aggressive behavior. Still, the courts had listened with apparent approval to a popular exposition of Henry Simon's positive program for *laissez faire*. It was not unreasonable to suppose that the decisions marked the advent of a tougher antitrust policy, and the only remedies commensurate with the severity of the courts' language were dissolution and divestiture. If the "new" Sherman Act meant anything, it signified a repudiation of the *United States Steel* decision and a resumption of the trust-busting program that the 1920 case had closed because the government could no longer present the courts with bad trusts.

The rule of *stare decisis*, however, would be quite intolerable if

---

of its otherwise innocent acts which "so permeates the entire texture and ties together the other threads as to result in an imperfect, an illegal product— unreasonable interference with competition and power to monopolize." 67 F. Supp. 626, 678.

[40] The Justice Department settled for a consent decree that dissolved A & P's central produce-buying agency and distributed its functions among the various operating companies. 1954 Trade Cases ¶67658.

[41] For one economist's exasperation at the arguments used by the government in the A & P case, see M. A. Adelman, "The A & P Case: A Study in Applied Economic Theory," 63 *Q. J. Econ.* 238 (1949).

judges felt obliged to proceed with a logician's consistency. The inevitable imprecision of language allows the courts some freedom to maneuver; unpalatable consequences can be avoided by the introduction of new categories and finer distinctions;[42] and a court can always enter a decree that bears little resemblance to the opinion rendered. This last line of retreat is especially likely in an antitrust case given the division of responsibility between the district and appellate courts; for the framing of a decree is the duty of the district court, notwithstanding that the most frequently cited opinions are those of the higher courts. It was within the power of the courts to decide that the new Sherman Act was, in fact, little different from the old. The reasons why they were almost certain to do so we shall consider in Chapter XVII.

---

[42] Thus the Court has semantically resolved the collective discrimination practiced by Hollywood producers against independent exhibitors in their access to films into "tacit collusion" and "conscious parallel action." The former is unlawful and enabled the exhibitor to recover treble damages in Bigelow v. RKO Radio Pictures, 327 U.S. 251 (1946). Conscious parallel action per se was held not to violate the Sherman Act in Theatre Enterprises v. Paramount Pictures, 346 U.S. 537 (1954). For the subtleties of this distinction, see Carl Kaysen, "Collusion under the Sherman Act," 65 *Q. J. Econ.* 263 (1951), and Michael Conant, "Consciously Parallel Action in Restraint of Trade," 38 *Minn. L. Rev.* 797 (1954).

Chapter XVII

THE LIMITS OF TRUST BUSTING

1. *Law and the conservative bias*

From 1938 onward, the antitrust agencies, armed with the favorable decisions noted in the last chapter and far greater budgets than ever before, sought dissolution and divestiture on an unprecedented scale. By the author's count—probably incomplete—some rearrangement of corporate structure was sought in no less than forty-four civil suits filed between December, 1936, and August, 1954.[1] The judicial ingenuity needed to nullify the vague promise of the new Sherman Act, however, was not lacking. Even the most cursory look at the results achieved by the important cases decided, compromised, or abandoned since 1938[2] confirms that the reluctance of the courts to disturb the

---

[1] Among the larger defendants are (or were) Aluminum Company of America, Great Atlantic & Pacific Tea, Pullman, Du Pont, Paramount, Loew's, RKO, Twentieth Century-Fox, Warner Brothers, National Lead, General Electric, Swift, Wilson, Armour, Cudahy, American Telephone & Telegraph, Pan American Airways, United Shoe Machinery, Timken Roller Bearing, Borden's, Proctor & Gamble, Colgate-Palmolive, Lever Brothers, Celanese Corporation, United Fruit, International Business Machines, Standard Oil of California, Columbia Gas and Electric, Minnesota Mining & Manufacturing, Pittsburgh Crushed Steel, and United States Rubber.

[2] Notably, United States v. Pullman Co., 53 Fed. Supp. 908 (E.D. Pa. 1944), 330 U.S. 806 (1947); United States v. National Lead Co., 332 U.S. 319 (1947); United States v. Yellow Cab Co., 338 U.S. 338 (1949); United States v. Paramount Pictures, 85 F. Supp. 881 (1949); United States v. Aluminum Co. of America, 44 F. Supp. 97 (S.D.N.Y. 1941), 148 F.2d 416 (2d Cir. 1945), 91 F. Supp. 333 (S.D.N.Y. 1950); Timken Roller Bearing Co. v. United States, 341 U.S. 593 (1951); United States v. Columbia Gas & Electric Co., Civil 16, *discontinued* July, 1953; United States v. New York Great Atlantic & Pacific Tea Co., 1954 Trade Cases ¶67658 (S.D.N.Y.); United States v. United Shoe Machinery Corp., 110 F. Supp. 295 (D. Mass. 1953); United States v. Armour & Co., Civil 48-C-1351, *discontinued* March, 1954; United States v. Western Electric Co., 1956 Trade Cases ¶68246 (D.N.J.); United States v. E. I. Du Pont de Nemours & Co., 353 U.S. 586 (1957); United States v. United Fruit Co., 1958 Trade Cases ¶68941 (E.D.La.).

corporate status quo has not changed. Indeed, only the decrees entered in the *Pullman*,[3] *Paramount*,[4] and *United Fruit*[5] cases were ambitious enough to merit consideration as possible exceptions to this conclusion. (The *Pullman* and *Paramount* suits are examined in the Appendix to this chapter; it is too early to assess the effects of the *United Fruit* divestiture agreed upon in February, 1958.[6]) Taken together the so-called big cases fought by the antitrust agencies in the last twenty years reveal a pattern of "legal victory—economic defeat." Since the hopes of most advocates of a more competitive economy still ride on trust busting, the reasons for this discrepancy between decision and decree are worth examining.

The disinclination of a court to break up major corporations even when it holds them guilty of violating the antitrust laws is often cited as another example of the alleged bias of judges in favor of established property rights. That this conservative bias exists is true enough; it is, of course, an indispensable feature of any legal system worthy of the name. The predictability that a preference for the status quo imparts to judicial behavior may not be the only desideratum of good law, but it is certainly an important one. Moreover, in antitrust cases, the normal judicial conservatism is re-enforced by the "fact" that dissolution and divestiture suits are conducted upon a premise which most judges and laymen really do not accept. Unlike the advocates of strong remedies, they are not convinced that the exercise of monopoly power which has been acquired by means neither actionable nor indictable per se violates the law to an extent justifying its elimination without a sympathetic attention to the position of workers and stockholders whose interests may be adversely affected by trust busting.[7]

---

[3] 53 Fed. Supp. 908 (E.D. Pa. 1944).

[4] 85 Fed. Supp. 881 (S.D.N.Y. 1949).

[5] United States v. United Fruit Co., 1958 Trade Cases ¶68941 (E.D.La.).

[6] By a consent judgment of February 4, 1958, the United Fruit Company agrees to use its assets to create a new firm capable of importing 9 million stems of bananas into the United States annually. This volume is equal to roughly 35 per cent of United's banana imports in 1957. Note, 3 *Antitrust Bulletin* 224, 225 (1958).

[7] The reasonable man's case against a rough handling for a good trust was clearly stated by Judge Sandborn when in 1914 he objected to a decree that ordered the International Harvester Company broken up into three units some years after its formation as a merger for market control. "Its business was conducted openly without legal challenge or attack, so far as this record shows, during all these years, and it is not improbable that many parties hold stock of the International Company which they purchased during these ten years in reliance upon these facts, the value of which a decree against the defendants will greatly

This view does not regard vested interests in monopoly as bona fide property rights merely by virtue of their established character, but it does assume, however inarticulately, that possible public gains must be weighed against possible private losses and that the more problematical the public benefit, the greater the weight of private claims. Thus it is one thing for the reasonable judge to order the termination of profitable leasing arrangements to the end that a secondhand market for shoemaking machinery may hasten the introduction of new equipment; it is quite another for him to transform a going concern into three smaller units in the hope that consumers will benefit in ways that the Antitrust Division cannot spell out in concrete terms.

2. *The possibilities for painless trust busting*

The advocates of trust busting sometimes object that the preoccupation of the courts with the fortunes of innocent parties is quite unnecessary; that the dangers to the interests of workers and stockholders in the plans for corporate reorganization put forward by the Justice Department are much exaggerated.[8] It is unlikely that the partisans of this thesis perceive its implications, for if a decree directing dissolution or divestiture does not hurt workers and stockholders, only the following inferences are possible.

1. The company had no appreciable monopoly power in the first place.

2. The company had previously refrained from making the most profitable use of whatever monopoly power it did possess (*i.e.*, the company was a "good" trust).

---

depreciate. So it is that in any event this suit does not appeal to the conscience of a chancellor with the force it might have had in 1903 or 1904 before the actual conduct of the business of the defendants had demonstrated its innocuous effect and no parties had been induced to act in reliance upon its freedom from attack." United States v. International Harvester Co., 214 Fed. 987, 1010 (D. Minn. 1914).

Significantly, the decree to which Judge Sanborn objected was never carried into effect but was replaced by a somewhat milder consent decree before the company's appeal was heard in the Supreme Court. Modification of this second decree was later denied to the government in United States v. International Harvester Co., 274 U.S. 693 (1927).

[8] Thus, two authorities have given this assurance with respect to the government's now abandoned plan to dissolve the Atlantic & Pacific Tea Company into seven regional chains without manufacturing subsidiaries or a central produce-buying agency. J. B. Dirlam and A. E. Kahn, "Integration and the Dissolution of the A & P Company," 29 *Ind. L. J.* 1 (1953).

3. Monopoly power residing in the company was not disturbed by dissolution or divestiture.

4. The unlawful power over price has been merely bequeathed or sold to other corporate units.

5. The fall in income sustained by the company as a consequence of its loss of monopoly power was offset by a fortunate development or concatenation of circumstances unrelated to the antitrust suit—for example, a fall in the cost of raw materials, an increased demand for the firm's output, tax relief, or profitable innovation. The company may have emerged unscathed from its dissection through luck or good management or any combination of the two.

6. Some monopoly power was eliminated by the decree, but such power had previously rested upon so precarious a foundation that it had never been capitalized into appreciably higher security prices or incorporated into established employee expectations.[9]

Hence, when proponents of trust busting contend that their measures will reduce monopoly power without inflicting a financial loss on hapless stockholders and employees, we can only conclude that they (a) are mistaken, (b) are employing a definition of monopoly power which an economist cannot accept, or (c) are deliberately eschewing attacks on the more formidable enclaves of monopoly power in the economy. And if capitalized monopoly *is* the target, their position is logically untenable. Not only does the destruction of monopoly power entail the imposition of a financial loss upon hapless parties, but the magnitude of the loss *is* the measure of "monopoly" eliminated.

3. *The labor stake in corporate market power*

Some authorities concede that stockholders may experience a capital loss as a consequence of the reduction of monopoly, but far from acknowledging that a company's workers may have a stake in its market power, they contend the latter must be numbered among the vic-

---

[9] One critic has suggested that there remains a further possibility for painless trust busting—the rapidly growing industry. But, strictly speaking, this possibility must be ruled out, since in a well organized capital market, growth prospects are presumably capitalized. Nevertheless, it is probably true that dissolution and divestiture are most likely to be ordered in the case of expanding industries. The contribution of a moderate decree to the already substantial uncertainty surrounding the future earnings of firms so situated is so problematical that it is more easily ignored by the courts.

tims of monopoly. A layman noting the market position of Ford, Chrysler, and General Motors, and the high wage scale of automobile workers may, perhaps, instinctively feel otherwise. In fact, the former view rests upon two tyrannies of abstraction:

1. If a purely competitive labor market is assumed, the wage rate is "given" to the employer and he presumably has no reason to share any monopoly gains with his workers.

2. If the employer operates in an imperfect labor market, he enjoys monopsony power, so that any exercise of his power over price in the products market necessarily depresses the wage scale and hence is inimical to the interest of his workers.

We need not dwell on the imperfections of the labor market nor on the fact that most firms which now figure in antitrust suits have entered into collective bargaining agreements. Only the monopsony effect of restrictive practices is relevant to policy. Unfortunately, the recognition of monopsony has lately served to obscure the intuitively more obvious truth that if company earnings are increased by monopoly, the employer is, for this reason alone, more vulnerable to union pressures. He is likely to consent to a higher wage scale because (a) he can afford it and (b) he stands to suffer a greater loss from strike action if he does not.

Some economists describe the vulnerability of monopolists to employee pressure by saying that monopoly may raise wage rates by increasing the value of labor's marginal product. But strictly speaking, this product is not really relevant to the setting of the wage rate of the amount of labor hired. If the employer has a free hand in varying the factor combination, he will attempt to equate the marginal revenue product of labor with the marginal cost of labor, and *ceteris paribus* the achievement of monopoly always lowers the marginal revenue product of labor.[10] If the employer does not have a free hand in varying the factor combination, he must make the best adjustment open to him. In fine, if its monopoly power increases, the firm will always prefer a lower wage bill and accept a higher one.

With the passing of time, any wage increase wrung from monopoly earnings is likely to cause some reduction of employment. Capi-

---

[10] The terms *value of labor's marginal product* and *marginal revenue product of labor* are used above with their generally accepted meanings in economics. The value of labor's marginal product is the sum which the public is willing to pay to obtain the output of the marginal unit of labor. The marginal revenue product of labor is the sum added to the firm's total revenue by the sale of the output of the marginal unit of labor.

tal is substituted for labor in the factor combination, and employer attrition whittles away the featherbedding made possible by such profits. Nevertheless, employment in plants where unions have secured wage increases or light work loads is seldom contracted by firing people. Rather the firm that finds itself with a marginal revenue product of labor that is below the marginal cost of labor corrects this discrepancy by failing to make good the normal wastage of manpower through resignation, death, and retirement. We may conclude, therefore, that organized employees who are in on the ground floor when monopoly power is gained by their employer are most unlikely to fail to benefit from its exercise. An attack upon the market position of the major automobile companies is perforce an attack upon the guaranteed annual wage of the industry's organized workers.

4. *Trust busting as an obsolete remedy*

In view of the obvious limitations of the legal fiction that makes the present employees and stockholders of a corporation responsible for the unlawful policies of past managements, it is doubtful the courts would knowingly impose harsh remedies even if it were clear that monopoly power could be touched in no other way. In fact, the need for the calculated doing of damage to property values and worker incomes is never made apparent in an antitrust case. Federal attorneys, as a matter of trial technique, resolutely deny that their proposals will adversely affect the interests of workers and stockholders, but by taking this position they are unable to prevent the defendant from suggesting to the judge that *if* his decree *should* harm these groups, *ipso facto* he will have impaired the efficiency of a going concern. Actually, the severity of what the courts regard as a "harsh" decree is much more likely to relate to the vagaries and imperfections of the capital market than to any contemplated destruction of monopoly power.[11] Thus, when stock divestiture is ordered, the investor is nor-

---

[11] A case in point is Timken Roller Bearing Co. v. United States, 341 U.S. 593 (1951). Here the Supreme Court refused to uphold the provision of the lower court decree directing the American company—a producer of antifriction bearings—to dispose of its one-third stock interest in a British firm manufacturing similar products. The Court was apparently influenced by the knowledge that currency controls would have prevented Timken from readily transferring the proceeds of divestiture out of the United Kingdom and so increased the danger that Timken might have taken a capital loss in changing its portfolio. See Walter Adams, "Dissolution, Divorcement, Divestiture: The Pyrrhic Victories of Antitrust," 27 *Ind. L. J.* 1 (1951).

mally allowed to retain ownership until a "fair" price obtains for his securities—provided voting rights are surrendered to an acceptable trustee. The probable consequences of trust busting for employee fortunates is a better index of how it promises to affect the firm's power over price, and our tacit assumption that workers are, so to speak, usually disinterested spectators in an antitrust action involving their employer indicates that we do not really expect a decree which will seriously disturb monopoly power in the short run.

In fact, once control over price has been capitalized into the value of securities owned by Johnny-come-latelies or incorporated into wage scales and fringe benefits, it is largely safe from judicial attack. Thus there would seem to be only two situations in which trust busting is likely to have an immediate, perceptible, and direct effect upon monopoly power.

The first is where any financial loss inflicted by the decree will fall upon the persons who have engineered the unlawful suppression of competition. Judges must ever affirm that a court of equity imposes no penalties for past conduct—that remedies are its sole concern, but, as one would expect, the most severe decrees involving dissolution and divestiture have been visited on companies whose major stockholders were personally responsible for the misconduct condemned. Now, however, the separation of legal ownership and actual control is so complete that the government has not much opportunity to employ trust busting as a *sub rosa* punishment.[12]

During the depression a lower court in declining to order the divestiture of a large block of railroad securities once visibly shuddered at the possible economic consequences of dumping "all this stock" on the market "in these troublous times." Pennsylvania R.R. v. Interstate Commerce Commission, 66 F.2d 37, 40 (3d Cir. 1933).

[12] Judging from the manner in which divestiture has been employed over the years, one might plausibly infer that a major object of antitrust policy is the substitution of management control for owner control in the large corporation. Court decrees have hastened this process in the Standard Oil companies, the tobacco companies that were originally a part of the Duke empire (American, Liggett & Myers, Reynolds, P. Lorillard, and British-American), and the Aluminium Company of Canada. And it seems probable that the recent Supreme Court decision directing the Du Pont Company to disgorge its stock in General Motors and United States Rubber and dissolving the holding companies to which the Du Pont family have transferred their shares in the chemical concern, will mainly benefit the salaried top managements of the three industrial giants.

The Antitrust Division obviously has no interest in promoting management control. If many antitrust suits contribute to this end, it is only because the shuffling of stock certificates that accompanies a dissolution or divestiture decree presents the managers with control of the company's proxy machine.

A dissolution or divestiture suit can also be prosecuted with some prospect of success when the target is monopoly power which cannot be capitalized; that is, when it is inseparably bound up with the acumen or charisma of particular individuals. In this circumstance, trust busting can promote competition by curbing the power and influence of the objectionable entrepreneur—by forcing the withdrawal from the market of a Duke or Rockefeller. In short, radical antimonopoly remedies can be anticipated only when it is possible for judges to "personalize" the issues, which is to say that so long as the courts refuse to impose decrees that seriously menace the interests of innocent parties, trust busting will never be employed to recast the structure of the economy.

These considerations provide a clue to a curious paradox in the enforcement of the antitrust laws. The budgets of the antitrust agencies have vastly increased since 1940;[13] yet the great victories of dissolution and divestiture were mostly won before 1920 by a handful of modestly paid lawyers and economists. Indeed, the economic impact of trust busting was largely registered in the *Standard Oil* and *American Tobacco* decrees of 1911. In these earlier cases, the labor union was not an interested onlooker; the major beneficiaries of monopoly were still active in the companies; the courts were understandably appalled at some of the tactics employed by the defendants; and the rapid rate of expansion in the defendants' industries suggested that no one would be seriously injured by dissolution and divestiture.[14] Nowadays, one must look a long way—certainly beyond the brotherhood of the large corporations—to find a potential candidate for trust busting that satisfies these conditions.

---

[13] As late as 1921—the first year in which the appropriations for the enforcement of the antitrust laws were itemized in the Justice Department's budget— the sum allowed for this purpose was only $147,000. C. D. Edwards, *Maintaining Competition* 296–97 (1949).

[14] It should also be noted that in the *Standard Oil* decree the Court— apparently through inadvertence—employed the remedy of gradual dissolution. Each stockholder in the dissolved company was given an equity in each firm turned loose from it proportional to his equity in the old concern, so that for some years after 1911 the "Rockefeller interest" by virtue of its stock holdings probably "co-ordinated" the policies of the Standard Oil companies. (The slight initial impact of the decree on the ownership structure of the Standard Oil properties, is emphasized in Federal Trade Commission, *Report on the Price of Gasoline* 155–60 (1915). Over the years, however, the marketing of additional securities, the withdrawal of the Rockefeller family from active participation in the oil industry, and the scattering of its Standard Oil holdings by sale and bequest slowly transformed the descendants of the oil trust into independent companies dominated by their respective managements.

The truth is that the really astounding success of the Justice Department against the oil and tobacco trusts led many observers to believe that all things are possible in equity; that if only enough cases could be brought to educate the courts in the finer points of libertarian economics, they would consent to order the destruction of the major corporations. The slender foundation of this hope was cogently exposed by Judge Wyzanski in the most recent *shoe machinery* case[15] when he observed:

> In the anti-trust field the courts have been accorded, by common consent, an authority they have in no other branch of enacted law. Indeed, the only comparable examples of the power of judges is the economic role they formerly exercised under the Fourteenth Amendment, and the role they now exercise in the area of civil liberties. They would not have been given, or allowed to keep, such authority in the anti-trust field, and they would not so freely have altered from time to time the interpretation of its substantive provisions, if courts were in the habit of proceeding with the surgical ruthlessness that might commend itself to those seeking absolute assurance that there will be workable competition, and to those aiming at immediate realization of the social, political, and economic advantages of dispersal of power."[16]

In fine, Judge Wyzanski affirms that the courts are allowed to retain the judge-made remedies of dissolution and divestiture only because their conservative bias is good surety that these remedies will not be much used.

5. *Alternatives to trust busting*

It is the burden of this chapter, then, that so far as trust busting is concerned, the new Sherman Act has become indistinguishable from the old; that this result was "inevitable" given judicial reluctance to disturb private rights in the interest of promoting nebulous public goals; that in most antitrust cases, this attitude is both understandable and commendable; and that on balance ambitious attempts at trust busting probably do the aims of free market policy as much harm as good. At best, dissolution and divestiture suits tie up the Justice De-

---

[15] United States v. United Shoe Machinery Corp., 110 F. Supp. 295 (D. Mass. 1953).

[16] *Ibid.* 348.

partment's limited means in lengthy suits which will probably be lost. At worst, the occasional securing of a dismembering decree which misses or but lightly touches monopoly power may delude the friends of antitrust policy into believing that the "big" case really can recast the structure of the American economy.

If these conclusions are accepted, a liberal of the Simons-Fetter school must needs rethink his tactics, and four courses of action would seem to be open to him.

1. The attempt to use antitrust policy for the purpose of changing the structure of the economy can be abandoned and the antitrust agencies either abolished or directed to investigate restrictive practices and punish an occasional malefactor.

2. He may return undaunted to the battle in the hope that he may yet persuade the courts—or failing this, the legislature—that dissolution and divestiture designed to injure hapless stockholders and workers is reasonable behavior. He cannot, of course, elect this approach unless he has convinced himself that failure to pursue an aggressive free market policy will ultimately place the country in dire jeopardy. (Some police-state variety of state socialism is generally made the end of the road for big-business capitalism by the ardent friends of trust busting.) For better or worse, most of us have not the confidence in our own prescience that this course requires.

3. The libertarian can discard the legalistic approach to antitrust problems and acknowledge monopoly power as a *de facto* property right which the state may not abruptly destroy without paying compensation. Thus, if the public interest is thought to require immediate dissolution in, say, the aluminum industry, the assets of the member firms could be acquired at their monopoly valuation and new firms organized and sold for what they would bring as competing units. To the extent that workers have managed to obtain part of the fruits of the industry's power over price, they, too, must be guaranteed against any sudden and appreciable loss of income sustained as a consequence of the compulsory reorganization.

4. Finally, the libertarian can abandon the regularized warfare of a trust-busting suit for guerrilla tactics. This entails recognizing that at this late date the large corporation is not to be destroyed by frontal assault, however much one may regret that it was allowed to entrench itself in the first place; and that the battle must also be maintained against those labor unions which by their own exertions and the active support of the federal government have cut themselves in on the prize of industrial monopoly. (The opponent of monopoly who

is not prepared to take on powerful members of the labor movement is really wasting his time.) For transforming competition among the giant few into something more acceptable, the libertarian will place his hopes in unspectacular Fabian sallies, notably the blocking of doubtful mergers, elimination of the secondary boycott, close scrutiny of the awarding of government favors, and curtailment of the patent privilege.

Whether measures of this sort will suffice to alter the face of the American economy in the foreseeable future is, of course, an unanswerable question. Their efficacy will depend partly upon the vigor with which they are pressed home but mostly upon the relative strengths of the forces making for or against industrial concentration that they can check and prod. Since mergers, patents, and government favors materially increased the levels of industrial concentration in the past we may reasonably hope that their curtailment will materially reduce industrial concentration in the future.

Appendix to Chapter XVII

THE PULLMAN AND PARAMOUNT CASES

1. *The Pullman decree*

Only two cases concluded under the "new" Sherman Act before January, 1958, seriously disturbed the corporate structures of important industries. The first involved the Pullman Company and the second the major Hollywood film producers. Although these suits established no new principles of law, they admirably illustrate the discrepancy between ideal and reality in trust-busting actions even under the most favorable circumstances.

For the thirty years prior to World War II, Pullman Incorporated through its two main subsidiaries—Pullman-Standard Manufacturing Company and the Pullman Company—manufactured, owned, and operated virtually all sleeping-car equipment carried on American railroads. In July, 1940, the Justice Department filed a civil action charging that the company had violated the Sherman Act by (a) having deliberately (and successfully) intrigued many years before to eliminate or absorb all rivals providing sleeping-car services and (b) scheming to ensure that the railroads carried only sleepers obtained on lease from Pullman.[1]

Various devices allegedly were used to secure this latter end. The company refused to sell its equipment to the railroads. It declined to furnish services on cars obtained from another manufacturer. By the use of long-term contracts with staggered expiration dates, it sought to ensure that its customer railroads would not be in a position to combine for the purpose of securing more favorable terms. The power of Pullman unlawfully secured in this manner was, according to the federal attorneys, employed to exact abnormally high charges for serv-

---

[1] For a recitation of the allegations in this case, see United States v. Pullman Co., 50 F. Supp. 123, 124–31 (E. D. Penn. 1943).

ice from the railroads and to slow down the introduction of improved equipment in order to prevent or minimize capital loss on its existing stock of cars.

As regards the bill of complaint, two observations may be ventured. First, the charges against the company were substantially true (though one may doubt that Pullman dealt with the country's railroads in quite the cavalier fashion depicted by the government). Second, the problem of securing better sleeper service on the railroads was more complicated than the government lawyers realized (or could acknowledge in court), being bound up with the drastic fall in railroad earnings after 1929 and the tangled mess of railroad reorganizations. Whether the restrictive practices of the Pullman Company would have excited much concern if the railroads had been in a stronger financial position is rather doubtful.

In its application for relief, the Justice Department sought to break the monopoly of Pullman on both the manufacture and the operation of sleeping cars. The first effort was unexceptionable, but the second was a doubtful incursion into the province of the Interstate Commerce Commission. The Justice Department, however, concentrated on the second goal only after the court had declined to help it toward the first. In the first case, Pullman Incorporated was merely directed to divest itself of either the manufacture or the operation of sleeping cars.[2]

Pullman officials indicated their willingness to withdraw from the operation side of their business (*i.e.*, to sell off the Pullman Company), but the federal lawyers insisted that the holding company be made to dispose of its manufacturing properties. The reasons for the government stand are not entirely clear, though it seems to have been inspired mainly by chagrin over the un-co-operative attitude of the management of Pullman Incorporated. Thus the federal attorney predicted that, given the probable postwar demand for new railroad equipment, the manufacturing side of the company's business would prove the most profitable, and they were loath to see it remain in the unclean hands of the Pullman management. They could also allege that stockholders would benefit if the company retained its operational service since the manufacturing properties could more readily be sold at a fair price.[3] The court refused to pass on the merits of these views. Pullman Incorporated was allowed to choose the form of divestiture,

---

[2] United States v. Pullman Co., 53 F. Supp. 908 (E. D. Penn. 1944).
[3] *Ibid.* 909–11

and it elected to sell its operating subsidiary to a buying group representing the major American railroads. Despite the protests of the Justice Department, this transaction was approved by the district court,[4] the Supreme Court,[5] and the Interstate Commerce Commission.[6] Thus the only readily apparent return from three years' litigation was the transfer of a public utility monopoly from one set of owners to another.

The view that the consumer interest benefited from this ending of vertical integration seems to rest on two contentions: (a) The industry can no longer pad its manufacturing costs in order to secure a higher rate base for sleeping-car fares. (b) More firms have entered upon the manufacture of sleeping cars as a consequence of the decree; hence the railroads have a wider choice of equipment and a better chance to improve sleeper service. The technique of padding accounting costs to raise the rate base has often been successfully employed by certain telephone companies whose charges are regulated by undermanned and often inept (or worse) state utility commissions, but it is difficult to believe that the experienced staff of the Interstate Commerce Commission was ever hoodwinked by such manipulation.

Those of us who hold a bias in favor of competition must count the entry of new manufacturing firms into the field a good thing; yet, given that sleeping-car fares are still subject to federal regulation, one can hardly accept the Pullman divestiture as a major blow to monopoly. In any event, a straightforward court order directing the Pullman Company to desist from refusing to furnish service on equipment that the railroads might acquire from other suppliers would have sufficed to ease the entry of new firms into the manufacture of sleeping cars.

Some observers consider the case important because it administered an unprecedented shock to the internal organization of a going concern. Pullman Incorporated—the ultimate holding company—in order to comply with a court ruling that directed it to withdraw from either the manufacture or the operation of sleeping cars, sold the rolling stock and goodwill of the Pullman Company for approximately 77 million dollars.[7] In the thirteen years before 1940 these properties had

---

[4] United States v. Pullman Co., 64 F. Supp. 108 (E. D. Penn. 1946).

[5] United States v. Pullman Co., 330 U.S. 806 (1947).

[6] *Pooling of Railroad Earnings and Service, Pullman Co.*, 268 I.C.C. 473 (1947).

[7] Pullman Incorporated obtained $36,567,500 from the sale of its modern equipment to individual railroads. *Annual Report, 1946* 15. It sold the stock of its operating subsidiary for $40,202,248. *Annual Report, 1948* 13.

accounted for roughly one-half the reported income of Pullman Incorporated.[8] The assumption is apparently that divestiture on this scale *could* have jeopardized the earnings of Pullman stockholders and employees.

This reasoning overlooks the fact that Pullman Incorporated chose divestiture in preference to dissolution, which would have entailed only a stock split and the granting of autonomy to the managers of the Pullman Company. Perhaps, from the standpoint of top management, divestiture is always preferable to dissolution since it conserves power. Nevertheless, in 1945 Pullman stockholders were probably well advised to exchange their antiquated equipment in a declining industry for such a sizable amount of cash. (Ninety per cent of Pullman's rolling stock was of predepression vintage at the time of the decree.[9])

Employees of the operating subsidiary were scarcely touched by divestiture. Indeed the safe assumption that railroad management would not prove a disturbing factor in labor relations seems to have influenced the Interstate Commerce Commission in its decision to permit the railroads to acquire the Pullman properties.[10]

2. *The motion picture case*

The actions against the major Hollywood producers—Paramount, Loew's, RKO, Warner Brothers, and Twentieth Century-Fox—represent in the opinion of one authority "probably the government's greatest economic victory in the 60-year history of antitrust enforcement."[11] In one sense this estimate is undoubtedly correct. In no other case involving a major corporaton has the government succeeded in gaining court approval for so many of its specific recommendations for relief. The Justice Department experienced no difficulty in securing a decree ending most of the features of film distribution which independent exhibitors had so often denounced as "unfair."[12] Struck down were non-competitive granting of runs on motion pictures, unreasonable

---

[8] *Annual Report, 1940* 4.

[9] *Pooling of Railroad Earnings and Service, Pullman Co.,* 268 I.C.C. 473, 475–76 (1947).

[10] *Ibid.,* pp. 490–91.

[11] Walter Adams, "The Aluminum Case: Legal Victory—Economic Defeat," 41 *Am. Econ. Rev.* 915, 915–16 (1951).

[12] United States v. Paramount Pictures, 70 F. Supp. 53 (S.D.N.Y. 1947).

clearance requirements, block booking, and pooling agreements among the defendants and between the defendants and independent exhibitors. Also eliminated was the form of resale price maintenance whereby the studios through their distributing companies set minimum admission charges at which their films could be shown.[13]

The district court, however, declined to grant the government's request that the major studios—the Big Five—should be compelled to withdraw from the ownership and management of theaters.[14] The opinion read by Augustus Hand concluded that no studio had acquired motion picture houses with the object of dominating the national market for films; that the control of theater circuits by the Big Five had not operated to exclude the Little Three—Universal, Columbia, and Republic—from exhibiting outlets in any important local market; and that the separation of the Big Five from their theater circuits would make no direct contribution to the elimination of unfair competition in the industry (which the court regarded as the main purpose of the proceedings). Judge Hand pointed out that most of the condemned competitive practices in distribution would almost certainly be employed by large independent exhibitors in their own interest unless they were explicitly restrained from doing so.[15] In short, the court concluded that the use of dissolution and divestiture against the Big Five did not promise either a higher level of ethics for the industry

---

[13] The unsavory aspects of film distribution have been probed exhaustively by federal agencies and Congressional committees over the years. The results are summarized in M. T. Huettig, *Economic Control of the Motion Picture Industry* (1944), and *The Motion Picture Industry* (TNEC Monograph No. 43, 1941).

[14] United States v. Paramount Pictures, 66 F. Supp. 323, 353 (S.D.N.Y. 1946).

[15] *Ibid.* 355.

For an example of what large independent exhibitors could do to smaller independents and the major studios in towns where the latter controlled no theaters, see Interstate Circuit v. United States, 306 U.S. 208 (1939).

In the 1930's two theater chains under a common management owned virtually all first-run houses in Dallas, Houston, San Antonio, Fort Worth, Austin, Galveston, Waco, Amarillo, and El Paso, and they demanded and obtained guarantees from all producers that any "A" feature exhibited by them would not reach the neighborhood houses too early, at too low prices, or on double bills. One letter to the local distributing agents of eight studios concluded bluntly: "In the event that a distributor sees fit to sell his product to subsequent runs in violation of this request, it definitely means that we cannot negotiate for his product to be exhibited in our 'A' theatres at top admission prices." 306 U.S. 208, 216.

or a lower scale of admission prices on motion pictures. The defendants were directed, however, to terminate their joint ownership of theaters or theater circuits with independent exhibitors.

The corporate superstructure of theater properties was so complicated by the time of the suit that it was impossible to tell exactly how many motion picture houses were actually "controlled" by the major studios. In 1945, according to figures cited by the court, of the country's 18,076 theaters, 1,636 were wholly owned by the major studios, 1,287 were jointly owned by a defendant and an independent exhibitor, and 214 were owned jointly by two of the studios. Every theater in which a studio had a stock interest greater than 5 per cent, however, was regarded by the court as under its domination. One defendant—Paramount—owned outright or with independent exhibitors 1,395 theaters, or nearly one-half of the 3,137 tied houses in the industry. According to evidence accepted by the court, the theaters comprising the circuits of the Big Five in 1945 paid approximately 45 per cent of the domestic film rentals received by all Hollywood producers.[16]

In May, 1948, the Supreme Court (after what a dissenting justice considered a perfunctory look at the 3,841-page court record) ruled that the government was entitled to additional relief.[17] The lower court then complied with the government's request that the film studios be compelled to withdraw from theater operation. In addition, the theater chains turned loose by divorcement were required to sell off theaters in some cities where they had more than one first-run outlet.

The rearrangement of corporate structures achieved by the *Paramount* case was impressive. But was there any material benefit to the public through the reduction of monopoly power? Given the complication introduced by the impact of television on movie attendance in recent years, this question cannot be answered with much confidence one way or the other.[18] For many years the central "fact" in film distribution has been the conflict between producer and exhibitor over the type of price discrimination to be practiced in the release of

---

[16] 70 F. Supp. 53, 67–68.

[17] United States v. Paramount Pictures, 334 U.S. 131 (1948).

[18] Doubtless the television revolution following so closely on the government's victory in the *Paramount* case affords sardonic satisfaction to all who doubt the worth of an antitrust policy in a world of innovation. It brings to mind the classic case of unnecessary effort, Q.R.S. Music Co. v. Federal Trade Commission, 12 F.2d 730 (7th Cir. 1926). Here the commission successfully attacked the hold of the firm on the market for the paper rolls used in player pianos, and in five years the market itself was extinct.

pictures. The producer wishes to ensure that anyone who will pay a dollar to see his latest epic today will not be discouraged from doing so by the knowledge that it will reach a cheaper theater within the week; the independent exhibitor commonly has every incentive to reduce admission prices in order to tap the lower-price market that producers prefer to reserve for exploitation at a later date.

Federal intervention in the industry was undertaken on the untestable assumption that the public interest in the conflict lay with the smaller exhibitor. (It is quite impossible to say how alternative policies of discrimination would affect the rate of motion picture attendance or the quality of films.) At the local level, the Big Five producers enjoyed some monopoly power by virtue of their participation in the gentlemen's agreements that prevail in localities where theater owners are few. This power was not touched by the separation of production from exhibition in the integrated companies; rather it was vested more securely in the managers of the freed theater circuits, who gained a free hand in the selection of price policies.

Only two benefits to the general public were indubitably conferred by the decree. In some towns, compliance with the divestiture provision increased the number of theater owners—or would have, had not television closed so many houses after 1945. The limitations placed on block booking have made it easier for the independent producer to find outlets on favorable terms for his offerings, with the result that the "A" film market is no longer so completely dominated by the major producers. On balance, the *Paramount* decree probably contributed to freer trade in the production and distribution of motion pictures.[19] But, so far as the author can discern, this result was a largely fortuitous by-product of the Court's effort to afford small theater owners some relief from the "unfair" pressures of the major producers.

---

[19] For a more confident statement of this view see Ralph Cassady, "Impact of the Paramount Decision on Motion Picture Distribution and Price Making," 31 *So. Calif. L. Rev.* 150 (1958).

Chapter *XVIII*

THE LAW OF LABOR MONOPOLY

1. *Labor unions and the antitrust laws*

Over the years the attention devoted to the impact of the antitrust laws on labor unions has greatly exceeded the importance of the subject. This is not to say that the activities of labor unions are not an important part of the monopoly problem. One may plausibly argue, as did Henry Simons, that policywise they present the toughest issues.[1] Neither the Attorney General nor the courts, however, have been disposed to probe the economics of labor monopoly in cases arising under the antitrust laws. Except for a brief period prior to World War II when Thurman Arnold[2] headed the Antitrust Division, federal officials by their inaction have given labor unions a virtual immunity from governmental supervision.[3] In private litigation, the courts have often affirmed that some activities of labor unions may violate the antitrust law, but they have long employed a double standard which accords far greater freedom of action to labor unions than to business firms.

In general, the "normal" activities of labor unions in no sense constitute unlawful combination regardless of their effect upon wages, employment, or the price of an industry's product. Under the antitrust laws, as under the common law,[4] an organized worker demand for

---

[1] *Economic Policy for a Free Society* (1948), especially 121–59.

[2] Arnold's modest proposals for bringing labor unions under the antitrust laws are set out in his *The Bottlenecks of Business* 240–59 (1940). They mainly aim at reducing the incidence of sympathy strikes and secondary boycotts.

[3] On at least one occasion their hands were tied by legislation. In appropriating funds for the enforcement of the antitrust laws for the fiscal year 1923, Congress directed that no part of the money should be spent in the prosecution of labor unions. 42 *Stat.* 613 (1922).

[4] The notable exception to the proposition that the common law offered no obstacle to a collective refusal to work was the short-lived doctrine that union efforts to organize workers could constitute "interference with contractual re-

improved working conditions backed by a collective refusal to work—and nothing more—has hardly ever subjected labor unions to criminal penalties, damage suits, or equitable restraints.[5]

2. *The case for leniency toward labor monopoly*

Probably only ardent social planners and authoritarians of various hues now believe that labor unions should be treated as conspiracies against the public interest when they try to improve the lot of their members by collective bargaining. Among moderate men, the wisdom of a double standard in antitrust policy is almost universally acknowledged. There is, however, some difference of opinion regarding the reasons why labor unions should be accorded immunities not granted to employer groups.

By one view, labor unions ought to enjoy immunity from the antitrust laws because the economic significance of their activities is negligible—they have no appreciable power over wages, hours, and working conditions. Doubtless the great majority of the 15 million-odd

---

lations" or "inducing breach of contract." While the origin of this doctrine can be traced to the old action against a third party who "enticed" one's servants away, it did not reach full flowering until Taff Vale Ry. v. Amalgamated Society of Railway Servants, (1901) A.C. 426 (H.L.); and Hitchman Coal Co. v. Mitchell, 245 U.S. 229 (1917).

In the English case, the employer's right to an injunction that would restrain a union from inducing his workers to break their contracts, though disputed by the defendant, was taken for granted by the court; the law lords were mainly concerned to show that a trade-union could be sued in its own name. In the American case, the Supreme Court in possibly the worst opinion since the *Dred Scott* decision actually enjoined the miners' union from organizing the employees of a coal company that used the "yellow dog" contract, *i.e.*, made non-membership in a union a condition of employment. The union's liability for enticing away the employer's "servants" was effectively ended in Britain by the Trade Disputes Act of 1906, 6 Edw. 7, c. 47 and in the United States by the Norris-La Guardia Act, 47 *Stat.* 70 (1932).

The history of the enticement doctrine is given in C. E. Carpenter, "Interference with Contract Relations," 41 *Harv. L. Rev.* 728 (1928). Its beginnings are discussed in W. L. Hodge, "Wrongful Interference by Third Parties with the Rights of Employers and Employed," 28 *Am. L. Rev.* 47 (1894).

[5] One authority has uncovered a number of early unreported cases in which the lower federal courts apparently treated union activities as unlawful under the Sherman Act in so far as they affected interstate commerce. E. E. Witte, *The Government in Labor Disputes* 65–66 (1932). Thus, in 1911 five Negro longshoremen at Jacksonville, Florida, were persuaded to plead guilty to a charge of restraining commerce by participating in a peaceful strike seeking recognition for their union.

union members in the United States belong to unions so weak that collective bargaining does little, if anything, for their incomes,[6] but the notion that the present place of railroad train crews in the top 15 per cent of American income recipients does not reflect the power of the railroad brotherhoods cannot be taken seriously. In any event, unless most labor leaders are wasting their time, the presumption must be that unions can—and sometimes do—perceptibly influence labor costs and hence the distribution of manpower and materials in the economy.

Many authorities, following the courts, argue that labor unions should not be treated as combinations in restraint of trade because they intend no harm to consumers of final products. That unions do not much worry about the effect of labor costs on the prices of final products is true enough. Indeed they are often criticized for precisely this oversight by economists who contend that the high wage policies of unions "cause" unemployment by raising prices to consumers and encouraging employers to change the factor combination.[7] But absence of wrong intent is no adequate reason for exempting labor unions from the consequences of their acts.

One may fall back on the venerable argument that labor unions are good because they countervail the employer's monopsony power in the labor market; that by making it impossible for him to depress wage rates by reducing his demand for labor, they may cause more, not less, labor to be hired. This argument is valid in so far as employers who are subject to union pressure have monopsony power and the union strength does no more than countervail such power. It may command respect in a case where skilled workers are pitted against their employer in an isolated community that offers them no comparable jobs, e.g., in many a West Virginia mining community. But the argument clearly does not hold for the vastly greater number of situations where

---

[6] As yet no one can say, with any high degree of precision, how much difference the growth of labor unions has made to the distribution of income in the United States. For the argument—buttressed by some statistical analysis— that unions may have raised the wage rates of 10 per cent of the labor force by 15 per cent while depressing the wage rates of all other workers by from 1 to 4 per cent, see Milton Friedman, "Some Comments on the Significance of Labor Unions for Economic Policy," in *The Impact of the Union* 204 (Wright ed. 1951).

[7] For a lucid statement of the representative economist's assumption that union success in raising wages above the competitive level "will contract the demand for labour, and make it impossible to absorb some of the men available," see J. R. Hicks, *The Theory of Wages* 179–97 (1932).

organized unskilled and semi-skilled workers confront employers in urban areas.

Again, an exemption of unions from the antitrust laws can be justified by invoking the distinction drawn by one economist between "price makers" and "price takers." By his analysis, the two conditions necessary for price making are (1) "a disparity in numbers between the two sides of the market, which disrupts personal contacts between buyer and seller and renders bargaining uneconomical" and (2) "the inexpertness of one side of the market which, of course, is always the side with the larger numbers."[8] Since efficient production requires the specialization of both manpower and machinery, employers and employees alike give hostages to one another in the form of Alfred Marshall's quasi-rent—that portion of the joint product that can be taken by one party without causing any other to diminish his efforts and hence reduce the size of the joint product itself. In the absence of collective bargaining, employers are doubtless well placed to appropriate the greater share of that part of the joint product whose division can be bargained over.[9]

The best reason for not treating labor unions as suspect conspiracies is, of course, that most people would view such a policy as grossly unfair. The commonplace view assumes that most labor disputes are private contests between masters and hands, that masters are richer than hands, and government intervention against unions would serve the unacceptable purpose of making the rich richer. This view further assumes, in effect, that (a) workers can command a higher total wage bill from an employer if collective bargaining is possible and (b) the gains of collective bargaining will mainly be exacted from the employer rather than the public.

In the short run, the first assumption is clearly valid, for the existence of quasi-rent ensures the "indeterminancy" of the wage rate and wage bill under collective bargaining. Nor is the validity of this assumption controverted by the probability that the wage bill of the

---

[8] Tibor Scitovsky, *Welfare and Competition* 16–22 (1951).

[9] Recognition of the employer's advantage in the bargaining over quasi-rents plete worker rationality is assumed, the implicit defense of collective bargaining that rests on the distinction between price makers and price takers does not hold. The long-run supply price of labor will merely be higher to an industry to the extent that technological developments have placed short-run bargaining advantage with employers.

employer will eventually decline as he becomes able to withdraw capital from the business or change his factor combination. Since some union members will also die, retire, or quit with the passing of time, thus relieving the employer of the necessity of firing anyone in the interest of profit maximization, workers understandably disregard the long-run effect of union policy upon the fortunes of their union and their employer.

The truth of the second assumption is not so self-evident. The allocation of the burden of a wage increase between employer and public will depend upon (a) the elasticity of demand for the employer's product, (b) the technical possibilities of substitution for labor in the factor combination, and (c) the willingness of the union to accept a reduction in employment, *i.e.*, its willingness to allow the employer to avail himself of the opportunity to minimize the impact of the wage concession upon his costs. In the case of a regulated public utility company which, as a matter of right, is entitled to a "fair return on a fair valuation of investment," the whole of any wage increase could conceivably be passed on to the public. In the case of most firms, the presumption is that consumer demand is quite elastic and, hence, that in the short run a wage increase is likely to be borne mostly by the employer.

In short, when attention is limited to the more immediate economic consequences of collective bargaining, the popular prejudice against having the State intervene to aid employers against unions turns out to be justified. The usual labor dispute is a clash of wills and bargaining skill between private parties over the distribution of quasi-rent in which the government is not particularly concerned. The long-run economic consequences of collective bargaining are likely to be blunted by the difficulty that the union will face in "covering the market," *i.e.*, organizing all workers in the industry so that unionized firms paying higher wages do not lose ground to their unorganized competitors; and by the inability of the union to keep employers from cutting down on labor in response to the concession of higher wages. We may conclude, then, that the public benefits to be gained by having the State intervene in the usual labor dispute over wages and hours are highly nebulous—a truth which most judges have perceived ever since we have had reported decisions.

Nevertheless, in so far as a union does manage to cover the labor market and gain control over the factor combination, the private conflict between an employer and his workers over the division of quasi-rent is transformed into a contest in which the public interest lies on the side of the employer—hence, the hostility of many economists to the idea of industry-wide bargaining. Indeed, if the life of the law were logic, the libertarian would be obliged to support measures that would allow unions to countervail the employer's bargaining power—but nothing more. This limitation could most directly be secured by confining collective bargaining to the company level and treating the concerted action of the organized employees of different firms as unlawful conspiracy. But as the admirers of Justice Holmes will never let us forget, the life of the law is, in fact, experience. This country should have no more encouraged by the Wagner Act (1935)[10] the spread of industry-wide bargaining and the secondary boycott than it should have permitted by inaction the wholesale mergers that produced the present level of corporate concentration in the economy; yet the error was made with a vengeance and the more favorably situated industrial workers encouraged to seek out and enjoy the advantages of market power. The libertarian may properly seek to withdraw this power by installments, but it would be immoral—and unthinkable politics—to attempt a frontal assault.

Unfortunately, union pressures which serve to redistribute quasi-rents are not easily distinguished from those which serve to benefit organized workers at the expense of the public; and so long as union tactics do not lead to violence, radically disrupt the provision of an important service, or grossly infringe the rights of third parties, neither legislators nor judges are interested in making any such distinction. For this reason proposed legislation that seeks only to suppress obnoxious union tactics would not greatly affect certain unions whose policies nevertheless perceptibly influence wages and prices. These bodies are so well entrenched already that a straightforward withdrawal of their members' labor is their strongest weapon; they have no need to resort to violence which, after all, is the expedient of the insecure.

The popular tendency to look with favor on decorous labor monopoly is not wholly irrational; and it admirably illustrates the premium which most of us place on a more peaceful conduct of labor relations. The economic significance of this indulgence should not be exaggerated. Only unions composed of highly skilled workers with a sense of professional solidarity (printers, high altitude steel workers, etc.) can hope to achieve it. Unions that organize mainly unskilled workers must either forgo substantial monopoly power or else seek it

---

[10] 49 *Stat.* 449.

through preferential legislation or tactics which are legally suspect. The railroad brotherhoods have successfully exploited the political approach to secure and advance their interests, while the teamsters' union with its predilection for mass picketing, secondary boycotts, and picket line "incidents" has shown the possibilities of direct action. Given the lack of popular hostility to decorous labor monopoly, it is not surprising that cases involving labor unions as combinations in restraint of trade fall, with unimportant exceptions, into one or more of the following classes.

1. Cases involving professional criminals who had seized the leadership of unions for the purpose of shaking down employers and union members.

2. Cases where union officials or members in the heat of battle committed acts which are crimes or torts, *e.g.*, physical assault on non-strikers or destruction of the employer's property.

3. Cases where union leaders, in order to advance the interests of their members, have knowingly lent their support to the activities of employers that violated the antitrust laws.

4. Cases in which the union employed labor weapons whose legal status has never been satisfactorily determined, notably "secondary" boycotts.

5. Cases where the interruption of production caused by a strike has jeopardized the public welfare.

6. Cases where the union's main concern in endeavoring to force an employer to terms lay not in advancing the interests of his organized workers but in preventing him from expanding his business at the expense of rivals who had entered into union contracts.

3. *Minor difficulties of unions under the antitrust laws*

Cases falling into the first two categories have produced no principles of law worth noting. Rather they exemplify the American practice of finding punishments for offenses which cannot be successfully prosecuted under more appropriate statutes. Labor racketeers are not easily convicted of the crimes of murder, arson, extortion, and felonious assault; prosecutors find it easier to produce evidence that they have unlawfully restrained interstate commerce.[11] In cases involving strike

---

[11] Thus the vicious live poultry racket, which flourished in metropolitan New York before 1935 and produced ten murders in five years, was attacked with some success under the antitrust laws. Clair Wilcox, *Competition and Monopoly in American Industry* 294–95 (TNEC Monograph No. 21, 1940).

violence, the modest penalties of the Sherman Act have proved more acceptable to juries than those prescribed by the ordinary criminal code,[12] though in recent years the courts have frowned on the use of the antitrust laws to afford remedies that are available under more appropriate acts. Thus, in the *Apex* case (1940)[13] the Supreme Court set aside an award of damages against a union whose members in a sit-down strike had wantonly destroyed the plaintiff's property. The majority opinion here argued that the Sherman Act was inapplicable since (a) strikers manifested no "intent" to affect the price of hosiery and (b) the firm's output was too small to make much difference one way or the other to the price of the industry's product; hence, the proper remedy for the plaintiff was a suit for damages in a state court. In *United States v. Gold* (1940)[14] the circuit court of appeals ruled that the palpably illegal acts by a furriers' union even though coupled with an obvious "intent" to affect the prices of fur goods were not enough. The criminal conviction of the defendants was reversed because, although they had attempted to shut down three non-union firms located in Newark, New Jersey, and supplying the New York market, "the operations of those firms were not shown to have been upon a large enough scale to make their cessation affect market conditions in New York."[15]

The rule that labor unions violate the antitrust laws when they knowingly assist an unlawful combination of employers was affirmed by the Supreme Court in *United States v. Brims* (1926).[16] In this case the officers of the carpenters' union were convicted of conspiring with building contractors and manufacturers of millwork to ensure that only the millwork of unionized mills was installed by their members in the Chicago area.[17] The co-operation apparently came about when con-

---

[12] On one occasion strikers offended against the Sherman Act by dynamiting a stretch of railroad track after warning passengers against travelling on the line. Vandell v. United States, 6 F.2d 188 (2d Cir. 1925).

[13] Apex Hosiery v. Leader, 310 U.S. 469.

[14] 115 F.2d 236 (2d Cir.).

[15] *Ibid.* 238.

[16] 272 U.S. 549.

[17] A similar case was earlier decided in a circuit court. Boyle v. United States, 259 Fed. 803 (7th Cir. 1919). In this case the court upheld a criminal conviction against manufacturers of electrical equipment and union leaders in the Chicago area. The manufacturers agreed to contracts with the union in return for an assurance that union men would not install certain competing electrical appliances imported from non-union plants outside the state. This case, however, was also complicated by an element of racketeering. Union leaders occasionally

tractors and manufactures that employed union carpenters found themselves at a competitive disadvantage vis à vis competitors that used non-union carpenters.

4. *The problem of the secondary boycott*

The controversial cases involving labor unions decided under the anti-trust laws fall mainly into the fourth category and turn upon the legal status of tactics that are popularly known as secondary boycotts. The most famous of these cases is, of course, *Loewe v. Lawlor*[18]—the affair of the Danbury hatters.

The United Hatters of North America, an A. F. of L. affiliate, sought to organize the Danbury, Connecticut, shop of Dietrich E. Loewe and his partner. Tempted by the pledge of a subsidy of $20,000 from members of the industry who were interested in humbling the union,[19] Loewe refused to sign a contract with the union; whereupon union leaders called a strike at the Danbury shop and had its products placed on the A. F. of L. "we don't patronize" list. The dispute began in July, 1902; litigation arising out of it was not settled until the case reached the Supreme Court for the second time, the final decision being given in January, 1915.

The case raised two main issues.[20] (1) Was the boycott enforced by the hatters' union against Loewe an unlawful restraint under the Sherman Act? (2) Were the individual members of the local Danbury hatters' union personally liable for damages suffered by the plaintiff as a consequence of their unlawful acts? Speaking for the Court, Justice Holmes emphatically answered both questions in the affirmative. Citing *Eastern States Lumber Dealers' Ass'n v. United States* (1913)[21] he held:

> Whatever may be the law otherwise, that case establishes that, irrespective of compulsion or even agreement to observe its intimation, the circulation of a list of "unfair dealers,"

---

accepted bribes to permit the installation of electrical equipment by non-union labor and smashed such equipment when "penalty" money was not paid.

[18] 235 U.S. 522 (1915).

[19] Elias Lieberman, *Unions Before the Bar* 57 (1950).

[20] Before the case went to the jury, the Supreme Court also heard argument on the general applicability of the Sherman Act to labor unions, but its decision that a labor union had no blanket exemption was never in much doubt. *Lawlor v. Loewe*, 208 U.S. 274 (1908).

[21] 234 U.S. 600.

manifestly intended to put the ban upon those whose names appear therein, among an important body of possible customers combined with a view to joint action and in anticipation of such reports, is within the prohibition of the Sherman Act if it is intended to restrain and restrains commerce among the States.[22]

Nor, according to Justice Holmes, did the trial judge err when he charged the jury that if union members "paid their dues and continued to delegate authority to their officers unlawfully to interfere with the plaintiffs' interstate commerce in such circumstances that they knew or ought to have known, and such officers were warranted in the belief that they were acting in the matters within their delegated authority, then such members were jointly liable, and no others."[23] By the terms of the jury verdict, the Danbury hatters were liable to pay $252,130 in damages to their injured employers.

The doubtful justice, if not the absurdity, of making individual union members liable for damages suffered by an employer in the course of a dispute was not considered by the Supreme Court. This doctrine of individual liability made sense only because American courts in 1915 still clung to the obsolete rule that a labor union, as an unincorporated association, could not be sued in its own name. Presumably, if the Danbury hatters were not individually liable for the unlawful damage done to Lawlor, then he had no remedy at all—an equally absurd situation. The Congressional reaction to the *Danbury hatters* decision, however, sufficed to produce the labor provisions of the Clayton Act which, at least in union circles, were thought to overrule the Supreme Court.[24]

The issue of the secondary boycott promptly returned to the courts following the passage of the Clayton Act in *Duplex Co. v. Deering* (1921).[25] In this case, the International Machinists' Union in its dispute with a manufacturer of newspaper printing presses sought to dissuade his customers from buying his machines. In addition, the union endeavored to persuade or coerce its own members and other organized workers into refusing to transport or service Duplex presses

[22] 235 U.S. 522, 534.

[23] *Ibid.* 534–35.

[24] The Executive Council of the American Federation of Labor welcomed the Clayton Act as precluding "the possibility of any similar suit being brought in the federal courts for the exercise of normal activities as performed by the Hatters since the enactment of the law." 22 *American Federationist* 116 (1915).

[25] 254 U.S. 443.

or do business with firms which used the Duplex presses. The case turned upon the definition of the "secondary" boycott and judicial interpretation of Congressional intent. The circuit court of appeals treated the plaintiff's request for an injunction as an application for relief from the effects of a secondary boycott, and it denied the injunction on the ground that the Clayton Act had specifically legalized this labor weapon. A majority of the Supreme Court held otherwise.

Justice Pitney, speaking for the Court, defined the secondary boycott as "a combination not merely to refrain from dealing with complainant, or to advise or by peaceful means persuade complainant's customers to refrain ('primary boycott'), but to exercise coercive pressure upon such customers, actual or prospective, in order to cause them to withhold or withdraw patronage from complainant through fear of loss or damage to themselves should they deal with it."[26] The majority opinion then cited the Congressional debates on the Clayton Act to support its ruling that Congress had never intended to legalize the secondary boycott, so defined. Unfortunately, in this case it is not clear whether the injunction was granted because (a) the machinists' union boycotted firms which dealt with Duplex, (b) the methods employed by the machinists' union to dissuade the Duplex customers were unsavory, e.g., refusing to repair their machines and branding their employees as "scabs," or (c) the defendant union officers were not themselves employees of Duplex or the local representatives of the striking Duplex employees.

For better or worse, this ambiguity was largely dispelled in *Bedford Cut Stone Co. v. Journeymen Stone Cutters' Ass'n* (1927).[27] In this case, the organized stonecutters under penalty of expulsion from the union refused to work on stone obtained from a quarry which had not signed a contract with the union. This refusal seemingly was a clear-cut instance of the "primary" boycott which had received the implied sanction of the Supreme Court in the *Duplex* case; yet the majority opinion inexplicably could perceive no basis for distinguishing it from this earlier case and reversed the lower court's refusal to enjoin the boycott.

United States v. Hutcheson (1941),[28] however, effectively overruled the *Duplex* and *Bedford* decisions. Here the A. F. of L. carpenters' union in the course of a jurisdictional dispute with the A. F. of L. machinists' union struck the Anheuser-Busch brewery at St. Louis and

---

[26] *Ibid.* 466.
[27] 274 U.S. 37.
[28] 312 U.S. 219.

called for a nationwide boycott of the company's product. A criminal indictment was returned against Hutcheson and other officers of the carpenters' union, but on appeal the Supreme Court sustained the defendant's demurrers denying that what was charged constituted a violation of the antitrust laws. While the majority opinion delivered by Justice Frankfurter is no model of clarity, it seems to say that (a) the unlawful acts alleged against the defendants were not covered by the antitrust laws since the unions had not combined with non-labor groups and (b) the *Duplex* and *Bedford* decisions had been overruled by the Norris-La Guardia Act whose aim "was to restore the broad purpose which Congress thought it had formulated in the Clayton Act but which was frustrated, so Congress believed, by unduly restrictive judicial construction."[29] In a concurring opinion Justice Stone preferred to rely upon a narrower doctrine. The indictment, he felt, was defective in that the activities of the union complained of neither caused, nor were intended to cause, an increase in the price of malt beverage.

By the *Hutcheson* decision the secondary boycott when employed by a labor union ceased to be a federal offense. This total exemption, however, was short-lived, since in the Taft-Hartley Act (1947)[30] the secondary boycott was resurrected as an "unfair" labor practice which the National Labor Relations Board could restrain by administrative order. As yet not enough cases have reached the Supreme Court to make clear the new law of boycott.[31]

At present the most important unanswered question is the legal status of a worker's obligation to handle—or refrain from handling—goods in transit to or from an employer engaged in a labor dispute—so-called "hot cargo."[32] A divided Supreme Court has held that when a worker is covered by a collective bargaining agreement that obligates him to handle hot cargo, he may be fired for refusing to cross another union's picket line.[33] In a recent case a divided Supreme Court also explicitly recognized the right of a union to negotiate a contract that

---

[29] 312 U.S. 219, 236.

[30] 61 *Stat.* 136.

[31] The evolution of the new law of secondary boycott is traced in Bernard Cushman, "Secondary Boycotts and the Taft-Hartley Law," 6 *Syracuse L. Rev.* 108 (1954), and C. P. Barker, "Evolution of the Secondary Boycott and Modification of 'Hot Cargo' Clause Defense," 11 *Sw. L. J.* 455 (1957).

[32] For the finer points of this uncertainty see J. F. Lawless, "Hot Cargo Clauses: A Problem in Their Application to Secondary Boycotts," 15 *Fed. Bar. J.* 76 (1955), and Note, "Hot Cargo Clauses," 25 *U. Chi. Rev.* 182 (1957).

[33] National L. R. Bd. v. Rockaway News Supply Co., 345 U.S. 71 (1953).

allows its members to refuse the handling of hot cargo; but, at the same time, the Court took the curious position that (a) such a contract is not enforceable and (b) if workers use the right to boycott hot cargo which their employer once conceded but now denies, they are guilty of an unfair labor practice.[34] Thus a secondary boycott is lawful if the employer agrees to abide by a hot cargo provision of a collective bargaining agreement and unlawful if he reneges—an unusual and unsatisfactory situation. Nevertheless, if organized workers can contract out of the obligation to handle the goods of employers engaged in labor disputes, the boycott provision of the Taft-Hartley Act will remain largely a dead letter. It is improbable that many employers who have conceded the union's right not to handle hot cargo in a contract will refuse to honor the concession when put to the test. Once again, the greater the monopoly power of a union, the less likely it is to run afoul of the law since employers are more disposed to respect scrupulously contracts with strong unions than with weak ones.[35]

5. Strikes that threaten the public safety

In the absence of explicit legislation dealing with strikes that create a public emergency, the temptation to use the Sherman Act for this purpose is not surprising. The remarkable thing is that before the Taft-Hartley Act, the Attorney General seems to have resorted to this expedient in only two major labor disputes—the Pullman strike of 1894 and the shopmen's strike of 1922.

---

[34] Carpenters' Local 1976 v. NLRB, 357 U.S. 93(1958).

In upholding the right of a union to seek a contract that allowed its members to refuse the handling of hot cargo, the Supreme Court followed Rabouin v. NLRB, 195 F.2d 906 (2d Cir. 1952).

Here the lower court reasoned that (a) the Taft-Hartley Act forbade only secondary boycotts by "employees," (b) the union had sought to dissuade only "employers" from handling hot cargo, and hence (c) the union had not committed an unfair labor practice. In this case the plaintiff had violated his contract with the union and the court was therefore loath to allow him to "profit from his own primary wrong."

[35] Not that the Taft-Hartley Act has been wholly without effect in modifying the *Hutcheson* decision. Thus in two cases decided in 1950 the Supreme Court condemned the efforts of unions by strikes and picketing to force an employer whose workers they did not represent to dismiss non-union men. National L. R. Bd. v. Denver Bldg. Council, 341 U.S. 675 (1951); Electrical Workers v. NLRB, 341 U.S. 694 (1951).

On both occasions, the lower courts affirmed the right of the government to use the Sherman Act in order to break strikes that were unduly interfering with the operation of major railroads, but in neither case was the lower court ruling endorsed by the Supreme Court. When a contempt proceeding was brought against Eugene Debs for failing to observe an injunction for his part in maintaining the Pullman strike, the Supreme Court refused to rule on the applicability of the Sherman Act to the case[36] but chose instead to treat the federal government's right to intervene as an inherent attribute of sovereignty. No case arising out of the shopmen's strike reached the Supreme Court.[37]

6. *Union pressures directed at consumer prices*

The presence or absence of union "intent" to affect the price of the employer's product lies close to the heart of the labor monopoly problem. It was most fully explored in the long litigation that comprised the two *Coronado* cases which remained in the courts from September, 1914, to October, 1927. The cases arose out of losses suffered by a coal company with mines in the neighborhood of Prairie Creek, Arkansas, in the course of its attempt to operate without an agreement with the United Mine Workers. Neither side came into court with particularly clean hands, though the miners had committed more clearly criminal acts—beating up of strikebreakers, destruction of mine property, and the other breaches of the peace that so often accompany a strike in the coal fields.

As the case moved up and down the federal courts through appeal and remand, judges and justices gave almost every possible ruling on the applicability of the Sherman Act to losses incurred by the company during the strike. In the first case, the action was dismissed by the trial judge for want of jurisdiction. By his findings, the union activities complained of did not constitute interference with interstate commerce and hence were not covered by the Sherman Act.[38] On appeal the action was reinstated by the circuit court on the ground that any interference with the physical movement of coal cars across state lines was perforce interference with interstate commerce.[39]

---

[36] *In re* Debs, 158 U.S. 564 (1895).

[37] For the position taken by the district court in the most important case arising out of the strike see United States v. Railway Employees' Dept. of A.F. of L., 290 Fed. 978 (N.D. Ill. 1923).

[38] Dowd v. United Mine Workers, 235 Fed. 1, 3 (8th Cir. 1916).

[39] *Ibid.* 9.

When the case came to trial, treble damages, interest, and costs totalling $745,000 were assessed against the union. The award was upheld in the circuit court of appeals,[40] except that $120,600 interest retroactive to July, 1914, was disallowed.[41] When the case finally reached the Supreme Court, Chief Justice Taft, speaking for the majority, depreciated the importance of any intent to restrain commerce, arguing that the union was not endeavoring to reduce the output of coal in the interests of higher prices; and that, in any event, the 5,000 tons shipped from the plaintiff's pits in his most prosperous weeks were an insignificant fraction of the national total of from 10 to 15 million tons a week.[42] According to the Chief Justice, the criminal acts of the union that damaged the plaintiff could more plausibly be explained by simple hostility to his effort to operate a non-union mine in a traditionally union territory. Therefore, the damage award was reversed.

The plaintiff thereupon returned to law, claiming that the strike against his mines was a part of the international union's design to protect high-cost union mines by preventing the cheaper coal of non-union mines from coming to market. New witnesses were presented by the plaintiff to bolster this charge, including the famous eavesdropping doctor who testified that in his hotel lobby he had heard union officers assert that the plaintiff must be defeated lest the largest union mine in the area abrogate its contract with the United Mine Workers.

The district court, however, refused to accept the new evidence as material and directed a verdict for the defendants, and the circuit court of appeals concurred. But on the plaintiff's appeal, the Supreme Court held that the potential weekly output of the plaintiff's mines was much greater than the court perceived at the first trial; hence the new evidence purporting to show the union's intent to raise the price of coal should have gone to the jury.[43] The third trial produced a hung jury, and to avoid a fourth, the case was settled in October, 1927, the union agreeing to pay $27,500 in damages.[44]

In fine, the *Coronado* doctrine, although often cited as a union defeat, ratified the exemptions of most labor disputes from the Sherman Act. Unions seldom worry much about the effect of a wage increase or hours reduction upon an employer's cost of production and

---

[40] United Mine Workers v. Coronado Coal Co., 258 Fed. 829 (8th Cir. 1919).

[41] United Mine Workers v. Coronado Coal Co., 259 U.S. 344, 347 (1922).

[42] *Ibid.* 412.

[43] Coronado Coal Co. v. United Mine Workers, 268 U.S. 295, 309 (1925).

[44] Lieberman, *Unions Before the Bar* 160.

price policy—that is, they hardly ever aim at "directly" restraining competition in the provision of final products.[45] Even when they do, the difficulties involved in proving such an unlawful intent in court leave injured parties little incentive to seek injunctions and treble damages.

7. *Ideal and reality in labor disputes*

We might note that, so long as the common law is not amended by statute, courts are compelled to undertake intervention in labor disputes which strengthens the hands of employers. By common law an employee may remain at his job in defiance of a strike call; the employer is entitled to replace strikers with whomsoever he can; non-strikers and strikebreakers are entitled to work without fear of bodily harm, damage to their property, or exposure to unreasonably abusive language; and the public may do business with the employer without being molested by union sympathizers. Consequently, at common law union members may only seek to bring pressure to bear on their temporary adversary by withdrawing their labor and peacefully petitioning for the support of non-strikers, strikebreakers, and the public. The history of violence in labor disputes, together with the enduring problem of sympathy strikes and secondary boycotts, indicates that organized workers are unwilling to limit their pressures to these weak measures. The nineteenth-century judge who, in an unguarded moment, doubted that a strike could be both lawful and effective was perilously close to the truth.[46]

The main obstacle to a more satisfactory conduct of collective bargaining lies, of course, in the discrepancy between the law and popular morality, for while most workers believe that they should have property rights in their jobs, the common law holds otherwise.

---

[45] For one of the few cases where a union deliberately sought to raise prices to consumers, see South Wales Miners' Federation v. Glamorgan Coal Co., (1905) A.C. 239 (H.L.). Here the union had contracts with mine owners tying the wage rate to the price of coal. When the price of coal showed signs of falling, the union would declare a "stop day" for its 100,000 members in order to reduce coal stocks.

In this case the House of Lords did not consider the consumer interest but ruled only that the union committed a wrong in "inducing" members to break their contracts. This decision was promptly overruled by the Trade Disputes Act of 1906, 6 Edw. 7, c. 47.

[46] See the interruption of counsel by Lord Justice Lindley in J. Lyons & Sons v. Wilkins, 1 Ch. 811, 820 (1896).

The courts cannot excuse palpably unlawful acts committed in the course of a labor dispute merely because the offenders are normally law-abiding citizens who experience no sense of wrongdoing in perpetrating strike violence.

Unfortunately, the common law's operational bias in favor of employers and non-union workers has not saved judges from the charge that they exhibit a concern for the rights of employers and non-union workers above and beyond the call of duty. Especially criticized is their liberality with injunctions in labor disputes.[47] In fact, the courts have been disposed to use injunctions to protect the public, employers, and non-union workers for the same reason that they have relied upon this remedy to enforce the rights of Negroes in the South. That is, in labor cases, as in civil rights cases, the premise that criminal prosecutions and tort actions afford "adequate" remedies to injured parties is palpably false. Damage suits and criminal prosecutions are slow, expensive, and allow the defendant the right of trial by a local jury. The injunction is speedy, cheap, preventative, and subjects the violator to summary punishment.

Most writers who deplore the readiness of judges to issue injunctions in labor disputes determinedly ignore the heart of the matter—the fact that organized workers, especially unskilled workers who are easily replaced, have a direct and substantial interest in coercion. These authorities cannot condone the use of unlawful intimidation as a labor weapon, but they can plead that union men are "goaded" into breaking the law by *agents provocateurs* or the conviction that police and judges will not deal fairly with them anyway.[48] Over the years there has been enough corruption and vindictiveness in local law enforcement to give these inferences a certain plausibility; nevertheless, the provocative tactics of employers in labor

---

[47] The literature on the use of injunctions in labor disputes is no longer manageable. The most comprehensive treatment of the problem for the early years is Felix Frankfurter and Nathan Greene, *The Labor Injunction* (1930). Later developments are traced in *State Court Injunctions: Report of the Labor Relations Subcommittee of the Senate Committee on Labor and Public Welfare*, S. Doc. No. 7, 82d Cong., 1st Sess. (1951).

[48] The position of the late Harold Laski is typical: "I freely admit that violence has often been used by the trade unions . . . . But I am bound to record my own view that most trade-union violence—jurisdictional disputes apart—has been due either to the denial of collective bargaining by the employers or to the fact that there is no level at which the power of government has not been used to protect employers' incitement to violence by men or acts organized for that purpose." *Trade Unions in the New Society* 58–59 (1950).

For an honest recognition of the union's need to intimidate potential strike-breakers, one must go back to Jack London, *War of the Classes* (1905).

disputes should not be exaggerated. The important truth is that since the law favors the employers in labor disputes, unlawful intimidation is most commonly the work of the union side.

The view that organized workers are provoked to breaking the law would be more plausible if its major inarticulate premise were correct, *i.e.*, that working-class solidarity is so great that strikes can only be broken by the use of terror and professional strikebreakers. In the United States at least, working-class solidarity of this order is a myth. In most areas, strikebreakers for unskilled and semiskilled jobs can be recruited without much difficulty when they can be guaranteed protection, and a significant minority of an employer's workers are probably people who must be coerced into respecting union discipline.[49] Moreover, since unlawful intimidation in labor disputes can usually be traced to men who are normally law-abiding citizens, criminal prosecutions and tort actions are of little avail. Indeed, a "fair" jury trial for men accused of misconduct in a labor dispute is generally precluded by the difficulty—often the impossibility—of securing a jury that is not hopelessly biased from the outset. Hence, if violence is to be eliminated from labor disputes, the state must devise new remedies for enforcing the law or remove some of the discrepancies between law and popular morality that produce crimes and torts which juries will not punish.

If this view is accepted, the Norris-La Guardia Act (1932),[50] which drastically limited the power of the federal courts to issue injunctions in labor disputes was a step in the wrong direction,[51] be-

---

[49] The indifference and hostility of a sizable fraction of the labor force to union leadership—and probably to the idea of collective bargaining itself—is underscored by the results of the NLRB elections held to settle the issue of union recognition. Under the Wagner Act such elections are conducted on a winner-take-all principle. The union which gets a majority of the votes cast obtains the sole right to bargaining collectively for all workers in the plant, and workers have the option of refusing to be represented by any union. From 1940 through 1950 roughly 18 per cent of those voting registered a preference for no union.

Since elections to decide worker representation are ordinarily held when unions are seeking to extend the area of collective bargaining or when rival unions are vying with one another for jurisdiction, the above percentage may exaggerate the strength of antiunion sentiment in the labor force; yet even in plants where the union principle is established, from 5 to 10 per cent of the workers will vote no-union whenever they get the chance. J. V. Spielmans, "Union Representation Elections," 60 *J. Pol. Econ.* 323–31 (1952).

[50] 47 *Stat.* 70.

[51] However, the contribution of the Norris-La Guardia Act to the weakening of law enforcement in labor disputes is easily exaggerated, since it was held not to touch the equity powers of state courts as regards "such traditionally local

cause it struck at the usefulness of one remedy which judges had managed to devise.[52] The injunction even in its pristine form, however, has not solved the problem of violence in labor disputes, and one can make a good case that the other line of action—a revision of the law to give workers property rights in their jobs—offers a more promising approach. Two legal innovations of the 1930's represent long steps in this direction and have probably done more to keep the public peace in labor disputes than all of the injunctions ever issued. By the Wagner Act (1935)[53] employees were afforded means to make collective bargaining compulsory upon their employers. By the Byrnes Act (1936),[54] which forbade the transportation of strikebreakers across state lines, professional thugs and hapless southern Negroes and poor whites were largely barred to employers as strikebreakers. The next step toward more peaceful labor relations would seem to be legislation denying employers the privilege of hiring replacements for workers called out on strike by the union which holds sole bargaining rights for them under the Wagner Act. There would still remain the problem of preserving the peace in the bitter disputes where some bona fide employees refuse to accept union discipline. Unfortunately, violence in labor disputes cannot be ascribed wholly to the obsolescence of the law of master and servant. It is also rooted in some serious defects of our national character.

---

matters as public safety and order and the use of streets and highways." Allen-Bradley Local v. Board, 315 U.S. 740, 749 (1942).

[52] According to a Supreme Court paraphrase: "Section 7 (of the Norris-La Guardia Act) deprives the courts of jurisdiction to issue an injunction in any case involving or growing out of a labor dispute, except after hearing sworn testimony in open court in support of the allegations of the complaint, and upon findings of fact to the effect (a) that unlawful acts have been threatened and will be committed unless restrained, or have been committed and will be continued unless restrained, and then only against the person or persons, association or organization making the threat or permitting the unlawful act or authorizing or ratifying it; (b) that substantial and irreparable injury to the complainant's property will follow; (c) that, as to each item of relief granted, greater injury will be inflicted upon the complainant by denial of the relief than will be inflicted on the defendant by granting it; (d) that the complainant has no adequate remedy at law, and (e) that the public officers charged with the duty to protect the complainant's property are unable or unwilling to furnish adequate protection." New Negro Alliance v. Sanitary Grocery Co., 303 U.S. 552, 561–62 (1937).

[53] 49 *Stat.* 449.

[54] 49 *Stat.* 1899.

Chapter *XIX*

MONOPOLY POLICY IN BRITAIN
SINCE 1890

1. *Monopoly as a minor problem*

We have seen that as late as 1890 the courts of Britain and the United States treated combinations in restraint of trade in much the same way. If it is an exaggeration to speak of a truly common law of monopoly, nevertheless judges in both countries reacted in much the same way to a common dilemma, *i.e.*, how to hold the balance between sanctity of contract and the rule which forbade them to enforce contracts that were against public policy. Cases were examined in the light· of the same few precedents, and since the federal courts had almost nothing to say about combinations in restraint of trade in the nineteenth century, the American state courts attached particular importance to the relevant decisions of the higher English courts.

With the Sherman Act this country set out on its experiment in antitrust policy. With the *Mogul* decision[1] it became an unambiguous principle of English law that one businessman may do anything to take custom away from another provided that the necessary injury is not motivated by personal malice and is not accomplished by acts which are clearly defined crimes or torts. A brief survey of monopoly policy in Britain since 1890 may suggest what might have been in the United States and perhaps better reveal the circumstances that encourage policy along one road rather than another.

A striking feature of monopoly policy in Britain is its manageability as a subject of study. The published materials are scant—a few reports by official bodies, a small number of books and articles that can be covered in a week's concentrated reading,[2] and a modest vol-

---

[1] Mogul Steamship Co. v. McGregor, Gow & Co., (1892) A.C. 25 (H.L.)

[2] A bibliography of the main works relating to monopoly in Britain is given by G. C. Allen in *Monopoly and Competition and their Regulation* 108–09 (Chamberlin ed. 1954).

ume of case law.[3] Moreover, the dominant note in this limited literature is one of diffidence. The evangelical fervor that pervades American work on monopoly is largely absent, for although British authors
may believe that restrictive practices ought to be discouraged, they
urge this view without much heat and generally regard the elimination
of such practices as a minor reform. The reasons for this moderation
are not difficult to discern.

For many years British economists discounted the importance of
monopoly as a policy problem on the ground that the nation's policy
of free trade (abandoned in 1931) precluded the development of
strong trusts. The acceptance of this assumption also implied that
mergers were commonly good things since if the creation of market
power was not a feasible objective, mergers were perforce motivated
by the prospect of realizing the economies of larger scale. (An unfortunate consequence of this attitude is that there exists little information on merger movements in Britain.[4]) In the words of one older
authority:

> Where trust methods have been obviously illegal, or where
> they flourish behind an oppressive tariff, what to do is plain.
> But the case is different in the United Kingdom where the
> continuance of amalgamations and associations depends solely
> upon their efficiency as instruments of production and distri-
> bution. . . . The point cannot be too much emphasized that
> we have not in this country to face the American problem or
> the German problem, but a problem of our own—the modifica-
> tion of society by a new organisation of industry, a more effi-
> cient method of production, evolving normally without arti-
> ficial stimulus. Patience, not hostility is our proper attitude.[5]

Again, the absence of marked hostility to corporate size has contributed to a less heated discussion of monopoly problems in Britain.

---

[3] Useful commentaries on the relevant case law are A. L. Haslam, *The Law
Relating to Trade Combinations* (1931); R. Y. Hedges, *The Law Relating to
Restraint of Trade* (1932); C. A. Cooke, "Legal Rule and Economic Function,"
46 *Econ. J.* 21 (1936); and D. K. Dix, *The Law Relating to Competitive Trading*
(1938).

[4] The publication of a book on mergers in the British economy, P. L. Cook
and Ruth Cohen, *The Effects of Mergers* was announced after this manuscript had
gone to press.

[5] H. W. Macrosty, *The Trust Movement in British Industry* 345 (1907).
For a more recent statement of the view that the existence of too many small
firms is a major source of economic waste in Britain, see Ian Bowen, *Britain's
Industrial Survival* 89–104 (1947).

This tolerance of size may reflect a somewhat higher level of business ethics or possibly the greater willingness of English courts to punish as torts the grossly unfair acts by which one firm injures another. (As is well known, for example, the law of libel and slander is much more strict in Britain than in the United States.) In any event, the objectionable business practices that produced an outcry against American trusts around 1900—notably the bogus independent, the fighting brand, commercial bribery, harassing patent suits, etc.—were never so ruthlessly and blatantly employed in Britain, though they may have been more widespread than was generally believed. A recent inquiry by the Monopolies Commission even turned up the classic "unfair" trade practice—the bogus independent that was being used by a near monopolist to maintain his position against troublesome smaller firms.[6]

The good temper of Britons in discussing monopoly also derives from the fact that the dividing line between business and government is not so rigid in Britain as in the United States. The older notion that a corporate body has a real, if ill-defined, responsibility to the State beyond mere compliance with the letter of the law has not wholly lost its force. In this country the Justice Department in its antitrust work must generally threaten a firm with legal action to get its way. In Britain the Board of Trade can apparently achieve this result by "suggesting" that certain trade practices be discontinued. One should remember, of course, that the reserve powers of a government body are more formidable in Britain than in the United States, i.e., bills drafted by civil servants and introduced by cabinet ministers do not get lost in Parliamentary committees. It follows that government departments in Britain tend to regard organized groups, especially trade associations, as useful adjuncts to the civil service.

Again, the attitude of British statesmen to monopoly control has necessarily been conditioned by the crises of the twentieth century, notably two world wars, the Great Depression, and the sudden transition from creditor to debtor status in the world economy. In the meeting of these emergencies, the restrictive agreement has undoubtedly served a number of worthy, if modest, ends. In wartime it has helped to ensure that the status quo among rival firms was maintained in the face of limited supplies and, temporarily at least, discouraged the development of black markets by confining scarce goods to known members of the trade. In peacetime it has discouraged price cutting that might sacrifice much needed foreign exchange or drive hard

---

[6] Monopolies and Restrictive Practices Commission, *Report on the Supply of Certain Industrial and Medical Cases* 92 (1956).

pressed firms into liquidation when there exists no ready alternative employment for their labor and capital.[7]

Finally the argument that monopoly is dictated by the economies of large scale is inherently more plausible when applied to Britain than to the United States. Given the smaller size of the domestic market in Britain, a single plant really may be able to supply the economy with the whole output of some product,[8] and *ceteris paribus* one would expect that the share of output accounted for by, say, the four largest firms in an industry would be greater in Britain than in the United States.[9]

2. *The courts and monopoly in Britain*

While the climate of opinion has been more tolerant of trade restraints in Britain than the United States, the role of the British courts in fostering these practices is commonly exaggerated. The most conspicuous feature of the British legal scene has not been the sympathy of the courts for the works of aspiring monopolists but rather the unwillingness of the latter to trust themselves to this sympathy. The reasons for this reluctance are not wholly clear. One barrister of the author's acquaintance attributes the disinclination of injured parties to go to law to the high cost of litigation. A more widely held view is that trade associations, knowing that the courts still affirmed the right to void agreements contrary to public policy, preferred to rely on such methods of private enforcement as they themselves could devise. By another view, trade associations feared the unpopular reaction that

---

[7] For one distinguished economist's defense of restriction as practiced by British industries, see Henry Clay, "The Campaign Against Monopoly and Restrictive Practices," 24 *Lloyds Bank Review* 14 (April, 1952). In opposing the new monopoly policy in Britain Clay maintains (a) it is unwise to hobble the collective activities of employers while leaving the activities of labor unions unsupervised, (b) the restrictive practices of British industries never wholly eliminate competition, and (c) collective agreements are more likely to promote stable production and employment than is atomistic competition.

[8] Thus, the former secretary of the Monopolies Commission in arguing that trust busting is not for Britain has pointed out that a single continuous ribbon machine for making electric light bulbs can more than supply the home market. Alix Kilroy, "The Task and Methods of the Monopolies Commission," 22 *Manchester School* 37, 41 (1954).

[9] For statistical evidence that concentration ratios are typically higher in British industries than in comparable American industries see Gideon Rosenbluth "Measures of Concentration," in *Business Concentration and Price Policy*, 57–95 (National Bureau of Economic Research, 1955).

they might provoke if restrictive agreements were subjected to the publicity of litigation. Whatever the reasons, the multitude of cartel agreements executed in Britain over the past sixty years has produced almost no litigation.[10]

The notion that modern English law has indulgently regarded trade restraints has been fostered by its insistence that contracts should not lightly be set aside—"that you are not to extend arbitrarily those rules which say that a given contract is void as being against public policy because, if there is one thing which more than another public policy requires it is that men of full age and competent understanding shall have the utmost freedom of contracting, and that their contracts when entered into freely and voluntarily shall be held sacred and shall be enforced by Courts of justice."[11] No doubt this admonition contains its grain of wisdom. Unhappily, it has been taken so seriously by English judges that as late as 1921, the Court of Appeal actually gave judgment for the plaintiff on a contract wherein the parties had pledged themselves to rig the bidding at a public auction of government surplus property.[12] While the courts have often observed that an agreement directly restraining competition could be void as being against public policy, no such agreement has been found unenforceable on this ground since 1855.[13]

If we except the *Nordenfelt* case[14] which was hardly typical—the competition suppressed was the defendant's right to sell munitions to foreign governments after he had agreed not to—the enforceability of a contract directly restraining competition first came before the courts in recent times in *United Shoe Machinery Company of Canada v. Brunet* (1909).[15] The case turned on the legality of the plaintiff's famous tying clause, the defendant having broken a contract in which he had pledged himself not to use the plaintiff's machines with equipment secured from third parties. A Canadian jury denied the plaintiff's

---

[10] The only decisions since 1890 in which the courts enforced the provisions of a cartel agreement appear to be Cade v. Daly, 1 Ir. R. 306 (1910); North Western Salt Co. v. Electrolytic Alkali Co., (1914) A.C. 461 (H.L.); Evans & Co. v. Heathcote, 1 K.B. 418 (1918); and English Hop Growers, Ltd. v. Dering, 2 K.B. 174 (1928).

[11] Sir George Jessel, M.R., in Printing and Numerical Registering Co. v. Sampson, 19 L. R. Eq. 462, 465 (1875).

[12] Rawlings v. General Trading Co., 1 K.B. 635 (1921).

[13] Hilton v. Eckersley, 6 El. & Bl. 47, 119 Eng. Rep. 781 (Q.B. 1855).

[14] Nordenfelt v. Maxim Nordenfelt Guns & Ammunition Co., (1894) A.C. 535 (H.L.).

[15] (1909) A.C. 330 (P.C.).

request for damages and an injunction in a verdict that was upheld by the Court of King's Bench in Ontario. On appeal, the Privy Council accepted that the plaintiff had not been injured but consented to enjoin further violation of the tying contract, observing:

> If the monopoly established by the appellants and their mode of carrying on their business be as oppressive as is alleged (upon which their Lordships express no opinion), then the evil, if it exists, may be capable of cure by legislation or by competition, but in their view not by litigation. It is not for them to suggest what form the legislation should take, or by what methods the necessary competition should be established.[16]

The status of the restrictive agreement was more fully considered a few years later in *North Western Salt Co. v. Electrolytic Alkali Co.*[17] The plaintiff was an incorporated association of salt producers controlling most of domestic production formed to keep up the price of salt by regulating supply. The defendants, who were not members of the association, agreed to sell it 18,000 tons of salt annually for four years, some portion of which was to be taken at a guaranteed price. The defendants also pledged themselves not to produce additional salt for sale, but their contract entitled them to buy back the whole or a part of their annual output at the plaintiff's current selling price and to act as distributors on the same terms as the plaintiff's other distributors. The plaintiff charged that the defendant sold salt in violation of the agreement and sought damages. The defense denied breach of contract and did not even bother to argue *pro forma* that the contract was unenforceable because the restraint imposed was against public policy. While the trial court ruled for the plaintiff, a majority of the Court of Appeal rather surprisingly decided that the agreement was against the public interest and, hence, unenforceable. According to Lord Justice Farwell:

> In the present case, no circumstances, in my opinion, could justify such a contract made for the mere purpose of raising prices, with the inseparable incident of depriving the members of the public of the choice of manufacturers, while hoodwinking them into the belief that choice is open to them; in

---

[16] *Ibid.* 344.
[17] (1914) A.C. 461 (H.L.).

any case, the special circumstances would have to be pleaded and proved by the plaintiffs.[18]

Nevertheless, this judgment was reversed by the House of Lords in a decision which, though not clearly "wrong," well illustrates the difficulties of allowing monopoly policy to arise out of the litigation of private parties. The Lord Chancellor (Haldane) conceded that the court must refuse damages to the plaintiff if the agreement was judged contrary to public policy. He ruled, however, that incompatibility with public policy could only be shown if (a) the agreement was illegal on its face or (b) its illegality had been pleaded by the defendant or (c) both. The Lord Chancellor's premise was apparently that a court of law is ill-equipped to gather and analyze information on market conditions and, consequently, that it ought to decide cases on the evidence brought forward by the interested parties.

Four years later in *Evans & Co. v. Heathcote* (1918)[19] one party did object that the disputed contract was against public policy but with no more success. Here the litigants belonged to a cartel—the Cased Tube Association—that was seeking to divide the output of metal bedstead tubing among its members. The cartel rested upon the common type of pooling agreement wherein each member was allotted a fixed percentage of the cartel's output. If he exceeded this percentage in any month, he paid a fine into the common fund from which compensation was paid to members who had not sold their share. The Court of Appeal accepted that the contract was not enforceable at common law. But it ruled that the Cased Tube Association was a trade-union in the eyes of the law and consequently, though the market-sharing scheme was not "directly" enforceable, it was not against public policy for the court to show indulgence by enforcing the agreement indirectly. The plaintiff was allowed to recover a sum owed to him by the cartel on an "account stated"—a remedy descended from equity.[20]

Although the courts have declared their willingness to enforce reasonable cartel agreements, they have seldom been called upon to do so. The modern case law of monopoly in Britain has mainly grown

---

[18] *Ibid.* 465. The passage is quoted by Lord Haldane. The opinions in the Court of Appeal, 3 K.B. 422 (1913) are not fully reported.

[19] 1 K.B. 418 (1918).

[20] Essentially the English remedy of account is a means whereby the court allows the plaintiff to recover money admittedly due him when his other remedies would fail. See E. H. T. Snell, *Principles of Equity* 573–77 (24th ed. 1954), or S. M. Leake, *Principles of the Law of Contract* 82–88 (8th ed. 1931).

out of the efforts of trade associations to enforce collective resale price maintenance.[21] The right of an individual manufacturer to negotiate a contract governing the resale price of his product was upheld in the House of Lords as early as 1915,[22] and six years later collective resale price maintenance was, for all practical purposes, made legal. In *Ware and De Freville v. Motor Trade Ass'n*[23] the plaintiffs, who were not members of the association, sold a car above the price set by the association. The defendant thereupon placed the names of the plaintiff on a published list of firms not eligible to receive supplies from its members, and the plaintiff sued to restrain them from putting his name on the so-called stop list on the ground that it libellously implied that he was "unfairly" engaged in business. The court held otherwise because "in the absence of evidence of special circumstances giving a libellous tendency to the words," the statement that you propose to do what you have a legal right to do is not capable of a defamatory meaning.[24]

A momentary pause was perhaps given to the enforcement of resale price maintenance in the curious *Rex v. Denyer* (1926).[25] Here an agent of the Motor Trade Association demanded £257 from one Read—a dealer not a member of the association—from whom he had purchased a car below list price on penalty of publishing the dealer's name on a stop list. When Read complained to the police, Denyer—the trade association officer who had made the demand—was indicted, convicted of attempted blackmail, and his conviction upheld in the Court of Criminal Appeal. According to the court, "there is not the remotest nexus or relationship between a right to put the name of Mr. Read upon the stop list, and a right to demand from him £257 as the price of abstaining from that course."[26] Two years later a dealer who had been similarly threatened by the Motor Trade Association failed in his effort to recover a sum paid to it before the decision in *Rex v. Denyer,* one member of the Court of Appeal remarking that in his opinion the *Denyer* case was wrongly decided.[27] The un-

---

[21] For a description of the machinery of collective resale price maintenance by the former secretary of the Motor Trade Association, see K. C. Johnson-Davies, *Control in Retail Industry* (1945).

[22] Dunlop Pneumatic Tyre Co. v. New Garage, (1915) A.C. 79 (H.L.).

[23] 3 K.B. 40 (1921).

[24] *Ibid.* 73.

[25] 2 K.B. 258 (1926).

[26] *Ibid.* 268.

[27] Opinion of Lord Justice Scrutton in Hardie & Lane v. Chilton, 2 K.B. 306, 320 (1928).

certain legal status of collective resale price maintenance was ultimately resolved in a friendly action when the House of Lords rejected the plaintiff's contention that it was unlawful for the Motor Trade Association to demand money from him because he had sold a car above list price on pain of black-listing him.[28] This doctrine was further strengthened in *British Motor Trade Ass'n v. Salvadori* (1949)[29] when the court granted an injunction restraining a non-member of the group from selling cars obtained without its knowledge above list price. In defense of this decision, it might be noted that, at that time, the government was striving both to keep down the price level at home and increase the export of cars, and that the Motor Trade Association's policy of price restraint accorded with these aims.

The courts have also been loath to afford relief to businessmen injured by the trade practices of their rivals, whether acting alone or in concert. Prodded by Parliament, the courts finally accepted the doctrine, unambiguously declared in the *Mogul* case,[30] that one may do anything to get rid of a business rival provided that one does not commit a wrong that is a well-defined tort. Unhappily, the evolution of a more civilized doctrine was impeded—and ultimately subverted—by the introduction of two irrelevant issues, the definition of malice and the extent of a trader's right to command the courts' protection against breach of contract. These issues were irrelevant because a case of "mere malicious purpose" must occur "seldom if at all in business transactions"[31] and because the agreements which figured in the litigation were mostly oral bargains between employers and workmen that could be terminated with, at most, a few days' notice by either party. That is, they had little in common with the contracts of the business world which the court was accustomed to construe and enforce in suits between the parties directly involved.

The opinions in the *Mogul* case, whatever their defects, had the considerable merit of ignoring the plaintiff's claims that the defendant had been actuated by malice and had enticed third parties to break their contracts with the plaintiff. The action of the defendants in combining to take custom away from the plaintiff by means which were not illegal or actionable per se was treated as "normal" business conduct—as, of course, it was in the nineteenth century. If the law

---

[28] Thorne v. Motor Trade Ass'n, (1937) A.C. 797 (H.L.).

[29] 1 Ch. 556 (1949).

[30] Mogul Steamship Co. v. McGregor, Gow & Co., (1892) A.C. 25 (H.L.).

[31] Lord Kincairney in Scottish Co-operative Wholesale Society, Ltd. v. Glasgow Fleshers' Trade Defence Ass'n, 35 S. L. Rep. 645, 651 (1898).

lords had decided otherwise, they would have created one or more new torts. The *Mogul* doctrine was simply freedom of contract carried to its logical conclusion.

The courts, however, were apparently unconvinced by their own arguments setting forth the virtues of *laissez faire,* so that one year later in *Temperton v. Russell*[32] they did not scruple to condemn an exercise of contractual freedom that was held to be against the public interest. In this case a master mason supplied materials to a firm of builders involved in a labor dispute. The union, after unsuccessfully seeking to dissuade him from this course, called his workers out on strike and threatened to withdraw labor from any supplier or customer of Temperton who continued to deal with him. The union was not actuated by malice in the ordinary sense of the word but merely wished to persuade Temperton to acquiesce in their demands. The court could have said that the type of union pressure applied to Temperton was against public policy. Instead it chose to rely upon old precedents of doubtful relevance[33] and upheld the award of damages against Russell on the ground that, as a union official, he had maliciously and wrongfully enticed people to break and refuse to enter contracts with Temperton.

A few years later in *Allen v. Flood*[34] the pendulum swung again to the *Mogul* doctrine when the House of Lords refused to allow workmen who had been dismissed as a result of a jurisdictional dispute to obtain damages from the union officers who had been responsible for their injury. The incompatibility of *Allen v. Flood* and *Temperton v. Russell* as regards the rights and responsibilities of organized workers was too glaring to stand for long. In the celebrated *Taff Vale* case[35] the House of Lords chose to rely upon the latter decision, the majority of the law lords reasoning that (a) the railway had "contracts" with its workers, (b) the local branch of the national union in bringing these workers out on strike "knowingly" caused them to break

---

[32] 1 Q.B. 715 (1893).

[33] Notably Lumley v. Gye, 2 El. & Bl. 216, 118 Eng. Rep. 749 (Q.B. 1853), and Bowen v. Hall, 6 Q. B. D. 333 (1881). In the first case, a theater manager recovered damages from another impresario who had persuaded a performer to break her contract with the plaintiff. In the second case, the plaintiff recovered against the defendant who had enticed an artisan—one of the few who knew the secret of manufacturing white glazed brick—to break a contract of exclusive service with the plaintiff.

[34] (1898) A.C. 1 (H.L.).

[35] Taff Vale Ry. Co. v. Amalgamated Society of Railway Servants, (1901) A.C. 426.

their contracts, (c) the strike was called to "injure" the railway and hence was motivated by malice, and (d) the national union could be sued for damages since it supported the strike.

Actually the facts of the case were as follows.[36] The Taff Vale Railway had for some years been on bad terms with the union. A dispute arose concerning the refusal of the company to promote an active union member which culminated in a strike by 1,227 men in August, 1900. As a condition of employment, employees were obliged to give two weeks' notice before quitting. Through bad union planning, only 356 strikers had worked out their notices, although another 465 strikers had given a week's notice. The national officers of the union did not authorize the strike but agreed to support it when presented with a *fait accompli*. The company therefore sued the national union for "inducing" breach of contract and certain damage suffered in the course of the strike. The point deserving emphasis is that the action for inducing breach of contract rested upon the most pettifogging technicality. Had the union members followed their local representatives' advice and given two weeks' notice at the same time, the company would have had no case, and in any event, since the company had two weeks' notice of the strike date, it suffered no loss that it could not reasonably have foreseen.

For better or worse, the unfairness of the *Taff Vale* decision provoked the extreme reaction of the Trade Disputes Act of 1906[37] which, going beyond the recommendations of a Royal Commission that had included Sydney Webb,[38] gave unions and their officers virtual immunity for all damage inflicted upon employers or third parties in the course of a labor dispute—an immunity which extended to those trade associations which chose to take the legal status of labor unions. The Act of 1906 is often cited as liberal, even radical legislation; yet, in truth, it merely directed the courts to adhere faithfully to the *Mogul*

---

[36] For the background of the *Taff Vale* case see the evidence of Ammon Beasley, General Manager of the Taff Vale Railway, before the Royal Commission on Trade Disputes and Trade Combinations in 1906; and Mr. Justice Wills' address to the jury in the case reprinted in the appendices to the minutes of evidence taken by the commission.

[37] 6 Edw. 7, c. 47.

[38] The majority report signed by Sidney Webb seems to accept the law of the *Taff Vale* decision. It merely recommends legislation "to declare that to persuade to strike, *apart from inducing breach of contract* is not illegal" and to confer protection against damage suits on union funds set aside for benevolent purposes. *Report of the Royal Commission on Trade Disputes and Trade Combinations* 16 (1906).

doctrine as, indeed, the courts did in the few subsequent cases involving an injury to a rival's trade not actuated by personal malice.[39]

3. *Parliamentary attitudes toward monopoly*

Although in 1918 a committee of the Ministry of Reconstruction had recommended the creation of an agency that would pay close attention to the activities of trade associations and the progress of industrial concentration,[40] no legislation was introduced. In 1929 when the question was next examined by a committee of the Board of Trade, it was concluded (not unreasonably) that "in the circumstances of the present industrial situation, the case for immediate legislation for the restraint of such abuses as may result from combinations cannot be said to be an urgent one."[41] Instead, by a long series of acts in the interwar years, Parliament lent its support to a restriction of competition in one sector of the economy after another, especially in agriculture, coal mining, and iron and steel. This legislation was, of course, directed toward a more worthy end than the enrichment of special interests at the expense of the country generally.[42] The serious unemployment that prevailed in Britain for most of the years between 1918 and 1939 caused distress that the government was obliged to relieve. At the same time, the "excess" capacity in industry that was the physical counterpart of this unemployment discouraged the introduction of new equipment and, to some extent, no doubt slowed the economy's rate of growth. Government policies that had the effect of restricting competition were therefore designed either to relieve distress or to bribe industries into accepting reorganization and re-equipment schemes that were calculated to improve their efficiency.

There is no profit in debating the wisdom of this legislation. It was doubtless unfair to industries without political influence and cannot have done much to modernize the capital plant of the British economy in the interwar years since industries suffering excess capacity had little incentive to undertake the "rationalization" expected

---

[39] Notably, Sorrell v. Smith, (1925) A.C. 700 (H.L.); and Crofter Hand Woven Harris Tweed Co. v. Veitch, (1942) A.C. 435 (H.L.).

[40] *Report of the Committee on Trusts*, Cmd. No. 9236, 11 (1918).

[41] *Final Report of the Committee on Industry and Trade*, Cmd. No. 3282, 192 (1929).

[42] A detailed discussion of this legislation is A. F. Lucas, *Industrial Reconstruction and the Control of Competition* (1937).

of them in exchange for legislation restricting competition. So long as the government's deflationary policy discouraged full employment and a world-wide depression made full employment exceedingly difficult in an economy heavily dependent on exports, the encouragement given to restrictive practices by Parliament probably did no great damage.[43]

After 1945, however, this legislation together with the extralegal cartel controls that had grown up under the *Mogul* doctrine left the country with a mass of restrictive practices that could be justified neither as cheap charity to depressed industries nor as encouraging the modernization of the country's industrial plant. The wear and tear of six years of war had wiped out excess capacity as a barrier to the introduction of new equipment, while the need to increase exports to offset the loss of overseas investments during the war made those cartel arrangements that gave aid and comfort to inefficient firms politically unpopular. Consequently the first step toward a policy looking toward a freer flow of trade was taken in the Monopolies and Restrictive Practices Act of 1948.[44] It is unlikely that this legislation reflected a sudden Parliamentary conversion to the philosophy of Thurman Arnold. More probably it was inspired by an apprehension that restrictive practices were injuring the export trade at a time when the economy was striving to increase its holdings of foreign exchange.

The Act of 1948 established a Monopolies and Restrictive Practices Commission under the supervision of the Board of Trade with power to undertake such investigations as the board might set for it. If an investigation revealed restrictive practices against the public interest, the board, after laying the commission's report before Parliament and obtaining its endorsement, could issue an order directing an end to the practices. Investigation was thus the main task of the Monopolies Commission and, in creating a climate of opinion favorable to the necessary enforcement machinery, it played a role in Britain comparable to the original Industrial Commission in the United States.[45]

---

[43] For the view that the restrictive practices of the interwar years were not so innocuous, see W. A. Lewis, *Monopoly in British Industry*, Fabian Research Series No. 91 (1945).

[44] 11 & 12 Geo. 6, c. 66.

[45] For an examination of the Monopolies Commission's free market bias and its limits, see Alex Hunter, "The Monopolies Commission and Economic Welfare," 23 *The Manchester School* 22 (1955).

A longer step toward a more competitive policy was taken with the Restrictive Trade Practices Act of 1956.[46] By its two most important provisions this legislation apparently forbids the more extreme forms of collective resale price maintenance[47] and establishes a Restrictive Practices Court before which a wide range of agreements must come to be justified. The original Monopolies Commission is not abolished, but the 1956 Act directs that henceforth it shall concern itself with restrictive practices of firms which produce one-third or more of the industry's output.

The enforcement machinery created by the 1956 Act has a number of interesting features. No criminal penalties are provided. The Restrictive Practices Court is composed of five judges drawn from the High Court and lay members not to exceed ten in number. Decisions shall be by majority vote save that questions involving matters of law shall be settled by the law members only. The findings of the Restrictive Practices Court are final on questions of fact. On questions of law the rulings of this court may be appealed by the disappointed party to the Court of Appeal and, ultimately to the House of Lords. Readers familiar with the difficulties that have arisen in the United States because antitrust cases have been tried by judges who know little economics or a Federal Trade Commission whose rules of evidence and procedure were often regarded with suspicion by judges will probably view the mixed court as a promising innovation.

The preparation of the Crown's case against registered restrictive agreements is entrusted to a registrar who stands in roughly the same relationship to the Restrictive Practices Court as does the general counsel of the National Labor Relations Board to its members; that is, the registrar must work closely with the court without taking orders directly from it. At present, the registrar would seem to have two main functions. He must ultimately bring all registered agreements before the court, though the Board of Trade may decide the order in which

---

[46] 4 & 5 Eliz. 2, c. 68.

[47] The future of collective resale price maintenance is in some doubt. While the Act of 1956 seems to forbid categorically any co-operation by rival manufacturers to detect and punish violations of resale price maintenance, one authority believes that they may still agree among themselves to prescribe resale prices and authorize a trade association to exercise their rights of enforcement. K. C. Johnson-Davies, "Trade Associations and the Restrictive Practices Act," 3 *Brit. J. Admin. L.* 12 (1956). If trade associations can enforce resale price maintenance, it is most probable that "in practice" collective resale price maintenance will continue.

he brings them. When he finds that a restrictive agreement that falls within the scope of the Act has not been registered, he must sue in the High Court to compel registration.

In general, while the wording of the 1956 Act is not quite so ambiguous as the Sherman and Clayton acts, it is vague enough. The definition of a restrictive agreement that must be registered is reasonably clear. It is any agreement between two or more parties in the United Kingdom "in the production or supply of goods, or in the application to goods of any process of manufacture, whether with or without other parties, being an agreement under which restrictions are accepted by two or more parties" as regards (a) prices, (b) terms of purchase or sale, (c) quantity or type of goods bought or sold, (d) methods of manufacture, and (e) division of the market.

The Act, however, proceeds to list several species of agreement that satisfy this definition but need not be registered. (The most important of these exemptions confer immunity upon agreements relating to collective bargaining, patents, trade-marks, exclusive agency rights, and government-approved rationalization schemes for industry.) The Act then provides that the court shall treat registered restrictive agreements as contrary to the public interest unless the parties to the agreement rebut this presumption by successfully pleading one or more of seven specified defenses. The legality of a registered agreement may be established showing that it (a) is essential to public health or safety, (b) confers some other substantial benefits upon consumers, (c) countervails someone else's monopoly power, (d) countervails someone else's monopsony power, (e) cannot be abrogated without the risk of serious unemployment in the industry, area or country at large, (f) helps the export trade, or (g) is "reasonably required" to achieve any other end that the court believes to be worthy.

In declining to ban all cartel agreements by fiat, Parliament has seemingly declared in favor of the rule of reason in construing such contracts that American courts have resolutely rejected for sixty years. Most economists (other than some specialists in antitrust matters) doubt the wisdom of treating all cartel agreements as unlawful per se since, like the authors of the 1956 Act, they can imagine a number of situations in which restrictions on competition might be desirable. It remains to be seen whether the decisions of the Restrictive Practices Court will confirm the fears of the American authorities who have long warned that the introduction of a reasonableness test would make an effective cartel policy unworkable.

To an American observer the weakness of the new policy in Britain is more conspicuous than its promise. The possible legal loopholes are virtually unlimited[48] and the enforcement machinery weak, though in no sense negligible. (The registrar of Restrictive Practices has begun his work with a staff of 122 including 21 executive officers,[49] and the first president of the Restrictive Practices Court is the distinguished High Court Judge, Mr. Justice Devlin.) But then the growth of antitrust policy in the United States has been leisurely to say the least. The new legislation in Britain represents a good beginning in replacing the *Mogul* doctrine with a body of case law that is better calculated to foster competition.

4. *Retrospect and prospect*

In summary, the differences in the British and American approaches to the problems of monopoly control since 1890, though real enough, are easily exaggerated. As regards cartels, British courts have said that restrictive agreements, if reasonable, are enforceable. American courts

---

[48] A major loophole in monopoly policy was apparently sanctioned in the only case that has so far reached the High Court under the 1956 Act. *Re* Austin Motor Co. Ltd.'s Agreements, 3 All E. R. 62 (Ch.D. 1957). Austin—a manufacturer of motor cars and parts—had, before 1956, marketed its products through wholesale and retail dealers who were closely tied to Austin and to one another by "multipartite" agreements. For example, a contract might both bind a Bristol wholesaler to handle only Austin parts and all Bristol retailers to buy Austin parts from the wholesaler. Such contracts were clearly subject to registration after 1956.

Austin thereupon abandoned the use of multipartite agreements and sought the same control of distribution through "bipartite" agreements which allowed Austin to prescribe, in detail, the terms on which each wholesaler and retailer could buy and sell its products. Austin then claimed that the new contracts were covered by the provision of the 1956 Act which exempted from registration "any agreement for the supply of goods between two persons, neither of whom is a trade association. . . ." This contention was accepted by the High Court when the Solicitor-General sued to compel registration.

The force of the Austin case as a precedent, however, is problematical. The decision turned upon the narrowest of issues, *i.e.*, were Austin's new contracts, on their face, two-party agreements exempt from registration? The presiding judge expressed surprise that the Solicitor-General had not tried to show that Austin's new contracts were merely the old contracts in a different guise. He indicated that he would willingly have heard argument on this point had it been raised. *Ibid.* 70. The *Austin* case is discussed by Cyril Grunfeld in 21 *Modern L. Rev.* 83 (1958).

[49] *Manchester Guardian*, April 17, 1957.

have said that all cartel agreements, reasonable or unreasonable, are both void and render the parties liable to criminal prosecution. In fact, British courts have but seldom lent their support to restrictive agreements, and the antitrust agencies in the United States have never commanded the resources that would have enabled them to drive collusion underground. But American cartel policy has sufficed to discourage overt collusion among the hundred or so largest firms—those that can be kept under the scrutiny of the small staffs of the antitrust agencies—and to eliminate the more elaborate types of co-operation among smaller firms. Since cartel agreements tend to prolong the life of the least efficient member—and the tighter the agreement the greater the protection conferred—this is no mean achievement. Nevertheless, it is a mistake to make these differences in cartel policy mainly responsible for British and American differences in industrial progress. British difficulties are more obviously due to the capital consumption of two wars, a neglect of technical education, and the brake exerted on investment by the unemployment of the interwar years.

As regards the treatment of monopoly in the large firm, the United States has, of course, taken a stronger line, but here again one should not make too much of the differences. While mergers have gone unsupervised in Britain and trust busting is as yet unknown, the United States has so far put forth a very limited effort in these areas; so that while the ownership structure of the American economy would be more concentrated today had the antitrust agencies never functioned, the centrifugal force of federal policy has not been great.

In the matter of labor monopoly, policy has been shaped by nearly identical considerations in both countries. Disliking the disorders and vindictive harassments of non-union workers that so often figured in labor cases, British and American courts ineptly sought to discipline unions by making them liable for interference with an employer's right to freedom of contract. In both countries, this development of the law was expressly repudiated by the legislature without, unfortunately, any attention to the factors which caused judges to render such bad decisions. The right of a labor union to employ secondary boycotts and enforce compulsory membership was ultimately conceded in Britain and the United States, though the American concessions came later and, except for the interval between the *Hutcheson* decision (1941)[50] and the Taft-Hartley Act (1947),[51] have not been

---

[50] United States v. Hutcheson, 312 U.S. 219.
[51] 61 *Stat.* 136.

so unqualified. But then the encouragement given to compulsory collective bargaining by the Wagner Act (1935)[52] has no counterpart in British law, so that it would be difficult to maintain that the policy bias against competition in the labor market is more marked in Britain than in the United States.

Perhaps the most surprising feature of monopoly policy in Britain is the as yet small influence of socialist tradition. The nationalization program of the postwar Labour government made no great inroads on the competitive sector of the economy. The industries transferred to national ownership were mainly public utilities—many of them already in the hands of local government authorities—whose acquisition would have been dictated by a rigorous adherence to Henry Simons' positive program for *laissez faire*[53] (though centralization has increased the monopsony power of the industries involved). In each of the industries transferred to national ownership after 1945, the way to nationalization was prepared by inquiries recommending more central control in the interest of greater efficiency and "the enormous weight of the restrictions of more than half a century of regulative Acts."[54] Indeed, one can plausibly argue that the postwar victory of the Labour party merely gave the *coup de grâce* to the industries chosen for nationalization; that the opposition had already performed most of the organizational spadework and provided it with an abundance of technical arguments to justify nationalization.

Possible exceptions to the generalization that nationalization after 1945 did not much increase monopoly in Britain are coal, steel, and road transport. The last two of these industries were largely returned to private ownership by a Conservative government in 1953.[55] In coal, the deterioration of capital equipment and labor relations had gone so far by 1945 that nationalization was probably due as much to *ad hoc* politics as socialist principle, *i.e.*, the industry was destined for a sweeping, state-imposed reorganization after World War II regardless of the outcome of the 1945 election.

The future of nationalization is, of course, another matter. For while the leadership of the Labour party will promise only the return of the steel industry to national control, an influential minority of socialists is committed to an increase in the area of public ownership.

---

[52] 49 *Stat.* 449.

[53] *Economic Policy for a Free Society* 40–77 (1948).

[54] H. A. Clegg and T. E. Chester, *The Future of Nationalization* 18 (1953).

[55] 1 & 2 Eliz. 2, c. 15; 1 & 2 Eliz. 2, c. 13.

The most we can say is that Parliamentary opinion seems to be hardening into the conviction that industries addicted to restriction must either give up many of their practices or accept more stringent government control. The choice which is ultimately made will no doubt be influenced by the information brought to light by the Monopolies Commission and the Court of Restrictive Practices.

Finally, this brief comparison of monopoly policy in Britain and the United States reveals the effect of subtle, albeit important, differences in the role of judge-made law. The arguments employed by judges in explaining their decisions—and indeed their major inarticulate premises—are strikingly similar in both countries. But as precedent is a more powerful god in English law, so considerations of public policy are a more suspect foundation for a ruling.[56] "A series of decisions based upon grounds of public policy, however eminent the judges by whom they were delivered, cannot possess the same binding authority as decisions which deal with and formulate principles which are purely legal."[57] British courts are therefore less willing to embark upon uncharted seas or construe away the force of unpopular precedents—hence, the tendency to look to Parliament rather than to the courts for the law relevant to new problems. Still, not too much should be made of the greater force of precedent in Britain. By the Monopolies Act of 1956 the courts in Britain have been directed to an enterprise in which they receive little guidance from either the words of the statute or the existing body of case law.

---

[56] The reasons for the greater weight of precedent in English law are considered by A. L. Goodhart, "Case Law in England and America," in *Essays in Jurisprudence and the Common Law* 50–74 (1931). By his analysis the decline of *stare decisis* in the United States is mainly due to the uncontrollable flood of American decisions, the predominant position of constitutional questions in American law, the American need for flexibility in legal development, the comparative method of teaching in American law schools, and the restatement of the laws by the American Law Institute.

[57] Lord Watson in Nordenfelt v. Maxim Nordenfelt Guns & Ammunition Co., (1894) A.C. 535, 553 (H.L.).

Chapter XX

THE ACHIEVEMENTS OF
ANTITRUST POLICY

1. *A limited effort*

The total amount of money spent to enforce the antitrust laws over sixty-five years would not buy a medium-size naval vessel, and even if one adds to this figure the costs incurred by private parties in antitrust suits, the resulting sum probably would not finance a modern aircraft carrier. But then where the functions of the State are concerned, money outlay is a poor yardstick of a project's effect on economic welfare. Conceivably the economic consequences of antitrust policy have been, for better or worse, greater than the modest budgets of the enforcement agencies would suggest. We may therefore ask without being naive or cynical, Are there any good reasons for supposing that the structure of the American economy would now be perceptibly different had there been no attempt at an antitrust policy?

We should, of course, prefer to frame an answer to a more important question, Would the *performance* of the American economy have been perceptibly different had the antitrust agencies never functioned? Would the distribution of income have been less fair? Would national income have grown at a slower rate? As yet the evidence that would permit direct answers to these questions which would carry conviction has not been assembled. Given the difficulty of defining—much less measuring—economic welfare and the problems inherent in any effort to apportion credit for economic progress, it is unlikely that any amount of empirical work will yield answers that satisfy even the fraternity of specialists. The impact of antitrust policy on economic performance we must infer from its impact (if any) on the structure of the American economy. Since this treatise has accepted that collusion among rivals and "artificial" market power in the single firm are unfair ways of changing the distribution of income, it follows that their

302

containment or reduction increases economic welfare. For the reasons argued in Chapter IV, the connection between market structure and economic progress is still obscure, so that we should refrain from inferring that competition does more for economic progress than monopoly.

2. *Cartels and antitrust policy*

In the domain of cartel regulation, the direct impact of the antitrust laws has been slight. Some considerable fraction of the national income—perhaps as much as one-half—originates in firms that are viewed as engaging only in "intrastate commerce" and hence beyond the reach of the federal power. (Not that the Supreme Court has evidenced much concern for States' rights in antitrust matters; the antitrust agencies have never had the funds which would allow them to litigate the boundaries of federal jurisdiction.) The state government effort against cartels has been too cynically frivolous to merit our attention.[1] In industries where the federal government undoubtedly has the authority to act, its challenge to cartel monopoly has been praiseworthy but not much more effective. The poverty of the federal antitrust agencies and the poor political returns to be had from the harassment of cartels have meant that fear of prosecution has not discouraged businessmen from viewing collusion as a normal method of conducting business. But then the amount of federal surveillance needed to ensure that *all* businessmen will think twice before co-operating to restrain competition is staggering to contemplate. The total elimination of collusion should probably be written off as a technical impossibility. At any rate the striving for this goal can only commend itself to one who believes that the biggest government is preferable to the smallest private monopoly.

Antitrust policy, however, has achieved two notable successes in the control of cartels. In the handful of industries that the antitrust agencies elect to police with their limited resources, the threat of prosecution has succeeded in discouraging—and sometimes eliminating —overt collusion. Indeed, in industries that have been visited with the expense and publicity of litigation, notably oil, tobacco, steel, meat

---

[1] A few states are honorable exceptions to this generalization. Thus from 1947 through 1952 the Attorney General of Texas filed 33 cases for antitrust violations, "practically all of them involving price fixing and territorial restrictions." Dan Moody and C. B. Wallace, "Texas Antitrust Laws and their Enforcement— Comparison with Federal Antitrust Laws," 11 *Sw. L. J.* 1, 24 (1957).

packing, and automobiles, officials of rival firms often go to humorous lengths to make sure that they do not have dealings with one another without legal counsel present. Strictly speaking, the whole theory of oligopoly or tacit collusion as manifested in price leadership, market sharing, delivered pricing, etc., is a tribute to the occasional effectiveness of antitrust policy, for these roundabout and inefficient ways of restraining competition are unknown within legal frameworks that permit overt collusion. There is, after all, no point in guessing about the future price policy of a competitor when it is possible to ask him outright for such information.

Second, the development of the doctrine that collusion to restrain competition is illegal per se has rendered the restrictive agreement unenforceable and, thus, has largely eliminated the more elaborate—and profitable—types of co-operation, especially the use of the income-pooling agreement. (The decline of income pooling is perhaps the most striking feature of cartel history in the United States over the last sixty years.) The disappearance of the legally enforceable combination in restraint of trade can be traced mainly to the expansion of federal jurisdiction and the respect accorded federal decisions in state courts. It was not an "inevitable" development. Nothing in the history of regulation at the state level indicates that the legislator's view of monopoly has undergone any great change since the nineteenth century. Price "chiselers" are still regarded as unsavory people—as they often are. The most vigorous competitors are frequently those businessmen who give tax collectors, safety inspectors, and price controllers the most difficult time. And restrictive policies which serve to increase the incomes of certain local citizens at the expense of outsiders are still denoted "fair" competition in state legislatures. The repudiation of the reasonableness test by state courts in cartel cases after 1890 is, more than anything else, a tribute to the prestige and influence of the federal bench.

The victory of the per se doctrine has not been without its costs. When firms lose the right to have their contracts construed in the light of some reasonableness test, their obvious move is agitation to secure statutory exemption from the antitrust laws. Just as any increase in the rate of income taxation (at any rate in the United States) is accompanied by an increase in the number and types of exemptions, so the increasing effectiveness of antitrust policy has led to special treatment for politically powerful or obviously unfortunate industries. At the federal level, the list of industries virtually exempt from the antitrust laws has come to include railroads, trucking, inland waterways, airlines, banking, pipelines, farmer co-operatives, and shipping. At the state level, there is scarcely an important "intrastate" industry that has not somewhere received back from the legislature the rights of collusion taken away by the court.[2]

We should not make too much of the tie between the rise of the per se doctrine and the spread of special-interest legislation. A statute that confers the State's blessing on collusion is always worth having; the refusal of the courts to enforce contracts restraining competition merely gives interested parties a further incentive to seek this boon. When the balance is struck, however, the rule that the courts, unless directed otherwise by the legislature, will not enforce a private agreement that restricts competition is the supreme achievement of antitrust policy in the United States. It is a sobering thought that this result could have been achieved by a brief, explicitly worded statute that required no enforcement machinery, and that even without such legislation, English courts since 1890 have hardly ever enforced contracts restraining composition.

3. *Close combination and antitrust policy*

The harassing of cartels by antitrust suits, though it may be a worthy thing, does not stir the imagination. The success of antitrust policy, rightly or wrongly, is commonly measured by its consequences for the world of big business, and the enduring importance of the large corporation is often cited as evidence of the inutility of antitrust policy.

We have seen that, so far as corporate concentration is concerned, the antitrust agencies have set two main tasks for themselves. They have sought to check the further progress of concentration by preventing mergers which threaten a reduction of competition, and they have sought to rectify the mistakes of history by dissolving and divesting established corporations that exercise more control over the market than is needed for efficient operation. The success of antitrust policy is generally taken to have been negligible in both ventures, the only serious differences of opinion relating to the reasons for failure. One view ascribes it to the futility of standing out against "historical necessity" on the assumption that something—usually "the advantages of large-scale production"—makes progressive concentration inevitable.

---

[2] At the state level, occupational licensing laws alone numbered over 1,200 in 1952 with licensed occupations including tree surgeons, egg graders, dry cleaners, pest controllers, and horseshoers. 25 *State Government* 275, 276 (1952).

A second view contends that corporate concentration has remained unaffected because "antitrust policy has never been tried"; that enforcement agencies have always lacked the resources that would make possible an effective surveillance of mergers and an all-out assault on unwarranted concentration.

The first premise of these estimates—that antitrust suits have not perceptibly affected corporate concentration—should not pass without comment. While the ownership structure of the American economy might not have been much different had the antitrust agencies never functioned, prima facie, it could not have been the same. Thus of the hundred largest industrial corporations in 1948,[3] nineteen have had their fortunes affected by dissolution or divestiture. Nine of the one hundred largest firms in 1948 (excluding the present American Tobacco Company and Standard Oil Company of New Jersey) gained their autonomy through court decrees, notably the companies severed from the oil and tobacco trusts in 1911. Many smaller firms also owe their independence to federal intervention. Moreover, it is most unlikely that the decline in corporate consolidations after 1910 was wholly unrelated to the rise of the antitrust agencies. We may suspect, for example, that in the oft-litigated industries of steel, meat packing, automobiles, and tobacco processing, mergers were discouraged by the prospect of provoking an antitrust suit.

Actually the main impact of antitrust policy on the structure of the economy has probably resulted from its influence on two industries—oil and steel. In 1948 the Standard Oil Company of New Jersey had an estimated 7.2 per cent of the assets of the hundred largest industrial firms, while four other oil companies created by the 1911 decree had a combined total of 8.7 per cent of the assets of the hundred largest. (Not that the oil trust had it been left undisturbed in 1911 would necessarily have grown as rapidly as have the modern Standard Oil companies.) The fear that the absorption of major rivals would provoke litigation certainly accounts for some of the decline in the relative importance of the United States Steel Corporation.[4] This company held 22.3 per cent of the assets of the hundred largest firms

---

[3] A. D. H. Kaplan, *Big Enterprise in a Competitive System* 153–54 (1954).

[4] According to one writer, the expansion of the United States Steel Corporation has been inhibited, almost from the start, by fear of antitrust action. Acting on the advice of Judge Gary, the corporation is held to have deliberately reduced its share of the output of major steel products between 1901 and 1911 in order to strengthen its defense in the dissolution suit which Gary foresaw. I. M. Tarbell, *The Life of Elbert H. Gary* 257–58 (1925).

in 1909 and only 5.2 per cent in 1948.[5] In fine, antitrust policy has perceptibly reduced concentration in American industries.

The tie between corporate size and industrial efficiency we explored in Chapter IV. For our present purposes, it will suffice to note that this connection, however close, is irrelevant to the alleged failure of antitrust policy to affect corporate concentration. The belief that judges and lawmakers co-operate with historical necessity is a rationalist heresy that can no longer be taken seriously. The view that antitrust policy failed to make a more obvious impact on the structure of the economy because the enforcement agencies were undernourished also invites qualification. That the machinery for devising an antitrust policy was virtually nonexistent when it was most needed—in the era of the Corporate Revolution—is true enough. In recent years, however, the funds of the Antitrust Division have permitted it to press for dissolution and divestiture on a scale that would have radically altered the structure of the economy—had it been granted.

Some authorities have suggested that the limited success of the Sherman Act can be blamed on the inability of the federal government to match the legal talent that the corporate defendants command; that "the people have been represented, in the main, by men of very meagre legal ability."[6] Undoubtedly private attorneys in antitrust cases get paid more than federal attorneys—and there are more of them. (Is there any branch of public business law where this is not true?) Even so, it is difficult to name an important case that the government lost mainly because its attorneys were outclassed in advocacy by the opposition. Nor, at least in recent years, do government briefs appear to have been seriously marred by hasty preparation.

So far as ingenuity in argument goes, the honors in antitrust cases have gone mainly to the government side, but this is because the federal attorneys have faced a more challenging task. Defense lawyers concentrate on cultivating the apprehension, never far below the level of consciousness in the mind of the court, that dissolution and divestiture *might* jeopardize operating efficiency and technological progress. To checkmate this maneuver the federal attorneys must bear the burden of educating the courts in the intricacies of economic analysis and industrial technology—a task which is often, as in the *Columbia Steel* case,[7] a truly formidable undertaking.

---

[5] Kaplan, *Big Enterprise in a Competitive System* 145–54.

[6] The estimate of government lawyers by Justice Brandeis is quoted in A. L. Goodhart, *Five Jewish Lawyers of the Common Law* 27 (1949).

[7] United States v. Columbia Steel Co., 334 U.S. 495 (1948).

We may therefore reaffirm the thesis argued in Chapter XVII that the effort at trust busting has had so little success because it seeks a deliberate unsettling of property rights that offends the conservative bias of the courts. Nor, as we have seen, should this failure be taken as evidence that judges have consciously or unconsciously sabotaged Congressional intent. The conservative bias is all-pervasive in any legal system worthy of the name. If the courts have been reluctant to order dissolution and divestiture, the moral is only that judges strive to behave in a judicious manner. The road to trust busting on a grand scale must lie through the Congressional committee and federal bureau, not through the suit in equity. This is tantamount to saying that trust busting probably has little future as an antimonopoly measure in the United States.

The control of mergers offers a more promising line of action since the courts may reasonably enjoin the consummation of a merger that they would not set aside ten years later. The drift of case law has progressively increased the power of federal government to block mergers, and the resources of the antitrust agencies now enable them to maintain surveillance over the more important mergers in the economy. The consequences of a more careful screening of mergers for corporate concentration will throw considerable light on the merits of rival assumptions about economic "reality." If, as the author believes, technological progress is a centrifugal force making for decentralization, a close check on mergers should ultimately produce lower concentration ratios in important industries. If economists who see corporate size and concentration as mainly the product of internal growth are correct, then a close check on mergers will make little difference. The truth is that if antitrust policy is to be more than the policing of cartels, its future will be decided by the ability of the antitrust agencies to block mergers and the correctness of the assumption that monopoly power in the single firm, in general, can only be obtained and preserved by the absorption of rivals, suppliers, and market outlets.

The tendency of antitrust policy to become a permanent inquisition on the conduct of the country's two or three hundred largest corporations, resulting in endless consent decrees, is understandable given the courts' hostility to dissolution and divestiture. Nevertheless, the tendency is unfortunate. It multiplies uncertainty respecting the law and rests on the doubtful assumption that civil servants are competent to make decisions assessing the welfare consequences of particular business practices, *e.g.*, a patent exchange between two firms. Moreover, it may well be futile. For in the negotiation of a complicated consent decree governing the conduct of a firm, one may presume both that the passage of time will soon make the decree irrelevant and that, since the defendant knows more about his operations than the government, he probably had the best of the compromise in the first place. In any event the ultimate object of policy is not a more detailed surveillance of the business world by the antitrust agencies but rather an economy sufficiently free of monopoly that such surveillance is largely unnecessary.

4. *Final reflections*

Let us end on a seemly note of caution. Antitrust policy as it has been fashioned by the campaigns of the antitrust agencies is considerably less than the whole of monopoly policy. Against the modest, albeit growing, success of these agencies in maintaining and fostering competition must be set such damaging defeats as the Wagner Act,[8] the Motor Carriers Act,[9] and the inability of the Federal Trade Commission itself to determine whether the main object of policy is the protection of competition or the preservation of competitors. Likewise we should not forget the commonplace truth that the free market is a value that is frequently and properly sacrificed in the interest of achieving other ends. One can, for example, make a good case for restricting competition in the interest of more peaceful labor relations, the protection of people too young or ill-informed to look after their own interests, national defense, or industries that have been visited by some sudden adversity. Nevertheless, we may insist that advocates who call for restrictions on competition as a means of promoting more important or pressing goals shall bear the burden of proof. If the history of legislation proves anything, it is that (a) the "regulation" of competition is generally initiated by parties whose incomes will be increased by its restriction, (b) these parties will insist, as a matter of course, that what benefits them benefits the public, (c) this claim may be false, and (d) even if it is true "up to a point"—as is quite likely—private interests cannot be trusted to conduct the analysis. And "within limits," of course, no opprobrium attaches to him who seeks to advance his own fortune at the expense of other people's freedom to trade. Businessmen and labor leaders who do not seek for themselves all

---

[8] 49 *Stat.* 449 (1935).
[9] 49 *Stat.* 543 (1935).

monopoly power that the law will allow do not inspire confidence. Let us hope, however, that the critical study of antitrust problems can create a climate of opinion that regularly frustrates such striving for private advantage at public expense.

Index of Cases

(The page numbers in italics indicate discussion of a case.)

Index of Authors

Adams, F. M.
187

Adams, Henry Carter
71, 74, 84

Adams, Walter
71, 251, 260

Adelman, M. A.
44, 47, 62, 63, 69, 198, 244

Allen, F. L.
26, 215

Allen, G. C.
283

Andrews, P. W. S.
38

Arnold, Thurman
264

Arrow, K. J.
76

Aspinall, Arthur
119

Bain, J. S.
20, 53, 68

Barger, Harold
73

Barker, C. P.
275

Barnes, D. G.
114

Barnes, I. R.
225

Baumol, W. J.
96

Beach, C. F.
125

Beckerath, Herbert von
30

Bennett, W. B.
172

Berry, T. S.
128, 129

Bishop, J. P.
114

Blair, J. M.
49

Bloxam, G. A.
171

Bonbright, J. C.
44

Bork, Robert
227

Boulding, K. E.
37, 78, 83, 96

Bowen, Ian
284

Bowman, W. S.
202, 204

Bremer, C. D.
35

Bryan, J. W.
115

Bullock, C. J.
30

Burns, A. R.
93

Butters, J. K.
43, 62, 64, 67

Carpenter, C. E.
265

Index of Subjects